RONALD REAGAN
IN QUOTATIONS

RONALD REAGAN IN QUOTATIONS

*A Topical Dictionary,
with Sources,
of the Presidential Years*

Compiled by David B. Frost

McFarland & Company, Inc., Publishers
Jefferson, North Carolina, and London

Frontispiece: President Reagan addresses the nation from the Oval Office on the space shuttle *Challenger* explosion, January 28, 1986 (courtesy Ronald Reagan Library).

LIBRARY OF CONGRESS CATALOGUING-IN-PUBLICATION DATA

Reagan, Ronald.
Ronald Reagan in quotations : a topical dictionary, with sources, of the presidential years / compiled by David B. Frost.
p.   cm.
Includes bibliographical references and index.

ISBN 978-0-7864-6581-1
illustrated case binding : 50# alkaline paper ∞

1. Reagan, Ronald — Quotations.
2. United States — Politics and government — 1981–1989 — Quotations, maxims, etc.
3. Presidents — United States — Quotations.
I. Frost, David B., 1945–   II. Title.
E838.5.R432 2012b   973.927092 — dc23   2011030575

BRITISH LIBRARY CATALOGUING DATA ARE AVAILABLE

Front cover: President Reagan making remarks at Omaha Beach Cemetery for the 40th Anniversary of the D-Day landings, June 6, 1984 (courtesy Ronald Reagan Library)

Manufactured in the United States of America

McFarland & Company, Inc., Publishers
Box 611, Jefferson, North Carolina 28640
www.mcfarlandpub.com

To Julie,
without whose loving and patient support
this project could not have been completed

Table of Contents

Table of Contents

Introduction

In his Farewell Address to the Nation, President Ronald Reagan brushed aside the nickname "The Great Communicator," insisting that he was not a great communicator, but merely a communicator of "great things"— things, he added, that did not spring from his own brow, but instead "from the heart of a great nation — from our experience, our wisdom, and our belief in the principles that have guided us for two centuries."

Reagan's critics, then and now, dismissed many of his policy prescriptions as overly simplistic. Yet even among the harshest of his critics, there was, and continues to be, a general agreement that Ronald Reagan possessed a remarkable, perhaps unprecedented, ability to connect with the American people. Indeed, as President Obama said in an appreciation of Ronald Reagan written for a special edition of *USA Today* commemorating the centennial of Reagan's birth, "No matter what political disagreements you may have had with President Reagan — and I certainly had my share — there is no denying his leadership in the world, or his gift for communicating his vision for America."

Even today, more than two decades after Ronald Reagan left the White House, his words continue to connect with a broad swath of the American public. To countless millions of Americans, the words that he spoke while president give voice not only to much of their own political ideology, but also to much of what they believe America can and should be. Among the political media, rarely a day passes when a conservative radio or television talk show host does not invoke, sometimes almost reverentially, the name of Ronald Reagan in authentication of a particular political point of view. Among those Republicans who have sought the Presidency for themselves since Reagan left office, nearly all have sought to lay claim to the Reagan mantle. The Reagan Revolution clearly continues to occupy a prominent position in the American political landscape.

Ronald Reagan in Quotations is a compilation of more than 2,500 quotations selected from the speeches and other public addresses that he delivered to an audience, either in person or in a radio or television broadcast, during his eight years as president. Presidential statements, proclamations, and executive orders that were released to the public by the Office of the Press Secretary but which were not actually delivered by President Reagan have not been used as a source.

The quotations are organized topically into more than seventy primary subject areas, many with subsections, thereby providing ready access to Reagan's views across a range of policy issues. The title and date of the speech from which each quotation was taken, as well as, where appropriate, the speech's venue and audience, are also provided.

President Reagan's speeches and addresses are contained in *The Public Papers of the President: Ronald Reagan*, issued by the Office of the Press Secretary from January 20, 1980, to January 20, 1989. The documents were compiled and published by the Office of the Federal Register, a part of the National Archives and Records Administration. The documents are maintained in the Ronald Reagan Presidential Library, in Simi Valley, California, and are available online courtesy of the University of Texas.

ABORTION

1   "I, also, strongly believe ... that the protection of innocent life is and has always been a legitimate, indeed, the first duty of government. And, believing that, I favor human life. The national tragedy of abortion on demand must end." Remarks at the Centennial Meeting of the Supreme Council of the Knights of Columbus in Hartford, Connecticut (August 3, 1982).

2   "[I] believe that God's greatest gift is human life and that we have a sacred duty to protect the innocent human life of an unborn child. Now I realize that this view is not shared by all. But out of all the debate on this subject has come one undisputable fact, and this ... has been the uncertainty of when life begins. And I just happen to believe that simple morality dictates that unless and until someone can prove the unborn human is not alive, we must give it the benefit of the doubt and assume it is. And thus it should be entitled to life, liberty, and the pursuit of happiness." Remarks at Kansas State University at the Alfred M. Landon Lecture Series on Public Issues (September 9, 1982).

3   "I, too, have always believed that God's greatest gift is human life and that we have a duty to protect the life of an unborn child. Until someone can prove the unborn child is not a life, shouldn't we give it the benefit of the doubt and assume it is?" Radio Address to the Nation on Domestic Social Issues (January 22, 1983).

4   "[T]here is a subject that weighs heavily on all of us — the tragedy of abortion on demand. This is a grave moral evil and one that requires the fullest discussion on the floors of the House and Senate." Remarks at the Conservative Political Action Conference Dinner (February 18, 1983).

5   "Either the law protects human beings, or it doesn't." Remarks and a Question-and-Answer Session with Women Leaders of Christian Religious Organizations (October 13, 1983).

6   "Now, I know this issue is controversial. But unless and until it can be proven that an unborn child is not a living human being, can we justify assuming without proof that it isn't? No one has yet offered such proof; indeed, all the evidence is to the contrary. We should rise above bitterness and reproach, and if Americans could come together in a spirit of understanding and helping, then we could find positive solutions to the tragedy of abortion." Address to a Joint Session of Congress on the State of the Union (January 25, 1984).

7   "We cannot pretend that America is preserving her first and highest ideal, the belief that each life is sacred, when we've permitted the deaths of 15 million helpless innocents since the Roe versus Wade decision — 15 million children who will never laugh, never sing, never know the joy of human love, will never strive to heal the sick, feed the poor, or make peace among nations. Abortion has denied them the first and most basic of human rights. We are all infinitely poorer for their loss." Remarks at the Annual Conference of Religious Broadcasters (January 30, 1984).

8   "We cannot proclaim the noble ideal that human life is sacred, then turn our backs on the taking of some 4,000 unborn children's lives every day. This as a means of birth control must stop." Remarks at the Annual Convention of the National Association of Evangelicals in Columbus, Ohio (March 6, 1984).

9 "We must not forget that in reality, if there is any justice in the abortionist position, it would require that they establish beyond a doubt that there is not life in the unborn — and they can't do that." Remarks to Participants in the 1985 March for Life Rally (January 22, 1985).

10 "We cannot condone the threatening or taking of human life to protest the taking of human life by way of abortion." Remarks to Participants in the 1985 March for Life Rally (January 22, 1985).

11 "Abortion is either the taking of a human life or it isn't. And if it is — and medical technology is increasingly showing it is — it must be stopped. It is a terrible irony that while some turn to abortion, so many others who cannot become parents cry out for children to adopt. We have room for these children. We can fill the cradles of those who want a child to love." Address Before a Joint Session of the Congress on the State of the Union (February 6, 1985).

12 "We are a nation of idealists, yet today there is a wound in our national conscience. America will never be whole as long as the right to life granted by our Creator is denied to the unborn. For the rest of my time, I shall do what I can to see that this wound is one day healed." Address Before a Joint Session of Congress on the State of the Union (February 4, 1986).

13 "Each child is a unique, unrepeatable gift, and every child who escapes the violence of abortion is an immeasurable victory for life." Remarks to Participants in the March for Life Rally (January 2, 1987).

14 "Our positive stance on family and children is consistent with our heartfelt convictions on the issue of abortion. Here again, we're not just against an evil. We're not just antiabortion; we're prolife." Remarks at the Conservative Political Action Conference Luncheon (February 20, 1987).

15 "Every time a choice is made to save an unborn baby's life, it is reason for joy." Remarks at the Conservative Political Action Conference Luncheon (February 20, 1987).

16 "Many of you've [right-to-life activists] been attacked for being single-issue activists or single-issue voters. But I ask: What single issue could be of greater significance? What single issue could say more about a society's values than the degree of respect shown for human life at its most vulnerable: human life still unborn?" Remarks at a White House Briefing for Right to Life Activists (July 30, 1987).

17 "Many of the most compelling arguments against abortion are as old as our civilization. Indeed, I would submit that a reverence for all human life is one of the distinguishing marks of true civilization." Remarks at a White House Briefing for Right to Life Activists (July 30, 1987).

18 "[O]urs is not a nation founded upon centuries of shared history, like the nations of Europe or Asia. No, ours is a nation founded upon a shared and basic law, the Constitution. And because it is the Constitution that must reflect our most fundamental values — freedom, equality before the law, and yes, the dignity of human life — because of this, the duty of everyone here today is clear. We must not rest — and I pledge to you that I will not rest — until a human life amendment becomes a part of our Constitution." Remarks at a White House Briefing for Right to Life Activists (July 30, 1987).

19 "Many who turn to abortion do so in harrowing circumstances, and we must remind those who disagree with us, and sometimes even ourselves, that we do not seek to condemn, we do not seek to sit in judgment. Yes, we must take our stand without apology. Yet at the same time, it is our duty to rise above bitterness and reproach, to call upon all Americans to come together in a spirit of helping and understanding." Remarks at a White House Briefing for Right to Life Activists (July 30, 1987).

20 "[O]ur opponents tell us not to interfere with abortion. They tell us not to impose our morality on those who wish to allow or participate in the taking of the life of infants before birth. Yet no one calls it imposing morality to prohibit the taking of life after a child is born. We're told about a woman's right to control her own body. But doesn't the unborn child have a higher right, and that is to life, liberty, and the pursuit of happiness? Or would our critics say that to defend life, liberty, and the pursuit of happiness is to impose morality? Are we to forget the entire moral mission of our nation through its history?" Remarks to Participants in the March for Life Rally (January 22, 1988).

21   "When reverence for life can have no boundaries, when we begin to take some life casually, we threaten all life." Remarks to Participants in the March for Life Rally (January 22, 1988).

22   "Let us unite as a nation and protect the unborn with legislation that would stop all Federal funding for abortion and with a human life amendment making, of course, an exception where the unborn child threatens the life of the mother. Our Judeo-Christian tradition recognizes the right of taking a life in self-defense. But with that one exception, let us look to those others in our land who cry out for children to adopt." Address Before a Joint Session of Congress on the State of the Union (January 25, 1988).

23   "Imagine what so many deemed unworthy of life have missed. Imagine what the rest of us have missed for their absence. Life and the human spirit are absolutes, indivisible. Isn't it time we returned the right to life to the core of our national values, our national customs, and our national laws?" Remarks at the Annual Convention of the

National Religious Broadcasters Association (February 1, 1988).

24   "We cannot proclaim the noble ideal that human life is sacred and then turn our backs on the taking of some 4,000 unborn children's lives every day. This must stop." Remarks to the Student Congress on Evangelism (July 28, 1988).

25   "Many who seek abortions do so in harrowing circumstances. And just as tolerance means accepting that many in good faith hold views different from our own, it also means that no man or woman should sit in judgment on another. I believe ... that we must rise above bitterness and reproach to find positive answers to the tragedy of abortion." Remarks to the Student Congress on Evangelism (July 28, 1988).

26   "[W]e pray this nation will turn away from abortion and choose adoption instead. Saving innocent lives — we believe there's nothing more important than this." Remarks at a Republican Party Fundraising Dinner in Houston, Texas (September 22, 1988).

AGRICULTURE

27   "I've always thought that when we Americans get up in the morning and see bacon and eggs and toast and milk on the table, we should give thanks that American farmers are survivors. They're the real miracle workers of the modern world." Remarks to Representatives of Agricultural Publications and Organizations on United States Agricultural Policy (March 22, 1982).

28   "Farmers are in a business that makes a Las Vegas crap table look like a guaranteed annual income." Remarks at the Annual Convention of the National Corn Growers Association in Des Moines (August 2, 1982).

29   "With all the miracles of modern-day electronics, there is still no greater technological

revolution than modern-day American farming. Today, in the United States ... our food and agricultural system is the most productive in the world...." Remarks at the Annual Convention of the National Corn Growers Association in Des Moines, Iowa (August 2, 1982).

30   "You [the American farmer] are the real miracle workers of the world — keepers of an incredible system based on faith, freedom, hard work, productivity, and profit — a system that feeds and sustains millions of the world's hungry." Radio Address to the Nation on Agriculture and Grain Exports (October 15, 1982).

31   "[I]t doesn't take a Harvard-trained economist to see what this [the efficiency of the American farmer] means to our economy and the well-being of our people." Remarks to Representatives of the Future Farmers of America (July 29, 1983).

32 "Our farmers and ranchers produce the most wholesome and varied range of foodstuffs anywhere. In fact, our agricultural community has been so successful, it's too often been taken for granted." Remarks at a White House Ceremony Marking the Observance of National Agriculture Day (March 20, 1984).

33 "[G]od has blessed America with a vast and a fertile land. But it's the ingenuity and muscle and sweat that have made our farms the envy of the world. And the last thing our farmers need is government getting in the way and making the job even tougher." Remarks to National and State Officers of the Future Farmers of America (July 24, 1984).

34 "You know, this country is nothing without the farmer, and those who work the land have the right to know that there's a future in farming. Their children have the right to know that they'll still be able to work the family farm generations from now and make a decent living." Radio Address to the Nation on the Farm Industry (August 17, 1985).

35 "They [the statistics concerning farming's role in the economy] don't convey the strength and nobility of values, the deep faith in God, and love of freedom and independence, the many years of hard work and caring for friends and neighbors that began on the farm and made America the greatest Nation on Earth. Farming is hard work, maybe the hardest. The strength of our farmers has always been the strength of their dreams for the future — dreams that a son or a daughter working the fields, tending the herds, might decide to stay on that farm and be able to make a go of it. There is no price tag on traditions like these, only the stark realization that to lose our farmers would be to lose the best part of ourselves, the heart and soul of America. Well, we cannot let that happen. We cannot permit the dreams of our farmers to die." Radio Address to the Nation on the Farm Industry (September 14, 1985).

36 "America is grateful for its farmers; they're the best in the world." Remarks to National and State Officers of the Future Farmers of America (July 22, 1986).

37 "[U]ltimately, we want to get government out of farming so that our farmers can achieve complete economic independence." Remarks at the Illinois State Fair in Springfield (August 12, 1986).

38 "You know, I've been saying for some while now it's time to get speculators who merely want to take advantage of government subsidies out of the agricultural business and give farming back to the farmers." Address to the Nation on the Venice Economic Summit, Arms Control, and the Deficit (June 15, 1987).

39 "[T]he American people care about the family farmer, and so do I. But neither they nor I want a farm program that makes our farmers less competitive in the world market. And no one wants one that gives, as ours does, almost $14 million to one wealthy farmer and little or nothing to most family farmers, or one that puts Department of Agriculture extension service programs in counties where there are no farmers." Remarks at the National Federation of Independent Business Conference (June 23, 1987).

40 "I happen to believe that, when it comes to farming, the decisionmaking shouldn't be in the hands of the politicians, academics, or bureaucrats. It should be in the hands of the farmers." Remarks to State Officers of the Future Farmers of America (July 29, 1987).

41 "The solution to the world agricultural problem is to get government out of the way and let farmers compete." Remarks to the State Presidents of the American Farm Bureau Federation (July 13, 1988).

42 "You know, 'amazement' is the word for how most of the rest of the world views American agriculture. We grow more grain, we plant more soybeans, we raise more cattle and export more produce than any combination of countries in the world. American agriculture is one of the great success stories of our time." Remarks to Representatives of the Future Farmers of America (July 28, 1988).

43 "American agriculture is one of the great success stories of our time. As recently as 1949, a single American farmer could feed 19 people for a year. Today a single American farmer feeds 120 people for a year. American products are shipped around the world. And through all these decades, despite drought and misfortune, American agriculture continues to succeed." Remarks on Signing the Disaster Assistance Act of 1988 (August 11, 1988).

AMERICAN EXCEPTIONALISM

44 "[T]his Nation ... [is] the last, best hope of man on earth." Address Before a Joint Session of the Congress on the Program for Economic Recovery (February 18, 1981).

45 "Preservation of freedom is the gift of our Revolution and the hope of the world." Remarks at the New York City Partnership Luncheon in New York (January 14, 1982).

46 "This nation has no mission of mediocrity. We were never meant to be second-best. The spirit that built our country was bold, not timid. It was a spirit of pride, confidence, and the courage that we could do anything." Remarks at the New York City Partnership Luncheon in New York (January 14, 1982).

47 "The world's hope is America's future." Remarks at the New York City Partnership Luncheon in New York (January 14, 1982).

48 "Across the world, Americans are bringing light where there was darkness, heat where there was once only cold, and medicines where there was sickness and disease, food where there was hunger, wealth where humanity was living in squalor, and peace where there was only death and bloodshed." Remarks at Kansas State University at the Alfred M. Landon Lecture Series on Public Issues (September 9, 1982).

49 "Yes, we face awesome problems. But we can be proud of the red, white, and blue, and believe in her mission. In a world wracked by hatred, economic crises, and political tension, America remains mankind's best hope." Remarks at Kansas State University at the Alfred M. Landon Lecture Series on Public Issues Series (September 9, 1982).

50 "I've always believed that this blessed land was set apart in a special way, that some divine plan placed this great continent here between the oceans to be found by people from every corner of the Earth who had special love for freedom and the courage to uproot themselves, leave homeland and friends to come to a strange land, and where, coming here, they have created something new in all the history of mankind — a land where man is not beholden to government; government is beholden to man." Remarks at Kansas State University at the Alfred M. Landon Lecture Series on Public Issues (September 9, 1982).

51 "At the root of everything we're trying to accomplish is the belief that America has a mission. We are a nation of freedom, living under God, believing all citizens must have the opportunity to grow, create wealth, and build a better life for all those who follow. If we live up to those moral values, we can keep the American dream alive for our children and grandchildren, and America will remain mankind's best hope." Remarks at White House Ceremony Celebrating Hispanic Heritage Week (September 15, 1982).

52 "You know, it's long been my belief that America is a chosen land, placed by some Divine Providence here between the two oceans to be sought out and found only by those with a special yearning for freedom. This nation is a refuge for all those people on Earth who long to breathe free." Remarks at the Swearing-In Ceremony for New United States Citizens in White House Station, New Jersey (September 17, 1982).

53 "The task has fallen to us as Americans to move the conscience of the world, to keep alive the hope and dream of freedom. For if we fail or falter, there'll be no place for the world's oppressed to flee to. This is not a role we sought. We preach no manifest destiny. But like the Americans who brought a new nation into the world 200 years ago, history has asked much of us in our time. Much we've already given; much more we must be prepared to give." Remarks at a Conservative Political Action Conference Dinner (February 18, 1983).

54 "Our forefathers didn't shed their blood to create this Union so that we could become a victim nation. We're not sons and daughters of second-rate stock. We were born to carry liberty's banner...." Remarks and a Question-and-Answer Session with Members of the Commonwealth Club of California in San Francisco (March 4, 1983).

55 "The United States remains the last, best hope for a mankind plagued by tyranny and deprivation." Remarks at the Annual Members Banquet of the National Rifle Association in Phoenix, Arizona (May 6, 1983).

56 "It's always been my belief that by a Divine plan this nation was placed between the two oceans to be sought out and found by those with a special brand of courage and love of freedom." Message to the Nation on the Observance of Independence Day (July 3, 1983).

57 "We can be proud of our heritage, and we need never hide from our roots. The world we live in is not an easy one, but we've inherited a noble mission, a mission that casts a beacon of hope for all of the Earth's people." Remarks at the Annual Convention of the American Legion in Seattle, Washington (August 23, 1983).

58 "We all believe in America's mission. We believe that in a world wracked by hatred and crisis, America remains mankind's best hope. The eyes of history are upon us, counting on us to protect the peace, promote new prosperity, and provide for a better tomorrow." Remarks at the Fundraising Dinner of the Republican National Hispanic Assembly (September 14, 1983).

59 "We're a powerful force for good. With faith and courage, we can perform great deeds and take freedom's next step.... We will carry on the tradition of a good and worthy people who have brought light where there was darkness, warmth where there was cold, medicine where there was

disease, food where there was hunger, and peace where there was bloodshed." Address Before a Joint Session on the Congress on the State of the Union (January 25, 1984).

60 "More than 200 years after the patriots fired that first shot heard 'round the world, one revolutionary idea still burns in the hearts of men and women everywhere: A society where man is not beholden to government; government is beholden to man." Remarks at the Annual Conservative Political Action Conference Dinner (March 2, 1984).

61 "Just as America has always been synonymous with freedom, so, too, should we become the symbol of peace across the Earth." Remarks at the Annual Conservative Political Action Conference Dinner (March 2, 1984).

62 "[T]he greatest source of our strength is not weapons or laws, but, instead, the character of our people — our standards as individuals and our recognition of those values that transcend the politics of the moment." Remarks at the National Legislative Conference of the Independent Insurance Agents of America (March 27, 1984).

63 "The only territories we hold are memorials like this one [U.S. Ranger Monument at Pointe du Hoc, France] and the graveyards where our heroes rest." Remarks at a Ceremony Commemorating the 40th Anniversary of the Normandy Invasion, D-Day (June 6, 1984).

64 "[Y]ou don't have to travel too far in the world to realize that we stand as a beacon, that America is today what it was two centuries ago, a place that dreamers dream of, that it is what Winthrop said standing on the deck of the tiny *Arabella* off the coast of Massachusetts coast, with a little group of Pilgrims gathered around him, and he said, 'We shall be as a shining city for all the world upon the hill.'" Remarks at a Spirit of America Festival in Decatur, Alabama (July 4, 1984).

65 "[F]or those who yearn to be free, for those who fight for the right to worship, to speak freely, to write what they want, to enjoy the freedom God meant us to have. For all those people, America's not just a word; it is a hope, a torch shedding light to all the hopeless of the world." Remarks at a Spirit of America Festival In Decatur, Alabama (July 4, 1984).

66   "Ours is a society that rewards honest toil, risk-taking, and achievement, for the factory worker, the small businessman and ... the family farmer, because the promise for America is for everybody, no matter who you are, who your parents are, or what lonely corner of the world you may have come from." Remarks at the Missouri State Fair in Sedalia (August 19, 1984).

67   "The dream of America is much more than who we are or what we do. It is, above all, what we will be. We must always be the New World — the world of discovery, the world that reveres the great truths of the past, but that looks forward with unending faith to the promise of the future." Remarks During a Visit to the Goddard Space Flight Center in Greenbelt, Maryland (August 30, 1984).

68   "Well, America isn't about promises; it never has been. America is about promise. It's about possibility." Remarks at a Reagan-Bush Rally in Fountain Valley, California (September 3, 1984).

69   "I don't think you need convincing that America has no mission of mediocrity. We haven't come all this way just to wind up a second-best nation. Leave that tired vision to the fainthearted souls. We're not in this historic competition just to survive or just to do well, America is in this to win. The crown we're striving for is not a crown of pride or glory; ours is a battle for human progress, for excellence at every level of society." Remarks to Members of the High Technological Corridor Board in Nashville, Tennessee (September 13, 1984).

70   "America's greatest gift has always been freedom and equality of opportunity — the idea that no matter who you are, no matter where you come from, you can climb as high as your own God-given talents will take you." Remarks to Members of the Congregation of Temple Hillel and Jewish Community Leaders in Valley Stream, New York (October 26, 1984).

71   "A nation's greatness is measured not just by its gross national product or military power, but by the strength of its devotion to the principles and values that bind its people and define their character." Remarks to Members of the Congregation of Temple Hillel and Jewish Community Leaders in Valley Stream, New York (October 26, 1984).

72   "America must never give up its special mission in the world, never. There are new worlds on the horizon, and we're not going to stop until we all get there together. America's best days are yet to come." Remarks at a Reagan-Bush Rally in Media, Pennsylvania (October 29, 1984).

73   "We were born to be a special place between the two great oceans with a unique message to carry freedom's torch. To a tired and disillusioned world, we've always been a light of hope where all things are possible." Remarks at a Reagan-Bush Rally in Boston, Massachusetts (November 1, 1984).

74   "America will never give up, never go back — never. We were born to a special place between these two great oceans with a unique mission to carry freedom's torch. To a tired and disillusioned world, we have always been a light of hope where all things are believed to be possible." Remarks at a Reagan-Bush Rally in Rochester, New York (November 1, 1984).

75   "[A]s a people, we Americans have fought harder, paid a higher price, done more to advance the freedom and dignity of man than any other people who ever lived on this Earth." Remarks at a Reagan-Bush Rally in Rochester, New York (November 1, 1984).

76   "Ours is a land of the free because it is the home of the brave. America's future will always be great because our nation will always be strong. Our nation will be strong because our people will be free. And our people will be free because we will be united, one people under God, with liberty and justice for all." Remarks at a Reagan-Bush Rally in Rochester, New York (November 1, 1984).

77   "To a tired and disillusioned world, we've always been a New World and, yes, a shining city on a hill where all things are possible." Address to the Nation on the Eve of the Presidential Election (November 5, 1984).

78   "This, then, is our historic mission — it always has been — to present to the world an America that is not just strong and secure, but an America that has a cause and a vision of a future were all peoples can experience the warmth and hope of individual liberty." Address to the Nation on the Eve of the Presidential Election (November 5, 1984).

79 "We must challenge ourselves to hurdle the accepted limits of the past, to draw a new map of possibilities, and give new meaning to the word 'success.' Isn't that, after all, what it means to be Americans?" Radio Address to the Nation on Economic Growth (January 26, 1985).

80 "These golden hopes of mankind are here for us to protect and preserve. Let us resolve to pass that sacred heritage on to other generations of Americans and to make it someday, we hope and pray, the birthright of all the peoples of the world." Remarks at the Convention of the National Republican Heritage Groups Council (May 17, 1985).

81 "America has, since its founding, been a refuge for those suffering under the yoke of oppression. A belief in the dignity of man and government by the consent of the people lies at the heart of our national character and the soul of our foreign policy." Remarks on Signing the Bill of Rights Day and the Human Rights Day and Week Proclamation (December 10, 1985).

82 "Those who struggle for freedom look to America. If we fail them in their hour of need, we fail ourselves as the last, best hope of liberty." Radio Address to the Nation on Tax Reform and the Situation in Nicaragua (December 14, 1985).

83 "It's no accident that America is blazing the trail of progress through the 20th century and leading the race to the future. We live in a country that encourages enterprise and rewards initiative, a country where everyone is free to contribute and all can benefit from the success of others. Our society is inventive because we're free, and prosperous because each individual is secure to gather and keep the fruits of his labor. If we're ever mindful of our enduring principles — the natural rights to life, liberty, and property ... then America will always be the shining star among nations, leading the world on to a better tomorrow." Remarks to Students and Faculty at Thomas Jefferson High School of Science and Technology in Fairfax County, Virginia (February 7, 1986).

84 "In a world too often prey to the forces of violence and tyranny, America is once again a bulwark for peace and freedom." Radio Address to the Nation on the Defense Budget (March 1, 1986).

85 "For free men and women, for Americans, there will always be exciting times because the fu-ture is in our hands. People all over the world look to us; the future generations of Americans depend on us. This is not a burden; this is a challenge." Remarks at a Dinner for the Republican Congressional Leadership (March 10, 1986).

86 "[S]o many dictators have a special fear and hatred for the United States [because] American power, as long as it is used wisely and justly, is an undying symbol of hope for oppressed peoples around the world." Radio Address to the Nation on International Violence and Democratic Values (March 29, 1986).

87 "Today the world looks to America for leadership. They look to what they call our miracle economy for an answer to how they may give their people a better life. And they look to our courage and might to protect them from the forces of tyranny, brutality, and injustice." Remarks to Marine Corps Basic Training Graduates in Parris Island, South Carolina (June 4, 1986).

88 "Here in this green and gentle land people of all nations, people of all races and faiths, have learned to live in harmony to build one nation." Remarks at the High School Commencement Exercises in Glassboro, New Jersey (June 19, 1986).

89 "Call it mysticism if you will, I have always believed there was some divine providence that placed this great land here between the two great oceans, to be found by a special kind of people from every corner of the world, who had a special love for freedom and a special courage that enabled them to leave their own land, leave their friends and their countrymen, and come to this new and strange land to build a New World of peace and freedom and hope." Remarks at the Opening Ceremonies of the Statue of Liberty Centennial Celebration in New York, New York (July 3, 1986).

90 "We are the keepers of the flame of liberty. We hold it high tonight for the world to see, a beacon of hope, a light unto the nations." Remarks on the Lighting of the Torch of the Statue of Liberty in New York, New York (July 3, 1986).

91 "The world has never known a force as strong or decent as that of America when we're unified. Together we Americans settled this great continent that God put between two oceans for free men and women all over the world to find and cherish. Together we're transforming the world with our technology, making life longer with greater opportunities and more fulfilling for millions all over the Earth. And most of all, together we've led the forces of freedom around the world in this century." Remarks on Departure for Reykjavik, Iceland (October 9, 1986).

92   "America is a great and generous nation. We are the beacon of liberty and freedom to all the world." Address to the Nation on the Congressional and Gubernatorial Elections (November 2, 1986).

93   "We're entering our third century now, but it's wrong to judge our nation by its years. The calendar can't measure America because we were meant to be an endless experiment in freedom — with no limit to our reaches, no boundaries to what we can do, no end point to our hopes." Address Before a Joint Session of Congress on the State of the Union (January 27, 1987).

94   "You may call it mystical if you please. But I have always believed there was some divine plan that put this continent here between the two great oceans to be found by people from every corner of the world who had an extra ounce of courage and a love of freedom such that they would uproot themselves from family, friends, and their own country and come here to start a new life." Remarks to Students and Faculty at Purdue University in West Lafayette, Indiana (April 9, 1987).

95   "Now, we all know that story, but maybe sometimes we get a little indifferent and let it slip from our minds. It concerns people from every corner of the Earth. They had a little more drive, and they dreamed a little more than others around them, and they had that little extra ounce of courage to leave everything behind and make a long, difficult journey across the ocean to a new continent, a new world, and where they built a new nation called America." Remarks at the Harley-Davidson Company Employee-Management Forum in York, Pennsylvania (May 6, 1987).

96   "I've always believed there was a divine plan that put this continent here between the two great oceans for it to be found by people from every corner of the Earth who had an extra love of freedom and that extra ounce of courage that would enable them to tear themselves away from their homeland, family, and friends, and make their way to this strange land." Remarks at the

Commencement Ceremony for Area High School Seniors in Chattanooga, Tennessee (May 19, 1987).

97   "For many generations, we Americans were able to live in a splendid isolation, bordered as we were by the two vast oceans. But in this century, we've learned the hard way that those days are over; that, like it or not, this nation is the final repository of mankind's greatest dream: a dream of human freedom and a world at peace. For us to withdraw or retreat into isolationism again that we'd known for so many years, I think would be — well, it would simply turn back and give control to those who believe in violence and war, and they'd have the final say on the world that we live in." Remarks to Participants in the People to People International Youth Exchange Program (June 24, 1987).

98   "[T]hose that we follow, our ancestors, happen to be people with a special belief in freedom and courage in their hearts that made them tear up roots wherever they lived, leave family and friends if need be, and travel to this new land where — most cases they didn't even know the language before they got here — and do it because of that extra urge for freedom that just the rest of their neighbors didn't have. And we are kind of a miracle. I have always said — you may call it mysticism if you will — but there had to be some divine plan that placed these great continents here between the two great oceans to be found by that kind of people. And that, maybe, is our purpose in life." Remarks to Participants in the People to People International Youth Exchange Program (June 24, 1987).

99   "But I'll tell you what is unique about us, and it's here in this room, present with all of you. You can leave here and move to Japan, but you can't become Japanese. You can move to France; you can't become a Frenchman or a Frenchwoman — Greece and not become a Greek, Turkey — all of these. But anybody, anyplace, from any corner in the world can come to live in America and become an American. And I guess that we're the only place where that is true, and that's what we're all about. You know, it's the magic and the mystery and the majesty of freedom." Remarks to Participants in the People to People International Youth Exchange Program (June 24, 1987).

100   "[A]merica means a dream and the freedom to chase that dream. America means government of, by, and for the people, in a land where the sacred soul of humanity is not only respected but revered. America means justice under law. It means peace and decency. It means a bright Kansas Sun rising over fields that hard-working, broad-shouldered farmers have planted with prayers and plowed with hope." Remarks on the Occasion of Alfred M. Landon's 100th Birthday in Topeka, Kansas (September 6, 1987).

101   "Over the 200 years of our Republic, our economy has produced more wealth, more opportunity, and a higher standard of living for more people than has ever happened before." Remarks to the United States Chamber of Commerce on the Economy and Deficit Reduction (November 19, 1987).

102   "[W]e are uniquely situated to lead the world into a new era of economic cooperation, to make this 'city on a hill' that is America, a global city. The watchword of this new era will be freedom — free enterprise, free trade, freedom to travel, freedom of emigration. Freedom — the emancipation of peoples' creative energies around the world. That's the challenge that has opened up to us in the 1980s. All we need is the courage to meet it." Remarks and a Question-and-Answer Session with Members of the City Club of Cleveland, Ohio (January 11, 1988).

103   "On every continent and ocean in this century, Americans have left such stories [of military heroism]. Courage is our mark, freedom and democracy our gift to mankind." Remarks at the Annual Conference of the Veterans of Foreign Wars (March 7, 1988).

104   "It is a great gift God has given each of us — making us Americans. Who knows why some are so blessed. It's a mystery we cannot fathom but can only adore and be thankful for." Remarks at the Annual Meeting of the United States Chamber of Commerce (May 2, 1988).

105   "I know I've said this before, but I believe that God put this land between the two great oceans to be found by special people from every corner of the world who had that extra love for freedom that prompted them to leave their homeland and come to this land to make it a brilliant light beam of freedom to the world." Remarks at the Republican National Convention in New Orleans, Louisiana (August 15, 1988).

106   "Today, to a degree never before seen in human history, one nation, the United States, has become the model to be followed and imitated by the rest of the world." Remarks and a Question-and-Answer Session with Area Junior High School Students (November 14, 1988).

107   "America is leading the world into a bright and glorious tomorrow. And today more than at any point in human history, we can truly say that the future belongs to the free. And America is the land of the free." Remarks Upon Departure from the University of Virginia in Charlottesville (December 16, 1988).

108   "I've spoken of the shining city all my political life, but I don't know if I ever quite communicated what I saw when I said it. But in my mind it was a tall, proud city built on rocks stronger than oceans, wind-swept, God-blessed, and teeming with people of all kinds living in harmony and peace; a city with free ports that hummed with commerce and creativity. And if there had to be city walls, the walls had doors and the doors were open to anyone with the will and the heart to get here. That's how I saw it, and see it still." Farewell Address to the Nation (July 11, 1989).

109   "Whether we seek it or not, whether we like it or not, we Americans are keepers of the miracles. We are asked to be guardians of a place to come to, a place to start again, a place to live in the dignity God meant for his children. May it ever be so." Final Radio Address to the Nation (January 14, 1989).

AMERICAN SPIRIT

110   "We hear much of special interest groups. Well, our concern must be for a special interest group that has been too long neglected. It knows no sectional boundaries or ethnic or racial divisions, and it crosses political party lines. It is made up of men and women who raise our food, patrol our streets, man our mines and factories, teach our children, keep our homes, and heal us when we're sick — professionals, industrialists, shopkeepers, clerks, cabbies, and truck drivers. They are, in short, 'We the people,' the breed called Americans." Inaugural Address (January 20, 1981).

111   "Nothing binds our abilities except our expectations, and given that, the farthest star is within our reach." Remarks at a White House Luncheon Honoring Astronauts of the Space Shuttle Columbia (May 19, 1981).

112   "There's no crisis our people can't rise above, no problem we can't solve, and no challenge too great." Remarks on Presenting a Check for the Westway Project to Mayor Edward I. Koch in New York, New York (September 7, 1981).

113   "If there's one thing the American people aren't lacking, it is courage." Remarks on the Program for Economic Recovery at a White House Reception for Members of Congress (September 29, 1981).

114   "[W]e Americans are known for dreaming with our eyes wide open. We live our dreams and make them come true. Our ideas and energies combine in a dynamic force.... We call it the American spirit." Remarks on New Year's Day January 1, 1982 (January 1, 1982).

115   "America's greatest moments have come when America dared to be great — when we believed in ourselves, in our values and our courage, and when we reached out to each other to do the impossible." Remarks at the National Legislative Conference of the Building and Construction Trades Department, AFL-CIO (April 5, 1982).

116   "There are many blessings in this good world, but surely the greatest is the one that we all share: We're Americans." Remarks at the Na-

tional Legislative Conference of the Building and Construction Trades Department, AFL-CIO (April 5, 1982).

117   "America has always done well when we had the courage to believe in ourselves, our values, and our capacity to perform great deeds." Remarks at the Annual Meeting of the United States Chamber of Commerce (April 26, 1982).

118   "America's greatest moments have always come when we dared to be great, when we believed in ourselves and reached out to each other to do the impossible." Remarks at the Annual Meeting of the United States Chamber of Commerce (April 26, 1982).

119   "Time and again the American people — you — have worked wonders that have astounded the world. We've done it in war and peace, in good times and bad, because we're a people who care and who know how to pull together — family by family, community by community, coast to coast — to change things for the better. The success story of America is neighbor helping neighbor." Address to Nation on the Fiscal Year 1983 Federal Budget (April 29, 1982).

120   "We live our dreams. We make them come true. Our ideas and energies combine in a dynamic force.... And that force has always enabled America to overcome great odds, and it always will. We just refer to it as the American spirit." Remarks at Dedication Ceremonies for the U.S. Pavilion at the Knoxville International Energy Exposition (World's Fair) in Tennessee (May 1, 1982).

121   "[T]here resides in the American people a common wisdom, a basic decency that comes to the fore just when it's needed the most." Remarks at the Republican Congressional "Salute to President Ronald Reagan Dinner" (May 4, 1982).

122   "The character of the American people is our country's most precious asset, and, like any asset, it should never be taken for granted." Remarks at the Annual Foundation Luncheon of the

YMCA of Metropolitan Chicago in Illinois (May 10, 1982).

123 "Let's reject the nonsense that America is doomed to decline, the world sliding toward disaster no matter what we do. Like death and taxes, the doomcriers will always be with us. And they will always be wrong about America." Remarks at Kansas State University at the Alfred M. Landon Lecture Series on Public Issues (September 9, 1982).

124 "No other experience in American history runs quite parallel to the black experience. It has been one of great hardships, but also one of great heroism; of great adversity, but also great achievement." Remarks at a National Black Republican Council Dinner (September 15, 1982).

125 "Our commitment to self-determination, freedom, and peace is the very soul of America." Remarks at the Swearing-In Ceremony for New United States Citizens in White House Station, New Jersey (September 17, 1982).

126 "We're a nation of dreamers who've come here ... in search of an ideal: respect for the liberty and dignity of man." Remarks at a Swearing-In Ceremony for New United States Citizens in White House Station, New Jersey (September 17, 1982).

127 "Our country is a special place, because we Americans have always been sustained, through good times and bad, by a noble vision — a vision of not only what the world around us is today, but what we as a free people can make it tomorrow." Address Before a Joint Session of the Congress on the State the Union (January 25, 1983).

128 "We Americans have always been at our best when we've faced challenge — exploring and taming new frontiers, testing our talents and abilities and, yes, moving on. We're a nation that lionizes pathfinders, whether they be Daniel Boone or Charles Lindbergh." Remarks at a White House Ceremony Commemorating the Bicentennial Year of Air and Space Flight (February 7, 1983).

129 "The country sound has become a good-will ambassador for us all around the world — through its variety, spreading an understanding of our basic values, our high spirit and determined

self-reliance. And as others understand this music, they also understand and appreciate our deep-seated love of country, freedom, and God." Remarks at a White House Reception for Members of the Country Music Association (March 15, 1983).

130 "Our whole way of life is based on a compact between good and decent people, a voluntary agreement to live together in freedom, respecting the rights of others and expecting that our rights in turn will be respected." Remarks to the American Gathering of Jewish Holocaust Survivors (April 11, 1983).

131 "We apologize to none for our ideals or our principles, nor the prosperity that we have made for ourselves and shared with the world." Remarks During a White House Ceremony Commemorating Flag Day (June 14, 1983).

132 "The promise of America, the character of our people, the thrust of our history, and the challenge of our future all point toward a higher mission: to build together a society of opportunity, a society that rewards excellence, bound by a body of laws nourished with the spirit of faith, equity, responsibility, and compassion. The streets of America would not be paved with gold; they would be paved with opportunity. Success would depend upon personal initiative and merit." Remarks at the Annual Meeting of the American Bar Association in Atlanta, Georgia (August 1, 1983).

133 "Well, one should never sell the American people short. Once we put our minds to it, there's nothing Americans cannot accomplish if the Federal Government will just get out of the way." Remarks at the Annual Meeting of the National Association of Towns and Townships (September 12, 1983).

134 "Americans have proven that there's no mountain too high, forest too thick, desert so vast, or problem so perplexing that it can serve as a barrier to the progress of free men and women." Remarks at the 25th Anniversary Celebration of the National Aeronautics and Space Administration (October 19, 1983).

135 "An America that is militarily and economically strong is not enough. The world must see an America that is morally strong with a creed and a vision. We are such people. This is what has led us to dare and to achieve. For us values count. They are the wellspring of our American way of life...." Remarks at the Annual Convention of the Congressional Medal of Honor Society in New York City (December 12, 1983).

136   "For us, work, family, neighborhood, freedom, and peace are not just words; they're expressions of what America means, definitions of what makes us a good and loving people." Address Before a Joint Session of the Congress on the State of the Union (January 25, 1984).

137   "Some days when life seems hard and we reach out for values to sustain us or a friend to help us, we find a person who reminds us what it means to be Americans." Address Before a Joint Session of Congress on the State of the Union (January 25, 1984).

138   "The story of black Americans is one of valor in the face of hardship." Remarks at a White House Ceremony Marking the Observance of National Afro-American (Black) History Month (February 2, 1984).

139   "Well, on this Earth there's no such thing as inevitable; only men and women building our nation's destiny one day at a time." Remarks at the National Convention of the National Association of Secondary School Principals in Las Vegas, Nevada (February 7, 1984).

140   "Respect for the dignity of life, concern for our fellow man, extraordinary acts of charity and mercy — this is our heritage as Americans." Remarks to the New York Federation of Catholic School Parents (April 5, 1984).

141   "We believe in the dignity of each man, woman, and child. Our entire system is founded on an appreciation of the special genius of each individual, and of his special right to make his own decisions and lead his own life." Remarks at Fudan University in Shanghai, China (April 30, 1984).

142   "Our greatest strength, the most powerful force for good on this planet, is the character of the American people." Remarks at the Midyear Meeting of the National Association of Realtors (May 10, 1984).

143   "How can anyone in the United States of America, in the world today, be scared of anything? We are truly a shining city on a hill." Re-

marks at the Annual Convention of the Texas State Bar Association in San Antonio (July 6, 1984).

144   "The American ideal is not just winning; it's going as far as you can go." Remarks to American Athletes at the Summer Olympics in Los Angeles, California (July 28, 1984).

145   "America has always been greatest when we dared to be great." Remarks During a Visit to the Goddard Space Flight Center in Greenbelt, Maryland (August 30, 1984).

146   "America works best when we unite for opportunity, reaching for the stars and challenging the limits of our potential." Radio Address to the Nation on the Presidential Campaign (October 27, 1984).

147   "Like our Olympic athletes, this nation should set its sights on the stars and go for the gold." Remarks at a Reagan-Bush Rally in Springfield, Illinois (November 2, 1984).

148   "Two hundred years of American history should have taught us that nothing is impossible." Address Before a Joint Session of the Congress on the State of the Union (February 6, 1985).

149   "You know, every once in a while I've heard people say we don't have any heroes anymore. They haven't looked around their own neighborhood. You see them getting up, sending the kids off to school, going to work every morning, supporting their church and their charity and all the good things in this society. You bet they're heroes. It's through their sweat, toil, and tears that the foundations of our society are built...." Remarks on Tax Reform to Concerned Citizens (May 29, 1985).

150   "Our country is great because it is built on principles of self-reliance, opportunity, innovation, and compassion for the others." Remarks at the Presentation Ceremony for the "C" Flag Awards (June 14, 1985).

151   "All Americans who strive to excel, not because they are in competition with anyone else, but because they're in competition with their own imagination to be the very best possible in whatever job they have." Remarks to the Finalists in the Teacher in Space Project (June 26, 1985).

152   "The truth is, uncommon valor is often a common virtue in this country of ours. America's the land of the free because she is the home of the brave. These United States are built on heroism and sustained and protected by it." Remarks to Students and Faculty at Thomas Jefferson High School of Science and Technology in Fairfax County, Virginia (February 7, 1986).

153 "I've always thought there's nothing that can't be done if the people, the American people want to do it." Remarks at a Fundraising Luncheon for Senator Alfonse M. D'Amato in New York, New York (April 18, 1986).

154 "Instead of focusing on problems, America's looking for solutions. Instead of fretting about this or that shortcoming, we're out creating, building, and making things better. Instead of lamenting dangers, we're putting our best minds to work trying to find ways of making this a safer, more secure world." Radio Address to the Nation on the Strategic Defense Initiative (July 12, 1986).

155 "America didn't become great by being pessimistic and cynical. We didn't become the leader of the free world and the mightiest economic force on this planet by shrinking from challenges. The doom and gloomers are basically out of touch with the spirit of America — that can-do spirit that sees every problem as an opportunity and every obstacle as a challenge to be overcome." Remarks at a White House Briefing for Members of the Tax Reform Coalition (September 23, 1986).

156 "All we said was this: Give the American people a chance, and they'll come through. They'll make the difference. They'll get us out of the worst economic mess since the Depression. And they have, building one of the mightiest prosperities in our history...." Remarks at a White House Briefing for Members of the Deficit Reduction Coalition (July 10, 1987).

157 "This land of freedom was built, and is still being built, by men and women who, without chroniclers, without heralds, have brought a warrior's courage to the challenges of everyday life. America is a land of heroes." Remarks at the Presentation Ceremony for the Young American Medals for Bravery and Service (November 13, 1987).

158 "[A]merica wasn't built by people who said, I can't. Every pioneer who crossed our frontier said, I can. Every man or woman who ever started a new business, discovered a new invention, explored a new idea said, I can.... The two most important words anyone can ever learn are those words: I can. You know, I've always thought that the best hope for America's future was to get as many things as possible out of the gloomy, pessimistic halls of Washington and back to the optimistic air of the real America, where people don't say, I can't, they say, I can." Remarks and a Question-and-Answer Session with Area High School Seniors in Jacksonville, Florida (December 1, 1987).

159 "[W]e Americans are a dynamic and energetic lot, people of enterprise and an abiding love of freedom. We believe in God and care about others who are in need. We are proud and independent. [W]e believe our country should be strong, but we desire peace. Have no doubt about that. The longing for peace runs deep here, second only to our fervency for the preservation of our liberty." Remarks at the Welcoming Ceremony for General Secretary Mikhail Gorbachev of the Soviet Union (December 8, 1987).

160 "Only those who don't know us believe that America is a materialistic land. But the true America is not supermarkets filled with meats, milk, and goods of all descriptions. It is not highways filled with cars. No, true America is a land of faith and family. You can find it in our churches, synagogues, and mosques — in our homes and schools." Address to the American and Soviet Peoples on the Soviet–United States Summit Meeting (December 8, 1987).

161 "One other thing we Americans like — the future — like the sound of it, the idea of it, the hope of it. Where others fear trade and economic growth, we see opportunities for creating new wealth and undreamed-of opportunities for millions in our own land and beyond. Where others seek to throw up barriers, we seek to bring them down. Where others take counsel of their fears, we follow our hopes. Yes, we Americans like the future and like making the most of it." Address Before a Joint Session of Congress on the State of the Union (January 25, 1988).

162 "What Washington too often doesn't understand, but I know you do, is that the source of our recordbreaking expansion will not be found poring over the computer models and equations of high-priced consulting firms, but by peering into the American heart. And there you'll find optimism about the future, trust in the strength of ordinary people, and faith in the power of freedom." Remarks at a Luncheon Hosted by WOC Radio and the Quad-Cities Chamber of Commerce in Davenport, Iowa (July 14, 1988).

APARTHEID

163 "The system of apartheid means deliberate, systematic, institutionalized racial discrimination, denying the black majority their God-given rights. America's view of apartheid is simple and straightforward: We believe it's wrong. We condemn it, and we're united in hoping for the day when apartheid will be no more." Remarks and a Question-and-Answer Session with Reporters on Signing the Executive Order Prohibiting Trade and Certain Other Transactions Involving South Africa (September 9, 1985).

164 "I have said that apartheid is abhorrent. It's time that the Government of South Africa took steps to end it and to reach out for compromise and reconciliation to end the turmoil in that strife-torn land." Remarks on Signing the Bill of Rights Day and the Human Rights Day and Week Proclamation (December 10, 1985).

165 "America's view of apartheid has been and remains clear. Apartheid is morally wrong and politically unacceptable. The United States cannot maintain cordial relations with a government whose power rests upon the denial of rights to a majority of its people based on race." Remarks to Members of the World Affairs Council and the Foreign Policy Association (July 22, 1986).

166 "The primary victims of an economic boycott of South Africa would be the very people we seek to help. Most of the workers who would lose jobs because of sanctions would be black workers. We do not believe the way to help the people of South Africa is to cripple the economy upon which they and their families depend for survival." Remarks to Members of the World Affairs Council and the Foreign Policy Association (July 22, 1986).

ARTS AND HUMANITIES

167 "The human need to create and enjoy heart is as profound as the urge to speak. In fact, it's through art that we best understand ourselves and can be understood by those who come after us." Remarks at the Awards Presentation Ceremony for the President's Committee on the Arts and Humanities (May 17, 1983).

168 "No one realizes the importance of freedom more than the artist, for only in the atmosphere of freedom can the arts flourish. Artists have to be brave; they live in the realm of idea and expression, and their ideas will often be provocative and unusual. Artists stretch the limits of understanding. They express ideas that are sometimes unpopular. In an atmosphere of liberty, artists and patrons are free to think the unthinkable and create the audacious; they are free to make both horrendous mistakes and glorious celebrations. Where there's liberty, art succeeds." Remarks at a Luncheon for Recipients of the National Medal of Arts (April 23, 1985).

169   "So it is that in matters of culture today, Americans look not so much to the Old World as to the New — to America itself — and they do so with pride." Remarks at a Presentation Ceremony for the National Medal of Arts (July 14, 1986).

170   "We believe in freedom not only because it reflects the most moral system of human interaction, not only because it leads to economic progress but also because it nourishes the artistic and creative spirit of man." Toasts at the State Dinner for President Jose Sarney Costa of Brazil (September 10, 1986).

171   "[Y]ou can never be lonely if you've got a book to read. My idea of the worst thing in the world that can happen to me is to be caught in a hotel room some night with nothing to read." Remarks at a White House Ceremony for the Elementary School Recognition Program Honorees (September 12, 1986).

172   "The arts and the humanities teach us who we are and what we can be. They lie at the very core of the culture of which we're a part, and they provide the foundation from which we may reach out to other cultures so that the great heritage that is ours may be enriched by, as well as itself enrich, other enduring traditions. We honor the arts not because we want monuments to our own civilization but because we are a free people. The arts are among our nation's finest creations and the reflection of freedom's light." Remarks at a Luncheon for Recipients of the National Medal of Arts (June 18, 1987).

173   "[I]t is not the place, and should not be the place, for government officials to determine what is good art and what is bad art. That path is a dangerous one for a democratic society — well, for any society, to take. No, the determination of such things should be left to women and men of taste and education, and indeed, finally, to history itself." Remarks on Receiving a Report from the President's Committee on the Arts and Humanities (November 17, 1988).

BERLIN WALL

174   "This year [1981] marks the 20th anniversary of the Berlin Wall, a border of brutality that assaults the human spirit and the civilized mind. On one side of the wall, people live in dignity and democracy; on the other side, domination and defeat." Remarks at the Welcoming Ceremony for Chancellor Helmut Schmidt of the Federal Republic of Germany (May 21, 1981).

175   "The Berlin Wall is a dramatic example of the desperate and cruel extremes to which totalitarian regimes will go to deny their subjects contact with other Europeans. From the Baltic Sea to Southeastern Europe, a murderous barrier of minefields and barbed wire, manned by guards who shoot to kill, stands as a monument to the inhumanity of those who would make the individual the servant of the state." Statement on the Twentieth Anniversary of the Berlin Wall (August 13, 1981).

176   "What can the world think of rulers who must build prison walls around their own nation? What can the world think of leaders who fear that their own people will flee their homeland at the first opportunity?" Statement on the Twentieth Anniversary of Berlin Wall (August 13, 1981).

177   "The Berlin Wall, that dreadful gray gash across the city, is in its third decade. It is the fitting signature of the regime that built it." Address to Members of the British Parliament (June 8, 1982).

178 "The Iron Curtain wasn't woven to keep people out; it's there to keep people in. The most obvious symbol of this is the Berlin Wall. And you know, if I had a chance I'd like to ask the Soviet leaders one question — in fact, I may stuff the question in a bottle and throw it over the wall when I go there today. I really want to hear their explanation. Why is the wall there? Why are they so afraid of freedom on this side of the wall? Well, the truth is they're scared to death of it because they know that freedom is catching, and they don't dare leave their people have a taste of it." Remarks on Arrival in Berlin (June 11, 1982).

179 "In Berlin, a gray, grim monument of steel and stone stands as a reminder of those whose self-proclaimed goal is the domination of every nation on Earth. The tragedy of our time is that goal has been so widely achieved." Remarks on Signing the Captive Nations Week Proclamation (July 19, 1982).

180 "Only a counterfeit revolution builds walls to keep people in and employs armies of secret police to keep them quiet. The real revolution lives on the principle that the government must rest on the consent of the governed...." Remarks at a White House Ceremony Marking the Implementation of the Caribbean Basin Initiative (October 5, 1983).

181 "Ahead of us may be a time when the artificial barriers that divide Germany, and indeed all Europe, are cast away, a time when there will be no need for weapons or barbed wire or walls in Berlin. These are not dreams. I believe from the bottom of my heart we have every reason for confidence. The future is on the side of the free." Toast at the State Dinner in Bonn, Federal Republic of Germany (May 5, 1985).

182 "But just as we all know what peace is, we certainly know what peace is not. Peace based on repression cannot be true peace and is secure only when individuals are free to direct their own governments. Peace based on partition cannot be true peace. Put simply: Nothing can justify the continuing and permanent division of the European Continent. Walls of partition and distrust must give way to greater communication for an open world." Address to the 40th Session of the United Nations General Assembly in New York, New York (October 24, 1985).

183 "I will stand in front of the wall that runs like an open wound through the heart of Europe, the wall that represents all that is most hostile to our democratic values of freedom and human rights. A regime that so fears its own people it must imprison them behind a wall is a regime that will always be a source of tension in Europe. It will always be at odds with free people everywhere." Address to Western Europe From the Venice Economic Summit (June 5, 1987).

184 "Today I say: As long as this gate is closed, as long as this scar of a wall is permitted to stand, it is not the German question alone that remains open, but the question of freedom for all mankind." Remarks on East-West Relations at the Brandenburg Gate in West Berlin (June 12, 1987).

185 "There is one sign the Soviets can make that would be unmistakable, that would advance dramatically the cause of freedom and peace. General Secretary Gorbachev, if you seek peace, if you seek prosperity for the Soviet Union and Eastern Europe, if you seek liberalization: Come here to this gate! Mr. Gorbachev, open this gate! Mr. Gorbachev, tear down this wall!" Remarks on East-West Relations at the Brandenburg Gate in West Berlin (June 12, 1987).

186 "[T]his wall will fall. For it cannot withstand faith; it cannot withstand truth. The wall cannot withstand freedom." Remarks on East-West Relations at the Brandenburg Gate in West Berlin (June 12, 1987).

187 "[N]o American who sees firsthand the concrete and mortar, the guardposts and machine-gun towers, the dog runs and the barbed wire can ever again take for granted his or her freedom or the precious gift that is America. That gift of freedom is actually the birthright of all humanity; and that's why, as I stood there, I urged the Soviet leader, Mr. Gorbachev, to send a new signal of openness to the world by tearing down that wall." Address to the Nation on the Venice Economic Summit, Arms Control, and the Deficit (June 15, 1987).

188 "As I said of the Berlin Wall, a nation that's so frightened of its own people that it treats them like prisoners will always be a source of tension in the world. If Mr. Gorbachev's actions match his words then — I said it there: Tear down the wall! Open the gate!" Remarks at a Senate Republican Policy Committee Luncheon (June 16, 1987).

189 "It's becoming more evident every day that collectivism is a dismal failure. Nowhere is that more clear than in Berlin, a bastion of freedom that I visited last week. The wall there divides a city, as you know, and imprisons a population. It's a monument to a repressive, stagnant system that today remains a force in the world only because of its military might and its power to subjugate and destroy." Remarks at a Fundraising Reception for Senator Orrin G. Hatch of Utah (June 17, 1987).

190 "[P]eople have put up small crosses on the free side of the wall — memorials to those who were killed trying to get over. On one side, the 'death strip'; on the other, memorials to those who fell crossing it. No place on Earth can you see more clearly the contrast between the prison that is communism and the spirit of liberty that lives in all of humanity." Radio Address to the Nation on the 26th Anniversary of the Berlin Wall (August 8, 1987).

191 "Today's Berlin Wall is very different from the crude strip of barbed wire that the people of Berlin woke up to the following morning 26 years ago. Changes have included the addition of guard towers, tank stops, razor-sharp metal fences, floodlights, ditches, and dog runs. The wall itself is now 12 feet high, concrete, and painted white so that anyone climbing it will make an easy target." Radio Address to the Nation on the 26th Anniversary of the Berlin Wall (August 8, 1987).

192 "I stood there alongside the cruel [Berlin] wall that symbolizes so powerfully the scar that divides the European continent. It's time for that wound to heal and that scar to disappear. Wouldn't it be a wonderful sight for the world to see, if someday General Secretary Gorbachev and I could meet in Berlin and together take down the first bricks of that wall...?" Address to the People of Western Europe on Soviet–United States Relations (November 4, 1987).

193 "To the Soviets today I say: I made my Berlin proposals almost 9 months ago. The people of Berlin and all of Europe deserve an answer. Make a start. Set a date, a specific date, when you will tear down the Wall. And on that date, bring it down." Address to the Citizens of Western Europe (February 23, 1988).

194 "Armaments are only the symptom, not the cause, of a much deeper division between free societies and the unfree. That division is at its heart a moral division. Perhaps it is best symbolized by the Berlin Wall and the horrible barrier that cuts down the center of Europe, dividing nations, peoples, families." Radio Address to the Nation Following the North Atlantic Treaty Organization Summit Meeting in Brussels, Belgium (March 5, 1988).

195 "Unfortunately, for Germans, as well as Americans, a horrendous scar continues to mar the hopes and prospects of a united Germany, free of totalitarian shackles. I'm speaking of course about the cruel and unnatural division of Europe and Germany, which is symbolized by the Berlin Wall — the wall that stands as a gash dividing those who hope and those who despair, and those who are free to do as they may and those who do only what the state will allow." Remarks at a Ceremony Commemorating German-American Day (October 6, 1988).

BROTHERHOOD

196 "Americans are brothers not because we share the same past and the same ancestry, but because we share the same ideals and the same hopes for the future." Remarks in New York City on Receiving the Charles Evans Hughes Gold Medal of the National Conference of Christians and Jews (March 23, 1982).

197 "Let us be true to our God and native land by standing by the ideals of liberty and opportunity that are so important to our heritage as free men and women. Let us prove again that America can truly be a promised land, a land where people of every race, creed, and background can live together in freedom, harmony, and prosperity. And let us proclaim for all to hear that America will have brotherhood from sea to shining sea." Remarks at a National Black Republican Council Dinner (September 15, 1982).

198 "In reaching out in brotherhood to our fellow citizens, we help stem the tide of historic challenges to mankind's advancement — starvation, disease, poverty, and war. Recognizing the precariousness of man's life on this planet, we strive to undergird the work of men and women of goodwill to bring about a world built upon the true values of fellowship and mutual respect." Message on the Observance of Brotherhood/Sisterhood Week, 1984 (February 17, 1984).

199 "In the history of our nation we've had problems with ill-spirited divisiveness — one race thinking it was better than another, one generation thinking it was superior to another. We've had religious divisions. We've had our share of bigotry. We've had tensions between this class or this group and that. And one of the good changes of recent years is that we've outgrown a lot of that nonsense. But we must commit ourselves to doing better. We are and must remain a pluralistic society, but we're also one nation together. We're brothers and sisters equal in the eyes of God and equal under the law." Remarks and a Question-and-Answer Session at the "Choose the Future" Conference in Chicago, Illinois (September 5, 1984).

200 "We're a little like climbers who begin their ascent from opposite ends of the mountain. The harder we try, the higher we climb, and the closer we come together — until that moment we reach the peak and we are as one." Remarks at the Annual Meeting of the Boards of Governors of the Individual Monetary Fund and the World Bank Group (September 25, 1984).

201 "As an older American, I remember a time when people of different race, creed, or ethnic origin in our land found hatred and prejudice installed in social custom and, yes, in law. There's no story more heartening in our history than the progress that we've made toward the brotherhood of man that God intended for us. Let us resolve there will be no turning back or hesitation on the road to an America rich in dignity and abundant with opportunity for all our citizens." Inaugural Address (January 21, 1985).

202 "Let us resolve that we, the people, will build an American opportunity society in which all of us — white and black, rich and poor, young and old — will go forward together, arm in arm. Again, let us remember that our heritage is one of blood lines from every corner of the Earth, we are all Americans, pledged to carry on this last, best hope of man on Earth." Inaugural Address (January 21, 1985).

203 "The truth is, it is only under freedom that a true fellowship of the spirit can exist. Love is not something that can be mandated by law or enforced by bureaucracy. It is when people voluntarily help one another, giving of themselves freely, that they receive the blessings of the soul which God has promised. This is an important part of freedom, the shining light which is a beacon to all who live in the darkness in tyranny — the fundamental truth that free people do indeed love and care for one another." Remarks at the Annual Convention of the Lions Club International in Dallas, Texas (June 21, 1985).

BUDGETARY AND FISCAL POLICIES

Budgetary and Economic Forecasts

204   "There are too many imponderables for anyone to predict deficits or surpluses several years ahead with any degree of accuracy." Address Before a Joint Session of the Congress Reporting on the State of the Union (January 26, 1982).

205   "While I don't believe in the accuracy of long-range projections, we're required to acknowledge them in our budgeting." Address to Nation on the Fiscal Year 1983 Budget (April 29, 1982).

206   "[I]'m sure all of you've grown a little weary of the great seers and prophets in the financial and political worlds, some optimistic, some pessimistic, who, even though they don't know how to predict accurately, at least know how to predict often." Remarks at the Republican Congressional "Salute to President Ronald Reagan Dinner" (May 4, 1982).

207   "I hope you'll keep in mind that economic forecasting is far from a perfect science. If recent history is any guide, the experts have some explaining to do about what they told us would happen but never did." Radio Address to the nation on the Economic Recovery Program (January 21, 1984).

208   "And you know, it's said that if you lined up all the economists in the world end to end, they still wouldn't reach a conclusion. Now, I feel free to tell that joke because my degree was in economics." Remarks to State Chairpersons of the National White House Conference on Small Business (August 15, 1986).

209   "The long-term solution to the plague of deficit spending, however, is not prudence this year or next. What's needed is reform that will bring discipline and accountability to the budget process." Radio Address to the Nation on the Federal Budget (February 20, 1987).

210   "The budget process is, indeed, a sorry spectacle: deadlines delayed or missed completely, huge continuing resolutions that camouflage the worst kind of special interest spending. Budget process? It's more like a magic show. It's wink and blink and smoke and mirrors and pulling rabbits out of hats, but almost all that ever comes up are designs to hide increases for the special interests." Radio Address to the Nation on Budget Reform (March 21, 1987).

211   "Simply put, the entire budget process has become a profound national embarrassment: every year, budget deadlines delayed or missed completely, monstrous continuing resolutions, billion-dollar hideouts for boondoggles and special interests. To tell you the truth, the whole process reminds me of the hit movie *The Little Shop of Horrors*. The budget isn't exactly like the man eating plant in the movie. And it isn't mean, it isn't green, and it doesn't come from outer space. But it does say, 'Feed me! Feed me! Feed me!'" Remarks at the 1987 Reagan Administration Executive Forum (March 30, 1987).

212   "[Our] economic expansion still has plenty of economists puzzled. You know economists; they're the sort of people who see something works in practice and wonder if it would work in theory." Remarks at the 1987 Reagan Administration Executive Forum (March 30, 1987).

213   "[T]he congressional budget process itself, with its missed deadlines and its gigantic catchall spending bills, is fatally flawed." Remarks and a Question-and-Answer Session with Southeast Regional Editors and Broadcasters (May 15, 1987).

214   "So, for now let me just reduce to three simple sentences what the whole budget issue comes down to: Some in Congress want to bust the budget. I won't let them. And the American people won't either." Remarks and a Question-and-Answer Session with Economic Reporters (June 16, 1987).

215   "That so-called budget process has become an embarrassment to the American way of governing." Remarks at the Dictaphone Corporation Employee Appreciation Day Picnic in Melbourne, Florida (June 22, 1987).

216   "The budget process has broken down; it needs a drastic overhaul. With each ensuing year, the spectacle before the American people is the same ... budget deadlines delayed or missed completely, monstrous continuing resolutions that pack hundreds of billions of dollars worth of spending into one bill, and a Federal Government on the brink of default." Address Before a Joint Session of Congress on the State of the Union (January 25, 1988).

Deficit Reduction

217   "Now, I know you've been told by some that we should do away with the tax cuts in order to reduce the deficit. That's like trying to pull a game out in the fourth quarter by punting on the third down." Radio Address to the Nation on the Program for Economic Recovery (April 3, 1982).

218   "Only a constitutional amendment will do the job. We've tried the carrot, and it failed. With the stick of a balanced budget amendment, we can stop government squandering, overtaxing ways, and save our economy." Address to Nation on the Fiscal Year 1983 Federal Budget (April 29, 1982).

219   "It's extremely difficult for the Congress to withstand the pressures for more spending. That's why I asked Congress to pass ... a constitutional amendment to require a balanced budget...." Radio Address to the Nation on the Program for Economic Recovery (May 1, 1982).

220   "Why is this government incapable of doing what their families, municipalities, and State governments do as a matter of course — spend within the limits of their revenues...? We must and will not, permit prospects for lasting economic recovery to be buried beneath an endless tied of red ink. Americans understand that the discipline of a balance budget amendment is essential to stop squandering and overtaxing." Remarks to Reporters on the Proposed Constitutional Amendment for a Balanced Federal Budget (July 12, 1982).

221   "The United States Congress breathes on a respirator that's pumping money, money, money. And the best way to pull the plug on its big spending ways is a balance budget amendment to our Constitution." Remarks at a Nevada Republican Party Rally in Reno (October 7, 1982).

222   "Governments don't reduce deficits by raising taxes on the people. Governments reduce deficits by controlling spending and stimulating new wealth, wealth from investments of brave people with hope for the future, trust in their fellow man, and faith in God." Radio Address to the Nation on Small Business (May 14, 1983).

223   "The liberal thesis — that we can whack the deficit by soaking the rich and cutting defense spending — is just plain wrong." Remarks at the Biennial Convention of the National Federation of Republican Women in Louisville, Kentucky (October 7, 1983).

224   "[I]t's time for the Federal government, in the best federalist tradition, to learn something from successful experiments in State and local laboratories of governments. The evidence from States and many municipalities is overwhelming. The executive branch needs a powerful weapon to cut out porkbarreling and special interest expenditures buried in large, catchall appropriations bills. It is time for Congress to give the President the authority to veto single line items in the Federal budget...." Remarks at Eureka College in Eureka, Illinois (February 6, 1984).

225   "Those who would be heroes trying to reduce deficits by raising taxes are not heroes. They have not addressed the point I made in the State of the Union: Whether government borrows or increases taxes, it will be taking the same amount of money from the private economy and, either way, that's too much." Remarks at the Annual Conservative Political Action Conference Dinner (March 2, 1984).

226   "How we come to grips with the deficit problem means a great deal. Any solution that places the emphasis on raising taxes is no solution at all. It's a formula for failure, because we'd be taxing ourselves right back into a recession." Remarks at a Luncheon with Community Leaders in Fairbanks, Alaska (May 1, 1984).

227   "My approach to deficit reduction is ... no secret. We should reduce deficits first and foremost by continuing our economic growth and by reducing wasteful government spending." Radio Address to the Nation on Deficit Reduction and Taxation (August 4, 1984).

228   "[W]e need to give the office of the Presidency the tool it needs [the line item veto] to cut out the porkbarreling and special interest expenditures the liberals in Congress are so fond of." Remarks at the Annual Convention of the American Legion in Salt Lake City, Utah (September 4, 1984).

229   "We do not believe, as some propose, that higher taxes on income, capital, and labor is the way to reduce budget deficits. That was a bad policy before, and it's bad policy today. Entrepreneurs must not be discouraged; they must be encouraged." Remarks and a Question-and-Answer Session at the "Choosing a Future" Conference in Chicago, Illinois (September 5, 1984).

230   "We must act to protect future generations from government's desire to spend its citizens' money and tax them into servitude when the bills come due. Let us a make it unconstitutional for the Federal Government to spend more than the Federal Government takes in." Inaugural Address (January 21, 1985).

231   "A dynamic economy, with more citizens working and paying taxes, will be our strongest tool to bring down budget deficits." Inaugural Address (January 21, 1985).

232   "First, as surely as night follows day, you'll hear that we can't make lasting progress bringing deficits down until we agree to a tax increase. Wrong. Our problem isn't that you're paying too little taxes; it's that government is spending too much money." Radio Address to the Nation on the Fiscal Year 1986 Budget (February 2, 1985).

233   "When your families do well, government spends and borrows. When you don't do well, government spends and borrows. Our future economic success depends on the economy growing faster than government spending. That's why

raising taxes would boomerang. Economic growth would slow, revenues would decline, and the budget deficit would swell." Radio Address to the Nation on the Fiscal Year 1986 Budget (February 2, 1985).

234   "As we lighten government's burden on our private sector through budget control, we should remember that no amount of cutting and no paring will help if we, at the same time, add to the burden by raising taxes. All we should be doing is shifting the load from one saddlebag to another." Remarks to Congressional Leaders During a White House Briefing on the Fiscal Year 1986 Budget (February 4, 1985).

235   "The case for a line-item veto should by now be obvious. The Governors of 43 States have used this authority effectively, and such authority has only once been withdrawn, only later to be reinstated." Message to the Congress Transmitting the Annual Economic Report of the President (February 5, 1985).

236   "We want to adopt the wisdom understood in every American household: that government shouldn't live beyond its means, that it shouldn't spend more than it takes in. We need that balanced budget amendment." Remarks at a White House Meeting with Members of the National Governors' Association (February 25, 1985).

237   "Now, whether government borrows or increases taxes, it will be taking the same amount of money from the private economy, and either way, that's too much. We must bring down government spending. We need a constitutional amendment requiring a balanced budget." Remarks at the Annual Dinner of the Conservative Political Action Conference (March 1, 1985).

238   "When push comes to shove [spending cuts versus raising taxes], I guess it's always easier to let the taxpayer take the fall." Remarks at a White House Meeting with Members of the American Business Conference (March 13, 1985).

239   "If the Democrats in the House can't bring themselves to cut wasteful Federal spending, there's always another option: Give me what 43 Governors already have — a line-item veto. I'll take the political heat; in fact, I'll enjoy it." Remarks at the Annual Republican Senate/House Fundraising Dinner (March 16, 1985).

240   "The tax-increasers are like those soldiers after World War II out on some of those Pacific islands who didn't know the war had ended. They've lost the fight, and they're now reduced to hit-and-run attacks on budget reform." Remarks at a White House Meeting with the Deficit Reduction Coalition (April 16, 1985).

241   "When it comes to taxes, what we need is simplification and reform, not increases." Remarks and a Question-and-Answer Session with Regional Editors and Broadcasters (April 18, 1985).

242   "[W]e should use this opportunity to trim programs that are wasteful, ineffective, and unnecessary — many of which never should have been funded with Federal tax dollars in the first place. To keep pouring your tax dollars into ... unworthy programs at the current levels while at the same time limiting worthwhile, efficient, and absolutely necessary programs would be a travesty. A freeze is a decision not to make a decision, a retreat in the face of special interest pressure." Remarks at the Midyear Conference of the National Association of Realtors (April 23, 1985).

243   "[U]nlike a spending freeze, which would not reduce deficits nearly enough and which would make no distinction between worthy and wasteful programs, our plan recognizes that all spending is not created equal. Some programs are vital to our national security and domestic welfare and must be given first priority. Others are no longer affordable or were not proper Federal responsibilities to begin with." Address to the Nation on the Federal Budget and Deficit Reduction (April 24, 1985).

244   "The across-the-board freeze they [the "big spenders" in Congress] advocate would limit worthwhile and absolutely needed programs while at the same time freeze in wasteful and inefficient ones. A freeze is really a decision not to make a decision. It is a retreat in front of special interest pressure." Radio Address to the Nation on the Bonn Economic Summit and the Federal Budget (April 27, 1985).

245   "[R]aising taxes will simply make it more likely that Congress will increase spending." Radio Address to the Nation on the Bonn Economic Summit and the Federal Budget (April 27, 1985).

246   "[T]here are still a few people, also, who want to raise your taxes. There are also a few people who still claim the Earth is flat. As far as we're concerned, those questions were answered a long time ago — both of them." Remarks at the Annual Republican Senate/House Fundraising Dinner (May 16, 1985).

247   "The Chief Executive of the United States should have the same tool to control spending as 43 Governors have today in this land. It'll provide leverage against pork-barreling at the taxpayers' expense. The only ones threatened by it are the big spenders and the special interests. The line-item veto is long overdue." Remarks at a Fundraising Dinner for Senator Mack Mattingly in Atlanta, Georgia (June 5, 1985).

248   "[F]reezes and other one-time measures ... are not solutions that would permit us to get a handle on Federal overspending, they would only postpone the inevitable." Radio Address to the Nation on the Federal Budget (June 22, 1985).

249   "We cannot reduce chronic overspending by Congress with a mere carrot of friendly appeals to good intentions. We must also be able to bear down with a rod of real discipline." Remarks and a Question-and-Answer Session with Reporters (August 5, 1985).

250   "Give me a line-item veto.... Give me the authority to veto waste, and I'll take the responsibility, I'll make the cuts, I'll take the heat." Address Before a Joint Session of Congress on the State of the Union (February 4, 1986).

251   "America doesn't need higher taxes; it needs less deficit spending. Raising taxes would knock the legs out from under economic growth, leaving us with higher taxes and higher spending." Remarks at a Senate Campaign Fundraiser for Former Governor Christopher S. (Kit) Bond in St. Louis, Missouri (February 12, 1986).

252   "We all know ... that there are those who believe the answer to high deficit spending is to increase your taxes — and then increase them again. Well, that's their answer to just about every problem — rob Peter to pay Paul. They don't realize Peter went bankrupt a long time ago." Remarks at a Senate Campaign Fundraiser for Representative W. Henson Moore in New Orleans, Louisiana (March 27, 1986).

253   "[G]ive me the line-item veto. I'll take the political heat. In fact, I'll enjoy it. As a Governor, with the line-item veto on budgets, I did it 943 times in 8 years without being overridden once." Remarks to State Chairpersons of the National White House Conference on Small Business (August 15, 1986).

254 "All it [the line item veto] would mean is that the President could selectively sign or veto individual spending items, that he wouldn't have to take the fat along with the meat." Radio Address to the Nation on the Reform of the Budget Process (November 8, 1986).

255 "I have long supported passing a constitutional amendment that would make balanced budgets mandatory. Then we wouldn't have to fight this battle all year, every year. America could greet the future confident that the monster of deficit spending was locked away forever in its cage." Radio Address to the Nation on Deficit Reduction (February 28, 1987).

256 "As I've been saying right along, the problem is the congressional budget process itself. Congress just refuses to exercise any budget discipline. That's why it's essential that the President be given the power to step in and cut out the waste." Radio Address to the Nation on International Trade and the Deficit (May 2, 1987).

257 "Polls show that 70 percent of the American people support a balanced budget amendment and have for years, but we can't even get an up and down vote in Congress. The reason: The big spenders don't want a balanced budget, pure and simple." Remarks at the Annual Meeting of the National Association of Manufacturers (May 28, 1987).

258 "Our founders intended the President to represent the broad national interest, including the interest in an overall limit on spending. That's why they gave the President the veto. But in recent years, Congress has found ways to encroach on Presidential veto power. This year, for example, the Government is being financed out of a single, gigantic, catchall resolution. My choice: sign or shut down the Government." Remarks at the Annual Meeting of the National Association of Manufacturers (May 28, 1987).

259 "Using taxes to cure deficits is like using leeches to cure anemia. We're not going to counter one evil with another; we're going to eliminate them both. Deficits are going the way of high

taxes: They're both being mowed down to make way for a new era of growth and opportunity." Remarks at a Senate Republican Policy Committee Luncheon (June 16, 1987).

260 "Raising taxes to bring down deficit spending is kamikaze economics. Raising tax rates, when all is said and done, would leave our government with less, not more, revenue. It would crash into our economy, sink growth and job creation, and lower the tax base. We could end up with the worst of all worlds: higher taxes, higher deficits, higher unemployment, and economic decline." Remarks at a Fundraising Reception for Senator Orrin G. Hatch of Utah (June 17, 1987).

261 "Well, the line-item veto simply means that when they're passing a piece of legislation that ordinarily the President would want to sign and be able to sign, but then somebody sticks a couple of spending measures in there that have nothing to do with the original bill, the President ought to have the right to sign that bill after he has vetoed those particular spending measures and gotten them out of the bill." Remarks on Arrival in Melbourne, Florida (June 22, 1987).

262 "The veto power of the President ... is no longer the potent force for fiscal responsibility as set down in the Constitution. This was clear last year when all government appropriations were thrown into one gigantic, catchall resolution. And for me, it was a take-it-or-leave-it, all-or-nothing choice — doing damage to long-respected constitutional checks and balances. The first step in reestablishing these checks and balances is giving the President the authority to cut out the fat, yet leave the meat, of legislation that gets to his desk." Remarks Announcing America's Economic Bill of Rights (July 3, 1987).

263 "The only force strong enough to stop this nation's massive runaway budget is the Constitution. Only the Constitution — the document from which all government power flows, the document that provides our moral authority as a nation — only the Constitution can compel responsibility." Address to the Nation on the Iran Arms and Contra Aid Controversy and Administration Goals (August 12, 1987).

264 "Unfortunately, expenses, special interest provisions, are often added to needed legislation. We can no longer afford this costly all-or-nothing way of doing business. The President should be able to cut the fat yet keep the meat of spending bills that reach his desk. The tool needed to cut that fat is the line-item veto." Radio Address to the Nation on Fiscal Integrity and Efficiency in the Federal Government (August 22, 1987).

265 "Every time Congress increases taxes, the deficit does not decrease, spending increases." Radio Address to the Nation on the Federal Debt Ceiling Increase and Deficit Reduction (September 26, 1987).

266 "But one way or another we owe it to our children to see that before the decade is out the Constitution of the United States of America includes a balanced budget amendment. The first man to ask for that was Thomas Jefferson, who at the time of ratification of the Constitution said it has one glaring omission: it does not have a clause prohibiting the Federal Government from borrowing." Remarks at a Luncheon Hosted by the New Jersey Chamber of Commerce in Somerset (October 13, 1987).

267 "Our opponents say they're against deficits, but they want to end the deficit by raising your taxes. I want to end it by cutting their spending. That's not going to be easy. Few Americans realize it, but a little more than a decade ago our government had a major shift in the checks and balances of budgetmaking power. The President's relative role was diminished, and the Congress' enhanced. And before that, Federal debt with inflation taken out had been steady or declining for a quarter of a century. Since then it's been in a climb. And this is why I've said it's time for the President to have ... a line-item veto." Remarks at a Luncheon Hosted by the New Jersey Chamber of Commerce in Somerset (October 13, 1987).

268 "One thing I can tell you is that everyone knows now that the [deficit] problem will not be solved simply by raising the taxes of the American people." Remarks at a White House Briefing for Members of Business Partners (November 19, 1987).

269 "Each year, I'm given a choice: hold my nose and swallow it whole, wasteful spending and all, or veto the entire bill, closing down much of the Federal Government. I do not believe that this is what the Founding Fathers had in mind when they gave the President the power to veto individual appropriations bills." Radio Address to the Nation on Foreign Issues and the Budget (December 19, 1987).

270 "The Constitution gives the President the authority to veto legislation and the Congress the authority to override that veto. When our forefathers framed that historic document, I'm sure they did not envision the dilemma a President faces today: Either veto the legislation needed to run the Government or sign into law a bill that does little to promote the national welfare." Remarks and a Question-and-Answer Session with Members of the City Club of Cleveland, Ohio (January 11, 1988).

271 "[S]ome people, complaining about the deficit — and no one complains about it louder than I do — when they complain about it, they cite our reducing taxes in these last several years. Well, I think someone should pay attention to the fact that every time we have reduced the rates, we have increased the total revenue paid in taxes by the people to the Government because there is an incentive for people to earn more and to go out and to experiment, and so forth. And so, no, the deficit has not been caused by the cut in taxes. The deficit would increase if we yielded to those who want us to increase taxes." Remarks and a Question-and-Answer Session with Members of the City Club of Cleveland, Ohio (January 11, 1988).

272 "Doesn't the new practice of creating gigantic continuing resolutions require a new and better response? Can anything but enactment of a line-item veto provide the leverage we need to curb wasteful and unnecessary spending?" Remarks and a Question-and-Answer Session with the Members of the Center for the Study of the Presidency (March 25, 1988).

273 "We also must get control of Federal spending, once and for all. Congress has had control of the budget process for 14 years and made a mess of it. One thousand page continuing resolutions you can hardly lift — forget about vetoing by the line, I'm ready to veto by the pound. But it's time to strengthen the President's hand in the budget process. It's too late for me to have the benefit of this, but it's time to give the Presidency ... a line-item veto." Remarks at the Annual Meeting of the United States Chamber of Commerce (May 2, 1988).

274   "And I promise you this, even after I leave office, I will never stop campaigning for the tools needed to limit the insatiable fiscal appetite of government. To protect our prosperity, the President needs the line-item veto, and America needs a constitutionally mandated balanced budget." Remarks at the Annual Republican Congressional Fundraising Dinner (May 11, 1988).

275   "To solve the deficit problem, it is essential that we restore the constitutional balance and repair the system. We need to give the President greater authority to limit spending — that means the line-item veto.... Congress must reform its faulty budget process. And we need a balanced budget amendment to the Constitution so the Federal Government does not spend more than it takes in." Radio Address to the Nation on the Federal Budget Deficit (December 17, 1988).

276   "Higher taxes mean slow economic growth, and economic growth combined with budget realism is the key to eliminating the deficit. George Bush's lips have been eloquent on this subject...." Radio Address to the Nation on New Year's Eve (December 31, 1988).

277   "Raising taxes would be the surest way to kill the economic goose that lays the golden eggs. So, I leave as I came: dead-set against any new taxes. And even if there were a tax increase, history shows that Congress would almost certainly spend the additional money. It wouldn't be used to reduce the deficit; it would just mean that you had to pay for an even bigger government." Radio Address to the Nation on the Federal Budget and Executive Salaries (January 7, 1989).

Deficits

278   "[What] we're trying to do is alter the economic situation in our country by changing one simple two-letter word, economic control by government to economic control on government." Toasts at a Dinner Honoring the Nation's Governors (February 24, 1981).

279   "The one sure way to reduce projected deficits, bring down interest rates, and still encourage growth is to reduce government's share of the gross national product." Remarks on the Program for Economic Recovery at a White House Luncheon for Editors and Broadcasters from Southeastern States (April 16, 1982).

280   "The American people need deeds, not just promises, to be convinced deficits will be reduced." Message to the House of Representatives Returning Without Approval a Fiscal Year 1982 Supplemental Appropriations Bill (June 25, 1982).

281   "I've said before on occasion that balancing the budget is like protecting your virtue. You just have to learn to say no." Remarks at a Rally Supporting the Proposed Constitutional Amendment for a Balanced Federal Budget (July 19, 1982).

282   "There is a better way. Balance the budget by bringing to heel a Federal establishment which has taken too much power from the States, too much liberty with the Constitution, and too much money from the people." Remarks at a Rally Supporting the Proposed Constitutional Amendment for a Balanced Federal Budget (July 19, 1982).

283   "Others insist that a constitution should not embody economic theory. Well, I've got news for them. A wise and frugal government which does not take from the mouth of labor the bread it has earned is not economic theory. The integrity to stand for sound money, and end to deficit national debt, and eventual retirement of the national debt is not economic theory. Those principles are at the very heart of a tried and proven system...." Remarks at a Rally Supporting the Proposed Constitutional Amendment for a Balance Federal Budget (July 19, 1982).

284   "You know, the actress Clara Bow once said of the famous Montana movie star, Gary Cooper — she said, 'When he puts his arms around me, I feel like a horse.' Well, for a conservative President like me to have to put his arms around a multibillion-dollar deficit, it's like holding your nose and embracing a pig. And believe me that budget deficit is as slippery as a greased pig." Remarks in Billings, Montana, at a Celebration Marking the Centennial of Billings and Yellowstone County (August 11, 1982).

285   "Governments don't reduce deficits by raising taxes on the people. Governments reduce deficits by controlling spending and stimulating new wealth, wealth from investments of brave people with hope for the future, trust in their fellow man, and faith in God." Radio Address to the Nation on Small Business (May 14, 1983).

286   "Incredibly, the liberal House leadership — the same people who now take the well of the House each morning to decry deficits — claimed, believe it or not, that a balanced budget would wreck our economy. That's a little like saying that good exercise, three square meals a day, and plenty of sleep at night will destroy your health." Remarks at the Biennial Convention of the National Federation of Republican Women in Louisville, Kentucky (October 7, 1983).

287   "[Waste, fraud, abuse, and mismanagement] grow and spread like an unchecked cancer, plundering your pocketbooks and hindering government's ability to provide essential public services in an efficient and timely manner." Radio Address to the Nation on Waste, Fraud, Abuse, and Mismanagement in the Federal Government (May 5, 1984).

288   "We got into this deficit mess not because government collects too little in taxes, but because government spends too much." Remarks by Telephone to the Annual Convention of the National Association of Home Builders in Houston, Texas (January 29, 1985).

289   "The record suggests that in a democracy the scaling back of domestic spending may well be the most politically difficult act a government can undertake. Yet when we succeed, we'll know that we fought the good fight with intelligence and skill and that we put our nation on a course of prosperity for decades to come." Remarks at a Senate Republican Policy Committee Luncheon (March 19, 1985).

290   "Courage and leadership are crucial if we expect to bring deficits down in a manner that protects our security and permits continued strong economic growth." Radio Address to the Nation on the Federal Budget and the Central American Peace Proposal (April 6, 1985).

291   "Deficits slow growth; they don't create it." Remarks to Community Leaders in Madrid, Spain (May 7, 1985).

292   "We also know that if we leave the pork barrels intact, the same political pressure groups will be back next year trying to fill them with pork." Remarks at a White House Meeting with the Deficit Reduction Coalition (April 16, 1985).

293   "It's been said that any government that robs Peter to pay Paul is bound to have the support of Paul. I think it's time we noticed that we can't rob Peter anymore. He went bankrupt a long time ago." Remarks at the Midyear Conference of the National Association of Realtors (April 23, 1985).

294   "The simple truth is: No matter how hard you work, no matter how strong this economy grows, no matter how much more tax money comes to Washington, it won't amount to a hill of beans if government won't curb its endless appetite to spend." Address to the Nation on the Federal Budget and Deficit Reduction (April 24, 1985).

295   "Well, there is no magic money machine. Every dollar the government spends comes out of your pockets. Every dollar the government gives to someone has to first be taken away from someone else. So, it's our moral duty to make sure that we can justify every one of your tax dollars, that we spend them wisely and carefully and, just as important, fairly." Address to the Nation on the Federal Budget and Deficit Reduction (April 24, 1985).

296   "Slogans and easy answers, like a freeze or raising taxes, are not the way to go. The answer is responsible reduction of Federal spending. It will work if we have the courage to say no to the special interest groups." Radio Address to the Nation on the Bonn Economic Summit and the Federal Budget (April 27, 1985).

297   "While spending control is vital to the economic well-being of this nation, the highest priority of any American Government is preservation of the national security. The maintenance of a national defense second to none, indeed, the only legitimate justification for running a large annual deficit — as we ran every year of World War II — is preservation of the Nation, itself." Radio Address to the Nation on the Budget Deficit and the Middle East (October 5, 1985).

298   "We do not face large deficits because American families are undertaxed; we face those deficits because the Federal Government overspends." Address Before a Joint Session of Congress on the State of the Union (February 4, 1986).

299   "So, I think there's a lesson never to be forgotten here: It's people, not government, who create wealth, provide growth, and ensure prosperity. That may sound elementary enough, but the history or our economic difficulties, especially the terribly big deficits we run each year, stem directly from our failure to remember that government consumes wealth, it doesn't create it." Radio Address to the Nation on the Deficit (November 29, 1986).

300   "Following the theories of a noted English economist of the period, John Maynard Keynes, economists and politicians used to say that when bad times occur the only way to restore prosperity is to spend our way out of it with massive new government programs paid for by borrowing. 'We owe it to ourselves!' they used to chant. But everybody knows you can't spend yourself rich any more than you can drink yourself sober. And you can't prime the pump without pumping the prime." Radio Address to the Nation on the Deficit (November 29, 1986).

301   "I am willing to work with congressional leaders for a reasonable bill. But I have a special message to the new Congress: You can't have it both ways. You cannot decry deficits and then pass budget-busting legislation. The American people expect us to work together to eliminate the deficit." Radio Address to the Nation on the Fiscal Year 1988 Budget (January 3, 1987).

302   "They [the Founding Fathers] knew they had created a good document but not a perfect one. In fact, even two centuries ago, some of them, especially Thomas Jefferson, were troubled by one omission: the lack of a limitation on public borrowing by the Federal Government. They knew from firsthand experience how tyranny abused the fiscal powers of government, how excessive borrowing and heavy taxation led to inflated currencies and economic hardship. Well, even in their reservations about the Constitution the Founding Fathers were perceptive and wise." Radio Address to the Nation on Memorial Day and the Budget Deficit (May 23, 1987).

303   "Deficits are simply a destructive economic force. They are a giant drain on the productive economy like a huge, disguised tax on the private sector. In fact, the only thing worse than deficits is high taxes." Remarks at a Senate Republican Policy Committee Luncheon (June 16, 1987).

304   "Some say the deficit is the responsibility of the President. Well, the fact is, according to the Constitution, the President can't spend one nickel. Congress appropriates every cent in the budget and every single cent that makes up our deficit. Every year we consult with the people in the Cabinet and the agencies, the people who actually run these programs. We ask them what they need and then put together a responsible budget. Each year, Congress announces — sometimes before they even see it — that our budget is dead on arrival. Then they put together their own budget. I have a choice: Take it, pork and all, or veto it, and see the entire United States Government grind to a halt. This is no way to run a country." Radio Address to the Nation on Budget Reform (June 20, 1987).

305   "Yes, we can go ahead and keep borrowing. We can spend beyond our means. But one day the bills will come due. And even before they arrive, we'll be living with a government whose uncontrolled spending robs families and enterprising men and women of the savings and incentive to build for themselves, for our nation, and for the future. That's our choice: Close the deficit and lock economic expansion in place for the years ahead, or return to the days of inflation and stagnation." Radio Address to the Nation on Economic Growth and Deficit Reduction (June 27, 1987).

306   "When we cut spending, it must stay cut, no coming back to next year with new programs or replacing old reductions with new increases. From now on, deficit cuts, like diamonds, must be forever." Radio Address to the Nation on the Supreme Court Nomination of Douglas H. Ginsburg and the Federal Budget (October 31, 1987).

307   "In my years in the White House, I've seen one Member of Congress after another call for lower deficits and less spending and then go out and vote for more spending. Some ... just want more spending, period, but many are sincere. They're prisoners of a dilemma. If nearby districts or States get so many Federal dollars, they must bring at least as much home or look bad. So they swap increases for increases, and deficit spending goes up." Remarks at the Annual Meeting of the American Council of Life Insurance (November 16, 1987).

308   "Now, as popular as the notion seems to be within the Beltway, I cannot bring myself to operate under the assumption that our citizens are at fault because they're undertaxed and selfishly putting themselves above the national interest." Remarks to the United States Chamber of Commerce on the Economy and Deficit Reduction (November 19, 1987).

309   "I'm not saying there aren't problems [in the economy]. The one that sticks out like a sore thumb is that United States budget deficit. It's an embarrassment and a shame — most dangerous, perhaps, because it signals the complete breakdown of one of the most basic functions of the United States Government." Remarks and a Question-and-Answer Session with Members of the City Club of Cleveland, Ohio (January 11, 1988).

310   "You know, a few of us can remember when, not too many years ago, those who created the deficits said they would make us prosperous and not to worry about the debt, because we owe it to ourselves. Well, at last there is agreement that we can't spend ourselves rich." Address Before a Joint Session of Congress on the State of the Union (January 25, 1988).

311   "You may have heard a lot of campaign talk from our liberal friends recently about the Federal deficit and Federal debt. What you don't hear them say is that the President can't spend one dime of the Government's money without congressional appropriations. Only Congress can decide how much the Government spends. Only Congress can pass spending bills. Only Congress can determine how big the deficit will be, or if we're to have a deficit at all. In fact, it is against the law for the President to spend a penny more or a penny less than Congress directs him to spend. The President can't add to the deficit. He can't subtract from it either. That's Congress' job." Radio Address to the Nation on the Federal Budget and the Congressional Elections (October 15, 1988).

312   "[T]here's a simple way to reduce a deficit. And you know how you do it? You spend less money. It's so simple only a liberal could miss it." Remarks at a Fundraising Dinner for Senatorial Candidate George Voinovich in Cincinnati, Ohio (October 19, 1988).

313   "No, we haven't been able to balance the budget, because the President not only can't spend money, he can't save money. Only the Congress can do that. If a Department or Agency's got some money left over, the Congress says they've got to spend it. That's why we've got an awful lot of warehouses with office furniture in them — because the only way they know, sometimes, to spend up the surplus is to buy new furniture." Remarks at a Republican Campaign Rally in Berea, Ohio (November 2, 1988).

314   "[I]t's no secret that one of my great disappointments as I leave office is that the Federal budget itself is not yet balanced." Remarks to Administration Officials on Domestic Policy (December 13, 1988).

Inflation

315   "Inflation is not just high prices; it's a reduction in the value of money." Address to the Nation on the Economy (February 5, 1981).

316   "I know the ladies know about inflation. Once upon a time you used to put some money in your purse and go to the market and buy a bag full of groceries. Now you take a bag full of money, go to the market, and bring the groceries home in your purse." Remarks on Arrival at Point Mugu Naval Air Station, California (February 19, 1981).

317   "They never answer the one question that I keep asking.... Why is it inflationary if the people keep their own money and spend it the way they want to and it is not inflationary if the government takes it and spends the way it wants to." Remarks on the Program for Economic Recovery at a White House Reception for Business and Government Leaders (June 11, 1981).

318   "[F]looding the market with money ... will be the answer ... for a short period of time [a]nd then in about two years you will have another recession worse than the one you have just got through fixing with inflation higher and unemployment higher." Remarks at a Meeting with Participants in the American Business Conference (September 28, 1982).

319   "Winning the war against inflation is probably the best economic legacy we could leave to the next generation." Radio Address to the Nation on International Trade (August 6, 1983).

320   "No American should undermine confidence in this nation's currency. A strong dollar is one of our greatest weapons against inflation." Remarks at the Annual Conservative Political Action Conference Dinner (March 2, 1984).

321   "Inflation was not some plague borne on the wind; it was a deliberate part of their official economic policy, needed, they said, to maintain prosperity. They didn't tell us that with it would come the highest interest rates since the Civil War." Remarks Accepting the Presidential Nomination at the Republican National Convention in Dallas, Texas (August 23, 1984).

322   "Inflation and high interest rates are not caused by people living too well; inflation and high interest rates are caused by government living too well." Remarks and a Question-and-Answer Session at the Economic Club of Detroit in Detroit, Michigan (October 1, 1984).

323   "[I]nflation was the quiet thief ... stealing our savings." Remarks at a Reagan-Bush Rally in Medford, Oregon (October 22, 1984).

324   "There is ... no crueler burden on the poverty-stricken and the elderly than inflation." Remarks at a White House Briefing for Supporters of Welfare Reform (February 9, 1987).

Reaganomics

GENERAL

325   "That plan [the Reagan plan for economic prosperity] is based on four commonsense fundamentals: continued reduction of the growth in Federal spending; preserving the individual and business tax reductions that will stimulate saving and investment; removing unnecessary Federal regulations to spark productivity; and maintaining a healthy dollar and a stable monetary policy...." Address Before a Joint Session of the Congress Reporting on the State of the Union (January 26, 1982).

326   "We will not play hopscotch economics, jumping here and jumping there as the daily sit-

uation changes. We have faith in our program, and we're sticking with it." Address Before a Joint Session of the Indiana State Legislature in Indianapolis (February 9, 1982).

327   "Have we all become addicted to temporary bailouts, failing to realize that the only answer must be a restoration of our economy from sea to shining sea?" Remarks at the Annual Convention of the National League of cities in Los Angeles, California (November 29, 1982).

328   "An economic recovery is something like a seedling. For awhile it grows underground, and you don't see it above ground, and then it shoots up and seeds sprouting all over the place. And that's what we're starting to see all around the Nation right now, the shoots of a recovery beginning to push up through the recession...." Remarks to Employees at the Chrysler Corporation of St. Louis Assembly Plan in Fenton, Missouri (February 1, 1983).

329   "The word is 'Reaganomics.' Somewhere along the line, our economic program got tagged with that label. To tell you the truth, it isn't a name I would have chosen. It sounds like a fad diet or an aerobic exercise. But we seem to be stuck with it. With every anchorman on the evening news, a goodly share of political pundits, and more than a few politicos using it, it has a good chance of becoming standard Americana." Radio Address to the Nation on the Economic Recovery Program (February 5, 1983).

330   "[R]ecession is giving way to a rainbow of recovery, reflecting a renaissance in enterprise. America is on the mend." Remarks and a Question-and-Answer Session with Members of the Commonwealth Club of California in San Francisco (March 4, 1983).

331   "[I] think the greatest and most positive indicator of all is they aren't calling it Reaganomics anymore. They never should have called it that. It was the result of that Republican majority that we finally have in the Senate after more than a quarter of a century of living in the wilderness and a combination of good, sound, and prominent Democratic Congressmen and Republicans in the House that made that economic plan go into effect." Remarks at a Fundraising Dinner for Senator John Tower in Houston, Texas (April 29, 1983).

332 "In the name of fairness, let's stop trying to plunder family budgets with higher taxes, and start controlling the real problem — Federal spending. In the name of growth, let's stop talking about billions more for dependency and start creating enterprise and new incentives for opportunity — so we can keep the dream alive for millions of aspiring whites, back, and Hispanics. In the name of America, let's stop spreading bondage and start spreading freedom." Remarks at the Annual Meeting of the American Bar Association in Atlanta, Georgia (August 1, 1983).

333 "[I] don't mean a miracle [the economic turnaround] like a magic trick; I mean a miracle of determination, hard work, and teamwork." Remarks at a Luncheon Sponsored by the Senate Republican Policy Committee. (January 24, 1984).

334 "I remember saying back when things looked the worst that too much pessimism could be deadly. Well, some people criticized me for trying to sugar-coat bad news. I merely wanted us to remember that there's a psychological factor in recession, and too much hammering at it makes recession worse." Radio Address to the Nation on the Economic Recovery Program (March 10, 1984).

335 "Some might attribute our success to the 'luck o' the Irish.' Well, maybe we have enjoyed a bit of luck. But believe me, the real reason is an economic program based on common sense." Radio Address to the Nation on the Economic Recovery Program (March 17, 1984).

336 "Now, this isn't a Keynesian recovery produced by big-spending bureaucrats tinkering with aggregate demand. In fact, I don't know of a single Keynesian who predicted it. Instead, this recovery was created by the incentives of tax rate reductions, which shifted resources away from government back to American producers, savers, and investors." Remarks on Signing the Annual Report on the State of Small Business (March 19, 1984).

337 "Lasting economic recovery [has] to be built on the solid rock of the American free enterprise." Remarks at a White House Meeting with the American Retail Federation (May 16, 1984).

338 "[Y]ou can tell our program is working ... the critics don't call it Reaganomics anymore." Remarks and a Question-and-Answer Session with Regional Editors on Foreign and Domestic Issues (July 9, 1984).

339 "[W]e ... believe that we should work together to make a bigger pie, so everyone can have a bigger splice." Remarks at a Meeting with Reagan-Bush Campaign Leadership Groups (October 30, 1984).

340 "The American miracle of which the world now speaks is a triumph of free people and their private institutions, not government." The President's News Conference [prepared statement] (February 21, 1985).

341 "If we're concerned about young people, a youth employment opportunity wage would cost the Government nothing, yet would provide employment opportunities to so many kids who are not [now] frozen out of those summer, part-time, weekend, after-school jobs." Remarks at the Midyear Conference of the National Association of Realtors (April 23, 1985).

342 "And you know, I said this before, but I'm going to repeat it, I was certain our program was working when they stopped calling it Reaganomics." Remarks at the Annual Meeting of the Chamber of Commerce of the United States (April 29, 1985).

343 "John Kenneth Galbraith [who had earlier said that Reaganomics was "an unprecedented experiment in economic policy, and it has failed"], where art thou now?" Remarks at the Annual Meeting of the Chamber of Commerce of the United States (April 29, 1985).

344 "We came to believe that government was more the problem than the solution, that the massive growth of government spending was weighing down the private sector, and that huge increases in taxes and regulations were stifling individual initiative and destroying opportunity for our people. In our country we've always held it as an article of faith that freedom works, and I came into office determined to give freedom a chance." Remarks to Community Leaders in Madrid, Spain (May 7, 1985).

345 "Instead of trying to redistribute existing wealth, we've tried to produce more. Instead of imposing more controls and regulations, we've sought to free our peoples entrepreneurial spirit. Instead of channeling more of our resources into bureaucracy, we've sought to expand private investment." Toast at the State Dinner in Madrid, Spain (May 7, 1985).

346 "I believe the worth of any economic policy must be measured by the strength of its commitment to American families, the bedrock of our society. There is no instrument of hard work, savings, and job creation as effective as the family. There is no cultural institution as ennobling as family life. And there is no superior, indeed no equal, means to rear the young, protect the weak, or attend the elderly. None." Address to the Nation on Tax Reform (May 28, 1985).

347 "In the past 5 years, the American people — not the politicians, not the elites, not the heavy-browed intellectuals, but the American people — singlehandedly turned our country around. And all we in Washington did was try to get the Government out of your way." Remarks to Citizens in Bloomfield, New Jersey (June 13, 1985).

348 "I've often said and believe it must always remain our goal: We cannot be satisfied until the United States can outproduce, outcompete, and outsell anybody, anywhere in the world." Remarks at the Annual Convention of the United States Jaycees in Indianapolis, Indiana (June 19, 1985).

349 "No American seeking opportunity through an expanding economy can break free if government erodes their take-home pay with new taxes. Minorities and women can't break free if government destroys their earning power with protectionist measures that raise prices and eventually cripple the job market and our economy as well. And workers searching for jobs and advancement can't break free if government upsets the marketplace with harebrained ideas like federally mandated comparable worth, a proposal that would take salary decisions out the hands of employers and employees and give government the power to determine what a fair salary is." Radio Address to the Nation on Economic Growth and Minorities (July 27, 1985).

350 "The American economy can be a mighty engine for progress, a mighty force for good in this world; but we have to leave it free, unshackled from high taxes and unburdened by excessive government. We must not hobble it with overregulation or smother it in antitrade, anti-

growth legislation. If we liberate the energies and imagination of the American people and allow them the wherewithal to build their dreams, America will be a dynamo leading the world into ... a new era of prosperity the likes of which this world has never before seen. That is our goal, and that's our challenge." Remarks at a White House Meeting with Members of the American Business Conference (April 15, 1986).

351 "The Europeans call our economic performance — to my face they've called it the American miracle. In fact, it is thousands of individual miracles of faith, hard work, and imagination — thousands of entrepreneurs and small business people like you." Remarks to State Chairpersons of the National White House Conference on Small Business (August 15, 1986).

352 "You know, I really discovered that what we were doing was working when they stopped calling it Reaganomics." Remarks at a Campaign Rally for Senator Jeremiah A. Denton in Montgomery, Alabama (September 18, 1986).

353 "Now, there are those who would tell you that everything we've accomplished has been a matter of luck, or just a part of an uncontrollable business cycle, or even the result of the celestial effects of Halley's Comet. But, my friends, America's progress can be traced not to personalities, not to chance, but to the dramatic change in philosophy we carried to Washington after the 1980 election — and to you, the American people." Remarks at a Republican Party Rally in Detroit, Michigan (September 24, 1986).

354 "That recovery [the American economic recovery] wasn't brought on by raising taxes. It wasn't brought on by protectionism — trade barriers, tariffs, and quotas — which is simply another form of taxes. Our economic renaissance was brought on because we cut tax rates and keep cutting them. We slashed unnecessary and counterproductive regulations and held back the destructionist threat to world trade while aggressively working to open markets abroad." Remarks at the Presentation Ceremony for the "E" and "E Star" Awards (May 18, 1987).

355 "[M]ost economists agree that raising the minimum wage reduces employment. Economists call it disemployment, but it amounts to the same thing: fewer jobs than there would have been."

Remarks at a White House Briefing for Minority Business Owners (July 15, 1987).

356 "[A]merica's economic miracle. You don't know what it means to go over there [in Europe] to those economic summits anymore and have those leaders of other countries use that term. I didn't invent it. They wanted to ask me and talk about the American miracle." Remarks to Broan Manufacturing Company Employees in Hartford, Wisconsin (July 27, 1987).

357 "[R]aising the minimum wage laws, most economists agree, reduces employment. And it's minorities, young people, and the poor that are hit the hardest." Remarks at the Presentation Ceremony for the Minority Enterprise Development Week Awards (October 7, 1987).

358 "And now, over the years, there's been a lot said about the so-called Reagan luck. Well, being of Irish extraction, sometimes I'm inclined to believe such things. However, I can assure all of you that the great economic expansion our country has enjoyed has had more to do with low tax rates, deregulation, and responsible Federal policies than with leprechauns. In fact, the only people who still seem to believe in tooth fairies and leprechauns are those who've tried to tell us that if we only raise taxes the budget deficit will disappear." Remarks at the 1988 Reagan Administration Executive Forum (January 19, 1988).

359 "The American people know what limited government, tax cuts, deregulation, and the move towards privatization have meant: It's meant the largest peacetime expansion in our history." Remarks at the Annual Conservative Political Action Conference Dinner (February 11, 1988).

360 "Well, to tell you the truth, I'm sort of proud of being an American, proud that since 1983 the United States has created six times as many jobs as has Western Europe." Radio Address to the Nation on Free and Fair Trade (May 14, 1988).

361 "[I]t's important to remind ourselves that in dealing with the economy we're dealing with human creativity. This insight has represented the underpinning of our economic expansion. We cut tax rates, reduced government regulation, and restrained Federal spending; and we unleashed the creativity of individuals and businesses. We gave them freedom to create; to keep the rewards of

their own risktaking and hard work; and to reach for new, bold ideas." Remarks at the Business Roundtable Annual Dinner (June 22, 1988).

362 "When George Bush and I took office, the other party, which had long controlled Washington, had left America with its economic and foreign policy in disarray.... Yes, soaring prices and a sinking economy — that's what the other fellows, with all their lip service about compassion, inflicted on the American people. The economists called it stagflation. The Democrats termed it malaise. The liberal pundits said it was part of America's inevitable decline. But we came in and said the only thing that was inevitable was that bad policies produce bad results. We said there may be no easy solutions, but there's a simple solution: Get government out of the way and let free people and a free economy work their magic." Remarks at a Campaign Fundraising Luncheon for Representative Connie Mack in Miami, Florida (June 29, 1988).

363 "What does all this mean [the improved economy]? It means that getting the Government off your backs and out of your pockets has worked." Radio Address to the Nation on the Economy (July 16, 1988).

364 "The policies that pulled America out of economic stagnation, rising unemployment, declining family income, and double-digit inflation have made America's economy a global success story. These policies are the wave of the future. Country after country is reducing taxes, cutting regulation, reducing the role of government, and letting entrepreneurs and working people build new factories, new jobs, and new futures for themselves and their families. It's sweeping the world, but like hamburgers and baseball, it all began right here in the United States." Remarks to the Employees of United States Precision Lens, Inc., in Cincinnati (August 8, 1988).

365 "Now, some people are telling you to take for granted the economic growth of today and of the last 7 years. Their message is: You can take prosperity for granted. It's time for a change; take a chance on us. Well, that's sort of like someone telling you that you've stored up all the cold beer you could want, so now you can unplug the refrigerator. But, no more than with a refrigerator, you can't unplug our progrowth economic policies and expect things to stay the same." Remarks to the Employees of United States Precision Lens, Inc., in Cincinnati, Ohio (August 8, 1988).

366   "Leaders all over the world have asked how we achieve this growth and prosperity. Well, my answer is simple: less government, more freedom, and moving toward a more open and equitable international economy." Radio Address on the Economy and Welfare (September 3, 1988).

367   "Incentive economics works because it places the individual at the center of the economy and unleashes the full human power of invention, production and, yes, compassion and generosity. It recognizes the creativity that is lodged in each person, the power of will and the act of faith that launches even great enterprises." Remarks at a Dinner Honoring Representative Jack F. Kemp of New York (December 1, 1988).

(Reaganomics) ECONOMIC BILL OF RIGHTS

368   "In this bicentennial year of our Constitution, I'm reminded that the Bill of Rights was adopted by our forefathers to protect the people from the threat posed by government of that age to our basic political liberties. Now, over 200 years later, the chief danger of big government is the threat to our economic liberties, to our basic right to earn our own keep and keep what we earn. Here the problem is a bloated Federal Government that over taxes, over spends, over borrows, and over regulates. In this day and time, what Americans need is an economic bill of rights...." Remarks at a Greater South Brevard Area Chamber of Commerce Luncheon in Melbourne, Florida (June 22, 1987).

369   "Just as Jefferson understood that our political freedoms needed protection by and from government, our economic freedoms need similar recognition and protection. Those who attain political power must know that there are limits beyond which they will not be permitted to go, because beyond that point their intrusion is destructive of the economic freedom of the people." Remarks Announcing America's Economic Bill of Rights (July 3, 1987).

370   "Our forefathers fought for personal and national independence, yet 200 years later, our own overly centralized government poses a threat to our liberty far beyond anything imagined by the patriots of old." Remarks Announcing America's Economic Bill of Rights (July 3, 1987).

371   "[Our] economic freedoms ... are as sacred and sacrosanct as the political freedoms of speech, press, religion, and assembly. They ... [make] self-government and personal independence part of the American experience." Remarks Announcing America's Economic Bill of Rights (July 3, 1987).

372   "Just as our political freedoms need protection by and from the Government, our economic freedoms need the same recognition and protection." Remarks to Citizens in New Britain, Connecticut (July 8, 1987).

373   "I'm stumping for something I believe even more important, even more historic than tax reform. It's an Economic Bill of Rights [consisting of] ... four essential guarantees for all Americans: The freedom to work — and that means eliminating government barriers to opportunity; the freedom to enjoy the fruits of your own labor — and that means bringing to an end, once and for all, excessive government borrowing, spending, and taxation; and the freedom to own and control your own property, including intellectual property like technological innovations; the freedom to participate in a free market — and that means government must work to foster, not hinder, economic growth." Remarks to Community Leaders in Danville, Indiana (July 13, 1987).

374   "The aim of our Economic Bill of Rights is the same as that of the political Bill of Rights in the Constitution: freedom." Remarks to Community Leaders in Danville, Indiana (July 13, 1987).

375   "[The] Economic Bill of Rights [is] a bill that will restore to us the freedoms that our Founding Fathers believed we should always have, a bill of rights that will protect us and future generations from the needless and wrongful encroachment of government upon our lives." Remarks at the Annual Convention of the National Association of Counties in Indianapolis, Indiana (July 13, 1987).

376   "Let's complete the civil rights movement by writing a guarantee of the American dream into the Constitution, a guarantee that America will always be, for our children and our children's children, the land of opportunity." Remarks at a White House Briefing for Minority Business Owners (July 15, 1987).

377   "I've promised to spend not just the remainder of my Presidency but the rest of my public life campaigning for an Economic Bill of Rights that will once and for all secure our economic freedoms." Remarks to Civic and Community Leaders in North Platte, Nebraska (August 13, 1987).

378   "[T]he past two decades have witnessed an expansion of many of our civil rights but that our economic liberties have been too often neglected, even abused. Well, it's time that abuse stopped. And that's what this Economic Bill of Rights is designed to do — to give our economic rights the same guarantees, the same constitutional protections as our other civil rights. This country was built free and strong not only because individuals were free to speak their minds but also because they were free to prosper. For too long, we forgot that. Let's never let government again take away our freedom to prosper." Remarks to Civic and Community Leaders in North Platte, Nebraska (August 13, 1987).

379   "I pledge to you: I'm not leaving office until your paycheck is, once and for all, safe from those who want to tax it and spend it into oblivion. For too long, the advocates of big government have been treating your paycheck, your savings, even your pensions, like they're government property. And they act as if they're being generous when they let you keep a little of it. Well, those days are over. In America, government is the servant, not the master, and we intend to keep it that way." Remarks to Citizens in North Platte, Nebraska (August 13, 1987).

(Reaganomics) SPENDING

380   "You and I, as individuals, can, by borrowing, live beyond our means, but for only a limited period of time. Why, then, should we think that collectively, as a nation, we're not bound by that same limitation?" Inaugural Address (January 20, 1981).

381   "We forgot or just overlooked the fact that government — any government — has a built in tendency to grow." Address to the Nation on the Economy (February 5, 1981).

382   "Government has only two ways of getting money other than raising taxes. It can go into the money market and borrow, competing with its own citizens and driving up interest rates, which it has done, or it can print money, and it's done that. Both methods are inflationary." Address to the Nation on the Economy (February 5, 1981).

383   "Over the past decades we've talked of curtailing government spending so that we can then lower the tax burden. Sometimes we've even made a run at doing that. But there were always those who told us that taxes couldn't be cut until spending was reduced. Well, you know, we can lecture our children about extravagance until we run out of voice and breath. Or we can cure their extravagance by simply reducing their allowance." Address to the Nation on the Economy (February 5, 1981).

384   "Spending by government must be limited to those functions which are the proper province of government. We can no longer afford things simply because we think of them." Address Before a Joint Session of the Congress on the Program for Economic Recovery (February 18, 1981).

385   "If you will forgive me, you know someone has once likened government to a baby. It is an alimentary canal with an appetite at one end and no sense of responsibility at the other." Address of the President and Prime Minister Pierre Elliott Trudeau of Canada Before a Joint Session of Parliament in Ottawa. (March 11, 1981).

386   "There are just too many people in this town [Washington, D.C.] who think this money belongs to the Government. Well, it doesn't. It's your money." Remarks at the National Conference of the Building and Construction Trades Department, AFL-CIO (March 30, 1981).

387   "Let's cut through the fog for a moment. The answer to a government that's too big is to stop feeding its growth." Address Before a Joint Session of the Congress on the Program for Economic Recovery (April 28, 1981).

388   "I've said many times, government doesn't tax to get the money it needs; government always finds a need for the money it gets." Remarks in Chicago, Illinois, at the Citizens for Thompson Fundraising Dinner for Governor James T. Thompson (July 7, 1981).

389   "They [America's declining economic trends] began when this Nation started down the path of government intervention, of 'tax and tax, spend and spend, elect and elect.' Let no one fault the motives of those who implemented such policies. They only intended to help, but they based their efforts on an impossible equation. If I can't pay for my need, and you can't pay for yours, we can't solve our problem by hiring our government to take the money from both of us to give to each other." Remarks in Chicago, Illinois, at the Citizens for Thompson Fundraising Dinner for Governor James T. Thompson (July 7, 1981).

390   "At home, our enemy is no longer Redcoats but red ink." Remarks on Signing a Proclamation Commemorating the 200th Anniversary of the British Surrender at Yorktown, Virginia (September 14, 1981).

391   "What we don't need is more spending, and what we don't need are taxes, and what we do need is a lot less of both." Remarks at an Ohio Republican Fundraising Reception in Cincinnati (November 30, 1981).

392   "Higher government spending and taxation do not work. Protectionist tariffs do not work. Always they are sold as short-term solutions. But inevitably, a quick-fix leads to long-term addiction, and [with it] the disease of higher interest rates, inflation, and economic stagnation...." Text of Remarks to the European Management Forum Symposium in Davos, Switzerland (January 28, 1982).

393   "[W]e must have an economic program of taxes ... that will stimulate and offer incentives to the economy to broaden the base of the economy so that even the government will get the revenues it needs, but from smaller assessments against each individual." Remarks at a Rally for United States Senator David D. Durgenberger in Bloomington, Minnesota (February 8, 1982).

394   "[D]eficits are not caused by our lowering taxes. Deficits are caused by government spending too much." Remarks at the Los Angeles, California, County Board of Supervisors' Town Meeting (March 3, 1982).

395   "Oppressive taxation is like a ball and chain on our economy, weighing it down by discouraging initiative, by punishing hard work, by making investment no longer worth the risk.... Quick fixes are not the answer to what ails our economy." Address Before a Joint Session of the Tennessee State Legislature in Nashville (March 15, 1982).

396   "[F]eeding more dollars to government is like feeding a stray pup. It just follows you home and sits on your doorstep asking for more." Remarks at the Annual Washington Policy Meeting of the National Association of Manufacturers (March 18, 1982).

397   "Big government has a way of spending all the money it can get its hands on, and then some." Remarks at the National Association of Realtors' Legislative Conference (March 29, 1982).

398   "We don't have a trillion-dollar debt because we haven't taxed enough; we have a trillion-dollar debt because we spend too much." Remarks at the National Association of Realtors' Legislative Conference (March 29, 1982).

399   "We must not mortgage our children's future to pay for the mistakes of today. The choice before our generation is grave but clear: We must either face and solve our problems now or surrender to them forever." Remarks at the National Association of Realtors' Legislative Conference (March 29, 1982).

400   "[I]n the quest for economic literacy, high tax rates don't soak the rich, they only create more tax shelters or an outright capital drain. Reducing high tax rates provides incentives to get more people paying taxes again." Remarks at the Annual Meeting of the United States Chamber of Commerce (April 26, 1982).

401   "[O]ur loyalty lies with little taxpayers, not big taxspenders." The President's News Conference [prepared statement] (June 30, 1982).

402   "Let's quit kidding ourselves. Pretending government could spend like there is no tomorrow and not hurt anyone has ended up punishing everyone — and the needy most of all." Remarks at a Rally Supporting the Proposed Constitutional Amendment for a Balanced Federal Budget (July 19, 1982).

403   "If I could correct 40 years of fiscal irresponsibility in 1 year, I'd go back to show business as a magician. You know, that might be more fun pulling rabbits out of a hat than jackasses out of the way in Washington." Remarks in Billings, Montana, at a Celebration Marking the Centennial of Billings and Yellowstone County (August 11, 1982).

404   "There's only one major cause of our economic problems: government spending more than it takes in and sending you the bill. There's only one permanent cure: bringing government spending in line with government revenues." Radio Address to the Nation on the Economy (September 25, 1982).

405   "And I just wish everyone in Washington could understand what millions of Republicans and Democrats at the grassroots learned a long time ago: You can't drink yourself sober; you can't spend yourself rich; and you can't prime the pump without pumping the prime." Remarks at a Meeting with Republican Congressional Candidates (October 6, 1982).

406   "The Federal budget must not become a roadblock on the path to long-term economic recovery." The President's News Conference (January 5, 1983).

407   "We must not saddle our children with the debts of their parents." Remarks at a Fundraising Dinner for Senator Charles Percy in Chicago, Illinois (January 19, 1983).

408   "You can't drink yourself sober or spend yourself rich, and you can't prime the pump without pumping the prime." Remarks at the Conservative Political Action Conference Dinner (February 18, 1983).

409   "Well, Federal money doesn't buy happiness, except for the bureaucrats and the special interests that luxuriate in those programs." Remarks at the Fundraising Dinner of the Republican National Hispanic Assembly (September 14, 1983).

410   "[G]overnment can only spend what it borrows or taxes away from the people." Remarks at a Fundraising Dinner for Senator Strom Thurmond in Columbia, South Carolina (September 20, 1983).

411   "You, the people, should not be forced to subsidize their [the "big spenders" in Congress] extravagance. They should force themselves to spend within your means." Radio Address to the Nation on the First Session of the 98th Congress (November 19, 1983).

412   "People should have the freedom to keep more of the money they earn and spend it the way they want to and not have the government taking more and more of their money to spend the way

it wants to." Remarks at a Spirit of America Rally in Atlanta, Georgia (January 26, 1984).

413   "[I] just don't believe the people can be bought with promises anymore that have to be paid for out of the Treasury. They know who eventually ends up paying for all those promises." Remarks at the Southern Republican Leadership Conference in Atlanta, Georgia (January 26, 1984).

414   "You know, we could say they [the liberals] spend money like drunken sailors, but that would be unfair to drunken sailors." Remarks Accepting the Presidential Nomination at the Republican National Convention in Dallas, Texas (August 23, 1984).

415   "The liberals in Washington who were so sure that we could spend ourselves rich and drink ourselves sober were surprised to see the economic mess they'd created. They didn't understand the real problem in Washington and the real reason for our recent economic woes was really very simple.... Government is too big, and it spends too much money." Remarks at the Annual Convention of the American Legion in Salt Lake City, Utah (September 4, 1984).

416   "Some people have labored so long at making government bigger, they've developed a knee-jerk addiction to tax increases. And every time their knee jerks, we get kicked...." Remarks to Members of the High Technological Corridor Board in Nashville, Tennessee (September 13, 1984).

417   "Raising taxes will not encourage people ... to work harder or be more productive; raising taxes will not stimulate investment; raising taxes will not give businesses the incentive to innovate and to make their companies more competitive. America doesn't need higher taxes." Remarks at a Reagan-Bush Rally in Corpus Christi, Texas (October 2, 1984).

418   "We must never again abuse the trust of working men and women by sending their earnings on a futile chase after the spiraling demands of a bloated Federal Establishment." Inaugural Address (January 21, 1985).

419   "The defense of our nation is the one budget item which cannot be dictated solely by domestic considerations." Remarks to Congressional Leaders During a White House Briefing on the Fiscal Year 1986 Budget (February 4, 1985).

420   "Every dollar the Federal Government does not take from us, every decision it does not make for us will make our economy stronger, our lives more abundant, our future more free." Address Before a Joint Session of the Congress on the State of the Union (February 6, 1985).

421   "The public treasury is a trust, not a gift shop." Remarks at the Annual Legislative Conference of the National Association of Counties (March 4, 1985).

422   "[T]axes and spending are like the foundation of a big house called growth. If our tax and spending policies are sound and balanced, the foundation will be rock solid, and the house of growth will stand and endure." Remarks to the Students and Faculty at St. John's University in New York, New York (March 28, 1985).

423   "Well, there is no magic money machine. Every dollar the government spends comes out of your pockets. Every dollar the government gives to someone has to first be taken away from someone else. So, it's our moral duty to make sure that we can justify every one of your tax dollars, that we spend them wisely and carefully and, just as important, fairly." Address to the Nation on the Federal Budget and Deficit Reduction (April 24, 1985).

424   "Government spending programs aimed at building the infrastructure will not do the job. The efficiency, the ingenuity, and vitality of private enterprise and free people must be brought into play." Remarks at the Annual Conference of the Council of the Americas (May 21, 1985).

425   "Sometimes I think that government is like that old definition of a baby: an enormous appetite at one end and no sense of responsibility at the other." Remarks at the Annual Meeting of the National Association of Manufacturers (May 24, 1985).

426   "[T]he more the Government spends, the more resources it takes from the private sector, the greater the upward pressure on interest rates, and the lower the rate of economic growth. Whether the Government obtains its funds through taxation or borrowing, the root problem remains the same — government use of spending

to take over more and more of the economic life of our nation. This smothers the private sector incentives that keep our economy vibrant." Radio Address to the Nation on the Federal Budget (April 12, 1986).

427   "After delaying so long, some in Congress say I should just sign this spending-spree bill because otherwise the Government will be forced to shut down. Well, I hope they know where the keys to the building are, because if they don't act responsibly, I won't have any choice but to shut it down. If they want to put a real budget together by candlelight, it's okay by me." Radio Address to the Nation on the Fiscal Year 1987 Appropriations Bills (September 27, 1986).

428   "Highest among these [the tasks that America faces] is curbing the growth of our government's spending. No nation can survive if government becomes like the man who in winter began to burn the wallboards of his house to keep warm until he had no house left and froze." Remarks at the Annual Meeting of the Boards of Governors of the International Monetary Fund and World Bank Group (September 30, 1986).

429   "But I have to be frank: If the big spenders want a fight on the budget, they'd better strap on their helmets and shoulder pads. In this fourth and final quarter, I'm determined to go out there and win one for the American people and, yes — and one for the Gipper." Radio Address to the Nation on the Fiscal Year 1988 Budget (January 10, 1987).

430   "The American people don't want more spending; they want better results." Remarks at the Annual Meeting of the National Association of Manufacturers (May 28, 1987).

431   "It's my belief that liberty should be as important a concern in Toronto as it was in Moscow. Liberty in the economic sphere means low taxes. It means paring away needless regulations and reducing counterproductive government planning and interference. And it means keeping down barriers to international trade, here and around the world." Radio Address to the Nation on the Soviet–United States Summit Meeting in Moscow and the Toronto Economic Summit (June 4, 1988).

432   "[I] say if you're not part of the solution, you're part of the problem. And the problem is big spending. The solution is so simple only a liberal could miss it. We just have to spend less. What we've learned from hard experience — that big spending is as seductive as anabolic steroids. And I think it's time the big spenders were disqualified." Remarks at a Republican Party Fundraising Dinner in Detroit, Michigan (October 7, 1988).

(Reaganomics) TAXATION

433 "[B]usiness doesn't pay taxes. Oh, don't get the wrong idea. Business is being taxed, so much so that we're being priced out of the world market. But business must pass its costs of operation — and that includes taxes — on to the customer in the price of the product. Only people pay taxes, all the taxes. Government just uses business in a kind of sneaky way to help collect the taxes." Address to the Nation on the Economy (February 5, 1981).

434 "The taxing power of government must be used to provide revenues for legitimate government purposes. It must not be used to regulate the economy or bring about social change." Address Before a Joint Session of the Congress on the Program for Economic Recovery (February 18, 1981).

435 "[A] reduction in Federal tax rates does not necessarily result in a reduction in tax revenues. The economy expands, it reduces the burden for the individual, but the overall share goes up as the base of the economy is broadened." Remarks at the Mid-Winter Congressional City Conference of the National League of Cities (March 2, 1981).

436 "Well, you know it's been said that taxation is the art of plucking the feathers without killing the bird. It's time they realize the bird just doesn't have any feathers left." Remarks at the Mid-Winter Congressional City Conference of the National League of Cities (March 2, 1981).

437 "Improving productivity, you know, only requires two things: people who have better ideas and people who have savings who want to invest in those ideas. Now, we have the first. Our problem is today we don't have the second. So, this ... is why ... we must also enact tax rate reductions across the board." Remarks at a White House

Reception for Members of the Advertising Council (May 20, 1981).

438 "An economy that is stifled by restrictive tax rates will never produce enough to balance the budget...." Remarks at a White House Reception for the Republican National Committee (June 12, 1981).

439 "You see, if we're sincere about giving the American people real tax reduction, then we have to do better than the typical one-shot, here today and gone tomorrow rebates of the old. We must make the people a commitment, the kind of commitment that says if you work or save more tomorrow than you did today, then your reward will be higher. More of every added dollar that you earn will be yours to keep." Remarks About Federal Tax Reduction Legislation at a White House Luncheon for Out-of-Town Editors and Broadcasters (July 22, 1981).

440 "It's been said that government performs its highest duty when it restores to its citizens taxes oppressively collected." Remark About Federal Tax Reduction Legislation meeting of the House Republican Conference (July 24, 1981).

441 "[P]ushing everyone into higher tax brackets only chase[s] the wealthy into tax shelters and encourage[s] the growth of the underground economy." Remarks on the Program for Economic Recovery at a White House Luncheon for Editors and Broadcasters from Southeastern States (April 16, 1982).

442 "The people in this economy are, I'm sure, honest people in most of their activities; they just have a double standard where taxes are concerned. They can be the friendly neighborhood fix-it man, a mechanic, craftsman, or member of the professions. They have one thing in common — they prefer to be paid in cash. The underground economy is a kind of cash-and-carry barter system — no checks, no records or bookkeeping, and thus no tax." Radio Address to the Nation on Taxes, Tuition Tax Credits, and Interest Rates (April 24, 1982).

443 "[T]he best way to help the people of this country is to stop taking excessive percentages of their earnings away from them and to allow them not only to keep their earnings and to have a job to work at but to see that the tax dollar they've put in their savings is worth as much 2 or

3 years from now as it was when they put it in, and not having 10 cents or 12 cents in value taken off every year by way of inflation." Remarks at a Utah Republican Party Picnic in Hooper (September 10, 1982).

444   "The unfair thing about our present income tax system [i.e. "bracket creep"] is that it's based on the number of dollars you earn, not their value. As you earn a greater number of dollars, you're pushed into a higher tax bracket, and the government takes a higher percentage of your paycheck, even though you might only be receiving a cost-of-living raise to stay even with inflation." Radio Address to the Nation on a House Budget Proposal (March 26, 1983).

445   "Like Federal employees, taxpayers also work for the government — they just don't have to take a civil service exam." Radio Address to the Nation on Federal Income Taxes (April 9, 1983).

446   "The liberal Democratic tax policy seems to boil down to this: America makes, Government takes." Radio Address to the Nation on Federal Income Taxes (April 9, 1983).

447   "Too many people in Washington and across the country still believe that we can raise more revenues from the economy by making it more expensive to work, save, and invest in the economy." Remarks at a California Republican Party Fundraising Dinner in Long Beach (June 30, 1983).

448   "There's an old saying that in levying taxes, as in shearing sheep, it's best to stop when you get to the skin." Remarks at the Annual Meeting of the National Association of Towns and Townships (September 12, 1983).

449   "Well, Federal money doesn't buy happiness, except for the bureaucrats and the special interests that luxuriate in those programs." Remarks at the Fundraising Dinner of the Republican National Hispanic Assembly (September 14, 1983).

450   "The American people aren't undertaxed; the Government in Washington is overfed. You know, I sometimes think the main difference between ourselves and the other side is we see an America where every day is the Fourth of July and they see an America where every day is April 15." Remarks at a Reagan-Bush Rally in Endicott, New York (September 12, 1984).

451   "We want to take a free country and make it freer. Part of human freedom is economic freedom.... We believe that when you tax something you put a kind of artificial limit on its production. When you put heavy income taxes on a working man or woman, you make it less worth their while to work hard and get ahead. But let them keep more of the fruits of their labor, and you encourage greater work and greater production. You encourage investment, and the economy grows. Jobs are created and more people work and pay their modest taxes, and the healthy spiral continues." Remarks at a Luncheon with Community Leaders in Buffalo, New York (September 12, 1984).

452   "We must simplify our tax system, make it more fair and bring the rates down for all who work and earn." Inaugural Address (January 21, 1985).

453   "The present tax code burdens some of our citizens too heavily while permitting others to avoid paying their fair share. It makes honest people feel like cheats, and it makes cheats pose as honest citizens. It allows the underground economy to thrive and wastes millions of man-hours on needless paperwork and regulations. It drives money needed for growth, investment, and jobs into unproductive tax shelters. It acts as the single biggest obstacle to enterprise and economic expansion." Remarks at a White House Meeting with Members of the National Governors' Association (February 25, 1985).

454   "To put it simply, our tax system is unfair, inequitable, counterproductive, and all but incomprehensible. I've mentioned before, and this is absolutely a fact, that even Albert Einstein had to write to the IRS for help with his Form 1040." Remarks at a White House Meeting with Members of the National Governors' Association (February 25, 1985).

455   "One of the first rules of economics is if you tax something, you get less of it. High tax rates discourage work, risk-taking, initiative, and imagination. And they're really a tax on hope, optimism, and our faith in the future. And they penalize the very people that give the most — the risk-takers, the entrepreneurs who create whole new businesses and industries, often out of no more than a dream and some hard work." Remarks at a White House Meeting with Members of the American Business Conference (March 13, 1985).

456   "We know that our tax code is unfair. We know that it's complicated beyond belief. Millions of Americans need professional assistance just to complete their returns. And we know that it has bred another problem every bit as serious — the wasting of economic resources." Radio Address to the Nation on Tax Reform (April 13, 1985).

457   "[F]or everyone who finds a shelter, someone else is left out in the cold ... for everyone who avoids paying his fair share, someone else has to make up the shortfall by paying a heavier tax burden." Remarks at the Annual Meeting of the National Association of Manufacturers (May 24, 1985).

458   "Steeply rising income tax rates punish success, discourage hard work and initiative, and cut into savings. And meanwhile, tax loopholes and shelters divert investment away from the productive economy and into areas that are often economically stagnant. Now, this is what happens when the Government tries to run the economy through the tax code. Tax considerations become paramount in business decisions, and the rationale and efficient allocation of resources by the market is distorted out of all recognition. Our economy becomes enmeshed in a bureaucracy instead of energized by opportunity. And economic growth slows, and with it, the creation of new jobs and businesses." Remarks at the Annual Meeting of the National Association of Manufacturers (May 24, 1985).

459   "The American people are always willing, even eager, to do their duty. But you quite naturally resent it when you see others shirking theirs. It rankles to know that your tax rates are so high because others who can afford high-priced lawyers and tax consultants are able to manipulate the system to avoid paying their fair share. And it simply adds insult to injury when, on top of a large tax bill to the IRS, you have to pay a professional to tell you how much you owe." Radio Address to the Nation on Tax Reform (May 25, 1985).

460   "For the sake of fairness, simplicity, and growth, we must radically change the structure of a tax system that still treats our earnings as the

personal property of the Internal Revenue Service; radically change a system that still treats people's earnings, similar incomes, much differently regarding the tax that they pay; and, yes, radically change a system that still causes some to invest their money, not to make a better mousetrap but simply to avoid a tax trap." Address to the Nation on Tax Reform (May 28, 1985).

461   "Death and taxes may be inevitable, but unjust taxes are not." Address to the Nation on Tax Reform (May 28, 1985).

462   "For too long our tax code has been a source of ridicule and resentment, violating our Nation's most fundamental principles of justice and fair play. While most Americans labor under excessively high tax rates that discourage work and cut drastically into savings, many are able to exploit the tangled mass of loopholes that has grown up around our tax code to avoid paying their fair share — sometimes to avoid paying any taxes at all." Message to the Congress Transmitting Proposed Tax Reform Legislation (May 29, 1985).

463   "It's been remarked that there are three stages of reaction to a new idea like our tax proposal. First stage is: 'It's crazy. It'll never work. Don't waste my time.' The second: 'It's possible, but it's not worth doing.' And finally: ' I've always said it was a good idea. I'm glad I thought of it.' Well, we're rapidly sweeping up on that third stage." Remarks on Tax Reform to Concerned Citizens (May 29, 1985).

464   "Thirty and forty years ago you didn't hear people brag at social get-togethers about how they got their tax bill down by exploiting this loophole and engineering that credit. But now you do. And it's not considered bad behavior. After all, goes this thinking, what's immoral about cheating a system that is itself a cheat? That isn't a sin, it's a duty." Remarks at the "Prelude to Independence" Celebration in Williamsburg, Virginia (May 30, 1985).

465   "Somewhere along the line, we stopped understanding that people worked not for the government, but for themselves; that they get up every morning and go out into the world to earn their bread, not to support a government, but to support their families." Remarks at the "Prelude to Independence" Celebration in Williamsburg, Virginia (May 30, 1985).

466 "When taxes are lowered, economic growth follows. And economic growth is good for just about everyone, especially the poor. It gives them a ladder they can use to climb out of poverty. And for those who aren't poor, but who are by no means rich — and that's most of the people in America — economic growth gives them options they never had before." Remarks at Northside High School in Atlanta, Georgia (June 6, 1985).

467 "Opportunity is key to the promise [of] the American dream, but high tax rates have transformed that difficult but rewarding climb up the ladder of success into a bitter and exhausting enslavement on the tax treadmill.... The tax system must no longer be poverty's accomplice." Remarks and a Question-and-Answer Session with Economic Editors During a White House Briefing on Tax Reform (June 7, 1985).

468 "It stands to reason that the more complex our tax code is, the more open it is to abuse." Remarks to Citizens in Chicago Heights, Illinois (June 28, 1985).

469 "[Y]ou didn't send us to Washington to feed the alligators; you sent us to drain the swamp. We didn't come to raise your taxes, but to lower them." Radio Address to the Nation on Economic Growth and Tax Reform (August 3, 1985).

470 "Some individuals go on so-called educational ocean cruises or purchase sky boxes at sports arenas and write them off as business expense. Now, I've been preaching the merits of free enterprise for years. Business people provide jobs and create wealth; I have nothing against them — on the contrary, they have my heartfelt admiration. What I am against is a tax system that allows some to take perfectly legal deductions that by any standards of fairness are an outrage." Remarks at a Senior Citizens Forum on Tax Reform in Tampa, Florida (September 12, 1985).

471 "It's time for Americans to take their money out of tax shelters and invest the money in America's future. Every day we live with the present tax code, we're slowing down economic growth, sacrificing jobs that would have been created, unfairly burdening families, and perpetuating an unjust system that only breeds cynicism and resentment in the American people." Remarks at a White House Luncheon for Elected Republican Women Officials (September 13, 1985).

472 "The practice of business is, in large measure, a moral endeavor; a practice in which men and women give of themselves, their strength, their intelligence, and imagination to unlock the mysteries of the material world on behalf of their fellow man. To inhibit this process through an oppressive system of taxation is, in a fundamental sense, to inhibit human development." Remarks to Business Leaders During a White House Briefing on Tax Reform (October 1, 1985).

473 "[I]ndustrial policy — that's a fancy name for Washington using the tax code to tell you how to run your business." Remarks to Business Leaders During a White House Briefing on Tax Reform (October 1, 1985).

474 "Let me suggest that over the long haul, the Federal Government simply can't raise revenue any faster than by cutting tax rates and then cutting tax rates again. It stimulates everybody to do better and more people go to work." Remarks at a Fundraising Dinner for Senator Robert W. Kasten, Jr., in Milwaukee, Wisconsin (October 15, 1985).

475 "[W]e must ... transform ... [our current] tax system, rotting from unfairness and complexity, a source of unending resentment and enmity, into one that is clear, simple, and fair for all, a system that could no longer run roughshod over Main Street America, but would ensure ... families and firms incentives and rewards for hard work and risk-taking in an American future of strong economic growth." Radio Address to the Nation on Tax Reform (May 10, 1986).

476 "You know, I've often wondered how much the Government really got from some of those tremendously high marginal rates. Because when I was back in Hollywood, where the pay scale is a little above the average, I know I would reach a point and then someone would send a script — and gee, it would look like a good part and something I'd like to do. But I'd already reached the 90-percent bracket. And there wasn't any way I was going to spend a couple of months working for 10 cents on the dollar. So, they didn't get much for their [high marginal tax] rate." Remarks to the Tax Reform Action Coalition (May 14, 1986).

477 "Throughout human history, taxes have been one of the foremost ways that governments intrude on the rights of citizens." Radio Address to the Nation on Independence Day and the Centennial of the Statue of Liberty (July 5, 1986).

478 "There's no way on God's good Earth that I will agree to an unraveling of what we've done with tax reform. Tax rates have come down, and they're going to stay down." Remarks at a White House Briefing for Women Entrepreneurs (December 3, 1986).

479 "One of the most important aspects of tax reform, however, isn't economic, but it's psychological. It's the complete discrediting of high marginal rates, and a new consensus is formed that when it comes to taxes, flatter is better. Poor Karl Marx." Remarks at a White House Briefing for the American Legislative Exchange Council (December 12, 1986).

480 "We must insist ... that there be a limit to the level of taxation, not only because excessive taxation undermines the strength of the economy but because taxation beyond a certain level becomes servitude. And in America, it is the Government that works for the people and not the other way around." Remarks Announcing America's Economic Bill of Rights (July 3, 1987).

481 "Taxation ... is more than mathematical calculations. It is the harnessing of free people; it is forced labor; and if it goes beyond reasonable bounds, it is a yoke of oppression. Raising taxes, then, should be serious business. It should not be done without a broad national consensus." Remarks Announcing America's Economic Bill of Rights (July 3, 1987).

482 "Remember back when it was a 90-percent bracket? I was in Hollywood at the time. You'd be surprised how many actors started turning down parts after they got in that bracket. Who wants to work for 10 cents on the dollar?" Remarks at a White House Briefing for Members of the Deficit Reduction Coalition (July 10, 1987).

BUSINESS

483 "When you're talking about the strength and character of America, you're talking about the small business community, about the owners of that store down the street, the faithful who support their churches and defend their freedom, and all the brave men and women who are not afraid to take risks and invest in the future to build a better America." Remarks at a White House Briefing on the State of Small Business (March 1, 1982).

484 "Our Nation is blessed with two important qualities that are often missing in other societies: our spirit of entrepreneurship and our capacity for invention and innovation. These two elements are combined in the small businesses that dot our land." Remarks on Signing the Small Business Innovation Development Act of 1982 (July 22, 1982).

485 "I've always believed that entrepreneurs are the forgotten heroes of America. In your dreams and in your courage to take great risks rest America's best hopes for more jobs, stronger growth, and a higher standard of living." Remarks and a Question-and-Answer Session at a Luncheon Meeting of the St. Louis Regional Commerce and Growth Association in Missouri (February 1, 1983).

486 "Our small business owners demonstrate through free enterprise that our national well-being is dependent on individual freedom to pursue our hopes, our dreams, and our creative ambitions." Remarks on Signing the Annual Report on the State of Small Business (March 18, 1983).

487 "Having one's own business is a powerful engine for social and economic progress." Remarks at a White House Ceremony Marking the Observance of Minority Enterprise Development Week (October 3, 1983).

488 "Small businesses are the biggest providers of new jobs, give the most employees the freedom to work part time, hire the most women, young people, and senior citizens. They embody innovation, provide economic diversity, and chart our path toward the products, markets, and jobs of the future." Remarks on Signing the Annual Report on the State of Small Business (March 19, 1984).

489 "You know, not too long ago, I was asked to explain the difference between a small businessman and a big businessman. And my answer was that a big businessman is what a small businessman would be if only government would get out of the way and let him alone." Remarks on Presenting the Small Business Person of the Year Award (May 9, 1984).

490 "You know, sometimes in Washington, there are some who seem to forget what the economy is all about. They give me reports saying the economy does this and the economy will do that, but they never talk about business. And somewhere along the way, these folks in Washington have forgotten that the economy is business. Business creates new products and new services; business creates jobs; business creates prosperity for our communities and our nation as a whole. And business is the people that make it work, from the CEO to the workers in the factories." Remarks at a White House Meeting with Business and Trade Leaders (September 23, 1985).

491 "Healthy, robust small business and keeping America out front are one and the same goal." Remarks on Receiving the Report of the National White House Conference on Small Business (December 23, 1986).

492 "One of America's greatest assets is the skill and professionalism of its businessmen and women, and entrepreneurs. The can-do spirit of our business community is in stark contrast to the inefficiency and poor performance often associated with other economic systems." Remarks at the Presentation Ceremony for the "E" and "E Star" Awards (May 18, 1987).

493 "Let's stop penalizing American business and treating it like an enemy." Remarks at the Federal Conference on Commercial Applications of Superconductivity (July 28, 1987).

494 "I learned that I was seeing then [when Reagan was hosting GE Theatre], as I've seen here today, the real source of this nation's economic growth and productivity—not government or bureaucracy. America's workers and entrepreneurs were making it happen back then and people like you are making it happen today." Remarks at a Forum for State Government Officials and Business Leaders in Somerset, New Jersey (October 13, 1987).

495 "[I]n a nation, as in a man or a woman, economic success is not a matter of bricks, mortar, balance sheets, or subsidies. No, if a national economy is to soar, first the inventive, enterprising, pioneering, dreaming entrepreneurial spirit of the Nation's people must soar." Remarks at the Annual Meeting of the United States Chamber of Commerce (May 2, 1988).

496 "[I]t's the individual who is always the source of economic creativity, the inquiring mind that produces a technical breakthrough, the imagination that conceives of new products and markets." Remarks and a Question-and-Answer Session with Members of the National Strategy Forum in Chicago, Illinois (May 4, 1988).

497 "Small business is about hopes and dreams. It's about making dreams come true— the dreams of men and women who lie awake at night and consider how they can improve their lot in life. Those dreams, those hopes, are a singular and great natural resource." Remarks at the Presentation Ceremony for the Small Business Person of the Year Awards (May 9, 1988).

CENTRAL INTELLIGENCE AGENCY

498 "[W]e must now summon all the nations of the world to a crusade for freedom and a global campaign for the rights of the individual, and you [the men and women of the CIA] are in the forefront of this campaign. You must be the cutting edge of freedom in peace and war, and in the shadowy world in between, you must serve in silence and carry your special burden. But let me assure you, you're on the winning side, and your service is one which free men will thank you and future generation honor you." Remarks on Signing the Intelligence Identities Protection Act of 1982 (June 23, 1982).

499 "You are the trip-wire across which the forces of repression and tyranny must stumble in their quest for global domination. You, the men and women of the CIA, are the eyes and ears of the free world." Remarks on Signing Intelligence Identities Protection Act of 1982 (June 23, 1982).

500 "[O]ur policies cannot be effective unless the information on which they're based is accurate, timely, and complete." Remarks at the National Leadership Forum of the Center for International and Strategic Studies at Georgetown University (April 6, 1984).

501 "An intelligence agency cannot operate effectively unless its necessary secrets are maintained even in this, the most open and free country on Earth." Remarks at Groundbreaking Ceremonies on the Addition to the Central Intelligence Agency Headquarters (May 24, 1984).

502 "[W]e can counter this hostile threat [foreign espionage] and still remain true to our values. We don't need to fight repression by becoming repressive ourselves ... [b]ut we need to put our cleverness and determination to work...." Radio Address to the Nation on Counterintelligence Activities (June 29, 1985).

503 "Espionage, spying, is not a game. It costs our country secrets and millions of dollars in stolen technology. It can also cost lives and threaten our national survival." Radio Address to the Nation on Efforts to Prevent Espionage Against the United States (November 30, 1985).

504 "While our security is tied to protecting certain secrets, there is no need to fight repression by becoming repressive ourselves." Radio Address to the Nation on Efforts to Prevent Espionage Against the United States (November 30, 1985).

505 "[O]ur secret services, our spies and intelligence agencies — from Nathan Hale to Midway, from OSS to CIA — have not written just a striking, stirring chapter in our history but have often provided the key to victory in war and the preservation of our freedom during an uneasy peace." Remarks at a Dinner for Former Members of the Office of Strategic Services (May 29, 1986).

506 "[W]hile you serve in silence; while your success must go without recognition, often even by your own families; while you cannot share with them or your fellow Americans the pride you feel in protecting and guarding their future; let me today, in this place, speak for all of them: We are grateful for what you do, for the sacrifices you make, for your selfless commitment to our country, and for the limitations on your personal freedom which you accept so your countrymen can live their lives in freedom and peace. We understand your burden, and we salute you. You carry on the struggle for freedom, and you, too, are heroes. America's proud of you, and we thank you." Remarks at the Dedication Ceremony for New Facilities at the National Security Agency at Fort Meade, Maryland (September 26, 1986).

507 "[O]ur intelligence community performs a vital role in the struggle against international terrorism and drug trafficking. It exposes and counters the huge, menacing apparatus of Soviet espionage and propaganda, and scouts future challenges. Unfortunately, many of your successes can only be celebrated in private." Remarks at the Swearing-in Ceremony for William H. Webster as Director of the Central Intelligence Agency (May 26, 1987).

508 "The CIA routinely places demands upon its employees that would elsewhere be deemed outrageous. Yet it offers them the satisfaction of keeping freedom's candle burning." Remarks at the Swearing-in Ceremony for William H. Webster as Director of the Central Intelligence Agency (May 26, 1987).

CLASS WARFARE

509 "Since when do we in America believe that our society is made up of two diametrically opposed classes — one rich, one poor — both in a permanent state of conflict and neither able to get ahead except at the expense of the other? Since when do we in America accept this alien and discredited theory of social and class warfare? Since when do we in America endorse the politics of energy and division?" Remarks at a Conservative Political Action Conference Dinner (February 26, 1982).

510 "Dependency on government should never be looked on as a chance to build a political constituency." Remarks at the Republican Congressional "Salute to President Ronald Reagan Dinner" (May 4, 1982).

511 "I have often described our opponents on the other side of the aisle as being people who can't see a fat man standing beside a thin one without automatically coming to the conclusion the fat man got that way by taking advantage of the thin one." Remarks at the Republican Congressional "Salute to President Ronald Reagan Dinner" (May 4, 1982).

512 "Well, maybe I'm old fashioned, but I don't think pitting one group of Americans against another is what the Founding Fathers had in mind. This nation was not built on a foundation of envy and resentment. The dream I've always believed in is, no matter who you are, no matter where you come from, if you work hard, pull yourself up and succeed, then by golly, you deserve life's prize." Remarks and a Question-and-Answer Session with Members of the Commonwealth Club of California in San Francisco (March 4, 1983).

513 "Fairness is not appealing to envy, pitting group against group. And fairness is not penalizing the initiative, hard work, savings, risk-taking, and investment that we need to create more jobs. True fairness means honoring our word. It means encouraging and rewarding every citizen who strives to excel and help make America great again." The President's News Conference (prepared statement) (June 28, 1983).

514 "We no longer believe that one man's gain is another man's loss. We have a new vision of America, one in which we are all pulling together rather than pulling apart, one where we're marching forward together as one, proud and united." Remarks to the Annual Meeting of the National Association of Manufacturers (May 29, 1986).

515 "We should applaud people who are trying to better their lot, not put them down." Remarks at the 1988 Reagan Administration Executive Forum (January 19, 1988).

COMMUNISM

516 "A new kind of colonialism [Communism] stalks the world today and threatens our independence. It is brutal and totalitarian." Remarks to the Permanent Council of the Organization of American States on the Caribbean Basin Initiative (February 24, 1982).

517 "The record is clear. Nowhere in its whole sordid history have the promises of communism been redeemed. Everywhere it has exploited and aggravated temporary economic suffering to seize power and then to institutionalize economic deprivation and suppress human rights." Remarks to the Permanent Council of the Organization of American States on the Caribbean Basin Initiative (February 24, 1982).

518 "This is May Day — May Day in the Soviet Union, whose citizens are being forced into an unnatural observance. We'll see, as we always do every May Day, the rockets on their carriages go by and the troops and the bayonets and so forth. They celebrate a government that promises a freedom it systematically denies; that proclaims justice while practicing tyranny; and that uses what it calls law as little more than a thin veneer for the edicts of a totalitarian [government]." Remarks at the Opening Ceremony for the Knoxville International Energy Exposition (World's Fair) in Tennessee (May 1, 1982).

519 "I think the greatest description of the difference between the two countries [the United States and the Soviet Union] is simply that one [the Soviet Union] has to put up fences and walls to keep its people in, and there's nothing like that that has to keep anyone in America. And thanks be to God." Remarks at the Opening Ceremony for the Knoxville International Energy Exposition (World's Fair) in Tennessee (May 1, 1982).

520 "Any system is inherently unstable that has no peaceful means to legitimize its leaders. In such cases, the very repressiveness of the state ultimately drives people to resist it, if necessary, by force." Remarks to Members of the British Parliament (June 8, 1982).

521 "[W]hen have you ever heard of a nation voluntarily requesting to become a member of the Warsaw Pact?" Remarks Upon Returning from the Trip to Europe (June 11, 1982).

522 "History shows that it is precisely when totalitarian regimes begin to decay from within, it is precisely when they feel the first real stirrings of domestic unrest, that they seek to reassure their own people of their vast and unchallengeable power through imperialistic expansion or foreign adventure." Remarks on Signing the Intelligence Identities Protection Act of 1982 (June 23, 1982).

523 "It [Communism] hasn't meant, as promised, a new classless society or the dictatorship of the proletariat. It has, instead, meant forced labor and mass imprisonment, famine and massacre, the police state and the knock on the door in the night. And it's also meant the growth of the largest military empire in the history of the world, an empire whose territorial ambition has sparked a wasteful arms race and whose ideological obsession remains the single greatest peril to peace among the nations." Remarks on Signing the Captive Nations Week Proclamation (July 19, 1982).

524 "The ominous growth of this danger, the human suffering that it's caused, is clearly the most important news event of our generation. And it is, as I've said, the tragedy of our time." Remarks on Signing the Captive Nations Week Proclamation (July 19, 1982).

525 "Responsible members of the world community do not threaten or invade their neighbors. And they restrain their allies from aggression." Address Before a Joint Session of Congress on the State of the Union (January 25, 1983).

526 "To those who would crush religious freedom, our message is plain: You may jail your believers. You may close their churches, confiscate their Bibles, and harass their rabbis and priests, but you will never destroy the love of God and freedom that burns in their hearts. They will triumph over you." Remarks at the Annual Convention of the National Religious Broadcasters (January 31, 1983).

527   "I believe that communism is another sad, bizarre chapter in human history whose last pages even now are being written. I believe this because the source of our strength in the quest for human freedom is not material, but spiritual. And because it knows no limitation, it must terrify and ultimately triumph over those who would enslave their fellow man." Remarks at the Annual Convention of the National Association of Evangelicals in Orlando, Florida (March 8, 1983).

528   "Democracy may not be perfect, but the brave people who risk death for freedom are not fleeing from democracy — they're fleeing to democracy from communism." Remarks at a Ceremony Marking the Annual Observance of Captive Nations Week (July 19, 1983).

529   "I challenge the Kremlin to explain why it refuses to provide anything but weapons of destruction to the undeveloped world. One explanation, of course, is that the Soviet system is incapable of producing enough food for its own population, much less enough to help others in need." Remarks on Signing the World Food Day Proclamation (October 14, 1983).

530   "The tide of history is a freedom tide, and communism cannot and will not hold it back." Toast at the State Dinner in Seoul, Korea (November 12, 1983).

531   "When men try to live in a world without God, it's only too easy for them to forget the rights that God bestows — too easy to suppress freedom of speech, to build walls to keep their countrymen in, to jail dissidents, and to put great thinkers in mental wards." Remarks at the Annual Convention of the National Association of Evangelicals in Columbus, Ohio (March 6, 1984).

532   "Well, I am an anti–Communist if you talk about communism for the United States. And in some Communist regimes, I'm very critical of

their violation of human rights and so forth. But I have never thought it was necessary for us to impose our form of government on some other country. The Communists don't share that view; they do seem to be expansionist." Remarks at a Luncheon with Community Leaders in Fairbanks, Alaska (May 1, 1984).

533   "Atheism is not an incidental element of communism, not just part of the package; it is the package. In countries which have fallen under Communist rule, it is often the church which forms the most powerful barrier against a completely totalitarian system. And so, totalitarian regimes always seek either to destroy the church or, when that is impossible, to subvert it." Remarks at a Conference on Religious Liberty (April 16, 1985).

534   "[I] can't help but remind all of us that some who take advantage of that right of democracy [free speech] seem unaware that if the government that they would advocate became reality, no one would have that freedom to speak up again." Address to a Special Session of the European Parliament in Strasbourg, France (May 8, 1985).

535   "Sooner or later we are all forced to shed whatever illusions we may have had about the nature of Communist regimes." Remarks at the Annual Republican Senate/House Fundraising Dinner (May 16, 1985).

536   "We are fully aware of the threat communism poses to human freedom. And don't let anyone tell you we're morally equivalent with the Soviet Union. I have heard that term used in places. This is a democratic country of free people, a democratic country where all people enjoy the right to speak, to worship God as they choose, and live without fear. We are morally superior, not equivalent, to any totalitarian regime, and we should be darn proud of it." Remarks at a Fundraising Dinner for Senator Paula Hawkins in Miami, Florida (May 27, 1985).

537   "Peace through strength rests on a secure foundation of values. Don't let anyone tell you that we're morally equivalent to the Soviet Union. This is a democratic country of free people. A democratic country where all of us enjoy the right to speak, to worship God as we please, and to live without fear. We're not equivalent — we're far superior to any totalitarian regime, and we should be darn proud of it." Remarks at a Fundraising Luncheon for Senator Don Nickles in Oklahoma City, Oklahoma (June 5, 1985).

538 "The time is now to understand that history will not wait upon a passive America. The time is now to understand that communism has already made its choice. It's an aggressive, implacable foe of freedom." Remarks at a Fundraising Luncheon for Senator Don Nickles in Oklahoma City, Oklahoma (June 5, 1985).

539 "If central planning were the way to a better world, we'd be importing our grain from the Soviet Union and not the other way around." Remarks at a Dinner for the Republican Congressional Leadership (March 10, 1986).

540 "[T]he true nature of communism. It is a cruel system that doesn't work. It produces misery, tyranny, and deprivation — and little else." Remarks at a Republican Party Rally in Miami, Florida (July 23, 1986).

541 "Marxist-Leninist regimes tend to wage war as readily against their neighbors as they routinely do against their own people. In fact, the internal and external wars often become indistinguishable." Address to the 41st Session of the United Nations General Assembly in New York, New York (September 22, 1986).

542 "[T]he mystique of communism has, at long last, been shattered. Young intellectuals can no longer be seduced by a philosophy that has so blatantly and demonstrably failed. The only thing produced in abundance by Marxism-Leninism has been deprivation and tyranny." Remarks on Signing the Human Rights Day, Bill of Rights Day, and Human Rights Week Proclamation (December 10, 1986).

543 "The other day, someone told me the difference between a democracy and a peoples democracy. It's the same difference between a jacket and straightjacket." Remarks on Signing the Human Rights Day, Bill of Rights Day, and Human Rights Week Proclamation (December 10, 1986).

544 "No matter how well-intentioned government controls and grandiose programs are, for the most part they are counterproductive. The inefficiency and misallocation of resources inherent in this approach undercut effective local and private sector programs. You know, if central planning worked, we'd be getting our grain from the Soviet Union and not the other way around." Remarks at the Annual Republican Congressional Fundraising Dinner (April 29, 1987).

545 "The totalitarian world produces backwardness because it does such violence to the spirit, thwarting the human impulse to create, to enjoy, to worship. The totalitarian world finds even symbols of love and of worship an affront." Remarks on East-West Relations at the Brandenburg Gate in West Berlin (June 12, 1987).

546 "Well, yes, our country has its shortcomings, but there's no moral equivalency between democracy and totalitarianism. There's no moral equivalency between turning the proud nations of Eastern Europe into satellites and joining the nations of Western Europe in the defense of their freedom. And, my friends, there's no moral equivalency between propaganda and the truth." Remarks at the 40th Anniversary Conference of the United States Advisory Commission on Public Diplomacy (September 16, 1987).

547 "[T]his [technological innovation] is good news for humanity, but it's bad news for statism. The centrally planned state can dig metal out of the ground or pump oil. Though less efficiently than a free economy, it can operate huge factories and run assembly lines. But it cannot fabricate the spirit of enterprise. It cannot imitate the trial and error of free markets, the riot of experiment that produces knowledge and progress. No government can manufacture the entrepreneur or light that spark of invention. All they can do is let their people go — give them freedom of mind and spirit." Remarks and a Question-and-Answer Session with Members of the City Club of Cleveland, Ohio (January 11, 1988).

548 "Nothing is less free than pure communism...." Farewell Address to the Nation (January 11, 1989).

CONSTITUTION

549 "All those other constitutions [of other countries] are documents that say 'We, the government, allow the people the following rights,' and our Constitution says 'We, the people, allow the government the following privileges and rights.' ... We give our permission to government to do the things that it does. And that's the whole story of the difference—why we're unique in the world...." Remarks to Delegates of the United States Senate Youth Program (February 5, 1981).

550 "Everybody has a constitution, but what makes ours different ... is all those other constitutions tell the people what the government will do for them and let them do, and ours is a constitution that says we, the people, will allow the government to do the following things, and anything we don't allow the government to do, government can't do." Remarks at a White House Reception for Women Appointees of the Reagan Administration (February 10, 1982).

551 "[L]et us give thanks that we live in a land of liberty safeguarded by our constitutional rights and protected by the rule of law." Remarks on Signing the Law Day U.S.A. Proclamation (April 16, 1986).

552 "Theirs [other countries' constitutions] all say, their constitutions, that the Government permits the people the following privileges, rights, and so forth. Ours says: We the people will allow the Government to do the following things, and it can't do anything other than what we have specifically given it the right to do. And as long as we keep that kind of a system in this country, we will be a superpower." Remarks at a White House Briefing for Republican Student Interns on Soviet–United States Relations (July 29, 1986).

553 "The United States Constitution is the impassioned and inspired vehicle by which we travel through history. It grew out of the most fundamental inspiration of our existence: that we are here to serve Him by living free—that living free releases in us the noblest of impulses and the best of our abilities; that we would use these gifts for good and generous purposes and would secure them not just for ourselves and for our children but for all mankind." Address Before a Joint Session of Congress on the State of the Union (January 27, 1987).

554 "[E]ach of these documents [the Declaration of Independence, the Articles of the Confederation, the Constitution, and the Bill of Rights] speak with a force far greater than all the armies that have ever marched: the force of the love of freedom that is born with the birth of every living soul." Remarks at the White House Ceremony Opening the "Roads to Liberty" Exhibit (March 11, 1987).

555 "Over the years, historical and legal scholars have continued to marvel at its [the Constitution's] wisdom and prudence. In some mysterious way it seemed to provide for every contingency; it set up a structure of government strong enough to maintain national unity but flexible enough to change with the times." Radio Address to the Nation on Memorial Day and the Budget Deficit (May 23, 1987).

556 "[T]he Constitution has blessed us with what I have to believe is the finest Government in history." Remarks to the Winners of the 1987 Elementary School Essay Project on the Constitution (June 1, 1987).

557 "[O]ur Constitution has proven a source of strength, stability, and unerring wisdom, serving longer than any other written constitution in the world. Think of that: Young as our country is, we're really, though, the oldest republic in the world." Remarks to the Winners of the 1987 Elementary School Essay Project on the Constitution (June 1, 1987).

558 "We're all heirs to the Constitution; we're all the Constitution's children. Being the heirs to the Constitution is our good fortune, but it also places upon us a responsibility: the responsibility to nurture and defend this country so that, when our turn comes, we, too, can pass on to our children a nation of greatness and freedom." Remarks to the Winners of the 1987 Elementary School Essay Project on the Constitution (June 1, 1987).

559   "The Constitution is the framework of our liberty and the guarantor of our rights. Its drafting two centuries ago was one of the few truly revolutionary acts in the annals of human government." Remarks at a Luncheon for Recipients of the National Medal of Arts (June 18, 1987).

560   "It was then, in 1787, that the revolution truly began; for it was with the writing of the Constitution, setting down as it were the architecture of democratic government, that the fine words and brave rhetoric of 1776 took on substance, that the hopes and dreams of the revolutionists would become a living, enduring reality. All men are created equal and endowed by their Creator with certain inalienable rights — until that moment, that was just a high-blown sentiment, the dreams of a few philosophers and their hotheaded followers." Remarks to the Winners of the Bicentennial of the Constitution Essay Competition (September 10, 1987).

561   "That [the American] revolution has been so successful that even those tyrannies that, in practice, reject every ideal and moral precept upon which our country is founded — even they put on the pretense of democracy, aping our Constitution and its democratic forms." Remarks to the Winners of the Bicentennial of the Constitution Essay Competition (September 10, 1987).

562   "Why does ours [the U.S. Constitution] work the way it does? And the answer is so simple that it almost escapes you. And yet it is so great that it explains the whole difference: three words — 'We the People.' All those other constitutions in the world are documents in which the government tells the people what they can do. And our Constitution is one in which we the people tell the Government what it can do, and it can do nothing other than what is prescribed in that document. So, if we can get the rest of the world to switch around someday, it will be heaven on Earth." Remarks to the Winners of the Bicentennial of the Constitution Essay Competition (September 10, 1987).

563   "Providing the rule of law for our fathers — as it does for us, as it will for our children and grandchildren — was the writing of the Constitution — several thousand words, mere words, on four sheets of parchment, but what power." Remarks at the 40th Anniversary Conference of the United States Advisory Commission on Public Diplomacy (September 16, 1987).

564   "All of us have an obligation to study the Constitution and participate actively in the system of self-government that it establishes. This is an obligation we owe, not only to ourselves but to our children and their children." Remarks at the Bicentennial Celebration of the United States Constitution (September 16, 1987).

565   "If our Constitution has endured, through times perilous as well as prosperous, it has not been simply as a plan of government, no matter how ingenious or inspired that might be. This document that we honor today has always been something more to us, filled with a deeper feeling than one of simple admiration — a feeling, one might say, more of reverence. One scholar described our Constitution as a kind of covenant. It is a covenant we've made not only with ourselves but with all of mankind." Remarks at the "We the People" Bicentennial Celebration in Philadelphia, Pennsylvania (September 17, 1987).

566   "[B]y protecting life, liberty, and property, and assuring the civil rights of all Americans, our Constitution has made our country free and prosperous and produced on this continent the greatest nation on Earth." Remarks at the Presentation Ceremony for the Minority Enterprise Development Week Awards (October 7, 1987).

567   "In these years, our country has come together to celebrate the signing and ratification of our Constitution. The more I reflect on that noble document, the more I'm drawn to the same conclusion as George Washington, that it is more than the product of human invention — that divine providence, as Washington believed, must have also lent a hand." Remarks and a Question-and-Answer Session with Members of the City Club of Cleveland, Ohio (January 11, 1988).

568   "[T]he most exciting revolution ever known to humankind began with three simple words: 'We the People,' the revolutionary notion that the people grant government its rights, and not the other way around." Address Before a Joint Session of Congress on the State of the Union (January 25, 1988).

569 "Our Constitution, our form of government, is built on a bedrock value: self-government, yes, but self-government with a purpose — which is individual liberty." Remarks at the Swearing-In Ceremony for Anthony M. Kennedy as an Associate Justice of the Supreme Court of the United States (February 18, 1988).

570 "[A]ll the other nations have constitutions. And I've read an awful lot of them. And many of them ... contain some of the same clauses that ours do.... The difference is so tiny in ours that it is overlooked, and yet it is so great it tells the entire difference. Three words: 'We the People'— our Constitution is a document in which we the people tell the Government what it can do,

and it can do nothing that isn't contained in that document. All those other constitutions are documents in which the Government is telling the people what it will let them do." Remarks and a Question-and-Answer Session with Members of the National Strategy Forum in Chicago, Illinois (May 4, 1988).

571 "Some people say Americans take our freedom for granted. I think that may be the most glorious gift of all. The Constitution we have makes it possible for all Americans to assume that political freedom is their birthright from the moment they open their eyes." Remarks at a Luncheon for Recipients of the Medal of Freedom (November 10, 1988).

CRIME AND JUSTICE

Criminal Justice System

572 "[T]he first principle of any [criminal] legal system is to punish the guilty and protect the innocent." Remarks at the Conservative Political Action Conference Dinner (March 20, 1981).

573 "It's time for honest talk, plain talk. There has been a breakdown in the criminal justice system in America. It just plain isn't working. All too often, repeat offenders, habitual lawbreakers, career criminals, call them what you will, are robbing, raping, and beating with impunity and, as I said, are quite literally getting away with murder. The people are sickened and outraged. They demand that we put a stop to it." Remarks at the Annual Meeting of the International Association of Chiefs of Police in New Orleans, Louisiana (September 28, 1981).

574 "[W]e should [not] be hesitant or feel guilty about ... [punishing] those who violate the elementary rules of civilized existence. Theft is

not a form of political or cultural expression; it is theft, and it is wrong. Murder is not forbidden as a matter of subjective opinion; it is objectively evil, and we must prohibit it. And no one but the thief and murderer benefits when we think and act otherwise." Remarks at the Annual Meeting of the International Association of Chiefs of Police in New Orleans (September 28, 1981).

575 "It's time ... that we acknowledge the solution to the crime problem will not be found in the social worker's files, the psychiatrist's notes, or the bureaucrat's budgets. It's a problem of the heart, and it's there we must look for the answer. We can begin by acknowledging some of those permanent things, those absolute truths I mentioned before. Two of those truths are that men are basically good but prone to evil, and society has a right to be protected from them." Remarks at the Annual Meeting of the International Association of Chiefs of Police in New Orleans (September 28, 1981).

576 "[F]or all our science and sophistication, for all our justified pride in intellectual accomplishment, we must never forget the jungle is always waiting to take us over. Only our deep moral values and our strong social institutions can hold back that jungle and restrain the darker impulses of human nature." Remarks at the Annual Meeting of the International Association of Chiefs of Police in New Orleans (September 28, 1981).

577   "[T]his rule [the exclusionary rule] rests on the absurd proposition that a law enforcement error, no matter how technical, can be used to justify throwing an entire case out of court, no matter how guilty the defendant or how heinous the crime. The plain consequences of treating the wrongs equally is a grievous miscarriage of justice. The criminal goes free, the officer receives no effective reprimand, and the only ones who suffer are the people of the community." Remarks at the Annual Meeting of the International Association of Chiefs of Police in New Orleans, Louisiana (September 28, 1981).

578   "Our laws represent the collective moral voice of a free society — a voice that articulates our shared beliefs about the rules of civilized behavior." Remarks on Signing Executive Order 12360, Establishing the President's Task Force on Victims of Crime (April 23, 1982).

579   "[The rules of civilized behavior] will lose their meaning and our citizens will lose faith in them if we concentrate solely on punishing criminals and ignore the suffering of those upon whom criminals prey. They should not be treated as ciphers on a statisticians chart. They are our fellow citizens ... [and] all of us have an interest in seeing that justice is done not only to the criminal but also for those who suffer the consequences of his crime." Remarks on Signing Executive Order 12360, Establishing the President's Task Force on Victim's Crime (April 23, 1982).

580   "Common sense tells us something is not right here. Common sense tells us we should do something about it ... [by] return[ing] some balance to our criminal justice system without infringing upon the rights of the defendant." Remarks on Signing the Missing Children Act and the Victim and Witness Protection Act of 1982 (October 12, 1982).

581   "[There are] certain enduring truths — the belief that right and wrong do matter, that individuals are responsible for their actions, that evil

is frequently a conscious choice, and that retribution must be swift and sure for those who decide to make a career of preying on the innocent." Remarks Announcing Federal Initiatives Against Drug Trafficking and Organized Crime (October 14, 1982).

582   "It's a nasty truth, but those who seek to inflict harm are not fazed by gun control. I happen to know this from personal experience." Remarks at the Annual Members Banquet of the National Rifle Association in Phoenix, Arizona (May 6, 1983).

583   "Don't they [gun control advocates] understand that most violent crimes are not committed by decent, law-abiding citizens? They're committed by career criminals. Guns don't make criminals. Hard-core criminals use guns. And locking them up, the hard-core criminals up, and throwing away the key is the best gun-control law we could ever have." Remarks at the Annual Members Banquet of the National Rifle Association in Phoenix, Arizona (May 6, 1983).

584   "It's often been said that no government can eliminate or end the illegal activities that provide much of the revenue and support for organized crime. Well, that's only true as far as it goes. I agree that government cannot stop or abolish the human impulses that make racketeering profitable. But I also believe we'd have the capacity to break apart and ultimately destroy the tightly knit regional and national networks of career criminals who live off those networks." Remarks on Establishing the President's Commission on Organized Crime (July 28, 1983).

585   "Shouldn't we have the right as citizens of this great country to walk our streets without being afraid and to go to bed without worrying the next sound might be a burglar alarm or a rapist? Of course we should. But in reality we don't. For too many years, the scales of criminal justice were tilted toward protecting rights of criminals. Those in charge forgot or just plain didn't care about protecting your rights — the rights of law-abiding citizens." Radio Address to the Nation on Proposed Crime Legislation (February 18, 1984).

586   "Nothing in the Constitution gives criminals the right to prey on innocent, law-abiding citizens." Radio Address to the Nation on Proposed Crime Legislation (February 18, 1984).

587 "Our criminal justice system is long overdue for reform. It is about time we take the handcuffs off law enforcement and put them on the thugs and murderers where they belong." Remarks at the National Legislative Conference of the Independent Insurance Agents of America (March 27, 1984).

588 "Our laws represent the collective moral voice of a free society." Remarks at a White House Ceremony Marking the Opening of the National Center for Missing and Exploited Children (June 13, 1984).

589 "[T]he American people have lost patience with liberal lenience and pseudointellectual apologies for crime. They're demanding that our criminal justice system return to realism; that our courts affirm values that teach us right and wrong matters, and that individuals are responsible for their actions, and retribution should be swift and sure for those who prey on the innocent." Remarks at the Annual Convention of the Texas State Bar Association in San Antonio (July 6, 1984).

590 "Believe me, we have it within our power to shatter the regional and national syndicates that make up organized crime in America. And this administration seeks no negotiated settlement, no détente with the mob. Our goal is to cripple their organization, dry up their profits, and put their members behind bars, where they belong." Remarks at the Annual Convention of the Texas State Bar Association in San Antonio (July 6, 1984).

591 "[I]t's not asking too much that Americans be able to take a walk after dark without having to cringe in fear." Remarks at a Reagan-Bush Rally in Austin, Texas (July 25, 1984).

592 "[W]e must rid ourselves once and for all of the old superstition that crime is somehow the fault of society and not the wrongdoer who preys on innocent people." Remarks at the Annual Convention of the American Legion in Salt Lake City, Utah (September 4, 1984).

593 "We do not seek to violate the rights of defendants. But shouldn't we feel more compassion for the victims of crime than for those who commit crime?" Address Before a Joint Session of the Congress on the State of the Union (February 6, 1985).

594 "[T]he values that are the basis for a free and a just society [are]: the belief that right and wrong matters, that individuals are responsible for their actions, and that punishment must be swift and sure for those who transgress against the rights of their fellow citizens." Remarks on Signing the Victims of Crime Week Proclamation (April 19, 1985).

595 "We are in this thing to win. There will be no negotiated settlements, no detente with the mob. It's war to the end where we're concerned. Our goal is simple: We mean to cripple their organization, dry up their profits, and put their members behind bars where they belong. They've had a free run for too long a time in this country." Remarks During a White House Briefing for United States Attorneys (October 21, 1985).

596 "The United States is the only nation in the world with such an expansive exclusionary rule. A rule that rests on the proposition that a law enforcement error, no matter how technical, can be used to justify throwing an entire case out of court, no matter how guilty the defendant or how heinous the crime. The plain consequence of treating the wrongs equally is a grievous miscarriage of justice. The criminal goes free, the officer is uncorrected, and the only ones who really suffer are the people in the community." Remarks at a White House Briefing on Proposed Criminal Justice Reform Legislation (October 16, 1987).

597 "I want courts that protect the rights of all citizens. No one has rights when criminals are allowed to prey on society." Remarks Announcing the Nomination of Douglas H. Ginsburg to Be an Associate Justice of the United States Supreme Court (October 29, 1987).

598 "The constitutional rights of the accused must be protected, but so must the rights of law-abiding citizens. Hardened criminals simply must not be allowed to prey upon the innocent." Remarks at the Swearing-In Ceremony for William Steele Sessions as Director of the Federal Bureau of Investigation (November 2, 1987).

599 "Being tough on crime doesn't require tortured constitutional reasoning. The Constitution itself is tough on crime; it was intended to 'establish justice' and 'ensure domestic tranquility.' It provides a system for discovering the truth, releasing the innocent, and punishing the guilty, not for subjecting the police to an endless guessing game about the rules." Remarks to Administration Supporters on Child Pornography and the Supreme Court Nomination of Anthony M. Kennedy (December 4, 1987).

600   "Crime is not a statistic: It is an outrage and a sin, and it must be fought." Remarks at a Campaign Fundraising Luncheon for Senator Pete Wilson in Irvine, California (August 23, 1988).

Illegal Drugs

601   "We're rejecting the helpless attitude that drug use is so rampant that we're defenseless to do anything about it. We're taking down the surrender flag that has flown over so many drug efforts; we're running up a battle flag. We can fight the drug problem and we can win." Remarks on Signing Executive Order 12368, Concerning Federal Drug Abuse Policy Functions (June 24, 1982).

602   "[Drug abuse is] one of the gravest problems that I think is facing our nation." Remarks on Signing the National Drug Abuse Education and Prevention Week Proclamation (September 21, 1984).

603   "[A]nother part of our strategy is a strong law enforcement/interdiction campaign aimed at stopping the drug flow before it reaches the customers. It's a complicated and frustrating job, but our commitment sends a message to every youngster in this country: Drug use is a threat, an ugly, life-destroying vice. And it's wrong." Remarks at a Fundraising Dinner for Senator Paula Hawkins in Miami, Florida (May 27, 1985).

604   "I'm particularly proud of the role that Nancy has played in ... the fight against drug abuse.... From one line that she used out in Oakland, California, answering a young person's question when she was speaking to them about what to do about it — and she said, 'Just say no.' And today Just Say No is a nationwide organization of young people that are pledged to say, 'Just say no.'" Remarks at a White House Briefing for Service Organization Representatives on Drug Abuse (July 30, 1986).

605   "[T]he solution does not lie simply within the realm of government, Federal or State.

It's time to go beyond government. All the confiscation and law enforcement in the world will not cure this plague as long as it is kept alive by public acquiescence. So, we must now go beyond efforts aimed only at affecting the supply of drugs; we must affect not only supply but demand." Remarks Announcing the Campaign Against Drug Abuse and a Question-and-Answer Session with Reporters (August 4, 1986).

606   "Today we must all be as one family in tackling this problem. The young fellow down the street using marijuana must no longer be a problem just for his own mother and father. The fellow at the next desk at work who gets stoned and at times is groggy on the job must no longer be just the boss's headache. The young coed, popping pills or snorting coke, must no longer be excused for just doing her thing. If we care, we'll be firm with these members of the American family. And if we care, we must act. And that doesn't mean, as you've been told, put them in jail — that means help free them from drugs." Remarks at the National Conference on Alcohol and Drug Abuse Prevention in Arlington, Virginia (August 6, 1986).

607   "It may be a while ago now, but I can remember how tough it is sometimes being young, and when I was a kid, we didn't have all the temptations and distractions of this modern society. I know that sometimes it takes all the courage you can muster to 'just say no,' to go with your conscience, what you know is right, rather than with the pack. But that effort is worth it. Don't get caught up in drugs." Radio Address to the Nation on Education and Drug Abuse (September 6, 1986).

608   "[D]rug abuse is not a so-called victimless crime. Everyone's safety is at stake when drugs and excessive alcohol are used by people on the highways or by those transporting our citizens or operating industrial equipment." Address to the Nation on the Campaign Against Drug Abuse (September 14, 1986).

609   "We're getting tough on drugs, and we mean business. To those who are thinking of using drugs, we say: Stop. And to those who are pushing drugs, we say: Beware." Remarks on Signing an Executive Order and a Message to Congress Transmitting Proposed Legislation to Combat Drug Abuse and Trafficking (September 15, 1986).

610 "Drug abuse is not a private matter. Using illegal drugs is unacceptable behavior. And the costs are paid by all of society." Remarks at a White House Kickoff Ceremony for National Drug Abuse Education and Prevention Week (October 6, 1986).

611 "When we all come together, united and committed, then those who are killing America and terrorizing it with slow but sure chemical destruction will see that they are up against the mightiest force for good that we know: the compassionate, but firm, resolve of the American people. And then they will have no dark alleyways to hide in." Remarks at a White House Kickoff Ceremony for National Drug Abuse Education and Prevention Week (October 6, 1986).

612 "Drug use is too costly for us not to do everything in our power, not just to fight it but to subdue it and conquer it." Remarks on Signing the Anti-Drug Abuse Act of 1986 (October 27, 1986).

613 "[D]rug abuse is not just an American problem, it's a critical worldwide problem." Remarks at a White House Meeting for the United States Ambassadors Conference on Narcotics (November 13, 1986).

614 "One of the most troubling issues facing our country is drugs. But it's a problem that, working together, I know we can lick." Radio Address to the Nation on Administration and Congressional Goals (November 15, 1986).

615 "We know the tremendous influence that movies and the media have over young minds. Though some are aware of their special responsibilities and are taking positive steps, it saddens me that my old industry hasn't gotten its act together and really begun to combat drug abuse. The movie industry should be part of the solution, not part of the problem." Remarks on Signing the Executive Order Establishing the White House Conference for a Drug Free America (May 5, 1987).

616 "And let's not kid ourselves — we can't expect children to excel in an environment of drugs and permissiveness. All Americans should stand shoulder to shoulder against this evil that undermines the moral fiber of the Nation and attacks our youth. It's time to get drugs off our campuses and out of our schoolyards." Remarks at

the Tuskegee University Commencement Ceremony in Alabama (May 10, 1987).

617 "Though some are aware of their special responsibilities and are taking positive steps, it saddens me that my old industry, the movie industry, hasn't gotten its act together and really begun to combat drug abuse. Too often drug use is still shown in a positive, upbeat way on the screen. When it comes to drug abuse, the movie industry should be part of the solution, not part of the problem." Remarks at the Commencement Ceremony for Area High School Seniors in Chattanooga, Tennessee (May 19, 1987).

618 "[A]ttacking the suppliers is not enough. As long as there is an illegal market for narcotics, the drug lords will find a way to meet the demand. That's why we cannot ignore the other half of our strategy. We need to keep up the pressure to prevent drug use. We want no new users, and we want those who are using drugs to stop." Radio Address on Drug Abuse and Trafficking (May 30, 1987).

619 "We all need to speak with one voice: Say no to drugs in the school; say no to drugs in the workplace; say no to drugs in the home. Together, say yes to a drug-free America." Radio Address on Drug Abuse and Trafficking (May 30, 1987).

620 "[B]efore I get started, I have a special message from Nancy. Whenever I speak to students, she asks me to remind you: For your families, for your friends, and just for yourselves, just say no to drugs and alcohol." Remarks and a Question-and-Answer Session with Area High School Seniors in Jacksonville, Florida (December 1, 1987).

621 "Drug use, some said, was a victimless crime. No one got hurt. No one suffered. So, what was the big deal? Well, I've often thought that this message that drugs weren't all that bad was part of a larger message. The same people who winked at us about drugs also told us that America's future was bleak. Too often they said that the traditional values of family and community were old fashioned and out of date. It was as if they'd lost faith in the future and wanted the rest of us to lose it, too." Radio Address to the Nation on Teenage Drug Abuse (January 16, 1988).

622 "Of all we've been able to do, I'm perhaps the proudest of what we've done to change attitudes in America about the use of drugs. It's no longer fashionable to use drugs. And by the end of this administration, I'd also like to be able to say that it's no longer tolerated." Remarks at the 1988 Reagan Administration Executive Forum (January 19, 1988).

623 "Drugs are ugly. Drugs are nothing to brag about. Drugs kill." Remarks and a Question-and-Answer Session with Students at Suitland High School in Suitland, Maryland (January 20, 1988).

624 "[W]e've heard the story of victimless crime before, and it's a bad one. The drug user is a victim. His employer is a victim. His fellow employees are victims. The family that depends on his wages are victims. And America—which is only as strong and as competitive as all of us together—America is the victim. It would be hard to find any crime with more victims than drug abuse." Remarks at a Seminar on Substance Abuse in the Workplace in Durham, North Carolina (February 8, 1988).

625 "The old line about drug use being a victimless crime is being replaced with an understanding that the money spent on drugs, even by casual users, ends up financing murderers in South America as well as on our own streets." Radio Address to the Nation on Drug Abuse and Aid to the Nicaraguan Democratic Resistance (February 27, 1988).

626 "[D]efeating the drug menace ... means understanding that drug use is not a victimless crime—that drugs kill and maim and finance the criminal underground. It means accepting the concept of user responsibility. It means realizing that those who use drugs are, in Nancy's words,

making themselves accomplices to murder." Radio Address to the Nation on Drug Abuse and Trafficking (April 16, 1988).

627 "We can show our love by teaching our children to just say no to drugs, by teaching them to choose life, by helping them to live in the world God made, not in an artificial, drug-induced world of false hopes and permanent darkness, of imaginary freedom, but absolute slavery." Remarks at a White House Ceremony Honoring Law Enforcement Officers Slain in the War on Drugs (April 19, 1988).

628 "[T]he drug problem is a national problem that demands national solutions and is too important for us to permit partisan bickering." Radio Address to the Nation on the Fight Against Illegal Drugs (June 25, 1988).

629 "But by far the most important development is the change in attitude in America. You can feel it. People are angry about illegal drugs. We're a patient people, but we've lost our patience." Radio Address to the Nation on the Resignation of Attorney General Meese and the War on Drugs (July 9, 1988).

630 "Some people are now saying we might as well just legalize the use of drugs. With my last breath in my body I will oppose this perverse and inhuman notion." Remarks to the United States Jaycees (September 20, 1988).

631 "We do not tolerate companies that poison our harbors and rivers, and we won't let people who are poisoning the blood of our children get away with it either." Radio Address to the Nation on Economic Growth and the War on Drugs (October 8, 1988).

DECLARATION OF INDEPENDENCE

632 "The Declaration of Independence does not say, life, liberty and happiness. It says, 'life, liberty, and the pursuit of happiness.' There are some things that are left to us to do." Remarks at a Rally Supporting the Proposed Constitutional Amendment for a Balanced Federal Budget (July 19, 1982).

633 "The explicit promise in the Declaration that we're endowed by our Creator with certain inalienable rights was meant for all of us. It wasn't meant to be limited or perverted by special privilege or by double standards that favor one group over another." Remarks at the Annual Meeting of the American Bar Association in Atlanta, Georgia (August 1, 1983).

634 "That declaration [the Declaration of Independence] inspired our nation to reach new heights of human freedom, but its promise wasn't complete until we abolished the shame of slavery from our land and, in the lifetime of many of us, wrote the civil rights statutes that outlawed discrimination by race, religion, gender, or national origin." Radio Address to the Nation on Civil Rights (June 15, 1985).

635 "The Declaration of Independence opened government to the people as never before. Each individual was acknowledged as possessing certain inalienable rights. And these rights in turn enabled our people to take part in their political system. Here was a true revolution, embodying the idea that government required the consent of those it governed. Overnight, Americans were acknowledged as citizens of a free land where they had once been only colonial subjects of a distant monarch." Message on the Observance of Independence Day, 1985 (July 3, 1985).

636 "The basic act of the American Revolution was not the call to arms but the Declaration of Independence, an act that in effect called the Nation into being and the act that has sustained our Republic for two centuries now." Remarks at the 40th Anniversary Conference of the United States Advisory Commission on Public Diplomacy (September 16, 1987).

DEMOCRACY

637 "Democracy depends on government being close to the people." Remarks at a White House Briefing for the National Association of Counties (February 22, 1982).

638 "Democracy allows for self-expression. It respects man's dignity and creativity. It operates by a rule of law, not by terror or coercion. It is government with the consent of the governed." Address Before the Bundestag in Bonn, Federal Republic of Germany (June 9, 1982).

639 "Diversity is one of the great strengths of democratic societies. Democracy only requires that we work together to understand each other, that we listen to each other, and that we address our differences seriously with mutual respect." Remarks to the People of Colombia Prior to the President's Visit (November 29, 1982).

640 "The development of democratic political institutions is the surest means to build the national consensus that is the foundation of true security." Address Before the Korean National Assembly in Seoul (November 12, 1983).

641 "One's country is worth dying for, and democracy is worth dying for, because it is the most deeply honorable form of government ever devised by man." Remarks at a Ceremony Commemorating the 40th Anniversary of the Normandy Invasion, D-Day (June 6, 1984).

642 "Democracy is far from perfect. But democracy does not wage war on its neighbors; it doesn't build walls to keep its people in; and it doesn't organize armies of secret police to spy on them and keep them quiet. Democracy reflects all the mistakes, all the frailties, but also the deepest hopes and dreams of the human spirit. And democracy rests upon a noble principle that has and always will make tyrants tremble: Government derives its legitimacy from the consent of the governed." Remarks on Signing the Captive Nations Week Proclamation (July 16, 1984).

643   "I firmly believe that democratic government is the birthright of every American." Remarks at a Summit Conference of Caribbean Heads of State at the University of South Carolina in Columbia (July 19, 1984).

644   "The trend to democracy not only underscores the desire of people to be free but also suggests a new recognition that free government is the surest path to economic progress." Remarks at the Western Hemisphere Legislative Leaders Forum (January 24, 1985).

645   "In my country, we've learned over and over again that democracy can only work when it is judged not in the short run but over the long term, when we keep in mind the principles upon which it is based and remember how right Winston Churchill was to remind us that democracy truly is the worst form of government, except for all the others." Address Before the Assembly of the Republic of Portugal in Lisbon (May 9, 1985).

646   "This democratic experience and economic development go hand in hand. History shows a strong, unbreakable link between political freedom and economic growth, between democracy and social progress." Address Before the Assembly of the Republic of Portugal in Lisbon (May 9, 1985).

647   "The great saving strength of democracy is that we can confront the truth about ourselves. Individuals of vision, courage, and leadership can set things right." Remarks Announcing Bipartisan Support for Balanced Budget and Emergency Deficit Control Legislation (October 4, 1985).

648   "[C]hange is never easy in a democracy." Remarks to Business Leaders During a White House Briefing on the Federal Budget and Deficit Reduction (October 18, 1985).

649   "Our government is elected by the people; it is not above the people or above the law. We believe the truth is found through debate and discussion. Truth does not burn in the fire or drown in the water." Radio Address to the Nation and the World on the Upcoming Soviet–United States Summit Meeting in Geneva (November 9, 1985).

650   "Down through history, there have been many revolutions, but virtually all of them only exchanged one set of rulers for another set of rulers. Ours was the only truly philosophical revolution. It declared that government would have only those powers granted to it by the people." Remarks Announcing America's Economic Bill of Rights (July 3, 1987).

651   "We know what real democracy constitutes; we understand its implications. It means the rule of law for the leaders as well as the people. It involves limitations on the power of the state over the people. It means orderly debate and meaningful votes. It means liberation of the captive people from the thralls of a ruling elite that presumes to know the people's good better than the people." Remarks on Soviet–United States Relations at the Town Hall of California Meeting in Los Angeles (August 26, 1987).

652   "Democracy doesn't mean selectively granting temporary freedoms in order to placate world opinion, but permanent, across-the-board human rights, guaranteed by a constitution and protected by the checks and balances of democratic government." Address to the Permanent Council of the Organization of American States (October 7, 1987).

653   "Democracy is made up of specifics — day-to-day freedoms — just as tyranny is made up of day-to-day oppressions. Is it sincere to talk about democracy but ignore the specific markers by which we can tell if democracy truly exists? I don't think so." Address to the Permanent Council of the Organization of American States (October 7, 1987).

654   "[D]emocracy takes time and personal effort." Remarks at a Luncheon for Members of Vote America (April 15, 1988).

655   "History has taught us that it is not weapons that cause war but the nature and conduct of the Governments that wield the weapons. So, when we encourage Soviet reforms, it is with the knowledge that democracy not only guarantees human rights but also helps prevent war and, in truth, is a form of arms control." Radio Address to the Nation on the Soviet–United States Summit Meeting in Moscow (May 28, 1988).

656   "Democracy is less a system of government than it is a system to keep government limited, unintrusive; a system of constraints on power to keep politics and government secondary to the important things in life, the true sources of value found only in family and faith." Remarks and a Question-and-Answer Session with the Students and Faculty at Moscow State University (May 31, 1988).

657   "The way of democracy is sometimes a complicated way and sometimes trying, but it is a good way, and we believe the best way." Remarks at the Exchange of Documents Ratifying the Intermediate-Range Nuclear Forces Treaty (June 1, 1988).

658   "[T]hat's what democracy is all about — a big agenda, America's agenda, for all of us to work on together, to build a bright tomorrow for our blessed land." Radio Address to the Nation on the Resignation of Howard Baker as Chief of Staff to the President and the Administration's Agenda (July 2, 1988).

DEVELOPING (THIRD WORLD) ECONOMIES

659   "Far too often, the governments of the developing countries undermine their own private sector — one of the essentials for commercial and industrial expansion — only to see [their] standards of living decline...." Remarks at a Ceremony Marking United States Membership in the African Development Bank (February 8, 1983).

660   "[T]he time has come ... to address the problems of the developing countries in a more forthright and less patronizing way. The fact is that massive infusions of foreign aid have proven not only ineffective in stimulating economic development in the Third World; in many cases they've actually been counterproductive. That kind of foreign aid is nothing more than welfare payments on a global scale and is just as ineffectual and degrading.... Our economic assistance must be carefully targeted and must make maximum use of the energy and efforts of the private sector." Remarks at the Annual Washington Conference of the American Legion (February 22, 1983).

661   "Economic and security assistance are not just a moral duty; they also serve our national interests. When conceived and administered well, assistance programs strengthen our foreign policy and enhance the security of our nation. By promoting economic development in needy countries, we bolster the vitality and security of the free world." Remarks on Receiving the Report of the Commission on Security and Economic Assistance (February 21, 1984).

662   "Americans want you [the people in developing economies] to succeed and to prosper. We have no desire to live as an island of plenty. We don't want jobs and higher standards of living just for our people. We don't want prosperity just at home. We'll be satisfied with nothing less than a worldwide recovery." Remarks at the Annual Convention of the Lions Club International in Dallas, Texas (June 21, 1985).

663   "Our policies toward the Third World should be aimed at establishing partners in trade, not recipients of aid. Our approach should be to keep open our markets, not to empty our Treasury." Remarks to the International Forum of the Chamber of Commerce of the United States (April 23, 1986).

664   "Our legacy must not be to engender dependence among debtor countries, but provide the incentives, the tools, and the opportunity for them to work, produce, and grow their way to self-sufficiency." Remarks to the International Forum of the Chamber of Commerce of the United States (April 23, 1986).

665 "[O]vercoming hunger and economic stagnation requires policies that encourage Africans' own productivity and initiatives. Such a policy framework will make it easier for the rest of the world, including the United States, to help. The laws of economic incentives do not discriminate between developed and developing countries. They apply to all equally." Address to the 41st Session of the United Nations General Assembly in New York, New York (September 22, 1986).

666 "The United States remains fully committed to doing its part in working with those developing nations that are struggling to improve the well-being of their people. Overcoming the obstacles to progress in these poorer nations is,

perhaps, the greatest management challenge in the world today." Remarks at the Annual Meeting of the Boards of Governors of the International Monetary Fund and World Bank Group (September 29, 1987).

667 "The success I'm talking about [in those countries with free markets] is in stark contrast to the misery and decline so evident in nations that have followed statist development models. In many parts of Africa, collectivism has brought decline even in countries rich in natural resources." Remarks at the Annual Meeting of the Boards of Governors of the International Monetary Fund and World Bank Group (September 29, 1987).

668 "We Americans are ready and willing to do our part, but setting things right will also require a commitment for tangible reform from African governments." Remarks Following Discussions with President Kenneth D. Kaunda of Zambia (October 8, 1987).

EDUCATION

General

669 "[E]ducation is the principal responsibility of local school systems, teachers, parents, citizen boards, and State governments. By eliminating the Department of Education less than 2 years after it was created, we cannot only reduce the budget but ensure that local needs and preferences, rather than the wishes of Washington, determine the education of our children." Address to the Nation on the Program for Economic Recovery (September 24, 1981).

670 "And finally — and don't think for a moment I've given up — we need to eliminate that unnecessary and politically engendered Department of Education." Remarks at the Conservative

Political Action Conference Dinner (February 18, 1983).

671 "[E]ducation does not begin with Washington officials or even State and local officials. It begins in the home, where it is the right and responsibility of every American." Radio Address to the Nation on Education (March 12, 1983).

672 "It's time to face the truth. Advocates of more and more government interference in education have had ample time to make their case, and they've failed." Radio Address to the Nation on Education (March 12, 1983).

673 "The classroom should be an entrance to life, not an escape from it." Radio Address to the Nation on Education (March 12, 1983).

674 "America can do better. We must move forward again by returning to the sound principles that never failed us when we lived up to them. Can we not begin by welcoming God back in our schools and by setting an example for children by striving to abide by His Ten Commandments and the Golden Rule." Radio Address to the Nation on Education (March 12, 1983).

675   "[B]etter education doesn't mean a bigger Department of Education. In fact, that Department should be abolished." Radio Address to the Nation on Education (March 12, 1983).

676   "I believe that parents, not government, have the primary responsibility for the education of their children. Parental authority is not a right conveyed by the state; rather, parents delegate to their elected school board representatives and State legislators the responsibility for their children's schooling." Remarks on Receiving the Final Report of the National Commission on Excellence in Education (April 26, 1983).

677   "[O]ur educational system is in the grips of a crisis caused by low standards, lack of purpose, ineffective use of resources, and a failure to challenge students to push performance to the boundaries of individual ability—and that is to strive for excellence." Remarks on Receiving the Final Report of the National Conference on Excellence in Education (April 26, 1983).

678   "Get a good education; that's the key to success. It will open your mind and give wings to the spirit." Radio Address to the Nation on Education (April 30, 1983).

679   "I believe common sense tells us that we don't have an education problem because we're not spending enough, we have an education problem because we're not getting our money's worth for what we spend." Remarks at the Annual Convention of the National Parent-Teacher Association in Albuquerque, New Mexico (June 15, 1983).

680   "To be an American means to understand that education is the key that opens the golden door of opportunity and, just as important, it's been the faithful guardian of our democracy." Remarks at the Presentation Ceremony for the Presidential Scholars Awards (June 16, 1983).

681   "America has always had a love affair with learning. From polished men of letters like Thomas Jefferson to humble, self-taught people like Abe Lincoln, Americans have put their faith

in the profound power of education to enrich individual lives and to make our nation strong." Remarks on Presenting Awards for Excellence in Education (September 28, 1983).

682   "God gives us sons and daughters with bright, eager minds, but it's up to us to cultivate and plant their seeds of knowledge." Remarks at the National Forum on Excellence in Education in Indianapolis, Indiana (December 8, 1983).

683   "I believe there are six [fundamental reforms] that can and will turn our schools around.... [W]e need to write stricter discipline codes, then support our teachers when they enforce those codes.... [W]e must end the drug and alcohol abuse that plagues hundreds of thousands of our children.... [W]e must raise academic standards.... [W]e must encourage good teaching.... [W]e must restore parents and State and local governments to their rightful place in the educational process.... And sixth and last, we must teach the basics." Remarks at the National Forum on Excellence in Education in Indianapolis, Indiana (December 8, 1983).

684   "Today American children need good education more than ever. But we can't get learning back into our schools until we get the crime and violence out." Radio Address to the Nation on School Violence and Discipline (January 7, 1984).

685   "Excellence [in education] must begin in our homes and neighborhood schools, where it is the responsibility of every parent and teacher and the right of every child." Address Before a Joint Session of the Congress on the State of the Union (January 25, 1984).

686   "America's schools don't need new spending programs; they need tougher standards, more homework, merit pay for teachers, discipline, and parents back in charge." Remarks at the Annual Conservative Political Action Conference Dinner (March 2, 1984).

687   "It [education] is as central as the family is central, as the towns we live in are central, and as our churches are central." Remarks at a White House Ceremony Marking the First Anniversary of the Report of the National Association on Excellence in Education (May 11, 1984).

688   "[E]ducation at its core is more than just teaching our young the skills that are needed for a job, however important that it. It's also about passing on to each new generation the values that serve as the foundation and cornerstone of our democratic free society — patriotism, loyalty, faithfulness, courage, the ability to make crucial moral distinctions between right and wrong, the maturity to understand that all that we have and achieve in this world comes first from a beneficent and loving God." Remarks at the Presentation Ceremony for the Presidential Scholars Awards (June 19, 1984).

689　"Learning cannot take place without discipline. School disorder destroys the learning atmosphere, drives good teachers out of teaching, and hurts minority and low income students who are concentrated in urban schools where the problem is most severe." Remarks at a Ceremony Honoring the 1983-1984 Winners in the Secondary School Recognition Program (August 27, 1984).

690　"[E]ducation has always played a crucial role in the life of our nation, teaching the sons and daughters of parents from around the world a common language, English, and a common way of life, democracy." Remarks at a White House Reception Marking the Beginning of National Historically Black Colleges Week (September 24, 1984).

691　"Discipline is important, not for its own sake, but as a way of instilling a virtue that is central to life in our democracy — self-discipline. And if it is sometimes difficult to assert rightful authority, we must ask: Who better to correct the student's arithmetic — his math teacher or, years later, his boss? Who better to teach the student respect for rules — his principal or, someday, the police?" Remarks at the Annual Meeting of the National Association of Independent Schools (February 28, 1985).

692　"Well, the answer is to restore State and local governments and, above all, parents to their rightful place in the educational process. Parents know that they cannot educate their children on their own. We must recognize, in turn, that schools cannot educate students without the personal involvement of parents." Remarks at the Annual Meeting of the National Association of Independent Schools (February 28, 1985).

693　"[W]e must go forward with the basics, making certain that all American students learn to read, write, and speak clearly, develop an ability to work with numbers, acquaint themselves with the fundamentals of American history, and come to understand the core values of Western civilization." Remarks at the Awards Presentation Ceremony for the Presidential Scholars (June 20, 1985).

694　"Few things could be more central to the life and health of our nation than the education of our children. Our schools hold the future of America in their hands. They will decide whether that future is enlightened, free, and informed, or shrouded in the darkness of ignorance." Radio Address to the Nation on Education (August 24, 1985).

695　"[E]xcellence is formed in the classroom by teachers, administrators, and parents working closely together to give their children the very best education possible, not by bureaucrats in the far-off city of Washington. When it comes to education, it's the classroom, not Washington, where the real action is." Radio Address to the Nation on Education (August 24, 1985).

696　"There can no longer be any question that an education founded on the basics works; that higher standards produce higher achievement; and that an orderly, disciplined classroom is a prerequisite for learning." Remarks at a White House Ceremony Honoring the Winners in the Secondary School Recognition Program and the Exemplary Private School Recognition Project (October 1, 1985).

697　"[T]he way to educational excellence is through incentives for achievement, higher standards for our students, and merit pay for teachers." Remarks at a Fundraising Luncheon for Virginia Gubernatorial Candidate Wyatt Durrette in Arlington, Virginia (October 9, 1985).

698　"An education is like a spaceship; it can take you anywhere." Remarks to the Students and Faculty at Martin Luther King, Jr. Elementary School (January 15, 1986).

699　"[S]ound educational practice is based on something Americans know a lot about: plain, old-fashioned common sense." Remarks on Receiving the Department of Education Report on Improving Education (March 4, 1986).

700　"Our children should master the basic concepts of math and science, and let's insist that students not leave high school until they have studied and understood the basic documents of our national heritage." Address Before a Joint Session of Congress on the State of the Union (January 27, 1987).

701   "Education, of course, is not just schooling, and it is not just for the young." Radio Address to the Nation on Administration Goals (January 31, 1987).

702   "When we talk about what works in education, we're really talking about preparing for America's future." Remarks to the National Governors' Association — Department of Education Conference in Columbia, Missouri (March 26, 1987).

703   "The secret to educational quality is not in the pocketbook; it's in the heart. It's in the simple dedication of teachers, administrators, parents, and students to the same basic, fundamental values that have always been the wellspring of success, both in education and life in our country. You don't need schools filled with high technology to give children a good education. You need schools that set high standards and pay attention to the basics of reading, math, science, language, and the meaning of our sacred national heritage. You need orderly schools that assign homework. You need schools with strong principals who have a sense of mission. You need committed teachers who lead students to do their best and keep regular tabs on progress. You need schools that teach a sense of right and wrong. And you need parents and communities that care." Remarks to the National Governors' Association — Department of Education Conference in Columbia, Missouri (March 26, 1987).

704   "When it comes to quality in a school, the important thing is not what goes in, but what comes out, not how much money is spent or how new the buildings are, but how well students read, write and do math and what they know about our sacred national heritage." Remarks on Arrival in Chattanooga, Tennessee (May 19, 1987).

705   "All across the Nation, communities have recognized that the key to a good education is not in the pocketbook, in how much we spend, but in the heart, in the values that guide learning. It's in mastering basics, the three R's — reading, writing, arithmetic. And it's in what you might call

the three F's, and those are faith, family, and freedom. The funny thing is, as schools begin to return to the basics of skill and character the test scores stopped falling and started up again." Remarks at the Presentation Ceremony for the Presidential Scholars Awards (June 17, 1987).

706   "One way of helping all our schools is by bringing more accountability into the educational system. That means merit pay to reward our best teachers, competency testing to maintain a high quality of instruction, achievement testing to measure the performance of schools and students, greater parental choice in determining their children's education, and programs like this that recognize the best schools in America." Remarks at a White House Ceremony Honoring the Winners of the Secondary School Recognition Program and the Exemplary Private School Recognition Project (October 5, 1987).

707   "A critical part of the rebirth of American education and getting back to basics is having our schools again teach old-fashioned ideas like right and wrong. Teaching traditional values does not trap our children into the past. These values are a bedrock from which young people will be able to launch themselves into the future, feeling secure in a world of change because they've been taught truths which never change: honor, justice, loyalty, and courage." Remarks at a White House Ceremony Honoring the Winners of the Secondary School Recognition Program and the Exemplary Private School Recognition Project (October 5, 1987).

708   "[T]he most important thing is not to throw quantities of money at education but to tie funding to results and to have a commitment to quality and to State and local control of schools." Radio Address to the Nation on Administration Goals (January 23, 1988).

709   "There's a lesson here that we all should write on the blackboard a hundred times: In a child's education, money can never take the place of basics like discipline, hard work, and, yes, homework." Address Before a Joint Session of Congress on the State of the Union (January 25, 1988).

710   "When we've looked at schools that work across the country, we've found that the key to what works is not money or being in a prosperous neighborhood but establishing a direction, that is, setting standards." Remarks on Receiving a Report on American Education (April 26, 1988).

711   "The education our children want is the ability to discover the answers to the basic questions we all have: Who am I? Where do I live? And what is the world around me like? Children yearn to learn, and their capacity for it is one of the God-given wonders. The education our children need is the ability to read, write, and reason as well as any student in any country in the world. They need it, and the Nation needs it, as well, if we're to prosper and grow. The education our children deserve is the kind no American should be deprived of, for it's the basic instruction in what it means to be an American." Radio Address to the Nation on Education (September 10, 1988).

712   "I believe that the education of all Americans must be rooted in the self-evident truths of Western civilization. These are the truths that have been passed down like precious heirlooms from generation to generation since the generations began. Since the founding of this Nation, education and democracy have gone hand in hand." Radio Address to the Nation on Education (September 10, 1988).

713   "Jefferson and the Founders believed a nation that governs itself, like ours, must rely upon an informed and engaged electorate. Their purpose was not only to teach all Americans how to read and write but to instill the self-evident truths that are the anchors of our political system — truths, to quote Jefferson, such as: 'all men are created equal, that they are endowed by their Creator with certain unalienable Rights, that among these are Life, Liberty, and the pursuit of Happiness.'" Radio Address to the Nation on Education (September 10, 1988).

714   "[W]hen a youngster's early educational experiences are not good ones — if the youngster goes through childhood baffled because nobody answers those basic questions about life and the universe — his thirst for learning will decrease. And when we lose our desire to learn, the world around us begins to shrink. Opportunities shrink. And our natural desire for self-improvement de-

teriorates. Tragically, we see this happen time and time again in schools that seem to serve more often as places that kids go during the day to kill time rather than places where they go to learn and grow." Remarks to Participants in the Elementary School Recognition Program (September 15, 1988).

School Choice

715   "Excellence demands competition among students and schools. And why not? We must always meet our obligation to those who would fall behind without our assistance. But let's remember, without a race there can be no champion, no records broken, no excellence — in education or any other walk of life." Remarks to the National Catholic Education Association in Chicago, Illinois (April 15, 1982).

716   "[P]arents who are sending their children, perhaps to a church school or an independent school at the same time they pay the full burden of supporting the public school ... should get some recognition of that fact and some relief for the fact that they are supporting two school systems." Remarks at a Utah Republican Party Picnic in Hooper (September 10, 1982).

717   "I happen to believe that as long as there is independent education in this country, all the way from the lowest grade on up through college and university, then we have academic freedom. I would hate to see the day when all education in our country was tax-supported and, therefore under political guidance and rule." Remarks and Question-and-Answer Session on Proposed Tuition Tax Credit Legislation with Editors of Religious Publications (September 14, 1982).

718   "[It is] vitally important ... for us to reverse the decline in American education, to take responsibility for the education of our children out of the hands of the bureaucrats and put it back in the hands of parents and teachers." Remarks at the Conservative Political Action Conference Dinner (February 18, 1983).

719   "At any time that we ever settle for a monopoly on education, then we settle for the evils that go with a monopoly." Remarks to Members of the National Catholic Association (April 7, 1983).

720   "We believe ... the independent, the parochial schools in this country, have offered a choice for the American people, and ... have helped, through their very presence, keep up the quality of education in schools through simple competition." Remarks to Reporters During a Meeting with Republican Senators on Tuition Tax Credit Legislation (November 15, 1983).

721   "Just as more incentives are needed within our schools, greater competition is needed among our schools. Without standards and competition, there can be no champions, no records broken, no excellence in education or any other walk of life." Address Before a Joint Session of Congress on the State of the Union (January 25, 1984).

722   "Parents should have greater freedom to send their children to the schools they desire and to do so without interference by local, State, or Federal levels of government. Diversity and competition among schools should be encouraged, not discouraged." Remarks at the Annual Meeting of the National Association of Independent Schools (February 28, 1985).

723   "A large part of the problem today is that too often schools cannot be held accountable. Accountability is improved when parents are able to choose between a variety of schools...." Remarks at the Awards Presentation Ceremony for the Presidential Scholars (June 20, 1985).

724   "[P]arents of disadvantaged children [should have] the right to choose the school that gives their children the best education. Affluent Americans already have that choice; why shouldn't the poor and the minorities, too?" Remarks at a White House Ceremony Honoring the Winners in the Secondary School Recognition Program and the Exemplary Private School Recognition Project (October 1, 1985).

725   "If one school doesn't do the job right, let them [the parents] send their children to a school that does." Radio Address to the Nation on Education and Drug Abuse (September 6, 1986).

726   "[E]ducational excellence depends on choice. I've long argued that parents should have more choice in determining the schools that their children will attend. I've long argued that more choice would lead to better education. And so, I've advocated tuition tax credits and education vouchers." Remarks and a Question-and-Answer Session with Students at Suitland High School in Suitland, Maryland (January 20, 1988).

727   "[I]ncreased choice leads to increased competition and better schools — so, better teachers, more accountability, but also better content." Remarks to Members of the National Governors' Association (February 22, 1988).

728   "Choice represents a return to some of our most basic notions about education. In particular, programs emphasizing choice reflect the simple truth that the keys to educational success are schools and teachers that teach, and parents who insist that their children learn." Remarks at a Briefing for the White House Workshop on Choice in Education (January 10, 1989).

Teachers

729   "One of the best ways to do this [improving education] is by rewarding excellence. Teachers should be paid and promoted on the basis of their merit and competence. Hard-earned tax dollars should encourage the best. They have no business rewarding incompetence and mediocrity." Address at Commencement Exercises at Seton Hall University in South Orange, New Jersey (May 21, 1983).

730   "Each of you [teachers], as tiring and routine as your daily duties sometimes seem, is a keeper of the American dream, the American future. By informing and exercising young minds, by transmitting learning and values, you are the link between all that is most precious in our national heritage and our children and grandchildren, who will someday take up the burdens of guiding the greatest, freest society on Earth." Remarks at the Annual Convention of the American Federation of Teachers in Los Angeles, California (July 5, 1983).

731   "All of us remember the teacher or teachers who gave us that one extra push, that one extra bit of help just when we needed it most — the people who profoundly influenced and changed our lives." Remarks at the Presentation Ceremony for the Presidential Awards for Excellence in Science and Mathematics Teaching (October 19, 1983).

732   "[Teachers] hold a critically important place in the life of our nation, not just because of the skills [they] impart, though that in itself would be enough, but because [they] shape the future by shaping the adults of the future." Remarks at a White House Ceremony Honoring the National Teacher of the Year (April 9, 1984).

733   "Today America boasts thousands of fine teachers, but in too many cases teaching has become a resting place for the unmotivated and the unqualified. And this we can no longer allow." Remarks at the Annual Meeting of the National Association of Independent Schools (February 28, 1985).

734   "Each gifted instructor, each leader helping restore excellence in education today is a vessel of hope for America — hope that ignorance may be cast away; hope that young minds may be awakened to new discovery; and yes, hope that we may always be free...." Remarks at a White House Ceremony Honoring National Teacher of the Year Theresa K. Dozier (April 18, 1985).

735   "[T]eachers ... deserve special gratitude. Their efforts ... [give us] the greatest gift that one person can give to another — a well-trained and perceptive mind." Remarks at the Awards Presentation Ceremony for the Presidential Scholars (June 20, 1985).

736   "[A]merica's teachers are the preservers and protectors of our heritage. [They] save our past from being consumed by forgetfulness and our future from being engulfed in ignorance." Remarks to the Finalists in the Teacher in Space Project (June 26, 1985).

737   "Teachers in the old days may have worn granny glasses and taught in one-room schoolhouses, while today's teachers jog to work and use computers in the classroom. But teachers still know what they're doing when they must tell Johnny to behave, ask questions in class, and do his homework every night. And good teachers still know what good teachers have always known: We don't need a lot of government interference and fancy gimmicks to produce good schools. What we need is to concentrate hard on basic academic subjects and fundamental moral values." Remarks on Receiving the Department of Education Report on Improving Education (March 4, 1986).

738   "To America's educators the challenge is to prepare our students for this changing world so that they can write clearly; so that illiteracy among this great and free people becomes a thing of the past and more children read at their level skill or above; so that every high school graduate has a basic understanding of mathematics and science and knows how to work a computer; and so that every graduate knows the meaning of our sacred American heritage." Remarks to Business Leaders at a White House Briefing on Economic Competitiveness (February 17, 1987).

739   "Anyone interested in immediate feedback or instant gratification doesn't belong in your [teaching] profession." Remarks at the Presentation Ceremony for the Excellence in Mathematics and Science Teaching Awards (November 18, 1987).

ELECTIONS AND VOTING

740   "I regard voting as the most sacred right of free men and women. We have not sacrificed and fought and toiled to protect that right so that now we can sit back and permit a barrier to come between a secret ballot and any citizen who makes a choice to cast it. Nothing — nothing will change that as long as I am in a position to uphold the Constitution of the United States." Remarks in

Denver, Colorado, at the Annual Convention of the National Association for the Advancement of Colored People (June 29, 1981).

741   "[I] regard voting as the most sacred right of free men and free women." Remarks in Denver, Colorado, at the Annual Convention of the National Association for the Advancement of Colored People (June 29, 1981).

742   "[W]e know that a government cannot be democratic if it refuses to take the test of free election." Remarks to the Permanent Council of the Organization of American States on the Caribbean Basin Initiative (February 24, 1982).

743   "Citizens must have complete confidence in the sanctity of their right to vote ... that the constitutional guarantees are being upheld, and that no vote counts more than another." Remarks on Signing the Voting Rights Act Amendment of 1982 (June 29, 1982).

744   "The free flow and open competition of ideas is the heart of our free societies. What a striking contrast this is with those nations of the world where the people have no role but must sit weakly by and wait for a small group of men to conclude their struggle for power behind closed doors and then rule without being held accountable to anyone." Remarks at a White House Luncheon for Delegates to the Conference on Free Elections (November 4, 1982).

745   "There's no more striking symbol of democracy than the picture of a citizen casting a ballot, electing a leader, choosing his or her own destiny." Remarks at a White House Luncheon for Delegates to the Conference on Free Elections (November 4, 1982).

746   "Democracy cannot be imposed from outside and it frequently evolves only after patient, incremental steps. It must be the product of free institutions — churches, labor unions, independent judiciary, and the press — and its life-giving, rejuvenating process is a citizen placing his vote in a ballot box...." Remarks at a White House Luncheon for Delegates to the Conference on Free Elections (November 4, 1982).

747   I do not underestimate the capabilities for repression of dictatorships.... But the imperishable democratic ideal and the democratic movement — these are stronger." Remarks at a White House Luncheon for Delegates to the Conference on Free Elections (November 4, 1982).

748   "Sometimes it's good to stop and think how unique we really are. We accept our right to vote as normal, but it is revolutionary. In the eyes of much of the world, it's a miracle." Radio Address to the Nation on the Congressional Agenda and the Economy (November 6, 1982).

749   "In a democracy, there is no greater expression of equal opportunity than the right to vote." Remarks at the Annual Meeting of the American Bar Association in Atlanta, Georgia (August 1, 1983).

750   "The future is best decided by ballots, not bullets." Address Before a Joint Session of Congress on the State of the Union (January 25, 1984).

751   "This historic room [the Oval Office] and the Presidency belong to you. It is your right and responsibility every 4 years to give someone temporary custody of this office and the institution of the Presidency." Address to the Nation Announcing the Reagan-Bush Candidacies for Reelection (January 29, 1984).

752   "When people enter the voting booth, that's the most private and protected moment of them all." Remarks and a Question-and-Answer Session with Reporters in Rochester, Minnesota (November 4, 1984).

753   "There has never been a transfer of power by bayonet in America and, God willing, there never will be." Remarks at the Inaugural Band Concert at the Capital Centre in Landover, Maryland (January 21, 1985).

754   "Good citizenship is vitally important if democracies are to continue. Good citizenship means trying to understand the issues and great questions of your day. It also means voting. To vote is to take part in this grand experiment called democracy in America." Remarks and a Question-and-Answer Session with Students of John A. Holmes High School of Edenton, North Carolina (May 13, 1986).

755   "The most powerful tool that you and I have with which to preserve our liberties and shape our own futures is our right to vote. Yet, tragically, in every election, millions of Americans fail to exercise this special privilege." Remarks to Members of the American Legion Auxiliary's Girls Nation (July 18, 1986).

756   "[W]e Americans are once again going to show the world the one thing that, more than any other, is the source of our strength. We'll go to the polls, and as a free people, we'll vote." Radio Address to the Nation on Voter Participation (October 18, 1986).

757   "Yes, every time we vote we're standing up, side by side, with the Founding Fathers, with the men of Valley Forge, with patriots and pioneers throughout history, with all those who dedicated their lives to making this a nation of the people, by the people, and for the people. Every time we vote we help to make America stronger." Radio Address to the Nation on Voter Participation (October 18, 1986).

758   "[O]f, course, 1988 is an election year, a year in which we will choose new officials at all levels and, yes, a new President. To tell you the truth, I've always loved election years — the rallies, the excitement, all of it so American. But more than the excitement, something of immense importance will be taking place, for this year we will be taking stock of ourselves as a nation and deciding in a free and peaceful democratic election — that is still the marvel of much of the world — where our highest hopes and dreams will lead us. Yes, in 1988, the 212th year of our independence and the 201st of our Constitution, ours remains a free nation truly ruled by we the people." Radio Address to the Nation on Administration Goals (January 2, 1988).

759   "[T]he first step in democratic involvement is voting." Remarks at a Luncheon for Members of Vote America (April 15, 1988).

760   "[G]overnment should derive its mandate from the consent of the governed, this consent being expressed in free, contested, regular elections. And there you have a first human right: the right to have a voice in government, the right to vote." Remarks and a Question-and-Answer Session with Members of the National Strategy Forum in Chicago, Illinois (May 4, 1988).

761   "This office [the Presidency] is not mine to give; only you, the people, can do that." Remarks at the Republican National Convention in New Orleans, Louisiana (August 15, 1988).

762   "Now, let me tell you a secret about the electorate: They tend to vote on the issues." Remarks at a Republican Party Fundraising Reception (October 11, 1988).

763   "So, my fellow Americans, on Tuesday, breathe in the intoxicating air of human freedom in every polling place and voting booth in this nation and reaffirm the words in the Declaration of Independence: 'All men are created equal.'" Radio Address to the Nation on the Upcoming Elections (November 5, 1988).

764   "There's nothing more glorious than the blessing that is our God-given freedom to choose those who will lead us, and there's no sight more moving than a lone American walking to that voting booth, casting a ballot in secret, and thereby determining the destiny of this great country." Radio Address to the Nation on the Upcoming Elections (November 5, 1988).

765   "[L]ast week the United States did something so exceptional that people around the world marveled at it. Last week the American people freely elected our government.... Soon, power will be peacefully transferred from those leaving office to those taking office. And, yes, we do this every election year, and that's what so much of the world marvels at. What we in America take for granted is something that's rare in history and all too remarkable on this globe, the Earth." Remarks and a Question-and-Answer Session with Area Junior High School Students (November 14, 1988).

ENERGY POLICY

766   "Now, we don't need an Energy Department to solve our energy problems. As long as we let the forces of the marketplace work without undue interference, the ingenuity of consumers, business, producers, and investors will do that for us." Address to the Nation on the Program for Economic Recovery (September 24, 1981).

767   "Here in America, in this administration, our national energy policy dictates that one of government's chief energy roles is to guard against sudden interruptions of energy supplies. In the past, we've tried to manage a shortage by interfering with the market process. The results were gas lines, bottlenecks, and bureaucracy. A newly created Department of Energy passed more regulations, hired more bureaucrats, raised taxes, and spent much more money, and it didn't produce a single drop of oil. In fact, American oil production continued to decline. Just as in today — and too many other cases — government did not solve the problem; it became the problem." Remarks at the Opening Ceremony for the Knoxville International Energy Exposition (World's Fair) in Tennessee (May 1, 1982).

768   "American industry has developed the strong technological base for the production of electricity from nuclear energy, and we owe it to our people to make it possible to use this technology to better their lives." Remarks on Signing the Nuclear Waste Policy Act of 1982 (January 7, 1983).

769   "Our renewed energy health is a testament to the ingenuity of the American people and the strength of American businesses, large and small. We have rightly placed our trust in our people and the belief that we were not running out of energy, only imagination." Message to the Congress Transmitting the Fifth National Energy Policy Plan (March 26, 1986).

770   "[N]o problems, however great, are going to be solved by turning the United States Senate over to the kind of people who thought the way to solve the energy crisis was to ration gasoline, control the price of oil, and win votes by demagoging about 'obscene profits.'" Remarks at a Campaign Rally for Senator Mark N. Andrews in Grand Forks, North Dakota (October 17, 1986).

ENVIRONMENT

771   "Well, unfortunately, there's been a kind of elitist attitude in Washington that vast natural resource areas must be locked up to save the planet from mankind. Well, we have a different philosophy, one based on respect for both man and nature. Our administration believes in the concept of stewardship, caring for the resources we have for the benefit of mankind." Remarks at the Annual Banquet of the National Rifle Association in Phoenix, Arizona (May 6, 1983).

772   "We favor economic development, but not within our national parks or our wilderness areas. We have not and never will propose that." Remarks at the Annual Banquet of the National Rifle Association in Phoenix, Arizona (May 6, 1983).

773   "I believe in a sound, strong environmental policy that protects the health of our people and a wise stewardship of our nation's natural resources." Radio Address to the Nation on Environmental and Natural Resources Management (June 11, 1983).

774   "Preservation of our environment is not a liberal or conservative challenge; it's common sense." Address to a Joint Session of the Congress on the State of the Union (January 25, 1984).

775   "[W]e also know that we must do this [protect and conserve the land] with a fine balance. We want, as men on Earth, to use our resources for the reason God gave them to us — for the betterment of man. And our challenge is how to use the environment without abusing it, how to take from it riches and yet leave it rich." Remarks at Dedication Ceremonies for the New Building of the National Geographic Society (June 19, 1984).

776   "I think there have been some who use the conservation movement as an excuse for blind and ignorant attacks on the entrepreneurs who help the economy grow — the farmers who make our food, the businesses that given us heat in winter and coolness in the summer. This kind of antagonism to all things that speak of business has tended to confuse the issue, blur responsibility, and overshadow sincere concern." Remarks at Dedication Ceremonies for the New Building of the National Geographic Society (June 19, 1984).

777   "If we've learned any lessons during the past few decades, perhaps the most important is that preservation of our environment is not a partisan challenge; it's common sense. Our physical health, our social happiness, and our economic well-being will be sustained only by all of us working in a partnership as thoughtful, effective stewards of our national resources." Remarks on Signing the Annual Report of the Council on Environmental Quality (July 11, 1984).

778   "We must and will be responsible to future generations, but at the same time let us remember that quality of life means more than protection and preservation. As Teddy Roosevelt put it, 'Conservation means development as much as

it does protection.'" Remarks on Signing the Annual Report of the Council on Environmental Quality (July 11, 1984).

779   "We can best serve the interests of the American people and generations yet to come by seeking to harmonize competing interests and to reconcile legitimate social goals. And in doing these things, we'll be a trusted friend to both the environment and to the people." Remarks on Signing the Annual Report of the Council on Environmental Quality (July 11, 1984).

780   "Some of America's greatest assets are, of course, the parks, national forests, and other public lands that have been set aside for the benefit and enjoyment of our people and for future generations." Remarks at the Presentation Ceremony for the Take Pride in America Awards (July 21, 1987).

781   "Those who would reduce the natural beauty of our land had better pay attention: 'They either clean up their act or get out of town!'" Remarks at the Presentation Ceremony for the Take Pride in America Awards (July 21, 1987).

782   "Our national parks, forests, waterways, monuments, and other public lands are national treasures that we hold in common. They are America's crown jewels, and we're the custodians who must preserve them, enjoy them, and pass them on to the next generation." Remarks at the Presentation Ceremony for the Take Pride in America Awards (July 26, 1988).

EQUAL OPPORTUNITY AND CIVIL RIGHTS

General

783   "And that responsibility [education in the home] ... includes teaching children respect fort skin color that is different than their own; re-

ligious beliefs that are different from their own. It includes conveying the message to the young as well as the old that racial discrimination and religious bigotry have no place in a free society." Remarks at the Annual Convention of National Religious Broadcasters (February 9, 1982).

784 "Well, let us come together as friends. We'll never find every answer, solve every problem, heal every wound, or live all our dreams. But we can do a lot if we walk together down that one path [the path of friendship] that we know provides real hope." Remarks at the Annual Convention of National Religious Broadcasters (February 9, 1982).

785 "No group should be bullied into silence by racial or ethnic slurs, or the fear of them. The language of hate — the obscenity of anti–Semitism and racism — must have no part in our national dialog." Remarks in New York City on Receiving the Charles Evans Hughes Gold Medal of the National Conference of Christians and Jews (March 23, 1982).

786 "Hatred, envy, and bigotry are as old as the human race itself, as too many tragic passages in the history of the world bear witness. What is new and daring and encouraging about the American experiment is that from the beginning, men and women strove mightily to undo these evils and to overcome the prejudice and injustice of the old world in the virgin soil of the new." Remarks in New York City on Receiving the Charles Hughes Gold Medal of the National Conference of Christians and Jews (March 23, 1982).

787 "[O]ur national character is based on a common identity with a single ideal, a shared value that overcomes our differences and unites us as a people. What has made us a nation is our love of liberty and our realization that we're part of a great historic venture, an experiment in freedom to test the ability of people to live together in freedom, respecting the rights of others and expecting that their rights, in turn, will be respected." Remarks Announcing the Formation of the Statue of Liberty–Ellis Island Centennial Commission (May 18, 1982).

788 "[T]he long struggle of minority citizens for equal rights, once a source of disunity and civil war, is now a point of pride for all Americans. We must never go back. There is no room for racism, anti–Semitism, or other forms of ethnic and racial hatred in this country." Remarks at the Annual Convention of the National Association of Evangelicals in Orlando, Florida (March 8, 1983).

789 "That declaration [of Independence] inspired our nation to reach new heights of human freedom, but its promise wasn't complete until we abolished the shame of slavery from our land and, in the lifetime of many of us, wrote the civil rights statutes that outlawed discrimination by race, religion, gender, or national origin." Radio Address on Civil Rights (June 15, 1983).

790 "We need unity, not divisiveness to see us through. If we're to remain strong and free and good, we must not waste the talents of one mind, the muscle of one body, or the potential of a single soul. We need all our people — men and women, young and old, individuals of every race — to be healthy, happy, and whole." Remarks at a White House Reception for the National Council of Negro Women (July 28, 1983).

791 "I've always believed that America can only be true to itself when its promise is shared by all our people. One of the best ways to make sure that happens is to build a healthy, growing economy that opens up more and more opportunity to our people." Radio Address to the Nation on the Soviet Attack on a Korean Civilian Airliner and on the Observance of Labor Day (September 3, 1983).

792 "Now, our minority actors should also get parts as lawyers and doctors, even cowboys — there were a great many black cowboys in our history. You know, this isn't the first time I've said things like this because for six terms I was president of the Screen Actors Guild, my union, and, believe me, we were working on this very problem then as a union." Remarks at a White House Ceremony Marking the Observance of Minority Enterprise Development Week (October 3, 1983).

793 "If the dream of America is to be preserved, we must not waste the genius of one mind, the strength of one body, or the spirit of one soul. We need all people — men and women, young and old, individuals of every race to be healthy, happy, and whole. This is our goal. We will not rest until all Americans can reach as high as their vision and God-given talents can take them." Remarks at a Spirit of America Rally in Atlanta, Georgia (January 26, 1984).

794 "As this special [spiritual] awakening gathers strength, we must remember that many in good faith will hold other views. Let us pledge to conduct ourselves with generosity, tolerance, and openness toward all. We must respect the rights and views of every American, because we're unshakably committed to democratic values. Our Maker would have it no less." Remarks at the Annual Convention of the National Association of Evangelicals in Columbus, Ohio (March 6, 1984).

795 "[N]o role is superior to another. What's important is that every woman have the right and opportunity to choose the role she wishes — or perhaps, try to fill them all." Radio Address to the Nation on Opportunities for Women (March 31, 1984).

796 "Let there be no doubt. This administration considers discrimination based on sex just as great an evil as discrimination based on religion or race...." Remarks at the Conference Luncheon of the Women Business Owners of New York (April 5, 1984).

797 "The struggle by all Americans for freedom from discrimination must be a spiritual struggle for brotherhood, must be a struggle for full participation at the ballot box; but just as important, it must be an economic struggle for opportunity in a growth economy that creates jobs, not welfare; wealth, not poverty; and freedom, not dependency. And this is a lesson America has been taking too long a time to learn." Remarks to Members of the National Association of Minority Contractors (June 27, 1984).

798 "I believe what black Americans need more, or most, is more opportunity, more enterprise, a bigger cash box, and economic emancipation." Remarks to Members of the National Association of Minority Contractors (June 27, 1984).

799 "Please spare us their [the liberal leadership in the House of Representatives] sermons on fairness and compassion. If they want minority Americans to have more opportunity, doing nothing isn't doing enough. Give enterprise zones a fair debate out there on the floor and then a chance for the representatives in government to vote on it. In the name of growth, let's stop talking billions for dependency and start creating opportunity [enterprise] zones for opportunity. And in the name of America, let's stop spreading bondage and start spreading freedom." Remarks to Members of the National Association of Minority Contractors (June 27, 1984).

800 "Because of the sweeping and exciting changes our country has undergone, it no longer makes sense to talk about a great divide between women and men. There are no longer any men's issues or women's issues, just issues that concern each of us as Americans." Remarks at Women Administration Appointees on Women's Equality Day (August 26, 1984).

801 "The United States of America is and must always remain a nation of openness to people of all beliefs. Our very unity has been strengthened by this pluralism. That's how we began; and this is how we must always be. The ideals of our country leave no room whatsoever for intolerance, anti–Semitism, or bigotry of any kind — none." Remarks at the Convention of B'nai B'rith (September 6, 1984).

802 "[W]e were founded as a nation of openness to people of all beliefs. And so we must remain. Our very unity has been strengthened by our pluralism." Remarks to Members of the Congregation of Temple Hillel and Jewish Community Leaders in Valley Stream, New York (October 26, 1984).

803 "We must never remain silent in the face of bigotry. We must condemn those who seek to divide us. In all quarters and at all times, we must teach tolerance and denounce racism, anti–Semitism, and all ethnic and religious bigotry wherever they exist as unacceptable evils. We have no place for haters in America — none, whatsoever." Remarks to Members of the Congregation of Temple Hillel and Jewish Community Leaders in Valley Stream, New York (October 26, 1984).

804 "If the dream of America is to be preserved, we must not waste the genius of one mind, the strength of one body, or the spirit of one soul. Let us encourage all Americans — men and women, young and old, individuals of every race, creed, and color — to succeed and to be healthy, happy, and whole. Our goal is a society of unlimited opportunity which will reach out to lift the weak and nurture those less fortunate." Address to the Nation on the Eve of the Presidential Election (November 5, 1984).

805 "Equal treatment and equality before the law — these are the foundations on which a just and free society is built." Radio Address to the Nation on Civil Rights (June 15, 1985).

806 "[A]merica had a conscience, and it was a good, strong one. It wouldn't let us hide from the truth, and it wouldn't let us sleep until we all, together, as a whole country, admitted that all people are equal and that in America there should be no second-class citizens. Our national conscience told us to change and start to be fair. And we listened and changed, and we started to be fair." Remarks to the Students and Faculty at Martin Luther King, Jr. Elementary School (January 15, 1986).

807 "We have a lot to be proud of, but nothing to be complacent about; we still have a way to go." Radio Address to the Nation on Martin Luther King, Jr., and Black Americans (January 18, 1986).

808 "[I] always thought being an American meant never being mean or small or giving in to prejudice or bigotry; that it did mean trying to help the other fella and working for a world where every person knows freedom is both a blessing and a birthright; that being an American also means that on certain special days, for a few precious moments, all of us — black or white, Jew or gentile, rich or poor — we are all equal, with an equal chance to decide our destiny, to determine our future, to cast our ballot." Remarks at a Republican Party Rally in Costa Mesa, California (November 3, 1986).

809 "You know, I spent a large part of my life in a profession where there was no question about the equal status of women and men, and that's the way I believe it should be in all lines of work." Remarks at a White House Briefing for Women Entrepreneurs (December 3, 1986).

810 "And I would challenge all of you [students] to pledge yourselves to building an America where incidents of racial hatred do not happen, because racism has been banned not just from the law books but from the hearts of the people. You should accept nothing less than making yours a generation free of bigotry, intolerance, and discrimination. If I might be presumptuous enough to offer this suggestion: A good place to start, a tangible contribution each of you can make, is to be totally intolerant of racism anywhere around you. If someone, even a friend, uses an ugly word referring to another's race or religion, let's make it clear we won't put up with it. Racial, ethnic, or religious slurs are vulgar, mean spirited; and there is no place for them in a democratic and free America." Address to High School Students on

Martin Luther King, Jr.'s Birthday (January 15, 1987).

811 "I was raised in a family that — my mother and father told my brother and myself that the greatest sin there was, was intolerance, prejudice against any other people for any reason. And we grew up with that, both of us, and I'm happy for it." Remarks to Students from Hine Junior High School on Abraham Lincoln (February 12, 1987).

812 "The civil rights movement earned the respect and gratitude of all good and decent Americans, even some who may at first have had reservations about what was happening. Yet changes in the law — and the political struggle itself — brought social progress that enormously strengthened the moral foundation of the United States." Remarks at the Tuskegee University Commencement Ceremony in Alabama (May 10, 1987).

813 "The civil rights movement was one of the proudest moments in our history, when our nation righted ancient wrongs, when we extended to all Americans God-given rights promised in our Constitution, and we made ourselves live up to our ideals." Remarks at a White House Briefing for Minority Business Owners (July 15, 1987).

814 "Civil rights are empty rights if not accompanied by economic opportunity." Remarks at a White House Briefing for Minority Business Owners (July 15, 1987).

815 "If the dream of America is to be strengthened, we must not waste the genius of one mind or the strength of one body or the spirit of one soul." Remarks at the Presentation Ceremony for the Minority Enterprise Development Week Awards (October 7, 1987).

816 "Equality before the law is the American standard. We can never allow ourselves to fall short. Discrimination is an evil, pure and simple, and cannot ever be tolerated." Remarks to State and Local Republican Officials on Federalism and Aid to the Nicaraguan Democratic Resistance (March 22, 1988).

817 "Let us never rest until every American of every race or background knows the full blessing of liberty, until justice for all is truly justice for all." Remarks Upon Returning from the

Soviet–United States Summit Meeting in Moscow (June 3, 1988).

Affirmative Action

818   "I don't look at people as members of groups; I look at them as individuals and as Americans. I believe you rob people of their dignity and confidence when you impose quotas. The implicit but false message of quotas is that some people can't make it under the same rules that apply to everyone else." Remarks at the Annual Meeting of the American Bar Association in Atlanta, Georgia (August 1, 1983).

819   "But economic opportunity doesn't guarantee equal opportunity. There are laws already on the books.... Those laws must be enforced; some must be strengthened." Remarks at the Republican Women's Leadership Forum in San Diego, California (August 26, 1983).

820   "Many of those big government programs had compassionate, indeed, noble intentions, but they also had serious adverse consequences. They marked a departure from creating wealth to creating dependency. I believe what black Americans need more, or most, is more opportunity, more enterprise, a bigger cash box, and economic emancipation." Remarks to Members of the National Association of Minority Contractors (June 27, 1984).

821   "As President, I will enforce civil rights to the fullest extent of the law. Yet, at the same time, we remain unalterably opposed to an idea that would undermine the very concept of equality itself— discriminatory quotas. Ours is a nation based on the sacredness of the individual, a nation where all women and men must be judged on their own merits, imagination, and effort; not what they are but on what they do." Remarks at the International Convention of B'nai B'rith (September 6, 1984).

822   "[B]using ... takes innocent children out of the neighborhood school and makes them pawns in a social experiment that nobody wants. We've found out it failed. I don't call that compassion." Remarks at a Reagan-Bush Rally in Charlotte, North Carolina (October 8, 1984).

823   "I'm sure that you have all seen the statue representing justice that presides in many of our courtrooms — the woman with the blindfold covering her eyes. Her eyes are covered because true justice should never depend on whether you're rich or poor, or black or white, or if you're Hispanic or Asian...." Radio Address to the Nation on Civil Rights (June 15, 1985).

824   "[T]here are some today who, in the name of equality, would have us practice discrimination. They have turned our civil rights laws on their head, claiming they mean exactly the opposite of what they say. These people tell us that the Government should enforce discrimination in favor of some groups through hiring quotas, under which people get or lose particular jobs or promotions solely because of their race or sex. Some bluntly assert that our civil rights laws only apply to special groups and were never intended to protect every American. Well, they couldn't be more wrong. The truth is, quotas deny jobs to many who would have gotten them otherwise, but who weren't born a specified race or sex. That's discrimination pure and simple and is exactly what the civil rights laws were designed to stop. Quotas also cast a shadow on the real achievements of minorities, which makes quotas a double tragedy." Radio Address to the Nation on Civil Rights (June 15, 1985).

825   "[T]he way to give minorities a fair shake is ... enterprise zones and a youth opportunity wage for teenagers." Remarks at a Fundraising Luncheon for Virginia Gubernatorial Candidate Wyatt Durrette in Arlington, Virginia (October 9, 1985).

826   "We're committed to a society in which all men and women have equal opportunities to succeed, and so we oppose the use of quotas. We want a colorblind society, a society that, in the words of Dr. King, judges people 'not by the color of their skin, but by the content of their character.'" Radio Address to the Nation on Martin Luther King, Jr., and Black Americans (January 18, 1986).

827   "[T]here are no such things as black values and white values or poor values and rich values. No ... there are only basic American values. [L]ower standards are double standards — and double standards are wrong." Remarks on Receiving the Department of Education Report on Improving Education (May 20, 1987).

828   "They [liberals] use our words and borrow our tunes, but the song is way out of key. When they say 'equality of opportunity,' they mean straight numerical quotas." Remarks at a Republican Party Fundraising Dinner in Houston, Texas (September 22, 1988).

FAMILY

829   "Home ownership is the symbol of the family unit, the neighborhood, and is essential if we're going to have social, economic, and political stability in our land." Remarks Following a Meeting with the Chairman and Vice Chairman of the President's Commission on Housing (June 17, 1981).

830   "Christmas means so much more because of one special child. But Christmas also reminds us that all children are special, that they are gifts from God, gifts beyond price that mean more than any presents money can buy. In their love and laughter, in our hopes for their future lies the true meaning of Christmas." Address to the Nation About Christmas and the Situation in Poland (December 23, 1981).

831   "Families are the bedrock of our nation — teachers of cooperation, tolerance, concern, and responsibility. Rebuilding America begins with restoring family strength and preserving family values." Remarks at the Annual Convention of the National Religious Broadcasters (February 9, 1982).

832   "[T]he world at times may seem cold and dark, but the family is the light in the window. It guides us and offers us warmth." Remarks at the San Gennaro Festival in Flemington, New Jersey (September 17, 1982).

833   "The future of our nation will be determined more than anything else by the character of our children." Remarks at a White House Reception for the National Coalition of Hispanic Mental Health and Human Services Organizations (September 23, 1982).

834   "[T]he family is basic to our nation's inner spirit. The family is our school of conscience, of service, of democracy, of love, of all things that we as a people esteem and treasure." Remarks on Signing the National Family Week Proclamation (November 12, 1982).

835   "Since men seem to have written most of our history books, the role of women and mothers in our communities and families has not always been given its due. But the truth is the wild west could never have been tamed, the vast prairies never plowed, nor God and learning brought to the corners of our continent without the strength, bravery, and influence of our grandmothers, great-grandmothers, and the women who came before them." Radio Address to the Nation on the Observance of Mother's Day (May 7, 1983).

836   "Families stand at the center of society, so building our future must begin by preserving family values. But how can families survive when big government's powers to tax, inflate, and regulate absorb their wealth, usurp their rights, and crush their spirit." Radio Address to the Nation on the American Family (December 3, 1983).

837   "Families stand at the center of our society." Address to a Joint Session of the Congress on the State of the Union (January 25, 1984).

838   "Family life has changed much down through the years. The days when we could expect to live in only one home and hold only one job are probably gone forever. Perhaps we will not go back to the old family ways, but I think we can and should preserve family values — values of faith, honesty, responsibility, tolerance, kindness, and love." Radio Address to the Nation on the American Family (June 16, 1984).

839 "[B]ig government becoming Big Brother, pushing parents aside, interfering with one parental responsibility after another, is no solution. It only makes bad situations worse...." Radio Address to the Nation on the American Family (June 16, 1984).

840 "The American family is the foundation of our country's goodness and strength. Take away the sense of purpose that raising a family gives to men and women, take away the love, support, and training that children get from their parents, and all that we hold dear in this land will be in jeopardy." Remarks to the National Campers and Hikers Association in Bowling Green, Kentucky (July 12, 1984).

841 "The family, after all, is the main generator of the good things that people bring to the society at large. We're nothing at all without the family...." Remarks at a Reagan-Bush Rally in Brownsville, Texas (October 2, 1984).

842 "[I]f families are strengthened, other social ills will be lessened." Message on the Observance of National Afro-American (Black) History Month, February 1985 (January 31, 1985).

843 "[O]ne other group deserves special honors, it's the largest of all — the working mothers of America. Some devote their full time to raising families, others combine that responsibility with jobs in the marketplace. Some are breadwinners; others are not. But all deserve our respect and thanks. All of these mothers work hard; in fact, they must be the hardest working people in America." Radio Address to the Nation on the Trip to Europe and Mother's Day (May 11, 1985).

844 "There is no instrument of hard work, savings, and job creation as effective as the family. There is no cultural institution as ennobling as family life. And there is no superior, indeed no equal, means to rear the young, protect the weak, or attend the elderly. None." Address to the Nation on Tax Reform (May 28, 1985).

845 "The tax system is crucial, not just to our personal, material well-being and our nation's economic well-being; it must also reflect and support our deeper values and highest aspirations. It must promote opportunity, lift up the weak,

strengthen the family, and perhaps most importantly it must be rooted in that unique American quality, our special commitment to fairness." Address to the Nation on Tax Reform (May 28, 1985).

846 "The family is the moral core of our society, the repository of our values, and the preserver of our traditions. The family's like a tree with its roots in the experience of past generations and its branches reaching boldly out into the future. Our families are the safe haven where we're taught charity, generosity, and love and from which spring our most cherished concepts of human dignity and the worth of each individual life. It's there that we learn to nourish the young and care for the elderly." Remarks on Tax Reform to Concerned Citizens (May 29, 1985).

847 "The family is the guardian of our most treasured possessions — our values of loyalty, chastity, and love and our belief in human dignity and the incalculable worth of each individual life — and through the family, each generation passes these values on to the next as a sacred inheritance. It's the family that civilizes us, that keeps us human, and ensures that our future will be humane." Remarks at a Fundraising Luncheon for Senator Jeremiah Denton in Birmingham, Alabama (June 6, 1985).

848 "[T]here's nothing more important to all of us and nothing more important to our society and our nation and our future than the family. The family is where our children learn a moral view; it's where the values of personal responsibility and loyalty and kindness are taught. And it's not saying too much to say as the family goes, so goes the nation." Remarks to Members of the Evangelical Press During a White House Briefing on Tax Reform (August 1, 1985).

849 "[I]t's been families pulling together that has provided the courage, willpower, and sense of security that have enabled millions of Americans to escape poverty and grab hold of the rungs on the ladder of opportunity." Radio Address to the Nation on Welfare Reform (February 15, 1986).

850 "Fatherhood can sometimes be walking the floor at midnight with a baby that can't sleep. More likely, fatherhood is repairing a bicycle wheel for the umpteenth time, knowing that it won't last the afternoon. Fatherhood is guiding a youth through the wilderness of adolescence toward adulthood. Fatherhood is holding tight when all seems to be falling apart; and it's letting go when it is time to part. Fatherhood is long hours at the blast furnace or in the fields, behind the wheel or in front of a computer screen, working a 12-hour shift or doing a 6-month tour of duty. It's giving one's all, from the break of day to its end, on the job, in the house, but most of all in the heart." Radio Address to the Nation on Flag Day and Father's Day (June 14, 1986).

851   "One of the healthiest and most encouraging signs of our times is a deep appreciation of the family, a keen realization that the family is the best school of good manners and good behavior, our most versatile support system, and our most efficient economic unit." Message on the Observance of Grandparents Day, 1986 (September 5, 1986).

852   "[A]ll those aspects of civilized life that we most deeply cherish — freedom, the rule of law, economic prosperity and opportunity — that all these depend upon the strength and integrity of the family. If you think about it, you'll see that it's in the family that we must all learn the fundamental lesson of life — right and wrong, respect for others, self-discipline, the importance of knowledge, and, yes, a sense of our own self-worth. All of our lives, it's the love of our families that sustains us when times are hard. And it is perhaps above all to provide for our children that we work and save." Radio Address to the Nation on Family Values (December 20, 1986).

853   "In some cases day care may be a necessity, but it can never replace the love and care of the parents themselves." Remarks to Members of the National Governors' Association (February 23, 1987).

854   "I've often thought that our mothers are the most hardworking of all Americans. Raising a family, as we all know, is a 24-hour-a-day duty. How often it was our mothers who picked us up when we fell, comforted us when we were sick, schooled us in our faith, and gave us the security and courage to go out and face the world. So let me just say to all America's mothers: Thanks, Mom, for a job well done." Radio Address to the Nation on Defense Spending (May 9, 1987).

855   "Parents who bring children into the world have a responsibility for these children, whether they live with them or not." Radio Address to the Nation on Welfare Reform (August 1, 1987).

856   "It's a preeminent responsibility for the family to care for and raise its children and a preeminent responsibility of society to nurture and protect the institution of the family." Remarks on Receiving the Report of the President's Child Safety Partnership (November 5, 1987).

857   "[L]et us make certain that the family is always at the center of the public policy process...." Address Before a Joint Session of Congress on the State of the Union (January 25, 1988).

858   "[O]ne of our most important responsibilities is to provide the very best opportunities for the generation that will follow us. Isn't that the dream of every parent, that their children's future will be even better than theirs? Our job is to make sure that government policies are geared to protecting and nurturing our most precious natural resource: our children." Remarks to Members of the National Governors' Association (February 22, 1988).

859   "The family provides children with a haven of love and concern. For parents, it provides a sense of purpose and meaning in life. When the family is strong, the Nation is strong. When the family is weak, the Nation itself is at risk." Remarks to the Student Congress on Evangelism (July 28, 1988).

860   "America cannot afford to waste any of its precious potential. Our children have to learn to read and write and reason. They must know math and science. But above all, they must realize their own worth and know the simple respect that is their birthright. I want them to feel proud of themselves, every one of them." Remarks on Signing the Youth 2000 Week Proclamation (September 9, 1988).

861   "Yes, the family is the bedrock of our nation, but it's also the engine that gives our country life. It is the reason that we produce. It's for our families that we work and labor so that we can join together around the dinner table, bring our children up the right way, care for our parents, and reach out to those less fortunate. It's the power of the family that holds the Nation together, that gives America her conscience, and that serves as the cradle of our country's soul." Remarks at a Business Leaders Luncheon in Sterling Heights, Michigan (October 7, 1988).

FOREIGN POLICY

862 "Harmony [in international relations] requires differences to be joined in pursuit of higher ideals." Remarks at the Welcoming Ceremony for Prime Minister Zenko Suzuki of Japan (May 7, 1981).

863 "Diplomacy is important, but friendship leaves an even more lasting impression." Remarks on Departure from Bonn, Federal Republic of Germany (June 11, 1982).

864 "Diversity is one of the great strengths of democratic societies. Democracy only requires that we work together to understand each other, that we listen to each other, and that we address our differences seriously with mutual respect." Remarks to the People of Colombia Prior to the President's Visit (November 29, 1982).

865 "We Americans covet no foreign territory, and we have no intention of becoming policeman to the world. But as the most powerful country in the West, we have a responsibility to help our friends keep the peace." Remarks at the Annual Convention of the American Legion (August 23, 1983).

866 "When our neighbors are in trouble, their troubles inevitably become ours." Remarks at a White House Ceremony Marking the Implementation of the Caribbean Basin Initiative (October 5, 1983).

867 "We're a nation with global responsibilities. We're not somewhere else in the world protecting someone else's interests; we're there protecting our own." Address to the Nation on Events in Lebanon and Grenada (October 27, 1983).

868 "[I]n making new friends, we don't discard the old." Remarks at a Meeting with Asian and Pacific-American Leaders (February 23, 1984).

869 "Great nations, if adversaries, cannot draw from each other's strength." Toast at a Welcoming Banquet Hosted by Premier Zhao Ziyang in Bejing (April 27, 1984).

870 "It's a good thing for the world when those who are not allies remain open to each other. And it's good to remember that competitors sometimes have mutual interests, and those interests can make them friends." Remarks Upon Returning from China (May 1, 1984).

871 "[W]e must continue to acknowledge our differences, for a friendship based on fiction will not long withstand the rigors of the world." Remarks Upon Returning from China (May 1, 1984).

872 "Change comes neither easily nor quickly in foreign affairs. Finding solutions to critical global problems requires lengthy and sustained efforts...." Radio Address to the Nation on the Trip to Europe (June 9, 1984).

873 "We're ready to be a friend to any country that is a friend to us and a friend of peace." Address to the 39th Session of the United Nations General Assembly in New York, New York (September 24, 1984).

874 "The United States welcomes diversity and peaceful competition. We do not fear the trends of history. We are not ideologically rigid. We do have principles, and we will stand by them, but we will also seek friendship and good will of all, both old friends and new." Address to the 39th Session of the United Nations General Assembly in New York, New York (September 24, 1984).

875 "Even the closest partners and allies may not always see things in exactly the same way. But we agree to keep each other's interests in mind, to keep one another informed, and to hear one another out on the issues which may arise between us. We, too, intend to give our neighbors the benefit of the doubt." Remarks Following a Meeting with Prime Minister Brian Mulroney of Canada (September 25, 1984).

876 "Well, as I said before, we don't want anyone to fear us. But as I said ... we don't care if they even don't love us. We just expect them to respect us. And that's why we'll be strong." Remarks at a Reagan-Bush Rally in Corpus Christi, Texas (October 2, 1984).

877   "We cannot play innocents abroad in a world that's not innocent; nor can we be passive when freedom is under siege. Without resources, diplomacy cannot succeed." Address Before a Joint Session of the Congress on the State of the Union (February 6, 1985).

878   "[T]he ultimate goal of American foreign policy is not just the prevention of war, but the expansion of freedom — to see that every nation, every people, every person, some day enjoys the blessings of liberty." Remarks to American Military Personnel and Their Families in Keflavik, Iceland (October 12, 1986).

879   "[L]ike it or not, we are the leader of the free world. And that is not a role we asked for; it's a role that was thrust upon us by history and by the hopes of those who aspire to freedom throughout the world. It is said that geography is destiny, but let me say that destiny is much more than that. We are a global power, with global interests and global responsibilities. We can ignore but we cannot escape this basic truth, and any retreat from our responsibilities endangers both our national ideals and our national interests." Remarks at a White House Briefing for the Citizens Network for Foreign Affairs (October 21, 1987).

880   "All Americans can agree on the fundamental objectives of our foreign policy. We want to promote democracy, because it is right, and because democratic governments are less likely to become involved in wars of aggression. We want a growing world economy where free enterprise works, because that's the kind of world in which men and women will live the best and most materially.... And we want to work with our friends and allies to prevent regional conflicts and enhance the security of friendly nations." Remarks at a White House Briefing for the Citizens Network for Foreign Affairs (October 21, 1987).

881   "[L]et us remember that perhaps the most fundamental consensus about our nation's role in the world is this: As Americans, it is our duty to ensure the peace while we work untiringly for freedom." Remarks to the Board of Trustees of the Center for Strategic and International Studies (December 14, 1987).

882   "America's first line of defense is found as much in our universities and the great works of humane learning as it is in all the NATO tank divisions on the German border. And the direction of our foreign policy is based as much on the great ideas that bind together the free nations of the world, as it is on the pace of all the peace conferences in Geneva." Remarks and a Question-and-Answer Session at a World Affairs Council Luncheon in Los Angeles, California (October 28, 1988).

883   "I'm a believer in a philosophy of world affairs summed up in a phrase I quoted to Mr. Gorbachev: Trust everybody, but cut the cards." Remarks at a Republican Campaign Rally in Berea, Ohio (November 2, 1988).

884   "The President and Congress ... share many responsibilities. But their roles are not the same. Congress alone, for example, has the power of the purse. The President is chief executive, chief diplomat, and commander in chief. How these great branches of government perform their legitimate roles is critically important to the Nation's ability to succeed, nowhere more so than in the field of foreign affairs. They need each other and must work together in common cause with all deference, but within their separate spheres." Remarks and a Question-and-Answer Session at the University of Virginia in Charlottesville (December 16, 1988).

885   "People around the world have much more in common than they do differences. The differences are between governments, and the problems are between governments. It's not people who begin wars or suppress freedom, it's governments that do that." Remarks at a Meeting with Soviet High School Students (January 13, 1989).

FOUNDING FATHERS

886   "This Nation was born when a band of men, the Founding Fathers, a group so unique we've never seen their like since, rose to such selfless heights. Lawyers, tradesmen, merchants, farmers — 56 men achieved security and standing in life but valued freedom more. They pledged their lives, their fortunes, and their sacred honor. Sixteen of them gave their lives. Most gave their fortunes. All preserved their sacred honor." Address at the Commencement Exercises at the University of Notre Dame (May 17, 1981).

887   "From their own harsh experience with intrusive government, the Founding Fathers made a great breakthrough in political understanding: They understood that it is the excesses of government, the will of one man over another, that has been a principle source of injustice and human suffering through the ages. The Founding Fathers understood that only by making government the servant, not the master, only by positing sovereignty in the people and not the state can we hope to protect freedom and see the political commonwealth prosper." Remarks at a Fundraising Dinner Honoring Former Representative John A. Ashcroft in Ashland, Ohio (May 9, 1983).

888   "The founders of our republic rooted their democratic commitment in the belief that all men are endowed by their Creator with certain inalienable rights. And so, they created a system of government whose avowed purpose was and is the protection of those God-given rights." Remarks at a Conference on Religious Liberty (April 16, 1985).

889   "Our Founding Fathers weren't neutral when it came to values." Radio Address to the Nation on Education (August 24, 1985).

890   "Our forefathers found their inspiration, justification, and vision in the Judeo-Christian tradition that emphasizes the value of life and the worth of the individual. It most certainly was never their intention to bar God from our public life." Radio Address to the Nation on Education (August 24, 1985).

891   "Well, they understood that private property — those Founding Fathers of ours — is one of the most important of civil rights, the most fundamental protection of the individual and the family against the excessive and always growing demands of the state. They knew that without economic liberty, political freedom may be no more than a shadow." Remarks at a White House Briefing for the American Legislative Exchange Council (December 12, 1986).

892   "How, with so much against them, could our Founding Fathers have dared so much, to declare for all the world and all future generations the rights of man, the dignity of the individual, the hopes of all humanity? Was it because they believed that God was on their side? Or was it because they prayed to discover how they might be on God's side? Our Founding Fathers knew that their hope was in prayer. And that's why our Declaration of Independence begins with an affirmation of faith and why our Congress opens every day with prayer." Remarks at the Annual National Prayer Breakfast (February 5, 1987).

893   "Barriers of distance and special interest might have divided them [the Delegates to the Constitutional Convention] and the people of their States from one another, but something even greater held them together. That something was a common dedication to the rights of man. It was their common devotion to the proposition that governments derive their just powers from the consent of the governed. And it was their mutual conviction that here on these American shores they would raise a light unto the nations — a light of self-government, of liberty, and of hope. Yes, many of the Founding Fathers traveled great distances to get to Philadelphia 200 years ago, but in a larger sense, mankind has traveled a great distance to that hall, as well." Remarks at the White House Ceremony Opening the "Roads to Liberty" Exhibit (March 11, 1987).

894   "Two hundred years ago, our Founding Fathers gave us a government of, by, and for the people. They believed that the Constitution they drafted would be a new order for the ages, and they were right. The dream of America has been a shining beacon for all mankind ever since then. It's the light of freedom and the torch of democracy, and it's drawn millions to our shores from all over the world." Remarks at a Rotary Club Luncheon in West Bend, Wisconsin (July 27, 1987).

895   "I think it's interesting to note that the reason the Bill of Rights was added to the document was that some believed the Constitution might not have been ratified otherwise. Such was our forefathers' devotion to liberty." Remarks at a White House Briefing for Human Rights Supporters (December 3, 1987).

896   "I suppose it's the destiny of every second generation or so to think for awhile that maybe they're wiser than our Founding Fathers. And it's the destiny of the generation that follows to realize that this almost certainly is not true and to try to bring the Nation back to its first principles." Remarks to Members of the National Governors' Association (February 22, 1988).

FREE MARKET CAPITALISM

897   "Our aim is to increase our national wealth so all will have more, not just redistribute what we already have which is just a sharing of scarcity." Address to the Nation on the Economy (February 5, 1981).

898   "[Our economic] system has never failed us, but ... we have failed [it] through a lack of confidence and sometimes through a belief that we could fine-tune the economy and get it tuned to our liking...." Address Before a Joint Session of the Congress on the Program for Economic Recovery (February 18, 1981).

899   "We believe that people will stay free when enterprise remains free, and we believe that there are no insurmountable problems when we let individuals make decisions outside the restricting confines of government." Remarks at the Welcoming Ceremony for Prime Minister Margaret Thatcher of the United Kingdom (February 26, 1981).

900   "There is no better Federal program than an expanding American economy." Remarks at the Mid-Winter Congressional City Conference of the National League of Cities (March 2, 1981).

901   "A declining economy is a poisonous gas that claims its first victims in poor neighborhoods, before floating out to the community at large." Remarks in Denver, Colorado, at the Annual Convention of the National Association for the Advancement of Colored People (June 29, 1981).

902   "We believe that on economic recovery, there are no Republicans and no Democrats, only Americans." Remarks on Federal Tax Reductions Following Meetings with Members of Congress (June 4, 1981).

903   "We who live in free market societies believe that growth, prosperity and, ultimately, human fulfillment are created from the bottom up, not the government down." Remarks at the Annual Meeting of the Boards of Governors of the World Bank and International Monetary Fund (September 29, 1981).

904   "We cannot have prosperity and successful development without economic freedom; nor can we preserve our personal and political freedoms without economic freedom. Governments that set out to regiment their people with the stated objective of providing security and liberty have ended up losing both. Those which put freedom as the first priority find they have also provided security and economic progress." Remarks at the Annual Meeting of the Boards of Governors of the World Bank and International Monetary Fund (September 29, 1981).

905   "In its most fundamental sense, it [economic development] has to do with the meaning, aspirations, and worth of every individual. In its ultimate form, development is human fulfillment, an ability by all men and women to realize freely their potential to go as far as their God-given talents will take them." Remarks at a Luncheon of the World Affairs Council of Philadelphia in Philadelphia, Pennsylvania (October 15, 1981).

906   "The road to prosperity and human fulfillment is lighted by economic freedom and individual incentive." Remarks to Reporters Upon Departure for the International Meeting on Cooperation and Development in Cancun, Mexico (October 21, 1981).

907   "Free people build free markets that ignite dynamic development for everyone." Remarks to Reporters Upon Departure for the International Meeting on Cooperation and Development in Cancun, Mexico (October 21, 1981).

908   "History demonstrates time and again, in place after place, economic growth and human progress make their greatest strides in countries that encourage economic freedom." Statement at the First Plenary Session of the International Meeting on Cooperation and Development in Cancun, Mexico (October 22, 1981).

909   "Only when the human spirit is allowed to invent and create, only when individuals are given a personal stake in deciding their destiny, in benefiting from their own risks, only then can society remain alive, prosperous, progressive, and free." Remarks at the New York City Partnership Luncheon in New York (January 14, 1982).

910   "Now, some of those I met with [other national leaders at meetings in Ottawa and Cancun] were a little surprised that I didn't apologize for America's wealth. Instead, I spoke at length of the free marketplace system and how that system could help them realize their aspirations for economic development and political freedom." Address Before a Joint Session of the Congress Reporting on the State of the Union (January 26, 1982).

911   "The greatest threat to freedom, even in today's perilous times, comes from no foreign foe. It comes from a dangerous habit many of our leaders fell into over several generations — letting the power and the resources that are the basis of freedom slip from the grassroots America into the hands of a remote central authority." Remarks at the Los Angeles California, County Board of Supervisors' Town Meeting (March 3, 1982).

912   "America's abundance was not a gift from government or anyone else. Free enterprise, not government, is the source from which our blessings flow...." Remarks at the National Association of Realtors' Legislative Conference (March 29, 1982).

913   "You know, there really is something magic about the marketplace when it's free to operate. As the song says, 'This could be the start of something big.'" Radio Address to the Nation on Taxes, Tuition Tax Credits, and Interest Rates (April 24, 1982).

914   "We believe advances in the human condition can only come from open markets, free trade, and stiff competition. Men and nations who ignore those forces will be lost to time." Remarks at the Opening Ceremony for the Knoxville International Energy Exposition (World's Fair) in Tennessee (May 1, 1982).

915   "[W]ith freedom and profit — the profit motive — America can still work miracles." Remarks at a Meeting with Participants in the American Business Conference (September 28, 1982).

916   "Rebuilding prosperity, I think, is the true meaning of fairness and compassion." Remarks and a Question-and-Answer Session at a Meeting with Employees of AccuRay Corporation in Columbus, Ohio (October 4, 1982).

917   "An essential element for growth, of course, is confidence in the future." Remarks at a Fundraising Dinner for Senator Charles Percy in Chicago, Illinois (January 19, 1983).

918   "[O]ne of the challenges facing all of us ... is a great lack of understanding among otherwise well-educated and intelligent people on ... the marketplace, how it functions and what is required to make it work. And much of what remains is prejudice." Remarks and a Question-and-Answer Session with Members of the Massachusetts High Technology Council in Bedford (January 26, 1983).

919   "Wealth is not created inside some think-tank on the Potomac; it is born in the hearts and minds of entrepreneurs all across Main Street

America." Remarks and a Question-and Answer Session with Members of the Commonwealth Club of California in San Francisco (March 4, 1983).

920 "There's an old economic axiom, still true today, that says, 'If people are not allowed to earn more by producing more, then more will not be produced.'" Remarks on Signing the Annual Report on the State of Small Business (March 18, 1983).

921 "[T]he plant can close no matter how essential it is to the employees and the townspeople. We know that America's economic strengths change and grow in different directions, sometimes without regard to the people who serve the old industries. This is the free market, and it's what gives our children and their children an economic future." Remarks at the National Conference on the Dislocated Worker in Pittsburg, Pennsylvania (April 6, 1983).

922 "[A]merica's prosperity was never a gift from government or anyone else. It was earned with imagination, invention, and backbreaking labor. Free enterprise, not government, is the source from which our prosperity flows...." Remarks at a Meeting of the National Association of Home Builders (May 16, 1983).

923 "An aspect of American history, distasteful to some, is the important role played by the profit motive. Well, I, for one, have no trouble with the profit motive. When people are free to work for themselves they work longer and harder. They'll do a better job because they're not just following orders, they're doing what they want to do. Profit motive unleashed an explosion of energy in America." Remarks at the Annual Convention of the Concrete and Aggregates Industries Associations in Chicago, Illinois (January 31, 1984).

924 "Free people build free markets that ignite dynamic development for everyone." Remarks at the National Leadership Forum of the Center for International and Strategic Studies at Georgetown University (April 6, 1984).

925 "Let's remember that technology is born of capital, and capital requires incentives for risk-taking and investment." Remarks to the Members of the High Technological Corridor Board in Nashville, Tennessee (September 13, 1984).

926 "We believe opportunity is the true engine of progress, the captain of great endeavors." Radio Address to the Nation on the Presidential Campaign (September 15, 1984).

927 "[T]he secret of a progressive new world is to take advantage of the creativity of the human spirit, to encourage innovation and individual enterprise, to reward hard work, to reduce barriers to the free flow of trade and information." Address to the 39th Session of the United Nations General Assembly in New York, New York (September 24, 1984).

928 "[N]o nation can have prosperity and successful development without economic freedom. Nor can it preserve personal and political freedoms without economic freedom." Remarks at the Annual Meeting of the Boards of Governors of the International Monetary Fund and the World Bank Group (September 25, 1984).

929 "[L]et us remember and draw strength from the most powerful, enduring truth in human history: Free men and women are not destined to be powerless victims of some capricious historical tide; free men and women are themselves the driving tide of history." Remarks at the Annual Meeting of the Boards of Governors of the International Monetary Fund and the World Bank Group (September 25, 1984).

930 "We don't want a world in which some nations go forward while others are left behind. We want a world in which all go forward together. And we can go forward together if countries give up spending what need not be spent and leave more in the hands of all the people who work and earn. Let them plant the seeds of wealth, and we'll see the smallest dreams awaken and grow into golden dreams for all mankind." Remarks at the Annual Meeting of the Boards of Governors of the International Monetary Fund and the World Bank Group (September 25, 1984).

931 "[W]e will not make any Federal commitments on behalf of projects that are not determined to be economically viable. To do otherwise would shift the burden of a high-risk business venture onto the shoulders of the American taxpayer." Statement on Signing the Bill Extending Conditional Loan Guarantee Agreements for Ethanol Fuel Production Facilities (April 16, 1985).

932 "This aspect of freedom, economic freedom, is one of the distinctive characteristics of life in our nation, as interwoven into the American legacy as freedom of speech and press. It has enabled our people to make our nation into a marvel of economic progress, and, as with all the freedoms that we enjoy, it's our duty to cherish and protect it." Remarks to Participants in the President's Inaugural Bands Parade at Walt Disney's EPCOT Center Near Orlando, Florida (May 27, 1985).

933 "We want to remember that while the creation of wealth is good — wealth, after all, generates jobs and prosperity — we must not let the creation of wealth become a preoccupation with material things." Remarks at Northside High School in Atlanta, Georgia (June 6, 1985).

934 "Free men, free minds, and free markets can and will make this a better world. It's only when people are free to challenge what exists and offer something new that mankind is able to step forward; only when people are free to dream and discuss untried ideas that a society remains vibrant; only when people are free in the marketplace to meet the needs of others as best they can that innovation and opportunity can become the order of the day." Remarks at the Annual Convention of the Lions Club International in Dallas, Texas (June 21, 1985).

935 "One of America's greatest assets is the skill and professionalism of its men and women of commerce and industry — the peppery, can-do spirit of our business community is in stark contrast to the inefficiency and poor performance often associated with other economic systems." Remarks to the International Forum of the Chamber of Commerce of the United States (April 23, 1986).

936 "The developing world has been told that it's necessary to give up freedom in order to achieve progress. Nothing could be further from the truth. Freedom and economic advance go hand in hand; they are two sides of the same coin. The mainspring of human progress is found not in controlling and harnessing human energy but in setting it free." Remarks to the International Forum of the Chamber of Commerce of the United States (April 23, 1986).

937 "To those countries whose economies are still enmeshed in statist policies, the American economy is a shining example that freedom not only works, it works wonders." Remarks to the Annual Meeting of the National Association of Manufacturers (May 29, 1986).

938 "[T]he freedom of the individual, not the power of the state, is the key to economic dynamism and growth." Address to the 41st Session of the United Nations General Assembly in New York, New York (September 22, 1986).

939 "[T]he United States believes the greatest contribution we can make to world prosperity is the continued advocacy of the magic of the marketplace — the truth, the simple and proven truth, that economic development is an outgrowth of economic freedom just as economic freedom is the inseparable twin of political freedom and democratic government." Address to the 41st Session of the United Nations General Assembly in New York, New York (September 22, 1986).

940 "We've seen that nations that have embraced the enduring principles of economic growth have become more prosperous and secure. And those that have not, have weakened, faltered, and fallen behind. We've heard many names given to these rediscovered economic insights — names describing policies of taxation, regulation, government spending, monetary management, and trade. But all those names and the many theories with which they are associated come down in the end to one name, one theory, one word. The word is 'freedom,' in this case economic freedom." Remarks at the Annual Meeting of the Boards of Governors of the International Monetary Fund and World Bank Group (September 30, 1986).

941 "Freedom works. The democratic freedoms that secure the God-given rights of man, and the economic freedoms that open the door to prosperity — they are the hope and, we trust, the destiny of mankind. If free trade is the lifeblood, free enterprise is the heart of prosperity." Address to a Joint Session of Parliament in Ottawa, Canada (April 6, 1987).

942 "[K]hrushchev predicted: 'We will bury you.' But in the West today, we see a free world that has achieved a level of prosperity and well-being unprecedented in all human history. In the Communist world, we see failure, technological backwardness, declining standards of health, even want of the most basic kind — too little food. Even today, the Soviet Union still cannot feed itself. After these four decades, then, there stands before the entire world one great and inescapable conclusion: Freedom leads to prosperity. Freedom replaces the ancient hatreds among the nations with comity and peace. Freedom is the victor." Remarks on East-West Relations at the Brandenburg Gate in West Berlin (June 12, 1987).

943   "This profound movement in recent years toward more limited government and freer trade has not only kept the global economy moving along at a steady pace, it's made it possible for the democratic nations to stand together and keep our defenses strong, while we promote the growth of democratic institutions in the world spread of freedom and peace." Remarks and a Question-and-Answer Session with Economic Reporters (June 16, 1987).

944   "Today the pivotal relationship between freedom and economic progress is becoming ever more important. The root cause of stagnation in the developing world, clearly, is not a lack of resources but a lack of freedom." Remarks on Receiving the Report of the Presidential Task Force on Project Economic Justice (August 3, 1987).

945   "In so many countries, what will change despair into confidence, deprivation into plenty, stagnation into upward mobility is a commitment to human freedom and an understanding of how that relates to the economic progress of mankind." Remarks on Receiving the Report of the Presidential Task Force on Project Economic Justice (August 3, 1987).

946   "Freedom of enterprise at an individual level builds countries from the bottom up; a lack of it, on the other hand, has the opposite effect." Remarks on Receiving the Report of the Presidential Task Force on Project Economic Justice (August 3, 1987).

947   "[F]reedom and opportunity are not just for the elite but the birthright of every citizen, that property is not just something enjoyed by a few but can be owned by any individual who works hard and makes correct decisions, that free enterprise is not just the province of the rich but a system of free choice in which everyone has rights, and that business, large or small, is something in which everyone can own a piece of the action." Remarks on Receiving the Report of the

Presidential Task Force on Project Economic Justice (August 3, 1987).

948   "Well, the Founding Fathers, Jefferson in particular, did not see economic and political freedom as the right only of the citizens of the United States but the right of all people, everywhere and for all time." Remarks on Receiving the Report of the Presidential Task Force on Project Economic Justice (August 3, 1987).

949   "I've long believed that one of the mainsprings of our own liberty has been the widespread ownership of property among our people and the expectation that anyone's child, even from the humblest of families, could grow up to own a business or a corporation." Remarks on Receiving the Report of the Presidential Task Force on Project Economic Justice (August 3, 1987).

950   "There has been much talk in the halls of this building about the right to development. But more and more the evidence is clear that development is not itself a right. It is the product of rights: the right to own property; the right to buy and sell freely; the right to contract; the right to be free of excessive taxation and regulation, of burdensome government." Address to the 42d Session of the United Nations General Assembly in New York, New York (September 21, 1987).

951   "Those who advocate statist solutions to development should take note: The free market is the other path to development and the one true path. And unlike many other paths, it leads somewhere. It works." Address to the 42d Session of the United Nations General Assembly in New York, New York (September 21, 1987).

952   "Some do not believe in democracy or in political, economic, or religious freedom. Some believe in dictatorship, whether by one man, one party, one class, one race, or one vanguard. To those governments I would only say that the price of oppression is clear. Your economies will fall farther and farther behind. Your people will become more restless. Isn't it better to listen to the people's hopes now rather than their curses later?" Address to the 42d Session of the United Nations General Assembly in New York, New York (September 21, 1987).

953   "[F]ree enterprise is the most powerful engine of economic progress known to humanity." Radio Address to the Nation on Philippine–United States Relations and the Situation in Central America (November 7, 1987).

954   "It's my belief that liberty should be as important a concern in Toronto as it was in Moscow. Liberty in the economic sphere means low taxes. It means paring away needless regulations and reducing counterproductive government planning and interference. And it means keeping down barriers to international trade, here and around the world." Radio Address to the Nation on the Soviet–United States Summit Meeting in Moscow and the Toronto Economic Summit (June 4, 1988).

955   "[O]ur own prosperity is only part of our achievement. We have also led the world toward a remarkable consensus: that economic freedom, not state planning and intervention, holds the key to growth and development. Yes, the other industrial democracies have joined us on this path. But it goes further than that. From India to Argentina, from Africa to China and even in the Soviet Union, the shackles of state economic domination are beginning to loosen. So, in winning this battle of ideas, we're helping to enrich and liberate the working people and entrepreneurs of the entire world." Radio Address to the Nation on Economic Growth and the Situation in Nicaragua (June 18, 1988).

956   "The future belongs to the flexible. It belongs to those countries that don't straitjacket the initiative of their people; to those who give reign to the creative, enterprising spirit that is in all people; to those who see the limit of government's understanding and its ability to respond to a world that is changing before our eyes." Remarks at the Business Roundtable Annual Dinner (June 22, 1988).

FREEDOM AND LIBERTY

General

957   "Above all, we must realize that no arsenal or no weapon in the arsenals of the world is so formidable as the will and moral courage of free men and women. It is a weapon our adversaries in today's world do not have. It is a weapon that we as Americans do have. Let that be understood by those who practice terrorism and prey upon their neighbors." Inaugural Address (January 20, 1981).

958   "There is no left or right. There's only an up or down: up to the ultimate in individual freedom, man's age old dream, the ultimate in individual freedom consistent with an orderly society — or down to the totalitarianism of the ant heap. And those today who, however good their intentions, tell us that we should trade freedom for security are on that downward path." Remarks at the Conservative Political Action Conference Dinner (March 20, 1981).

959   "We cherish liberty and hold it safe, providing hope for the rest of the world." Remarks of the President and Prime Minister J. Malcolm Fraser of Australia at the Welcoming Ceremony (June 30, 1981).

960   "When we unfurl our flags, strike up the bands, and light up the skies each July 4th, we celebrate the most exciting, ongoing adventure in human freedom the world has ever known." Message on the Observance of Independence Day, 1981 (July 3, 1981).

961   "Those principles [upon which our Constitution is based] must be reaffirmed by every generation of Americans, for freedom is never more than one generation away from extinction.

It can only be passed on to a new generation if it has been preserved by the old." Remarks at the Dedication of the James Madison Memorial Building of the Library of Congress (November 20, 1981).

962 "It's been said that if we lose this way of ours, this thing we call freedom, history will record with great astonishment that those who had the most to lose did the least to prevent its happening. That must not be said of us." Address Before a Joint Session of the Iowa State Legislature in Des Moines (February 9, 1982).

963 "Liberty belongs to the brave." Remarks at the National Legislative Conference of the Building and Construction Trades Department, AFL-CIO (April 5, 1982).

964 "[W]e are a free people who can work together voluntarily in a way no system based on tyranny ever will. That always has been and always will be America's ultimate strength." Radio Address to the Nation on the Observance of Independence Day (July 3, 1982).

965 "The price of freedom may be high, but never so high as the loss of freedom. We are a nation under God. Freedom is not granted to us by government; it is ours by divine right." Remarks at a Rally Supporting Proposed Constitutional Amendment for a Balanced Federal Budget (July 19, 1982).

966 "[F]reedom rests, and always will, on the individual — on individual talent, on individual integrity, and individual effort." Remarks at the Swearing-In Ceremony for New United States Citizens in White House Station, New Jersey (September 17, 1982).

967 "You know, the spirit of the American Revolution was born in an idea that remains true for all time. In freedom and opportunity are to flourish, limits must be placed on the size and authority of government. But no limit must be placed on the ability of any man or woman to reach for the stars, to go as far as their God-given talents will take them." Remarks and a Question-and-Answer Session During a United States Chamber of Commerce Teleconference on Job Training Programs (November 19, 1982).

968 "Our Revolution was born to liberate the individual and to create economic and social op-

portunity. It lives in one simple principle: Government must rest on the consent of the governed. This is still the most inspiring and successful and truly progressive political idea in the world today. It always has and always will make tyrants tremble." Remarks on Signing the World Communications Proclamation (December 16, 1982).

969 "We work and educate for freedom, for the service of the ideal of liberty, not for subservience to the State." Message to the Nation on the Observance of Independence Day (July 3, 1983).

970 "No future will outshine ours if we hold tight to the torch of freedom, if we remain true to the rule of law, and if we meet the challenge of providing opportunity to all our people." Remarks at the Annual Meeting of the American Bar Association in Atlanta, Georgia (August 1, 1983).

971 "No state can be regarded as preeminent over the rights of individuals. Individual rights are supreme." Remarks at the Annual Meeting of the Boards of Governors of the World Bank Group and the International Monetary Fund (September 27, 1983).

972 "People who live in tyranny ... can see freedom much more clearly. It shines like a candle in the midst of the darkness, and America's freedom shines through a world of stormy seas, giving hope to tens of millions of people for a better way of life." Remarks on Signing the Bill of Rights Day and Human Rights Day and Week Proclamation (December 9, 1983).

973 "Government which rests upon consent of the governed is a cardinal principle that enshrines the dignity of every individual." Radio Address to the Cuban People on the 25th Anniversary of Their Revolution (January 5, 1984).

974 "Only when people are given a personal stake in deciding their own destiny, benefiting from their own risks, do they create societies that are prosperous, progressive, and free." Address to a Joint Session of the Congress on the State of the Union (January 25, 1984).

975 "The challenges to peace and freedom that we face today are neither easy nor free from danger. But face them we must, and surmount them we can, providing that we remember the rights of individual liberty, and of government resting on the consent of the governed, are more than the sole possession of a chosen few; they are universal rights, gifts from God to men and women everywhere. And those rights are a crucial anchor for stability in a troubled world, a world where peace is threatened by governments that oppress their citizens, renounce God, and prey on their neighbors." Remarks on Arrival at Shannon Airport in Shannon, Ireland (June 1, 1984).

976   "Freedom motivates people of courage and creativity to strive, to improve, and to push back the boundaries of knowledge." Remarks at University College, Galway, Ireland (June 2, 1984).

977   "Yet, in free societies, differences are expected, indeed, encouraged. It is this freedom to disagree, to question, to state one's case even when in opposition to those in authority that is the cornerstone of liberty and human progress." Remarks at University College, Galway, Ireland (June 2, 1984).

978   "Freedom is the flagship of the future and the flashfire of the future. Its spark ignites the deepest and noblest aspirations of the human soul." Address Before a Joint Session of the Irish Parliament (June 4, 1984).

979   "The dream of human progress through freedom is still the most revolutionary idea in the world today. And it's also the most successful." Remarks to Representatives of the United States International Youth Year Commission (June 22, 1984).

980   "No one emigrates to Cuba or jumps over the wall into East Berlin or seeks refuge in the Soviet Union. Those who look for freedom seek sanctuary here." Address to the Nation on the Observance of Independence Day (July 4, 1984).

981   "We stand foursquare on the side of human liberty. And I pledge to you that we will maintain that stand as long as I am in this office." Remarks at the International Convention of B'nai B'rith (September 6, 1984).

982   "Free men and women are not destined to be powerless victims of some capricious historical tide; free men and women are themselves the driving force of history. And our future is never trapped in the hands of fate; our future will de-

pend on our own freedom, courage, vision, and faith." Remarks at the Annual Meeting of the Boards of Governors of the International Monetary Fund and the World Bank Group (September 25, 1984).

983   "America must remain freedom's staunchest friend, for freedom is our best ally and it is the world's only hope to conquer poverty and preserve peace. Every blow we inflict against poverty will be a blow against its dark allies of oppression and war. Every victory for human freedom will be a victory for world peace." Inaugural Address (January 21, 1985).

984   "Free people, given time, will find a way to solve what may appear to be unsolvable." Remarks at the Western Hemisphere Legislative Leaders Forum (January 24, 1985).

985   "There's never been a war between two free countries. If we're for democracy, we're for peace, domestically and internationally." Remarks at the Western Hemisphere Legislative Leaders Forum (January 24, 1985).

986   "Freedom is not the sole prerogative of a chosen few; it is the universal right of all God's children. Look to where peace and prosperity flourish today. It is in homes that freedom built. Victories against poverty are greatest and peace most secure where people live by laws that ensure free press, free speech, and freedom to worship, vote, and create wealth." Address Before a Joint Session of the Congress on the State of the Union (February 6, 1985).

987   "The abundance we enjoy should lay to rest the lie that freedom must be sacrificed for progress to be made. Freedom not only is right; freedom works. It builds societies that are humane and positive in spirit." Radio Address to the Nation on the Bonn Economic Summit and the Federal Budget (April 27, 1985).

988   "Despite the hectic pace of change in today's world, we know that by allowing the freest expression of individual human aspirations, we can surmount our challenges and build a more secure and peaceful future. We know this because of a simple truth which makes our societies strong: Freedom works." Remarks on Departure for Europe (April 30, 1985).

989   "Let us ask ourselves: What is at the heart of freedom? In the answer lies the deepest hope for the future of mankind and the reason there can be no walls around those who are determined to be free. Each of us, each of you, is made in the most enduring, powerful image of Western civilization. We're made in the image of God, the image of God, the Creator." Remarks to Citizens in Hambach, Federal Republic of Germany (May 6, 1985).

990   "[H]istory has no inevitable outcome; it's still the work of free men and women...." Remarks at the Convention of the National Republican Heritage Groups Council (May 17, 1985).

991   "History's not a static thing. History moves; it never stops. And the American Revolution continues as we continue to push back the barriers to freedom. We, like the patriots of yesterday, are struggling to increase the measure of liberty enjoyed by our fellow citizens." Remarks at the "Prelude to Independence" Celebration in Williamsburg, Virginia (May 30, 1985).

992   "Liberty not only spawns progress, but it is the genesis of true peace as well." Radio Address to the Nation on the 40th Anniversary of the End of the Second World War in the Pacific (August 10, 1985).

993   "One of the greatest threats to freedom is that it will ... be taken for granted.... It never should be." Toast at the State Dinner for Prime Minister Poul Schlüter of Denmark (September 10, 1985).

994   "[A]merica must remain freedom's staunchest friend, for freedom is our staunchest ally." Remarks at a White House Meeting with Reagan-Bush Campaign Leadership Groups (October 7, 1985).

995   "In free societies, government exists for the sake of the people, not the other way around. Government is not directed by the whims of any dictator or the mandate of any clique but by the good sense of the people through a democratic vote. In free societies, people do not live in fear. They never worry that criticizing the government will lead to a late knock on the door, an arrest by some goon squad. When people are free, their rights to speak and to pray are protected by law. And the goons are not running the jails; they're in the jails. In a free society, neighbors don't spy on neighbors; neighbors help neighbors. And that's the way God meant it to be." Remarks to

Citizens in St. George's, Grenada (February 20, 1986).

996   "In the cause of liberty, all free people are part of the same family. We should stand together as brothers and sisters." Remarks to Citizens in St. George's, Grenada (February 20, 1986).

997   "What was it that tied these profoundly different people [America's immigrants] together? What was it that made them not a gathering of individuals, but a nation? That bond that held them together, as it holds us together tonight, that bond that has stood every test and travail, is found deep in our national consciousness: an abiding love of liberty." Remarks on the Lighting of the Torch of the Statue of Liberty in New York, New York (July 3, 1986).

998   "[B]uilding free institutions and making them function effectively requires patience, perseverance, tolerance, luck, and plain hard work. But the results are worth it. Freedom unleashes the creative spirit of the human spirit and carries a nation to its greatest potential." Remarks at the Welcoming Ceremony for Prime Minister Muhammad Khan Junejo of Pakistan (July 16, 1986).

999   "[W]hen you [the young people in the audience] have children or grandchildren of your own, one of them will ask you about a November day a long time ago when a former sports announcer named Dutch Reagan came to town for the last campaign.... I hope you'll tell them for me that I said it wasn't true, that there are really no last, no final campaigns; that each generation must renew and win again for itself the precious gift of liberty, the sacred heritage of freedom." Remarks at a Republican Party Rally in Costa Mesa, California (November 3, 1986).

1000   "Well, in a free society ... the individual makes the ultimate decision as to the direction of his or her life. This freedom is one of the greatest sources of strength from which this or any country can draw, a wellspring of hope that can be seen in the optimism of free people." Remarks at the Tuskegee University Commencement Ceremony in Alabama (May 10, 1987).

1001   "America has achieved so much because across our blessed land, for more than two centuries, men and women have understood that America's greatest gift, the gift of freedom, is also a challenge. The challenge is to be all that we can be and, through meeting that challenge, to help build the future of this free nation." Remarks at the Commencement Ceremony for Area High School Seniors in Chattanooga, Tennessee (May 19, 1987).

1002   "The most vital factor in maintaining man's environment and ensuring that the needs of the Earth's population are taken care of is human freedom. It's freedom that energizes the creative spirit of mankind to meet the immense challenges of our modern age." Remarks at the Presentation Ceremony for the National Medals of Science and Technology (June 25, 1987).

1003   "[F]reedom is not something that can be touched, heard, seen, or smelled. It surrounds us, and if it were not present, as accustomed to it as we are, we would be alarmed, overwhelmed by outrage, or perhaps struck by a sense of being smothered. The air we breathe is also invisible and taken for granted, yet if it is denied even for a few seconds, we realize instantly how much it means to us. Well, so, too, with freedom." Remarks Announcing America's Economic Bill of Rights (July 3, 1987).

1004   "Freedom is not created by government, nor is it a gift from those in political power. It is, in fact, secured, more than anything else, by those limitations ... that are placed on those in government. It is absence of the government censor in our newspapers and broadcast stations and universities. It is the lack of fear by those who gather in religious services. It is the absence of official abuse of those who speak up against the policies of their government." Remarks Announcing America's Economic Bill of Rights (July 3, 1987).

1005   "Our forefathers fought for personal and national independence, yet 200 years later, our own overly centralized government poses a threat to our liberty far beyond anything imagined by the patriots of old." Remarks Announcing America's Economic Bill of Rights (July 3, 1987).

1006   "The American character ... is no accident, no fluke of nature. It was nurtured by the political and economic liberty that has been hailed and protected by generations of Americans. It's the source of power that turned a vast wilderness into an economy that has provided more oppor-

tunity and a higher standard of living for more people than any other in the history of mankind." Remarks on Receiving the Report of the Presidential Task Force on Project Economic Justice (August 3, 1987).

1007   "I've long believed that one of the mainsprings of our own liberty has been the widespread ownership of property among our people and the expectation that anyone's child, even from the humblest of families, could grow up to own a business or a corporation." Remarks on Receiving the Report of the Presidential Task Force on Project Economic Justice (August 3, 1987).

1008   "Freedom serves peace; the quest for peace must serve the cause of freedom." Address to the 42d Session of the United Nations General Assembly in New York, New York (September 21, 1987).

1009   "Under our system, government is strong enough to defend justice, but limited enough to guarantee freedom." Remarks at the Presentation Ceremony for the Minority Enterprise Development Week Awards (October 7, 1987).

1010   "[I]t is free people who will dominate the affairs of mankind. And let me predict that, someday, the realm of liberty and justice will encompass the planet. Freedom is not just the birthright of the few, it is the God-given right of all His children, in every country. It won't come by conquest. It will come, because freedom is right and freedom works. It will come, because cooperation and good will among free people will carry the day." Address to the People of Western Europe on Soviet–United States Relations (November 4, 1987).

1011   "Our country will never be able, simply, to put its faith in machines. The true bulwark of our freedom and national independence is to be found in the souls of our people. Our greatest defense lies in their love of liberty and strength of character. It is this that makes us a mighty force for good on this planet. It is this on which our security and our free system of government rely. It is the willingness to accept the heavy burden of responsibility that comes with liberty. Freedom, you see, is not meant for the faint of heart." Remarks to Members of the Reserve Officers Association (January 27, 1988).

1012 "[W]e accept no moral equivalency between the cause of freedom and the rule of totalitarianism." Remarks at the Annual Conservative Political Action Conference Dinner (February 11, 1988).

1013 "There is a titanic struggle in the world today. I've often characterized it as the struggle between freedom and totalitarianism, but you could as easily call it the struggle between the pen and the sword, between the first amendment of our Constitution and article 6 of the Soviet Constitution — that's the one that places the party over the country." Remarks at the Annual Convention of the American Society of Newspaper Editors (April 13, 1988).

1014 "We Americans make no secret of our belief in freedom. In fact, it's something of a national pastime." Remarks and a Question-and-Answer Session with the Students and Faculty at Moscow State University (May 31, 1988).

1015 "Freedom is the right to question and change the established way of doing things. It is the continuing revolution of the marketplace. It is the understanding that allows us to recognize shortcomings and seek solutions. It is the right to put forth an idea, scoffed at by the experts, and watch it catch fire among the people. It is the right to dream — to follow your dream or stick to your conscience, even if you're the only one in a sea of doubters. Freedom is the recognition that no single person, no single authority or government has a monopoly on the truth, but that every individual life is infinitely precious, that every one of us put on this world has been put there for a reason and has something to offer." Remarks and a Question-and-Answer Session with the Students and Faculty at Moscow State University (May 31, 1988).

1016 "[L]et us also remember that the freedoms we cherish are never more than a generation away from extinction. It's up to each of us to preserve, protect, and defend America's precious heritage. Some Americans have done just that on the battlefield; but all of us can do it each and every day. We can vote at election time. We can volunteer to help political campaigns for the candidates of our choice, as well as volunteer for work that's needed around our community. And we can simply raise our children well, do our jobs well, and live in God's light." Radio Address to the Nation on the Resignation of Howard Baker as Chief of Staff to the President and the Administration's Agenda (July 2, 1988).

1017 "When we look around the world, to Europe, Africa, Asia, and Latin America, we find that the bonds of language, faith, and kinship have not been replaced by a new order built on class struggle. The yearning for national independence has not been extinguished by the totalitarian state, and the tide of history has been revealed to all mankind to be a rising tide of freedom and national liberation." Remarks on Signing the Captive Nations Week Proclamation (July 13, 1988).

1018 "[M]y country has always believed that where the rights of the individual and the people are enshrined, war is a distant prospect. For it is not people who make war; only governments do that." Address to the 43d Session of the United Nations General Assembly in New York, New York (September 26, 1988).

1019 "As Americans, we know that freedom is as much a part of us as our blood. It's not a commodity. It can't be bought, can't be sold, and it can't be bartered away. No, my friends, despite the millions upon millions of words expended to describe its meaning, the truth is that the word 'freedom' is deceptively simple. It's a word that describes the God-given condition of the human soul. For what we know is this: God created us free, just as he created us man and woman. Indeed, since Adam ate of the Tree of Knowledge, there's nothing that defines us human beings so much as the fact that we're free." Remarks at a Luncheon for Recipients of the Medal of Freedom (November 10, 1988).

1020 "Our greatest freedom, the freedom to choose right from wrong, cannot be willed away by the tyrants. For God has given all humankind the gift of knowing right from wrong and the responsibility to choose between them." Remarks at a Luncheon for Recipients of the Medal of Freedom (November 10, 1988).

1021 "Yes, in America, freedom seems like the air around us: It's there; it's sweet, though we rarely give it a thought. Yet as the air fills our lungs, freedom fills our souls. It gives breath to our laughter and joy. It gives voice to our songs. It gives us strength as we race for our dreams." Radio Address to the Nation on the Celebration of Thanksgiving Day (November 19, 1988).

1022   "Tyranny fails. Freedom works." Remarks to the American Enterprise Institute for Public Policy Research (December 7, 1988).

1023   "[W]e've told the world the truth we've learned from the noble tradition of Western culture, and that is that the only answer to poverty, to war, to oppression is one simple word: freedom." Remarks to the American Enterprise Institute for Public Policy Research (December 7, 1988).

1024   "[M]an is not free unless government is limited. There's a clear cause and effect here that is as neat and predictable as a law of physics: As government expands, liberty contracts." Farewell Address to the Nation (January 11, 1989).

Speaking Out for Freedom

1025   "Now, some in this country say, 'Freedom is fine for us, but we can't worry about it for everyone else. Let's not stick out our necks anywhere.' Have they forgotten that freedom was not won here without the help of others? Have they forgotten that people who turn their backs on friends often lose what they cherish most for themselves? Have they forgotten that freedom is never more than one generation away from extinction?" Remarks at the National Legislative Conference of the Building and Construction Trades Department, AFL-CIO (April 5, 1982).

1026   "Our willingness to speak for freedom is no bargaining chip. It's an integral part of our foreign policy." Remarks and a Question-and-Answer Session in Los Angeles with Editors and Broadcasters from the Western Region of the United States (July 1, 1982).

1027   "Someone has said that when anyone is denied freedom, then freedom for everyone is threatened. The struggle in the world today for the hearts and minds of mankind is based on one simple question: Is man born to be free, or slave? In country after country, people have long known the answer to that question. We are free by divine right. We are masters of our fate, and we create governments for our convenience. Those who would have it otherwise commit a crime and a sin against God and man." Radio Address to the Nation on Solidarity and United States Relations with Poland (October 9, 1982).

1028   "It's our duty to speak out against the evil and the cruelty of misused state power. Unless we speak out, unless we give voice to the decent impulses of mankind and our own deepest held convictions, a kind of moral atrophy sets in, and we too may ultimately lose faith in the appeal and the power of our convictions." Remarks at a White House Luncheon for Delegates to the Conference on Free Elections (November 4, 1982).

1029   "For with the privilege of living in this kindly, pleasant, greening land called America, this land of generous spirit and great ideals, there is also a destiny and a duty, a duty to preserve and hold in sacred trust mankind's age-old aspirations of peace and freedom and a better life for generations to come." Remarks at the Conservative Political Action Conference Dinner (February 18, 1983).

1030   "Rulers of totalitarian states, however great the danger they pose to the rest of mankind, are aware of the shakiness of their rule and the fragility of their claims of legitimacy. And that's why they seek to stifle dissent. And that's why we must never stand by in silence as they do." Remarks on Signing a Resolution and a Proclamation Declaring National Andrei Sakharov Day. (May 18, 1983).

1031   We believe it is our duty to defend freedom, not just here at home but everywhere people are persecuted for their beliefs." Remarks at the Annual Convention of the Anti-Defamation League of B'nai B'rith (June 10, 1983).

1032   "The question isn't who has the most perfect democracy. The question is, who's trying to build democracy and who is determined to destroy it. Many nations, including the United States, which once condoned slavery, have evolved into better democracies over time. But nations which fall into the clutches of totalitarianism do not become free and democratic again. And freedom can't be lost in one nation without being diminished everywhere." Remarks at the Annual Convention of the Anti-Defamation League of B'nai B'rith (June 10, 1983).

1033   "There are those who believe that we should muffle our criticism of totalitarianism in the mistaken notion that this will further the cause of peace. But we Americans want nothing more than to remain free and at peace. Nevertheless, ignoring reality, giving up the moral high ground, refusing to speak the truth will not engender the respect needed for the preservation of peace and human liberty. Totalitarian regimes must know that free men will not cower. Then and only then can conflict be avoided." Remarks at a White House Reception for Baltic Americans (June 13, 1983).

1034   "We must not ignore those powerful forces who have no respect for our traditions of freedom and who would like to make the world over in their image." Remarks at the Presentation Ceremony for the Presidential Scholars Awards (June 16, 1983).

1035   "We must not turn our backs on our friends. We must not permit dictators to ram communism down the throats of innocent people in one country after another." Remarks at a California Republican Party Fundraising Dinner in Long Beach (June 30, 1983).

1036   "Many governments oppress their people and abuse human rights. We must oppose this injustice." Remarks at a Ceremony Marking the Annual Observance of Captive Nations Week (July 19, 1983).

1037   "This nation cannot simply ignore the suffering of oppressed peoples and remain true to our basic strengths and principles. We cannot follow a foreign policy based on the self-delusion that problems would not exist if we did not mention them. We cannot abdicate our obligation to speak out for those who cannot speak for themselves." Remarks at the Annual Convention of the Veterans of Foreign Wars in New Orleans, Louisiana (August 15, 1983).

1038   "Well, America is the lion's heart of democracy. We have an obligation to give that democracy a voice, even an occasional roar." Remarks at the Annual Convention of the Veterans of Foreign Wars in New Orleans, Louisiana (August 15, 1983).

1039   "We know it will be hard to make a nation [the Soviet Union] that rules its own people through force to cease using force against the rest of the world. But we must try. This is not a role we sought. We preach no manifest destiny. But like Americans who began this country and

brought forth this last, best hope of mankind, history has asked much of the Americans of our time. Much we have already given; much more we must be prepared to give." Address to the Nation on the Soviet Attack on a Korean Civilian Airliner (September 5, 1983).

1040   "Our country is the leader of the free world, and we morally cannot shirk that responsibility." Remarks at the Fundraising Dinner of the Republican National Hispanic Assembly (September 14, 1983).

1041   "We are all sovereign nations and therefore free to choose our own way as long as we do not transgress upon the sovereign rights of one another. But we cannot really be free as independent states unless we respect the freedom and independence of each of our individual citizens." Remarks at the Annual Meeting of the Boards of Governors of the World Bank Group and the International Monetary Fund (September 27, 1983).

1042   "The struggle for peace is indivisible. We cannot pick and choose where we will support freedom; we can only determine how. If it's lost in one place, all of us lose." Remarks and a Question-and-Answer Session with Editors and Broadcasters on the Situation in Lebanon (October 24, 1983).

1043   "When we feel strongly about a particular situation, we make our views known, often quite candidly, to the appropriate level of the government concerned." Remarks at a Reception for Korean Community Leaders in Seoul (November 12, 1983).

1044   "As Americans, it's our responsibility to speak out against blatant affronts to human rights." Remarks on Signing the Bill of Rights Day and Human Rights Day and Week Proclamation (December 9, 1983).

1045   "Now, we're not naïve. We're not trying to create imitations of the American system around the world. There's no simple cookbook recipe for political development that is right for all people, and there's no timetable. While democratic principle and basic institutions are universal, democratic development must take into account historic, cultural, and social institutions." Remarks at a White House Ceremony Inaugurating the National Endowment for Democracy (December 16, 1983).

1046   "Our willingness to speak out on these distinctions [between pluralistic systems which acknowledge their wrongs and shortcomings and systems that excuse their defects in the name of totalitarian ideology] is the moral center of our foreign policy. For us, human freedom is a first principle, not a bargaining chip. To fail to publicly enunciate the differences between totalitarian and democratic systems of government would be to forsake the moral high ground." Remarks at Eureka College in Eureka, Illinois (February 6, 1984).

1047   "The struggle between freedom and totalitarianism today is not ultimately a test of arms or missiles, but a test of faith and spirit. And in this spiritual struggle, the Western mind and will is the crucial battleground. We must not hesitate to express our dream of freedom; we must be reluctant to enunciate the crucial distinctions between right and wrong — between political systems based on freedom and those based on a dreadful denial of the human spirit." Address Before a Joint Session of the Irish Parliament (June 4, 1984).

1048   "[I]'ve always believed that a truly American foreign policy means more than the pragmatic business of getting along with other nations. It also means standing up for values like human freedom and our obligation to see that freedom is spread someday to all the nations of the Earth." Remarks at the Presentation Ceremony for the Presidential Scholars Awards (June 19, 1984).

1049   "When Soviet actions threaten the peace or violate a solemn agreement or trample on standards fundamental to a civilized world, we cannot and will not be silent. [T]o do so would betray our deepest values. It would violate our conscience and ultimately undermine world stability and our ability to keep the peace. We must have ways short of military threats that make it absolutely clear that Soviet actions do matter and that some actions inevitably affect the quality of the relationship." Remarks to Participants in the Conference on United States–Soviet Exchanges (June 27, 1984).

1050   "One of the great tragedies of our age is that ugly, sinister walls continue to deny for the millions trapped behind them the most basic yearnings of the human spirit. And let us make it plain that we must and will condemn all tyrants who deny their citizens human rights, whether they be dictators of the left or the right." Remarks on Signing the Captive Nations Week Proclamation (July 16, 1984).

1051   "[W]e have a moral responsibility to support anyone who aspires to live in a true democracy, free from Communist interference. If the democratic people do not stand together, we certainly will be unable to stand alone." Remarks at a Summit Conference of Caribbean Heads of State at the University of South Carolina in Columbia (July 19, 1984).

1052   "But we know there are occasions when quiet diplomacy is not enough, when we must remind the leaders of nations who are friendly to the United States that such friendship also carries responsibilities for them and for us. And that's why the United States calls for all governments to advance the democratic process and work toward a system of government based on the consent of the governed." Remarks on Signing the International Human Rights Day Proclamation (December 10, 1984).

1053   "We cannot break faith with freedom anywhere. This is our heritage and our moral obligation." Remarks at the 1985 Reagan Administration Executive Forum (January 25, 1985).

1054   "No evil is inevitable unless we make it so." Remarks at a Fundraising Dinner for the Nicaragua Refugee Fund (April 15, 1985).

1055   "I believe that the most essential element of our defense of freedom is our insistence on speaking out for the cause of religious liberty." Remarks at a Conference on Religious Liberty (April 16, 1985).

1056   "[H]istory is not on the side of those who manipulate the meaning of words like revolution, freedom, and peace. History is on the side of those struggling for a true revolution of peace with freedom all across the world." Remarks to Citizens in Hambach, Federal Republic of Germany (May 6, 1985).

1057   "Let us never forget that aggression and war are rarely the work of a nation's people, for it is the people who must bear the brunt and endure the worst of war. No, war and aggression in our century have almost always been the work of governments, one of the militarists and ideologues who may control them. And that is why war and aggression have a tiny constituency. Let democracy spread, let the people's voice be heard, and the warmongers will be made outcasts and pariahs. Let us not be afraid that in our crusade for freedom to proclaim to the world that the cause of democratic government is also the cause of peace." Address Before the Assembly of the Republic of Portugal in Lisbon (May 9, 1985).

1058   "[W]e have to continue to state in public the crucial moral distinctions between democratic government and the totalitarian state." Remarks at the Convention of the National Republican Heritage Groups Council (May 17, 1985).

1059   One of the most damaging lies of our era is the falsehood that people must give up freedom to enjoy economic progress...." Remarks at the Annual Conference of the Council of the Americas (May 21, 1985).

1060   "The truth is, it is only under freedom that a true fellowship of the spirit can exist. Love is not something that can be mandated by law or enforced by bureaucracy. It is when people voluntarily help one another, giving of themselves freely, that they receive the blessings of the soul which God has promised. This is an important part of freedom, the shining light which is a beacon to all who live in the darkness in tyranny — the fundamental truth that free people do indeed love and care for one another." Remarks at the Annual Convention of the Lions Club International in Dallas, Texas (June 21, 1985).

1061   "The American people have held high the torch of freedom for all those fighting for liberty around the world." Radio Address to the Nation on the 40th Anniversary of the United Nations General Assembly (October 19, 1985).

1062   "We champion freedom not only because it is practical and beneficial but because it is morally right and just. Free people whose governments rest upon the consent of the governed do not wage war on their neighbors. Free people blessed by economic opportunity and protected by laws that respect the dignity of the individual are not driven toward the domination of others." Address to the 40th Session of the United Nations General Assembly in New York, New York (October 24, 1985).

1063   "In this storm-tossed world of terrorists and totalitarians, America must always champion freedom, for freedom is the one tide that will lead us to the safe and open harbor of peace." Radio Address to the Nation on the State of the Union (January 25, 1986).

1064   "Fundamental conflicts between freedom and tyranny cannot be papered over by treaties. True peace will always demand clear-eyed, rock-hard realism and an enduring commitment to the values of political and economic freedom...." Remarks at a White House Meeting with the Board of Directors of the United States Institute of Peace (February 26, 1986).

1065   "Furthering democracy really is at the heart of what America's all about — the conviction that we as a people can never truly rest until every man, woman, and child on Earth knows the blessings of liberty." Remarks to Members of the American Legion Auxiliary's Girls Nation (July 18, 1986).

1066   "When we approach our dealings with Communist governments and the governments of other countries where freedom is under assault, we do so knowing that we have a special responsibility. We must not only be mindful to our own interests, but we must also keep faith with those millions of souls who live under oppression." Remarks on Signing the Captive Nations Week Proclamation (July 21, 1986).

1067   "[W]hen we proclaim our faith in God and the dignity of man, our love of freedom, and our fidelity to our Judeo-Christian values, when we do all this, we give hope to every freedom-loving soul that truth is strong and that the hollow shell of totalitarianism may one day crack and let its people go." Remarks at the Ethics and Public Policy Center Anniversary Dinner (November 18, 1986).

1068   "I've often spoken of freedom as the fresh and rising tide of the future. To speak so is not to threaten any people or nation; it is only to renew mankind's most sacred hope and oldest dream: a world where material wants are satisfied, where human freedom is enshrined, and peace and fellowship among nations prevail. Those goals should be celebrated and those truths should be pursued with no apologies to anyone." Remarks and a Question-and-Answer Session at a Los Angeles World Affairs Council Luncheon in California (April 10, 1987).

1069   "Preserving the peace is one of America's primary goals in world affairs. However, equally important to us is our commitment to championing the cause of freedom. Freedom and peace are inseparably linked...." Remarks at the Annual Republican Congressional Fundraising Dinner (April 29, 1987).

1070   "Our global commitment to freedom does not mandate the sending of arms or troops, but at the very least it means that any people whose liberty is denied or whose independence is violated — that these people know we Americans are on their side." Remarks to Captive Nations Conference Participants (July 24, 1987).

1071   "We are the keepers of the flame. It's up to us to foster the legacy of those who came before us and to ensure America remains a champion of liberty and a force for good in the world." Remarks to Captive Nations Conference Participants (July 24, 1987).

1072   "But while we sought arms reduction and defensive deterrence, we never lost sight of the fact that nations do not disagree because they are armed; they are armed because they disagree on very important matters of human life and liberty. The fundamental differences between totalitarian and democratic rule remained. We could not gloss over them, nor could we be content anymore with accepted spheres of influence, a world only half free. And that is why we sought to advance the cause of personal freedom wherever opportunities existed to do so. Sometimes this meant support for liberalization; sometimes, support for liberation." Remarks on Soviet–United States Relations at the Town Hall of California Meeting in Los Angeles (August 26. 1987).

1073   "We refused to believe that it was somehow an act of belligerence to proclaim publicly the crucial moral distinctions between democracy and totalitarianism." Remarks on Soviet–United States Relations at the Town Hall of California Meeting in Los Angeles (August 26, 1987).

1074   "[W]e believe that such public affirmations were not only necessary for the protection and extension of freedom but, far from adding to world tensions, crucial to reducing them and help-ing the pursuit of peace. Public candor and realism about and with the Soviets have helped the peace process. They were a signal to our Soviet counterparts that any compulsion to exploit Western illusions must be resisted, because such illusions no longer exist." Remarks on Soviet–United States Relations at the Town Hall of California Meeting in Los Angeles (August 26, 1987).

1075   "We stand against totalitarianism, particularly imperialistic expansionist totalitarianism. We are for democracy and human rights, and we're for a worldwide prosperity that only free economies can give and the pursuit of human happiness that only political freedom allows." Radio Address to the Nation on Soviet–United States Relations (August 29, 1987).

1076   "Not by force, not by coercion, but by speaking out, we have changed the course of history." Remarks at the 40th Anniversary Conference of the United States Advisory Commission on Public Diplomacy (September 16, 1987).

1077   "[T]his is our mission as a nation: to stand for freedom and to give hope." Remarks at the 40th Anniversary Conference of the United States Advisory Commission on Public Diplomacy (September 16, 1987).

1078   "Many ... critics also said that it was provocative to tell the truth about repression in the Soviet Union, about Soviet overseas adventures, about Soviet violations of past agreements. We said that the United States of America must never be afraid to tell the truth about anyone." Remarks and a Question-and-Answer Session with Area High School Seniors in Jacksonville, Florida (December 1, 1987).

1079   "[I]f peace is to have a chance, if the hope for freedom is to be kept alive, the United States must play a powerful and active role in world affairs. It is an awesome responsibility." Remarks to Members of the Reserve Officers Association (January 27, 1988).

1080   "Negotiations between East and West do not imply moral equivalency of our two systems or ways of life. We must never forget to say this publicly and say it repeatedly." Address to the Citizens of Western Europe (February 23, 1988).

1081   "We spoke plainly and bluntly. We rejected [the idea of] ... moral equivalency. We said freedom was better than totalitarianism. We said communism was bad. We said a future of nuclear terror was unacceptable. We said we stood for peace, but we also stood for freedom. We said we held fast to the dream of our Founding Fathers: the dream that someday every man, woman, and child would live in dignity and in freedom. And because of this, we said containment was no longer enough, that the expansion of human freedom was our goal. We spoke for democracy, and we said that we would work for the day when the people of every nation enjoyed the blessing of liberty." Remarks to the World Affairs Council of Western Massachusetts in Springfield (April 21, 1988).

1082   "We will never, ever, negotiate away the dream of every Cuban-American — a dream that I, too, hold in my heart — that Cuba will again join the family of free and democratic nations." Remarks at a Cuban Independence Day Ceremony (May 20, 1988).

1083   "[W]e should remember that reform that is not institutionalized will always be insecure. Such freedom will always be looking over its shoulder. A bird on a tether, no matter how long the rope, can always be pulled back." Remarks and a Question-and-Answer Session with the Students and Faculty at Moscow State University (May 31, 1988).

1084   "But our [the members of the North Atlantic Council's] consensus is built not only on what we're against but on what we're for. And we are against totalitarianism. We're for freedom and democracy — for them without hesitation or apology, and virtually, I would venture, without division. This is the first great truth to keep in mind. There may be divisions within our countries as to methods, but there are none as to fundamental goals." Remarks at the Annual Meeting of the Atlantic Council (June 13, 1988).

1085   "America will continue to encourage the movement toward freedom, democracy, and reform by holding firm to our principles and speaking openly and truthfully about human rights and the fundamental moral difference between freedom and communism. And America shall light the path as the whole world climbs out of the dark abyss of tyranny to freedom." Remarks

on Signing the Captive Nations Week Proclamation (July 13, 1988).

1086   "[W]e Americans champion freedom not only because it's practical and beneficial but because it is also just, morally right." Address to the 43d Session of the United Nations General Assembly in New York, New York (September 26, 1988).

1087   "[A]merica has always stood with those who stand for freedom. This is not to say that we eagerly jump into every fight. We don't. But we've always been ready to give a hand to those struggling for freedom when they needed it." Remarks at the National Defense University on Signing the Department of Veterans Affairs Act (October 25, 1988).

1088   "[O]ur public candor about human rights abuses and the fundamental moral differences between totalitarianism and democracy must continue. We must continue to speak aggressively for the cause of human freedom. We must be unafraid to point out the moral wrong of those who would repress liberty. We must be unashamed to say that economic growth and material prosperity are the result of economic freedom, not state planning." Remarks and a Question-and-Answer Session at a World Affairs Council Luncheon in Los Angeles, California (October 28, 1988).

1089   "We came to Washington together in 1981, both as anti–Communists and as unapologetic defenders and promoters of a strong and vibrant America. I'm proud to say I'm still an anti–Communist. And I continue to be dedicated to the idea that we must trumpet our beliefs and advance our American ideals to all the peoples of the world until the towers of the tyrants crumble to dust." Remarks to the American Enterprise Institute for Public Policy Research (December 7, 1988).

1090   "These noxious ideas [Socialist utopias] have not, to put it mildly, withstood the scrutiny of honest scholars and the testimony of those fortunate enough to escape from those national prison camps. Refugees have told us ... that where there is little freedom, there is little food...." Remarks to the American Enterprise Institute for Public Policy Research (December 7, 1988).

GOD AND COUNTRY

1091   "We are a nation under God, and I believe God intended for us to be free." Inaugural Address (January 20, 1981).

1092   "This is the real task before us: to reassert our commitment as a nation to a higher law than our own, to renew our spiritual strength. Only by building a wall of such spiritual resolve can we, as a free people, hope to protect our own heritage and make it someday the birthright of all men." Remarks at the Conservative Political Action Conference Dinner (March 20, 1981).

1093   "I also believe that this blessed land was set apart in a very special way, a country created by men and women who came here not in search of gold, but in search of God. They would be free people, living under the law with faith in their Maker and their future." Remarks at the Annual National Prayer Breakfast (February 4, 1982).

1094   "To preserve our blessed land, we must look to God." Remarks at the Annual Convention of the National Religious Broadcasters (February 9, 1982).

1095   "Where did we begin to lose sight of that noble beginning, of our conviction that right and wrong do exist and must be lived up to? Do we really think that we can have it both ways, that God will protect us in time of crisis even as we turn away from Him in our day-to-day life?" Remarks at the Annual Convention of the National Religious Broadcasters (February 9, 1982).

1096   "Pursuit of liberty and justice under God is still the most inspiring, the most successful, the most revolutionary idea the world has ever known." Remarks at a Mount Vernon, Virginia, Ceremony Commemorating the 250th Anniversary of the Birth of George Washington (February 22, 1982).

1097   "[S]tanding up for America also means standing up for God, who has blessed our land. I believe this country hungers for a spiritual revival. I believe it longs to see traditional values reflected in public policy again." Address Before a Joint Session of the Alabama State Legislature in Montgomery (March 15, 1982).

1098   "We have problems in our country, and many people are praying and waiting for God to do something. I just wonder if maybe God isn't waiting for us to do something. And while no one is capable of doing everything, everyone is capable of doing something." Remarks on Private Sector Initiatives at a White House Luncheon for National Religious Leaders (April 13, 1982).

1099   "I believe standing up for America also means standing up for the God who has blessed this land. We've strayed so far, it may be later than we think. There's a hunger in our land to see traditional values reflected in our public policy again." Remarks at the Annual Meeting of the United States Chamber of Commerce (April 26, 1982).

1100   "I've said before that the most sublime picture in American history is of George Washington on his knees in the snow at Valley Forge. That image personifies a people who know that it's not enough to depend on our own courage and goodness; we must also seek help from God, our Father and Preserver." Remarks at a White House Ceremony in Observance of National Day of Prayer (May 6, 1982).

1101   "Prayer has sustained our people in crisis, strengthened us in times of challenge, and guided us through our daily lives since the first settlers came to this continent. Our forbearers came not for gold, but mainly in search of God and the freedom to worship in their own way." Remarks at White House Ceremony in Observance of National Day of Prayer (May 6, 1982).

1102   "Ours is a nation grounded on faith, faith in man's ability through God-given freedom to live in tolerance and peace and faith that a Supreme Being guides our daily striving in this world. Our national motto, 'In God We Trust,' reflects that faith." Remarks Following a Meeting with Pope John II in Vatican City (June 7, 1982).

1103   "The Ten Commandments and the Golden Rule are as much a part of our living heritage as the Constitution we take such pride in. And we've tried — not always successfully, but always in good conscience — to extend these same principles to our role in the world." Remarks Following a Meeting with Pope John II in Vatican City (June 7, 1982).

1104   "This faith in the dignity of the individual under God is the foundation for the whole American political experiment. It is central to our national politics." Remarks at the Centennial Meeting of the Supreme Council of the Knights of Columbus in Hartford, Connecticut (August 3, 1982).

1105   "I think the American people are hungry for a spiritual revival. More and more of us are beginning to sense that we can't have it both ways. We can't expect God to protect us in a crisis and just leave Him over there on the shelf in our day-to-day living. I wonder if sometimes He isn't waiting for us to wake up and that He isn't maybe running out of patience." Remarks at Kansas State University at the Alfred M. Landon Lecture Series on Public Issues (September 9, 1982).

1106   "[P]rayer is one of the few things in this world that hurts no one and sustains the spirit of millions." Radio Address to the Nation on Prayer (September 18, 1982).

1107   "Faith in God is a vital guidepost, a source of inspiration, and a pillar of strength in times of trial. We can and must respect the rights of those who are nonbelievers, but we must not cut ourselves off from this indispensable source of strength and guidance." Remarks at a Candle-Lighting Ceremony for Prayer in Schools (September 25, 1982).

1108   "When Americans reach out for values of faith, family, and caring for the needy, they're saying, 'We want the word of God. We want to face the future with the Bible.'" Remarks at the Annual Convention of National Religious Broadcasters (January 31, 1983).

1109   "We face great challenges in this country, but we've faced great challenges before and conquered them. What carried us through was a willingness to seek power and protection from One much greater than ourselves, to turn back to Him and to trust in His mercy. Without His help,

America will not go forward." Remarks at the Annual National Prayer Breakfast (February 3, 1983).

1110   "Of the many influences that have shaped the United States of America into a distinctive Nation and people, none may be said to be more fundamental and enduring than the Bible." Remarks at the Annual National Prayer Breakfast (February 3, 1983).

1111   "[Our] commitment to freedom and personal liberty ... is grounded in the much deeper realization that freedom prospers only where the blessings of God are avidly sought and humbly accepted. The American experiment in democracy rests on this insight." Remarks at the Annual Convention of the National Association of Evangelicals in Orlando, Florida (March 8, 1983).

1112   "Freedom prospers when religion is vibrant and the rule of law under God is acknowledged." Remarks at the Annual Convention of the National Association of Evangelicals in Orlando, (March 8, 1983).

1113   "[T]he best thing about country music is its people — a large and God-fearing, patriotic bunch from the mainstream of America." Remarks to Members of the Country Music Association During a Television Performance (March 16, 1983).

1114   "And if we live our lives and dedicate our country to truth, to love, and to God, we will be part of something much stronger and much more enduring than any negative power here on Earth." Radio Address to the Nation on the Observance of Easter and Passover (April 2, 1983).

1115   "[I]f those of us who live for the Lord could remember that He wants us to love our Lord and our neighbor, then there's no limit to the problems we could solve or the mountains we could climb together as a mighty force for good." Remarks at the Annual Members Banquet of the National Rifle Association in Phoenix, Arizona (May 6, 1983).

1116   "We are a Nation under God, a living and loving God.... We cannot expect Him to protect us in a crisis if we turn away from Him in our everyday living. But you know, He told us what to do in II Chronicles. Let us reach out to Him. He said, 'If my people, which are called by my name, shall humble themselves and pray and seek my face and turn away from their wicked ways, then I will hear from Heaven and will forgive their sin and will heal their land.'" Remarks at a Dinner Honoring Senator Jesse Helms of North Carolina (June 16, 1983).

1117   "Much of the world is in turmoil, with the mass of humanity living in wretched conditions, suffering deprivation and tyranny. [A]ll of us can be grateful for this blessed land. God has placed in our hands the responsibility of watching over it." Remarks at the Hispanic Economic Outlook Preview Luncheon in Los Angeles, California (August 25, 1983).

1118   "[P]reserving America must begin with faith in the God who has blessed our land. And we don't have the answers; He does." Remarks and a Question-and-Answer Session with Women Leaders of Christian Religious Organizations (October 13, 1983).

1119   "The Christmas spirit of peace, hope and love is the spirit Americans carry with them all year round, everywhere we go. As long as we do, we need never be afraid, because trusting in God is the one sure answer to all the problems we face." Radio Address to the Nation on Christmas (December 24, 1983).

1120   "I recognize that we must be cautious in claiming that God is on our side, but I think it is all right to keep asking if we're on His side." Address to a Joint Session of the Congress on the State of the Union (January 25, 1984).

1121   "[T]he American dream isn't one of making government bigger; it's keeping faith with the mighty spirit of free people under God." Address to a Joint Session of the Congress on the State of the Union (January 25, 1984).

1122   "[I]n a world today that is so torn with strife where the divisions seem to be increasing, not people coming together ... I wonder if we have ever thought about the greatest tool that we have — that power of prayer and God's help." Remarks at the Annual National Prayer Breakfast (February 2, 1984).

1123   "All our material wealth and our influence have been built on our faith in God and the bedrock values that follow from that faith." Remarks at the Annual Convention of the National Association of Evangelicals in Columbus, Ohio (March 6, 1984).

1124   "Only when the fellowship of all men under the Fatherhood of God is recognized and acknowledged, only then will the world finally know true peace and understanding." Remarks at the Welcoming Ceremony for Pope John Paul II in Fairbanks, Alaska (May 2, 1984).

1125   "Far more can be accomplished by the simple prayers of good people than by all the statesmen and armies of the world. Only when the fellowship of all men under the Fatherhood of God is recognized and acknowledged, only then will the world finally know true peace and understanding." Remarks at the Welcoming Ceremony for Pope John II in Fairbanks, Alaska (May 2, 1984).

1126   "[L]et us also remember who we are and what we stand for. We're a nation under God, and His divine spirit of truth and love must guide and always remain central to our existence." Remarks on Signing the Captive Nations Week Proclamation (July 16, 1984).

1127   "It's probably true that politics is the prose of a culture, but religion is its poetry. Governments are passing things in the long history of the world, but faith and belief endure forever." Remarks at the St. Ann's Festival in Hoboken, New Jersey (July 26, 1984).

1128   "Those who created our country — the Founding Fathers and Mothers — understood that there is a divine order which transcends the human order. They saw the state, in fact, as a form of moral order and felt that the bedrock of moral order is religion." Remarks at an Ecumenical Prayer Breakfast in Dallas, Texas (August 23, 1984).

1129   "The truth is, politics and morality are inseparable. And as morality's foundation is religion, religion and politics are necessarily related. We need religion as a guide. We need it because we are imperfect, and our government needs the church, because only those humble enough to admit they're sinners can bring to democracy the tolerance it requires in order to survive." Remarks at an Ecumenical Prayer Breakfast in Dallas, Texas (August 23, 1984).

1130   "For all our problems, our differences, we are together as of old. We raise our voices to the God who is the Author of this most tender music. And may He continue to hold us close as we fill the world with our sound — in unity, affection, and love — one people under God, dedicated to the dream of freedom that He has placed in the human heart, called upon now to pass that dream on to a waiting and hopeful world." Inaugural Address (January 21, 1985).

1131   "Fifty-six percent of Americans believe that religion can answer all or most of today's problems. In fact, only one in five doubts the relevance of religion in the modern world. And we'll get them, too." Remarks at the Annual Convention of the National Religious Broadcasters (February 4, 1985).

1132   "Let us pray that America will always use her power wisely, justly, and humbly to defend our legitimate interests, to help those who are struggling for freedom. But let us pray, too, that God will give our country the humility to see our own faults and the strength to preserve our hard-won tradition of freedom to worship and religious tolerance." Radio Address to the Nation on International Violence and Democratic Values (March 29, 1986).

1133   "At its most fundamental level, of course, the American vision is the vision of all Western civilization — the belief in a just and living God, in individual responsibility, and in the importance of the family. And by reasserting, for example, the ancient belief in the goodness of creation — a belief found, among other places, in Genesis — we've been able to reawaken a sense of the goodness of our own land and our people. And by restating the belief that history has meaning, that it's a story unfolding according to the will of its creator — we've been able to reestablish a sense of our nation's own place, and that story is a land of opportunity and a defender of freedom." Remarks to Members of the National Fraternal Congress of America (September 25, 1986).

1134   "I grew up in a home where I was taught to believe in intercessory prayer. I know it's those prayers, and millions like them, that are building high and strong this cathedral of freedom that we call America; those prayers, and millions like them, that will always keep our country secure and make her a force for good in these too troubled times. And that's why as a nation we must embrace our faith, for as long as we endeavor to do good — and we must believe that will be always — we will find our strength, our hope, and our true happiness in prayer and in the Lord's will." Remarks at the Annual National Prayer Breakfast (February 5, 1987).

1135   "[B]oth Madison and Washington were to refer to the outcome of the Constitutional Convention as a miracle; and miracles, of course, have only one origin." Remarks at the "We the People" Bicentennial Celebration in Philadelphia, Pennsylvania (September 17, 1987).

1136   "I hope the General Secretary is watching this on TV. I'd like him to see what we're celebrating, because for us, Christmas celebrates the cause of peace on Earth, good will toward men." Remarks on Lighting the National Christmas Tree (December 7, 1987).

1137   "Whenever I consider the history of this nation, I'm struck by how deeply imbued with faith the American people were, even from the very first." Remarks to the Student Congress on Evangelism (July 28, 1988).

1138   "[A]s a nation we must embrace our faith, for as long as we endeavor to do good — and we must believe that will be always — we will find our strength, our hope, and our true happiness in prayer and in the Lord's will." Remarks to the Student Congress on Evangelism (July 28, 1988).

1139   "For the message of this most joyous holiday is that we are all — no matter what divides us — we are all loved by a force greater than ourselves, a love that surpasseth all understanding, a love that provides all the answers for those who feel lost and alone during these remarkable days. We are not alone; we're never alone." Radio Address to the Nation on the Holiday Season and the Earthquake in Armenia (December 24, 1988).

GOVERNMENT

General

1140　"We are a nation that has a government — not the other way around. And this makes us special among the nations of the Earth. Our government has no power except that granted it by the people." Inaugural Address (January 20, 1981).

1141　"All of us should remember that the Federal Government is not some mysterious institution comprised of buildings, files, and paper. The people are the government. What we create we ought to be able to control." Presidential News Conference [prepared remarks] (January 29, 1981).

1142　"Government's first duty is to protect the people, not run their lives." Remarks at the National Conference of the Building and Construction Trades Department, AFL-CIO (March 30, 1981).

1143　"[G]overnment has certain legitimate functions which it can perform very well ... but when it undertakes tasks that are not its proper province, it can do none of them as well or as economically as the private sector." Address at the Commencement Exercises at the University of Notre Dame (May 17, 1981).

1144　"For too long government has been fixing things that aren't broken and inventing miracle cures for unknown diseases." Address at the Commencement Exercises at the University of Notre Dame (May 17, 1981).

1145　"[W]e must always ask: Is government working to liberate and empower the individual? Is it creating incentives for people to produce, save, invest, and profit from legitimate risks and honest toil? Is it encouraging all of us to reach for the stars? Or does it seek to compel, command, and coerce people into submission and dependence?" Remarks at a Luncheon of the World Affairs Council of Philadelphia in Philadelphia, Pennsylvania (October 15, 1981).

1146　"Here in this land, for the first time, it was decided that man is born with certain God-given rights. We the people declared that government is created by the people for their own convenience. Government has no power except those voluntarily granted to it by the people." Remarks at the Bicentennial Observance of the Battle of Yorktown in Virginia (October 19, 1981).

1147　"Government is only as good as the people who make it work one day at a time." Remarks to Department of Transportation Employees in the Senior Executive Service (January 12, 1982).

1148　"Did we forget the function of government is not to confer happiness on us but to give us the opportunity to work out happiness for ourselves?" Remarks at the New York City Partnership Luncheon in New York (January 14, 1982).

1149　"No one denies that government has an essential role to protect those in need, to provide opportunity, to pave the way. But ultimately, it is individuals, millions of everyday citizens who brave new horizons, expand freedom, and create better lives for us all." Remarks at the New York City Partnership Luncheon in New York (January 14, 1982).

1150　"The best view of big government is the view in the rearview mirror as we leave it behind." Remarks at the New York City Partnership Luncheon in New York (January 14, 1982).

1151　"Did we forget that government is the people's business and every man, woman and child becomes a shareholder with the first penny of tax paid." Remarks to the New York City Partnership Luncheon in New York (January 14, 1982).

1152　"If we do nothing else in this administration, we're going to convince this city that the power, the money, and the responsibility of this country begins and ends with the people and not in some puzzle palace here on the Potomac." Remarks at the Inaugural Anniversary Dinner of the Administration of Ronald Reagan (January 20, 1982).

1153   "The Federal Government should only do what the people cannot do for themselves or through their locally elected leaders." Address Before a Joint Session of the Alabama State Legislature in Montgomery (March 15, 1982).

1154   "The Federal Government has, at great cost, been attempting to perform tasks that are not its proper function. Oh, those who led us down that path had good intentions; they just didn't see how far they were taking us from the Constitution." Address Before a Joint Session of the Tennessee State Legislature in Nashville (March 15, 1982).

1155   "Government exists to ensure that liberty does not become license to prey on each other." Remarks at Kansas State University at the Alfred M. Landon Lecture Series on Public Issues (September 9, 1982).

1156   "[T]he idea that local governments and the private sectors should work in harmony in tackling serious problems is about as old as our Republic. But somewhere along the line, in recent years, the people began looking to Washington as the solution to the problems. And after decades of relying on Federal solutions, I think the people are beginning to notice that many of the problems are not only still with us, but, in some cases, they're getting worse." Remarks on Presenting 1982 Awards of the HUD National Recognition Program for Community Development Projects (December 9, 1982).

1157   "Very simply, my idea of what the Federal Government should be doing is reducing the cost of government to the lowest practical point at which you can leave the most of your earnings in your pocket that is still possible and still do and fill the responsibilities of government." Remarks to Employees at the Chrysler Corporation of St. Louis Assembly Plant in Fenton, Missouri (February 1, 1983).

1158   "[F]amilies cannot proper and keep America strong if government becomes a Goliath that preys upon their wealth, usurps their rights, and crushes their spirit." Radio Address to the Nation on Federal Income Taxes (April 9, 1983).

1159   "I've always believed that the best thing the Federal Government can do to enhance progress in this country is to get out of the way and let the people get on with it." Remarks at Cinco de Mayo ceremonies in San Antonio, Texas (May 5, 1983).

1160   "[L]ike the Founding Fathers, we recognize the people as sovereign and the source of social progress. We recognize government's role in that process, but only under sharply defined and limited conditions. We remain aware of government's urge to seek more power, to disturb the social ecology and disrupt the bonds of cooperation and interchange among private individuals and institutions through unnecessary intrusion or expansion." Remarks at a Fundraising Dinner Honoring Former Representative John M. Ashbrook in Ashland, Ohio (May 9, 1983).

1161   "Instead of seeing the people and their free institutions as the primary vehicle of social change, our political opposition has looked at government and bureaucracy as the primary vehicle of social change. And this marked the onslaught of special interest politics, the notion that every noble social goal is the business of government, that every pressure group has its claim on the tax dollars of working people, that national legislation means brokering and bartering with the largest share going to the most powerful of the noisiest political constituency." Remarks at a Fundraising Dinner Honoring Former Representative John M. Ashbrook in Ashland, Ohio (May 9, 1983).

1162   "It's about time the notion that government is the servant, not the master, came back into fashion." Radio Address to the Nation on Organ Donorship and on Reform 88 (July 30, 1983).

1163   "Government must limit what it does, but it still must perform its responsibilities with care and professionalism." Remarks on Presenting the Presidential Rank Awards to Members of the Senior Executive Service (December 19, 1983).

1164   "There are many explanations for the American miracle, but government planning isn't one of them." Remarks at the Annual Convention of the Concrete and Aggregates Industries Associations in Chicago, Illinois (January 31, 1984).

1165   "If history suggests anything, it is that government, even when directed by well-meaning individuals, usually causes more problems than it solves." Remarks at an Iowa Caucus Rally in Des Moines (February 20, 1984).

1166   "The difference between the path toward greater freedom and a bigger government is the difference between success and failure; between opportunity and coercion; between faith in a glorious future and fear of mediocrity and despair; between respecting people as adults, each with a spark of greatness, and treating them as helpless children to be forever dependent; between a drab, materialistic world where Big Brother rules by promises to special interest groups, and a world of adventure where everyday people set their sights on impossible dreams, distant stars, and the kingdom of God." Remarks at the Annual Conservative Political Action Conference Dinner (March 2, 1984).

1167   "The American miracle is a product of freeing the energies of our people, not harnessing them to some central plan or bureaucratic program." Remarks at the Midyear Meeting of the National Association of Realtors (May 10, 1984).

1168   "Too much government has always meant the oppression of the human spirit and the stultification of human progress." Remarks at the Presentation Ceremony for the Presidential Scholars Awards (June 19, 1984).

1169   "We don't celebrate dependence day on the Fourth of July. We celebrate Independence Day." Remarks Accepting the Presidential Nomination at the Republican National Convention in Dallas, Texas (August 23, 1984).

1170   "Our government ... has no power or rights that we, the people, have not freely given to it. Now, this may seem as small distinction, but as I said, it is everything." Remarks at Naturalization Ceremonies for New United States Citizens in Detroit, Michigan (October 1, 1984).

1171   "There's a true and tested path to a bright and hopeful future; but it's not the path of good intentions by bigger government. It's the path of greater responsibility in government and greater opportunity for every man, woman, and child." Remarks and a Question-and-Answer Session at the Economic Club of Detroit in Detroit, Michigan (October 1, 1984).

1172   "Their [big government spenders] idea of compassion is bureaucratic compassion, which always begins with every family sending more to Washington, and ultimately leads to more suffering for those who need help the most." Remarks

Following a Meeting with Republican Members of Congress and Congressional Candidates (October 4, 1984).

1173   "As long as we remember that the difference between having faith in people and faith in big government is the difference between success and failure, we're going to be able to reach for the stars. And as long as we concentrate on hard work and high tech, not on hard times and high taxes, we can have the future of our dreams." Remarks and a Question-and-Answer Session at St. Agatha High School in Detroit, Michigan (October 10, 1984).

1174   "Now, we need government, of course. But when you go from government to big government — to government as the neighborhood bully — it's time for a change...." Remarks at a Reagan-Bush Rally in Warren, Michigan (October 10, 1984).

1175   "[A]merica's greatest progress for everyone — whites, blacks, young, and old — begins not in Washington, but in our homes, neighborhoods, workplaces, and voluntary groups across this land." Radio Address to the Nation on the Presidential Campaign (October 27, 1984).

1176   "There's a lot of politicians back there [in Washington] that haven't found out who they work for. They thought you worked for them. It's the other way around." Remarks at a Reagan-Bush Rally in Detroit, Michigan (November 1, 1984).

1177   "I still believe the government is the servant of the people and not the other way around." Remarks at the Annual Convention of the National Religious Broadcasters (February 4, 1985).

1178   "Protecting the environment, defending our people, and ensuring that justice is done — these are all special roles for government. Economic prosperity, however, requires the enterprise, work, and investment of the private sector." Remarks at the Signing Ceremony for the Joint Canada–United States Declarations in Quebec City, Canada (March 18, 1985).

1179   If we've learned anything, it is that government that is big enough to give you everything you want is more likely to simply take everything you've got. And that's not freedom, that's servitude. That isn't the way Americans were meant to live." Remarks to the Students and Faculty at St. John's University in New York, New York (March 28, 1985).

1180   "[I] see my job ... [as being] to get out of your way, to be a partner but not a senior partner, and to have policies that we are sure are not going to hinder the practice of the free economy." Remarks at a Symposium at the University of Tennessee in Knoxville (September 24, 1985).

1181   "Isn't it time the Congress got government out of the way and let the good times roll?" Radio Address to the Nation on the Federal Budget (April 12, 1986).

1182   "We don't need more government. We need more growth, strong, vibrant growth that will bring all Americans into the economic mainstream, light the forgotten streets of our inner cities with hope, and reach out to every corner of the world with opportunity." Remarks at a White House Meeting with Members of the American Business Conference (April 15, 1986).

1183   "Federal money is, as we all know, nothing more than local money that is given back, minus a carrying charge and coupled with complex guidelines and regulations." Toast at a White House Dinner Honoring the Nation's Governors (February 2, 1987).

1184   "I've thought from my own days as Governor that the best thing the Federal Government can do for the States is get out of your pockets and out of your way." Toast at a White House Dinner Honoring the Nation's Governors (February 22, 1987).

1185   "Lately I've noticed some talk in some quarters about how America's become selfish. Those who say that seem to think that more big government and higher taxes are signs of an elevated moral state in our Union. Well, I believe that's dead wrong. The greatness of this land of freedom is not in the strength of government but in the strength and decency that we as free men and women bring to our daily lives." Remarks at the Presentation Ceremony for the Presidential Scholars Awards (June 17, 1987).

1186   "Big government, huge bureaucracies, and central planning aren't the solutions; they are the problem." Remarks at a Fundraising Recep-

tion for Senator Orrin G. Hatch of Utah (June 17, 1987).

1187   "I've always believed that there's nothing government can do as well, other than a certain few things like national security, as the private sector can do if government gets out of its way and sets it free to do it." Remarks at a White House Luncheon for Members of the Volunteer International Council of the United States Information Agency (October 9, 1987).

1188   "You know, it's said that the 10 most frightening words in the English language are: 'Hello, I'm from the Government, and I'm here to help.' Well, any more of that kind of government help and our economy would have gone right down the tubes." Remarks at a White House Briefing for Members of the Small Business Community (October 29, 1987).

1189   "[T]he best thing the Government can do for free people is to get out of their way." Remarks to the United States Chamber of Commerce on the Economy and Deficit Reduction (November 19, 1987).

1190   "The Federal Government does a lot to shape the future. And there are many times when it would be helpful if government just left things alone." Remarks and a Question-and-Answer Session with Area High School Seniors in Jacksonville, Florida (December 1, 1987).

1191   "[M]ore often than not, the best thing government can do for a free people is get its hands out of their pockets and get out of their way." Remarks at the 1988 Reagan Administration Executive Forum (January 19, 1988).

1192   "Well, of course, sometimes government can help and should help — natural disasters like the drought, for example — but we need to look to a future where there's less, not more, government in our daily lives. It's that philosophy that brought us the prosperity and growth that we see today." Remarks to Representatives of the Future Farmers of America (July 28, 1988).

1193   "It's been said that a bureaucrat is someone who has a problem for every solution." Remarks at the Presentation Ceremony for the Distinguished Rank Awards (August 2, 1988).

1194   "Well, no bureaucrat, politician, government expert, or certified genius sitting in a

Federal office in Washington has ever been able to replace the economic miracle of free men and women working with their hands, their hearts, and their heads to build a better future for their families and a stronger economy for America. I have said this again and again, and I'm going to keep on saying it: It's not the Government, it is the American people who have made our nation the greatest country on Earth. Basically what our program did was get out of your way and let you do what you can do so well." Remarks to the Employees of United States Precision Lens, Inc., in Cincinnati, Ohio (August 8, 1988).

Economic Intervention

1195   "In this present crisis [slumping economy], government is not the solution to our problem; government is the problem." Inaugural Address (January 20, 1981).

1196   "Government can and must provide opportunity, not smother it; foster productivity, not stifle it." Inaugural Address (January 20, 1981).

1197   "Government can provide opportunity. It can pave the way. But ultimately, it is individuals ... who brave new horizons, expand freedom, and create better lives for us all." Remarks at a Luncheon with Members of the President's Task Force on Private Sector Initiatives (December 2, 1981).

1198   "The country is bursting with ideas and creativity, but a government run by central decree has no way to respond." Remarks at a Luncheon with Members of the President's Task Force on Private Sector Initiatives (December 2, 1981).

1199   "Government should promote a strong, vibrant, and private economy with policies that primarily rely upon free markets to organize and allocate our economic resources." Annual Report to Congress on the State of Small Business (March 1, 1982).

1200   "I'm convinced that in these last few decades the increased intervention by government in the marketplace, tax policies that took too great a percentage of overall earnings, plus burdensome and unnecessary regulations reduced economic growth and kept us from creating jobs for newcomers entering the job market." Radio Address to the Nation on the Observance of Labor Day (September 4, 1982).

1201   "A President's greatest responsibility is to protect all our people from enemies, foreign and domestic. Here at home the worst enemy we face is economic — the creeping erosion of the American way of life and the American dream that has resulted in today's economic stagnation and unemployment." Address to the Nation on the Economy (October 13, 1982).

1202   "[Some] urge that we embark on a giant public works program funded by government. Isn't that what we tried in all those seven other recessions since World War II? And all we got for that spending was a temporary quick fix, followed by more inflation and another recession, usually deeper than the one before." Radio Address to the Nation on the Economic Recovery Program (October 30, 1982).

1203   "If there's one lesson that we should have learned over the last two decades, it is that focusing totally on government as a vehicle for social improvement is the least effective method of improving the lives of people." Remarks on Signing a Statement on Minority Enterprise Development (December 17, 1982).

1204   "Government's legitimate role is not to dictate detailed plans or solutions to problems for particular companies or industries. No, government serves us best by protecting and maintaining the marketplace, by ensuring that the rules of free and fair trade, both at home and abroad, are properly observed, and by safeguarding the freedoms of individual participants." Statement on Establishment of the President's Commission on Industrial Competitiveness (August 4, 1983).

1205   "Millions of individuals making their own decisions in the marketplace will always allocate resources better than any centralized government planning process." Remarks at the Annual Meeting of the Board of Governors of the World Bank Group and the International Monetary Fund (September 27, 1983)

1206   "The primary economic responsibility of the Federal Government is not to make choices for people, but to provide an environment in which people can make their own choices." Message to the Congress Transmitting the Annual Economic Report of the President (February 5, 1985).

1207   "Let me make one thing very plain: Yes, we are sympathetic, and we will extend support. But American taxpayers must not be asked to bail out every farmer hopelessly in debt, some by hundreds of thousands of dollars, or be asked to bail out the banks who also bet on higher inflation." Radio Address to the Nation on Farm Credit Programs (February 23, 1985).

1208   "[O]ur national experience shows that when government grows beyond these two limited duties [maintaining a strong military and providing a safety net for those in genuine need], when government lays claim to more and more of our resources and begins, through massive regulation and high taxation, to impinge on our individual freedoms, then our economy grows not more prosperous but less so." Remarks to Participants in the President's Inaugural Bands Parade at Walt Disney's EPCOT Center Near Orlando, Florida (May 27, 1985).

1209   "The way to a better life for all Americans is to free the energy of our citizens, to let you the people make decisions with your own lives, and to do that by getting the Government out of your way. That's the plan for a more prosperous future. With freedom and the profit motive, there's nothing we can't do." Remarks to Citizens in Concord, New Hampshire (September 18, 1985).

1210   "A democratic government, indeed any government, is powerless to ordain economic growth or decree technological innovation. But this much a government can do: It can reward or punish specific economic activities. High tax rates represent punishment. Burdensome regulations represent punishment. But cutting taxes and eliminating needless regulations constitute rewards." Remarks at a White House Meeting with Members of the Business Council (February 19, 1986).

1211   "Even in free market economies, high taxes make people less free to work, save, and invest. Excessive regulation makes them less able to experiment and innovate. Too much government spending can rob those on the receiving end of a reason to labor, and those who must pay of their incentive to strive." Remarks at the Annual Meet-

ing of the Boards of Governors of the International Monetary Fund and World Bank Group (September 30, 1986).

1212   "If the Keynesian view had been correct — if government really could, in effect, fabricate prosperity — then, as the decade of the seventies wore on, we all would have noticed our standard of living going up. And instead, of course, just the opposite took place." Remarks to Students and Faculty at Purdue University in West Lafayette, Indiana (April 9, 1987).

Regulation

1213   "Regulation tends to smother innovation, discourage new investment, increase labor costs, and reduce competition." Remarks at the Mid-Winter Congressional City Conference of the National League of Cities (March 2, 1981).

1214   "Only 50 years ago, Americans still felt they could accomplish anything, and they did. Today, the descendants of these pathfinders peer through a maze of regulations and often give up even before they've tried." Remarks at the Mid-Winter Congressional City Conference of the National League of Cities (March 2, 1981).

1215   "We must remove government's smothering hand from where it does harm; we must seek to revitalize the proper functions of government. But we do these things to set loose again the energy and the ingenuity of the American people. We do these things to reinvigorate those social and economic institutions which serve as a buffer and a bridge between the individual and the state — and which remain the real source of our progress as a people." Remarks at the Conservative Political Action Conference Dinner (March 20, 1981).

1216   "This country is bursting with ideas and creativity, but a government run by central decree has no way to respond." Remarks at the Annual Meeting of the National Business Alliance. (October 5, 1981).

1217   "Regulations that inhibit our growth and prosperity would be incomprehensible to the colonists who revolted because of the Stamp Act." Remarks at the Bicentennial Observance of the Battle of Yorktown in Virginia (October 19, 1981).

1218 "We've lived too long ... lost in a jungle of government bureaucracy, tangled in a web of programs and regulations. And almost all of these government initiatives were intended to relieve suffering, enforce justice, or preserve an environment threatened by pollution. But for each ounce of blessing, a pound of freedom was quietly stolen." Address Before a Joint Session of the Iowa Legislature in Des Moines (February 9, 1982).

1219 "If the Federal Government had been around when the Creator was putting His hand to this State, Indiana wouldn't be here. It'd still be waiting for an environmental impact statement." Address Before a Joint Session of the Indiana State Legislature in Indianapolis (February 9, 1982).

1220 "The ultimate and overwhelming positive goal of my administration is to put limits on the power of government, yes, but to do it so that we liberate the powers and the real source of our national genius which will make us great again." Remarks at Kansas State University at the Alfred M. Landon Lecture Series on Public Issues (September 9, 1982).

Role of State and Local Government ("Federalism")

1221 "All of us need to be reminded that the Federal Government did not create the States; the States created the Federal Government." Inaugural Address (January 20, 1981).

1222 "I've long believed that State and local governments have a better chance to be efficient and responsive than does the Federal bureaucracy, which tries to fit solutions to problems that vary from one locale to another, and all too often they end up with their own bureaucracy the beneficiary of whatever program they administer." Remarks on the Nation's Economy at a White House Meeting with State Legislators and County Executives (February 9, 1981).

1223 "Unfortunately, our decentralized system of government has over the years been bent out of shape. The Federal Government too often

has treated State and local officials as if they were nothing more than administrative agents for Federal authority." Statement on Signing Executive Order Establishing the Presidential Advisory Committee on Federalism (April 8, 1981).

1224 "I believe, as our Founding Fathers did, that local governments should do as much as they can, because they can do so much so much better than distant officials in some faraway bureaucracy." Remarks About Federal Tax Reduction Legislation at a Meeting with State Legislators and Local Government Officials (July 23, 1981).

1225 "The Founding Fathers saw the federal system as constructed something like a masonry wall: The States are the bricks and the National Government is the mortar. For the structure to stand plumb with the Constitution, there must be a proper mix of that brick and mortar." Remarks at the Annual Convention of the National Conference of State Legislatures in Atlanta, Georgia (July 30, 1981).

1226 "As a former Governor himself, I believe that FDR would today be amazed and appalled at the growth of the Federal Government's power." Remarks at the Annual Convention of the National Conference of State Legislatures in Atlanta, Georgia (July 30, 1981).

1227 "Forcing Americans to accept the dictates of a swollen government in Washington instead of dealing with elected representatives in their city hall has to be one of the more serious mistakes of this century. City halls, county seats, and State legislatures are the very laboratories of democracy, and yet in past years we've closed our eyes to their findings. By removing the possibility of resolving our problems where they occur, too many of us have turned our backs on the genius of our system. Too many of us have stopped believing in our ability to govern ourselves." Remarks at the Inaugural Anniversary Dinner of the Administration of Ronald Reagan (January 20, 1982).

1228 "Prisoners of the past, they [those who have controlled government for nearly three decades], remain shackled to the myth that all wisdom, morality, and compassion begin at both ends of Pennsylvania Avenue." Address Before a Joint Session of the Alabama State Legislature in Montgomery (March 15, 1982).

1229   "A citizen with a problem should be able to take a bus to city hall for an answer; he shouldn't have to take a jet to Washington. Removing the possibility of solving problems where they occur, forcing Americans to accept the dictates of a faraway bureaucracy has to be one of the more serious mistakes of this century." Address Before a Joint Session of the Tennessee State Legislature in Nashville (March 15, 1982).

1230   "There has been a philosophy abroad in the land that the States should be reduced to administrative districts of the Federal Government. Well, don't you let that happen. This country will remain strong so long as it is a federation of sovereign States. It's unique in all the world in that respect." Remarks and Question-and-Answer Session at a Reception in Los Angeles, California, for Gubernatorial Candidate George Deukmejian (August 24, 1982).

1231   "[O]ne of the most unique things about America that I believe is more responsible for our freedom than anything else is the fact that in this country we were established to be a federation of sovereign States. We were not set up to have 50 administrative districts of the Federal Government." Remarks and Question-and-Answer Session at a Fundraising Reception in Columbus, Ohio, for Gubernatorial Candidate Bud Brown (October 4, 1982).

1232   "I have a dream that some day we can provide you [local governments officials] with the revenue sources that have been co-opted by the Federal Government, so that local money no longer has to make a round trip through Washington before you can see it back in your local area — minus a certain carrying charge." Remarks at the Annual Meeting of the National Association of Towns and Townships (September 12, 1983).

1233   "[Our country] was set up by the Constitution to be a federation of sovereign states, not administrative districts of a Federal government that retained all the power itself." Remarks at a Fundraising for Gubernatorial Candidate Jim Bunning in Louisville, Kentucky (October 7, 1983).

1234   "We're coming to the end of an era when politicians can sell the idea that the best solution to any problem is letting Washington do it because Federal money is free.... Well, Washington

money isn't free money.... It comes right out of those same pockets." Remarks at a Fundraising Dinner for Gubernatorial Candidate Jim Bunning in Louisville, Kentucky (October 7, 1983).

1235   "It is that ability of citizens to choose where they will live that has kept government at the State level from becoming tyrannical." Remarks at a Fundraising Dinner for Gubernatorial Candidate in Louisville, Kentucky (October 7, 1983).

1236   "Local government meeting local needs — that's a fundamental principle of good government. Many government workers here in Washington are diligent and dedicated; I've found that out. And yet they can't know the American people as well as [local government officials]." Remarks on Signing the Local Government Fiscal Assistance Amendments of 1983 (November 30, 1983).

1237   "We believe in neighborhoods. We believe that the closer political power is to the people it affects, the better it will be wielded." Remarks at the Annual Dinner of the National Italian American Foundation (September 15, 1984).

1238   "As long as we remember that the difference between having faith in people and faith in big government is the difference between success and failure, we're going to be able to reach for the stars." Remarks and a Question-and-Answer Session at St. Agatha High School in Detroit, Michigan (October 10, 1984).

1239   "[W]e must continue working to return power to levels of government closer to the people. We believe that when it comes to running county government, county officials will always do better from the county seat than bureaucrats could ever do from Washington." Remarks at the Annual Legislative Conference of the National Association of Counties (March 4, 1985).

1240   "You know, one thing that makes our country unique in all the world is that we are a federation of sovereign States. Now, there are those in recent years who have been in charge in Washington, and some who are still there, who would like to change that. They would like to make the Federal Government all-powerful and make the States simply administrative districts of that Federal Government. Well, our strength comes from this system that was designed to keep authority and autonomy over our domestic affairs as close to the people as possible." Remarks to Senate Campaign Supporters of Representative Ken Kramer in Denver, Colorado (September 8, 1986).

1241   "That's the greatest strength and source of freedom in our nation: that we are a federation of sovereign States." Remarks at the Republican Governors Association Dinner (October 7, 1986).

1242   "This country is great, and our freedom is sure as long as we continue to have a federation of sovereign States." Remarks at a White House Briefing for the American Legislative Exchange Council (December 12, 1986).

1243   "The constitutional foundations for federalism have been seriously eroded in recent decades. The fault is on both sides of the Federal-State line. Time and again, the National Government has intruded into the domain of the States. Too many State leaders have traded sovereignty for a few pieces of Federal silver." Remarks at a White House Briefing for Members of the American Legislative Exchange Council (May 1, 1987).

1244   "[T]here's no more important battle to finish than that of restoring government to the people. And that's what federalism is all about." Remarks at a White House Briefing for Members of the American Legislative Exchange Council (May 1, 1987).

1245   "So, let me say that as a Governor I always thought that before a new President began entertaining heads of state from around the world he should show that first things come first and spend an evening with the heads of our 50 sovereign States and our territories." Toast at a White House Dinner Honoring the Nation's Governors (February 21, 1988).

1246   "The founders gave us a Federal system in the first place, because the best government of, by, and for the people is not the National Government but State government." Toast at a White House Dinner Honoring the Nation's Governors (February 21, 1988).

1247   "[P]art of federalism is recognizing that the States are laboratories of democracy." Toast at a White House Dinner Honoring the Nation's Governors (February 21, 1988).

1248   "Perhaps the greatest test of federalism is how we meet the urgent need for welfare reform — how successful we are in fashioning local and community solutions to problems that would destroy families, or worse, keep families from forming in the first place. With a variety of innovative programs, the States are moving forward to meet this challenge, and I think we have reason to be optimistic that in the diversity of these approaches we may find new answers." Remarks to Members of the National Governors' Association (February 22, 1988).

1249   "[T]hose of us who have actually served at the State and local level know it's not in Washington but in the States, the cities, and communities of this country where the real work gets done. And we know from experience that the 10 most frightening words in the English language are, 'I'm from the Federal Government, and I'm here to help.'" Remarks to State and Local Republican Officials on Federalism and Aid to the Nicaraguan Democratic Resistance (March 22, 1988).

1250   "We took a lesson from the environmental movement, and now when any agency in the executive branch takes an action that significantly affects State or local governments, it has to prepare a federalism impact statement, which only seems proper to me. The Federalist system given us by our Founding Fathers is a precious natural resource, and every bit as much as our environment, it should be cherished and protected." Remarks to State and Local Republican Officials on Federalism and Aid to the Nicaraguan Democratic Resistance (March 22, 1988).

1251   "It's time, as I said to Congress, for the Federal Government to show a little humility, to let a thousand sparks of genius in the States and communities around this country catch fire and become guiding lights." Remarks to State and Local Republican Officials on Federalism and Aid to the Nicaraguan Democratic Resistance (March 22, 1988).

1252   "The Federal Government is so large and its mandate so very broad that when programs are instituted, flexibility and ability to adapt to local circumstances are very limited. And that's another way the States have it all over the Federal Government. You're low to the ground, you're flexible, you can change speeds and directions as nimbly as a high-performance sports car when you find out what works. The virtue of innovative programs at the State level is when they work you know it quickly and you can expand them, and when they don't you can rechannel the energies that went into them and look for new solutions." Remarks at the Republican Governors Club Dinner (October 4, 1988).

Trust the People

1253   "The American people are resilient. I think they realize that the wrongs done for several decades cannot be corrected instantly." Remarks at the Conservative Political Action Conference Dinner (March 20, 1981).

1254   "Trust the people. This is the one irrefutable lesson of the entire post-war period, contradicting the notion that rigid government controls are essential to economic development. The societies which have achieved the most spectacular broad-based economic progress in the shortest period of time are not the most tightly controlled, not necessarily the biggest in size, or the wealthiest in natural resources. No, what unites all of them is their willingness to believe in the magic of the marketplace." Remarks at the Annual Meeting of the Boards of Governors of the World Bank and International Monetary Fund (September 29, 1981).

1255   "Trust the people, trust their intelligence and trust their faith, because putting people first is the secret of economic success everywhere in the world." Remarks at a Luncheon of the World Affairs Council of Philadelphia in Philadelphia, Pennsylvania (October 15, 1981).

1256   "Americans should never have to consider themselves wards of the state. They're members of their communities, and the answers to their problems can be found on the streets where they live." Remarks at a Luncheon Meeting with Members of the President's Task Force on Private Sector Initiatives (December 2, 1981).

1257   "For too long we've been stalled in history, repeating mistakes of yesterday because our leaders have been afraid to share a new tomorrow. But our people are ready. Our people know that they can solve any problem, that no challenge is too great. They're fed up with promises and platitudes. They're calling for the government to have faith in the governed." Remarks at a Rally for Senator Malcolm Wallop of Wyoming in Cheyenne (March 2, 1982).

1258   "Trust the people — that's the secret weapon. Only when people are free to worship, create, and build, only when they can decide their destiny and benefit from their own risks — only then do societies become dynamic, prosperous, progressive, and free." Remarks at the Annual Meeting of the United States Chamber of Commerce (April 26, 1982).

1259   "[T]here resides in the American people a common wisdom, a basic decency that comes to the fore just when it's needed most." Remarks at the Republican Congressional "Salute to President Ronald Reagan Dinner" (May 4, 1982).

1260   "[T]he strength of this country lies in the minds, the motivation, and faith of people ... not the bureaucracy in Washington, D.C." Remarks and a Question-and-Answer Session at a Meeting with Employees of AccuRay Corporation in Columbus, Ohio (October 4, 1982).

1261   "[T]he future of free people doesn't depend so much on those who hold elected office. It depends on those outside government.... And while the history books may record events as they happened during this or that administration, the direction of a country is determined not so much by the leader as by the character of the people." Remarks at a Fundraising Dinner for Senator John Tower in Houston, Texas (April 29, 1983).

1262   "We don't ask the people to trust us. We say, 'Trust yourselves. Trust your values.' And working together, we'll make America great again." Remarks at a Republican Fundraising Dinner for Congressional Campaign Committees (May 12, 1983).

1263   "Our system is based on faith in people...." Remarks at a Fundraising Dinner for the Republican Majority Fund (September 27, 1983).

1264   "Like death and taxes, the doom-criers will always be with us. And they'll always be wrong about America until they realize progress begins with trusting people." Radio Address to the Nation on the Economic Recovery Program (January 21, 1984).

1265   "Trust the people—this is the crucial lesson of history and America's message to the world. We must be staunch in our conviction that freedom is not the sole possession of a chosen few, but the universal right of men and women everywhere." Remarks at the National Leadership Forum of the Center for International and Strategic Studies at Georgetown University (April 6, 1984).

1266   "As a result of that crisis that faced us ... we weren't [going to] ... pursu[e] a program based on the shifting sands of government expediency. Another quick fix certainly would have failed. There was only one way to go, and that was use three simple words as our guide: Trust the people." Remarks at a White House Meeting with the American Retail Federation (May 16, 1984).

1267   "I believe America works best when we trust the people—all our people. When we trust their vision, faith, judgment, and courage, when we give them opportunities to climb higher and reach for the stars, a million dreams can become the golden dream of America." Remarks and a Question-and-Answer Session at the Economic Club of Detroit in Detroit, Michigan (October 1, 1984).

1268   "[O]ur guiding philosophy has been that you know best what's right for you. You don't need a big government in Washington to tell you what's right for you." Remarks at a Reagan-Bush Rally in Brownsville, Texas (October 2, 1984).

1269   "[T]here's nothing wrong with America that our people can't and won't make right if government will just stand aside and get out of the way." Remarks Following a Meeting with Republican Members of Congress and Congressional Candidates (October 4, 1984).

1270   "We're the people who crossed the plains, scaled the mountains, won the west. We're the people who came up with the inventions that lit the world and filled it with sound and laughter. We're the people who twice in this century have fought in Europe and stood up for decency for all mankind. We're a people, in short, who don't need the supervision of government sophisticates to tell us what is right and good." Remarks at a Reagan-Bush Rally in Warren, Michigan (October 10, 1984).

1271   "The greatness of America doesn't begin in Washington; it begins with each of you—in the mighty spirit of free people under God, in the bedrock values you live by each day in your families, neighborhoods, and workplaces. Each of you is an individual worthy of respect, unique and important to the success of America. And only by trusting you, giving you opportunities to climb high and reach for the stars, can we preserve the golden dream of America as the champion of peace and freedom among the nations of the world." Address to the Nation on the Eve of the Presidential Election (November 5, 1984).

1272   "If the dream of America is to be preserved, we must not waste the genius of one mind, the strength of one body, or the spirit of one soul. Let us encourage all Americans—men and women, young and old, individuals of every race, creed, and color—to succeed and to be healthy, happy, and whole. Our goal is a society of unlimited opportunity which will reach out to lift the weak and nurture those who are less fortunate. [W]e are giving more help to more people ... [but] [o]ur work is not finished." Address to the Nation on the Eve of the Presidential Election (November 5, 1984).

1273   "So, let's forget political angles. Let's just trust the uncommon wisdom of the common people." Remarks at a White House Meeting with Members of the President's Private Sector Survey on Cost Control in the Federal Government (February 25, 1985).

1274   "[My] administration has always believed that the real source of America's economic and social progress is not national edicts and mandates that are issued from Washington, but the toil and creativity of her people working at the local level through their own private institutions and associations." Remarks at a White House Meeting with Members of the National Newspaper Association (March 7, 1985).

1275   "A lack of faith in freedom often stems from the belief that people are not capable of making the tough decisions necessary for a country's security and economic health. Americans have proven these cynics wrong time and again." Radio Address to the Nation on the Bonn Economic Summit and the Federal Budget (April 27, 1985).

1276   "Our free society is based on faith in the people." Radio Address to the Nation on the Bonn Economic Summit and the Federal Budget (April 27, 1985).

1277   "Our democratic governments are not built on the proposition that the people are always right; indeed, within the structure of our governments there are safeguards against the whims or passions of the majority. But democratic government is built on the proposition that there resides in the common people an uncommon wisdom, that over the long run the people and their right to political self-expression are the best protection against freedom's oldest and most powerful enemy — the unchecked growth and abuse of the power of the state." Address Before the Assembly of the Republic of Portugal in Lisbon (May 9, 1985).

1278   "I've always had the sneaking suspicion that not only can Americans run their own affairs better than government can, they can probably run the Government better than the bureaucrats and politicians." Remarks at a Fundraising Event for Senator Steven D. Symms in Boise, Idaho (October 15, 1985).

1279   "[S]ometimes I think Washington people forget that self-interest doesn't really count as much with the American people as it does in this town. But ... over the long run, the American people are a little more enlightened than that; that they respond readily to what's right and what's wrong, what's good and bad, and not just 'what's in it for me?'" Remarks and a Question-and-Answer Session with the American Society of Newspaper Editors (April 9, 1986).

1280   "And the future rests not in big, impersonal forces, but with us, in our own choices and actions as a people. In all the long history of mankind, no nation has ever afforded its people greater liberty or depended more for its very survival upon their own diligence than our own." Remarks and a Question-and-Answer Session with Members of the American Legion Boys Nation (July 25, 1986).

1281   "America's greatness doesn't reside in Washington, but in people like you whose hard work, dedication, and generosity keep America strong and keep our future free." Remarks at a Senate Campaign Fundraising Luncheon for Rep-

resentative W. Henson Moore in New Orleans, Louisiana (September 18, 1986).

1282   "Well, there's one thing about Washington: There are always plenty of people around to tell you why something can't be done. But what those people always forget is that there's a force in our nation more powerful than all the lobbyists and insiders put together. And that force is the people...." Radio Address to the Nation on Tax Reform (September 20, 1986).

1283   "Now, I know it's true that some here in the Capital think the people can't be trusted with such complex matters as foreign policy. But along with our Founding Fathers, I've always believed that the intuitive wisdom of the people is far more dependable over the long run than the temporary insights or parochial pursuits of the Washington experts. And that's why I've said right from the start that the first obligation of democratic leaders is to keep the people informed and seek their support on public policy." Radio Address to the Nation on the Meeting with Soviet General Secretary Gorbachev in Reykjavik, Iceland (October 4, 1986).

1284   "The power of the Presidency is often thought to reside within this Oval Office. Yet it doesn't rest here; it rests in you, the American people, and in your trust." Address to the Nation on the Iran Arms and Contra Aid Controversy (March 4, 1987).

1285   "The Constitution called for a limited government, and in the two centuries since then, many around the world have asked: How is it possible that self-government and limited government work so well in America? Well, the answer is simple, and you're a part of it. As the Frenchman de Tocqueville found, when we Americans want to do something, we don't wait for government. We join together, and do it ourselves." Remarks at a Luncheon for Members of the College of Physicians in Philadelphia, Pennsylvania (April 1, 1987).

1286   "[I]n the critical matchup between those who want to keep spending your money and raising your taxes and those of us who resist a return to the old policies of tax and tax, spend and spend, we have now reached breakpoint. That's why I've made a personal decision to do something no President should ever hesitate to do when he must, and that's go to you, the American people, and put the facts before you." Address to the Nation on the Venice Economic Summit, Arms Control, and the Deficit (June 15, 1987).

1287   "[T]o achieve what we achieved economically, we first had to make political changes. Our guide here was still the same: Trust the people — put the facts before them, then trust the people." Remarks at a White House Briefing for Members of the Deficit Reduction Coalition (July 10, 1987).

1288   "My friends, there is still a thing called common sense in America." Remarks at a White House Briefing for State and Local Officials on the Economic Bill of Rights (July 22, 1987).

1289   "[I]n choosing between big government and the American people, I'm old-fashioned. I stand with the men who wrote the glorious Constitution whose 200th birthday we celebrate this week. I put my trust in the people." Remarks at the Annual Meeting of the National Alliance of Business (September 14, 1987).

1290   "[I]t's so hard for government planners, no matter how sophisticated, to ever substitute for millions of individuals working night and day to make their dreams come true. The fact is, bureaucracies are a problem around the world." Remarks and a Question-and-Answer Session with the Students and Faculty at Moscow State University (May 31, 1988).

1291   "By now, it's clear that our approach works, that trusting the people leads to prosperity." Radio Address to the Nation on the Economy (July 16, 1988).

1292   "When people get to flattering me about this economic expansion, the longest in the peacetime history of our nation, I sometimes ask: What is it we really did to make all this happen for Americans? And the truth is, we just got out of your way. You did it; we didn't." Remarks to Representatives of the Future Farmers of America (July 28, 1988).

1293   "It is the American people who endured the great challenge of lifting us from the depths of national calamity, renewing our mighty economic strength, and leading the way to restoring our respect in the world. They are an extraor-

dinary breed we call Americans. So, if there's any salute deserved tonight, it's to the heroes everywhere in this land who make up the doers, the dreamers, and the lifebuilders without which our glorious experiment in democracy would have failed." Remarks at the Republican National Convention in New Orleans, Louisiana (August 15, 1988).

1294   "But you know, the American people always have a way of figuring out the facts." Remarks at a Republican Campaign Rally in Bowling Green, Kentucky (October 21, 1988).

1295   "[T]here's a special faith that has, from our earliest days, guided this sweet and blessed land. It was proclaimed in the Declaration of Independence and enshrined in the Constitution. It found a home in even our most remote frontier settlements, and from every corner of the globe, it has drawn tens of millions of tempest-tossed dreamers to our shores. Yes, it was what our founders meant when they inscribed on our great seal the words that in translation say, 'A new order for the ages.' It is a faith in the wisdom and redeeming power of a free people." Remarks to Administration Officials on Domestic Policy (December 13, 1988).

1296   "[T]he American people rounded up a posse, swore in this old sheriff, and sent us riding into town, where the previous administration had said the Nation's problems were too complicated to manage. Well, we said of course they are; so government should stop trying to manage them, stop putting its faith in the false god of bureaucracy, and trust the genius of the American people instead. Yes, we said, it's time to return to the principles of our founders: the principles of the Constitution and the principles of limited government — free enterprise and respect for family, community, and faith." Remarks to Administration Officials on Domestic Policy (December 13, 1988).

1297   "And let me offer lesson number one about America: All great change in America begins at the dinner table. So, tomorrow night in the kitchen I hope the talking begins. And children, if your parents haven't been teaching you what it means to be an American, let 'em know and nail 'em on it. That would be a very American thing to do." Farewell Address to the Nation (January 11, 1989).

HEALTHCARE

1298   "[T]he quality of American medicine is unsurpassed and on that we don't need a second opinion." Remarks at the Annual Meeting of the American Medical Association House of Delegates in Chicago, Illinois (June 23, 1983).

1299   "What our space shuttle is to technology, our health care is to medicine. In life-saving discoveries, in innovative treatment, in the overall quality of services, America's doctors have no peers." Remarks at the Annual Meeting of the American Medical Association House of Delegates in Chicago, Illinois (June 23, 1983).

1300   "A catastrophic illness can strike anyone — the young, the old, the middle aged. The single distinguishing characteristic is simply this: Whatever form it takes, a catastrophic illness costs money — lots of it." Radio Address to the Nation on Proposed Catastrophic Health Insurance Legislation (February 14, 1987).

1301   "[A]merican medicine is the best in the world, and on that we need no second opinions, because there are no other opinions. Our competitive system has produced the finest health care in history. And with each year that passes, it saves more lives, finds cures to more diseases, makes life better for more people than ever before." Remarks at a Luncheon for Members of the College of Physicians in Philadelphia, Pennsylvania (April 1, 1987).

1302   "[W]hile our quality is the highest in the world, so are our prices. Last year medical costs climbed seven times faster than the rate of inflation. It's getting to where many patients feel that the recovery room should be next to the cashier's office." Remarks at a Luncheon for Members of the College of Physicians in Philadelphia, Pennsylvania (April 1, 1987).

1303   "What our citizens must know is this: America faces a disease that is fatal and spreading. And this calls for urgency, not panic. It calls for compassion, not blame. And it calls for understanding, not ignorance. It's also important that America not reject those who have the disease, but care for them with dignity and kindness. Final judgment is up to God; our part is to ease the suffering and to find a cure. This is a battle against disease, not against our fellow Americans. We mustn't allow those with the AIDS virus to suffer discrimination." Remarks at the American Foundation for AIDS Research Awards Dinner (May 31, 1987).

1304   "We will — I will do all that God gives us the power to do to find a cure for AIDS. We'll not stop, we'll not rest, until we've sent AIDS the way of smallpox and polio." Remarks at a Panel Discussion on AIDS Research and Treatment (July 23, 1987).

1305   "What we need right now in the battle against AIDS is a good strong dose of common sense ... common sense to recognize that, when it comes to stopping the spread of AIDS, medicine and morality teach the same lessons. It's also common sense that ignorance about the extent of the spread of AIDS won't help anyone — those who have it, those who might get it, those who are looking for ways of preventing its spread." Remarks at a Panel Discussion on AIDS Research and Treatment (July 23, 1987).

HOLOCAUST

1306   "Well, I, for one, intend that this bully pulpit shall be used on every occasion, where it is appropriate, to point a finger of shame at even the ugliness of graffiti, and certainly wherever it takes place in the world, the act of violence or terrorism, and that even at the negotiating table, never shall it be forgotten for a moment that wherever it is taking place in the world, the persecution of people, for whatever reason — persecution of people for their religious belief— that is a matter to be on the negotiating table, or the United States does not belong at that table." Remarks at the First Annual Commemoration of the Days of Remembrance of Victims of the Holocaust (April 30, 1981).

1307　"Those who died cannot be with us, but they have a contribution to make. Their voices from the past cry out for us never to tolerate hatred or bigotry. Their voices can be heard even now." Remarks at a White House Ceremony Commemorating the Day of Remembrance of the Holocaust (April 20, 1982).

1308　"We must see to it that the immeasurable pain of the Holocaust is not dehumanized, that it is not examined clinically and dispassionately, that its significance is not lost on this generation or any future generation. Though it is now a dry scar, we cannot let the bleeding wound be forgotten. Only when it is personalized will it be real enough to play a role in the decision we make." Remarks to the American Gathering of Jewish Holocaust Survivors (April 11, 1983).

1309　"Good and decent people must not close their eyes to evil, must not ignore the suffering of the innocent, and must never remain silent and inactive in times of moral crisis." Remarks to the American Gathering of the Jewish Holocaust Survivors (April 11, 1983).

1310　"You know, when you talk about human life, I think that means seeing that the immeasurable pain of the Holocaust is never dehumanized, seeing that its meaning is never lost on this generation or on any future generation, and, yes, seeing that those who take our place understand: never again." Remarks to Members of the Congregation of Temple Hillel and Jewish Community Leaders in Valley Stream, New York (October 26, 1984).

1311　"How does life continue in the face of this crime against humanity? The survivors swore their oath: Never again. And the American people also made that pledge: Never again. And we've kept it." Remarks on Presenting the Congressional Gold Medal to Elie Wisel and on Signing the Jewish Heritage Week Proclamation (April 19, 1985).

1312　"Here lie people — Jews — whose death was inflicted for no reason other than their very existence. Their pain was borne only because of who they were and because of the God in their prayers." Remarks at a Commemorative Ceremony at Bergen-Belsen Concentration Camp in the Federal Republic of Germany (May 5, 1985).

1313　"[R]ising above all this cruelty, out of this tragic and nightmarish time, beyond the anguish, the pain and the suffering for all time, we can and must pledge: Never again." Remarks at a Commemorative Ceremony at Bergen-Belsen Concentration Camp in the Federal Republic of Germany (May 5, 1985).

1314　"We must make sure that from now until the end of days all humankind stares this evil in the face, that all humankind knows what this evil looks like and how it came to be. And when we truly know it for what it was, then and only then can we be sure that it will never come again." Remarks at the Site of the Future Holocaust Memorial Museum (October 5, 1988).

1315　"Some people say evil of this degree is incomprehensible. They say we will never understand it. Some people even say that the word 'evil' is insufficient to describe the Holocaust, and instead they use terms like mad, crazy, insane. I think they're wrong.... I believe the Holocaust is comprehensible. Indeed, we must comprehend it. We have no choice; the future of mankind depends upon it. And that's what we're here for: to lay the cornerstone for the United States Holocaust Memorial Museum, which will help us understand and make it impossible for us to forget." Remarks at the Site of the Future Holocaust Memorial Museum (October 5, 1988).

1316　"Those monsters who made the Holocaust — they chose death, with results almost too awful to grasp. The mind reels from the enormity of the crime. It begs to be set free from so terrible a fact, to wipe it from the memory. But people like Simon Wiesenthal have made us understand that we must not, we cannot, and we will not." Remarks at the Simon Wiesenthal Center Awards Presentation Ceremony in Los Angeles, California (October 30, 1988).

HUMAN RIGHTS

1317   "Everyday life confirms the fundamentally human and democratic ideal that individual effort deserves economic reward. Nothing is more crushing to the spirit of working people and to the vision of development itself than the absence of reward for honest toil and legitimate risk." Remarks at the Annual Meeting of the Boards of Governors of the World Bank Group and International Monetary Fund (September 29, 1981).

1318   "There have been revolutions before and since ours, revolutions that simply exchanged one set of rulers for another. Ours was a philosophical revolution that changed the very concept of government." Remarks at the Bicentennial Observance of the Battle of Yorktown in Virginia (October 19, 1981).

1319   "Democracy and respect for human rights is not the easiest course, but it is the most moral." Toasts at the Dinner for President Luis Herrera Campins of Venezuela (November 17, 1981).

1320   "To be alive and to be human is to struggle for what is right and against what is not." Remarks in New York City on Receiving the Charles Evans Hughes Gold Medal of the National Conference of Christians and Jews (March 23, 1982).

1321   "Human rights means working at problems, not walking away from them." Remarks at the Quadrennial Convention of the International Longshoremen's Association in Hollywood, Florida (July 18, 1983).

1322   "All Americans long for a safer world in which individual rights are respected and precious values flourish." Radio Address to the Nation on United States Foreign Policy (April 7, 1984).

1323   "In reaffirming the moral beliefs that began our nation, we strive to make the United States what we pray to God it will always be — a beacon of hope to all the persecuted and oppressed of the world. And we resolve that as a people we'll never rest until the blessings of liberty and self-government are extended to all the nations of the Earth." Remarks on Signing the International Human Rights Day Proclamation (December 10, 1984).

1324   "We must defend human rights everywhere, since countries which respect human rights are unlikely to unleash war or to impose their will on others." Radio Address to the Nation on the 40th Anniversary of the United Nations General Assembly (October 19, 1985).

1325   "The rights of the individual and the rule of law are as fundamental to peace as arms control. A government which does not respect its citizens' rights and its international commitments to protect those rights is not likely to respect its other international undertakings." Address to the Nation on the Upcoming Soviet–United States Summit Meeting in Geneva (November 14, 1985).

1326   "Those countries which respect the rights of their own people tend, inevitably, to respect the rights of their neighbors. Human rights, therefore, is not an abstract moral issue; it is a peace issue." Address Before a Joint Session of the Congress Following the Soviet–United States Summit Meeting in Geneva (November 21, 1985).

1327   "We've learned from history that the cause of peace and human freedom is indivisible. Respect for human rights is essential to true peace on Earth. Governments that must answer to their peoples do not launch wars of aggression. That's why the American people cannot close their eyes to abuses of human rights and injustice, whether they occur among friend or adversary or even on our own shores." Remarks on Signing the Bill of Rights Day and the Human Rights Day and Week Proclamation (December 10, 1985).

1328   "Our democratic system is founded on the belief in the sanctity of human life and the rights of the individual — rights such as freedom of speech, of assembly of movement, and of worship. It is a sacred truth to us that every individual is a unique creation of God, with his or her own special talents, abilities, hopes, and dreams. Respect for all people is essential to peace...." New

Year's Messages of President Reagan and Soviet General Secretary Gorbachev (January 1, 1986).

1329   "[T]he surest way to strengthen the foundation of peace is to support the growth of democracy and gain full respect for human rights." Remarks at a White House Meeting with the Board of Directors of the United States Institute of Peace (February 26, 1986).

1330   "[H]uman rights [is] the indispensable element for peace, freedom, and prosperity." Address to the 41st Session of the United Nations General Assembly in New York, New York (September 22, 1986).

1331   "Respect for human rights is not social work; it is not merely an act of compassion. It is the first obligation of government and the source of its legitimacy." Address to the 41st Session of the United Nations General Assembly in New York, New York (September 22, 1986).

1332   "Peace is more than just an absence of war. True peace is justice, true peace is freedom, and true peace dictates the recognition of human rights." Address to the 41st Session of the United Nations General Assembly in New York, New York (September 22, 1986).

1333   "[H]uman rights violations in the Soviet bloc remain unceasing, because they're institutionalized and sanctioned by the state ideology." Remarks at a White House Briefing on Soviet–United States Relations for the President's Commission on Executive Exchange (October 6, 1986).

1334   "Peace is not simply an absence of war, it's the presence of justice. Human rights, human freedom are its indispensable elements." Remarks at a White House Meeting with Human Rights Advocates (October 7, 1986).

1335   "It's love of freedom that binds a people who are so richly diverse. It unites us in purpose, and it makes us one nation. At birth, our country was christened with a declaration that spoke of self-evident truths, the foremost of which was that each and every individual is endowed by our Creator with certain unalienable rights. And our creed as Americans is that these rights — these human rights — are the property of every man, woman, and child on this planet and that a violation of human rights anywhere is the business of free people everywhere." Remarks on Signing the Human

Rights Day, Bill of Rights Day, and Human Rights Week Proclamation (December 10, 1986).

1336   "No nation will be at peace with its neighbors if it is not at peace with its own people. So, human rights is not just an internal issue; it's truly an issue of peace." Remarks and a Question-and-Answer Session at a Los Angeles World Affairs Council Luncheon in California (April 10, 1987).

1337   "Human rights, after all, is what our nation is all about." Radio Address to the Nation on Soviet–United States Relations (November 28, 1987).

1338   "[A]lthough we're making a serious effort to improve relations between the Soviet Union and the United States, we will not do it by compromising our national interests or diminishing our commitment to the universality of human rights." Remarks at a White House Briefing for Human Rights Supporters (December 3, 1987).

1339   "[O]n human rights [it is] difficult ... for the people of the Western democracies to have trust in a government that doesn't trust its own people and denies their human rights." Remarks and a Question-and-Answer Session with News Editors and Broadcasters (December 11, 1987).

1340   "[W]e Americans are concerned about human rights, including freedoms of speech, press, worship, and travel. We will never forget that a wise man has said: 'Violence does not live alone and is not capable of living alone. It is necessarily interwoven with falsehood.' Silence is a form of falsehood. We will always speak out on behalf of human dignity." New Year's Messages of President Reagan and Soviet General Secretary Gorbachev (January 1, 1988).

1341   "Arms reductions cannot and will not be pursued in isolation from other areas of deep concern to the American people and the other free people of the world. If relations with the Soviet Union are to improve, if we're to enter into a new period of rapprochement with our adversary, we must see greater respect for human rights. We need to see more freedom and a further opening of the emigration door." Remarks at the 1988 Reagan Administration Executive Forum (January 19, 1988).

1342   "We Americans ... often speak about human rights, individual liberties, fundamental freedoms. We know that the promotion of human rights represents a central tenet of our foreign policy. We even believe that a passionate commitment to human rights is one of the special characteristics that helps to make America, America. It was Lincoln himself who said that the Declaration of Independence granted liberty not to our nation alone but 'gave promise that in due time the weights should be lifted from the shoulders of all men.' And it's important to note that this American emphasis on human rights represents much more than merely a vague respect for human dignity. No, part of our heritage as Americans is a very specific and definite understanding of human rights, a definition of human rights that we can assert to challenge ourselves and our own institutions and that we can hold up as an example for all the world." Remarks and a Question-and-Answer Session with Members of the National Strategy Forum in Chicago, Illinois (May 4, 1988).

1343   "Ultimately, our view of human rights derives from our Judeo-Christian heritage and the view that each individual life is sacred." Remarks and a Question-and-Answer Session with Members of the National Strategy Forum in Chicago, Illinois (May 4, 1988).

1344   "All of us who are united by our belief in democracy will continue to press the Soviet Union to improve its practices in these vital areas, in short, to grant full recognition of fundamental human rights. To raise these issues is not only our inclination by tradition and principle but the Helsinki Final Act, our responsibility." Address to the Citizens of Western Europe (May 23, 1988).

1345   "The United States views human rights as fundamental, absolutely fundamental to our relationship with the Soviet Union and all nations. From the outset of our administration, we've stressed that an essential element in improving relations between the United States and the Soviet Union is human rights and Soviet compliance with international covenants on human rights." Remarks to Soviet Dissidents at Spaso House in Moscow (May 30, 1988).

1346   "On the fundamental dignity of the human person, there can be no relenting, for now we must work for more, always more." Remarks to Soviet Dissidents at Spaso House in Moscow (May 30, 1988).

1347   "Now, let us understand: If we would have peace, we must acknowledge the elementary rights of our fellow human beings. In our own land and in other lands, if we would have peace, the trampling of the human spirit must cease. Human rights is not for some, some of the time. Human rights, as the universal declaration of this Assembly adopted in 1948 proclaims, is 'for all people and all nations,' and for all time." Address to the 43d Session of the United Nations General Assembly in New York, New York (September 26, 1988).

1348   "[W]hen human rights concerns are not paramount at the United Nations, when the Universal Declaration of Human Rights is not honored in these halls and meeting rooms, then the very credibility of this organization is at stake, the very purpose of its existence in question." Address to the 43d Session of the United Nations General Assembly in New York, New York (September 26, 1988).

1349   "[I] think if we look closely enough here, we'll see at work not just a foreign policy successful at expounding the cause of freedom but a foreign policy successful precisely because its very purpose and meaning was defined by that cause and sprang from the greatest of all ideas of Western thought and civilization: freedom, human dignity under God." Remarks and a Question-and-Answer Session at a World Affairs Council Luncheon in Los Angeles, California (October 28, 1988).

HUMAN SPIRIT

1350   "The most powerful force in the world comes not from balance sheets or weapons arsenals, but from the human spirit. It flows like a mighty river in the faith, love, and determination that we share in our common ideals and aspirations." Remarks at the New York City Partnership Luncheon in New York (January 14, 1982).

1351   "The most powerful force for progress in this world doesn't come from government elites, public programs, or even precious resources like oil or gold. True wealth comes from the heart, from the treasure of ideas and spirit, and from the investment of millions of brave people with hope for the future, trust in their fellow men, and faith in God." Remarks at the Annual Meeting of the United States Chamber of Commerce (April 26, 1982).

1352   "God gave angels wings. He gave mankind dreams. And with His help, there's no limit to what can be accomplished." Remarks at a White House Ceremony Commemorating the Bicentennial Year of Air and Space Flight (February 7, 1983).

1353   "[O]nly when the human spirit is allowed to worship, invent, create, and produce, only when individuals are given a personal stake in deciding their destiny and benefiting from their own risks, only then do societies become dynamic, prosperous, and free." Remarks at the Annual Meeting of the Board of Governors of the World Bank Group and the International Monetary Fund (September 27, 1983).

1354   "The better future that we all yearn for will not be built by skeptics who spend their lives admiring the complexity of the problems. It'll be built by free men and women who believe in themselves." Remarks to Representatives of the United States International Youth Year Commission (June 22, 1984).

1355   "Oppression will never extinguish the instinct of good people to do the right thing." Remarks at the International Convention of B'nai B'rith (September 6, 1984).

1356   "[T]he deeds of infamy or injustice are all recorded, but what shines out from the pages of history is the daring of the dreamers and the deeds of the builders and the doers. These things make up the stories we tell and pass on to our children. They comprise the most enduring and striking fact about human history — that through the heartbreak and tragedy man has always dared to perceive the outline of human progress, the steady growth in not just the material well-being, but the spiritual insight of mankind." Address to the 39th Session of the United Nations General Assembly in New York, New York (September 24, 1984).

1357   "There are no constraints on the human mind, no walls around the human spirit, no barriers to our progress except those we ourselves erect." Address Before a Joint Session of the Congress on the State of the Union (February 6, 1985).

1358   "History is no captive of some inevitable force. History is made by men and women of vision and courage." Address Before a Joint Session of Congress on the State of the Union (February 4, 1986).

1359   "[T]he power of the human spirit ... the capacity of the individual, once released from the stultifying hand of government, to reach and climb, and build and dream, and to achieve and succeed, and make life better for all humankind." Remarks at a White House Briefing for Members of the Deficit Reduction Coalition (July 10, 1987).

1360   "There is no end to what the human spirit can achieve if it is left alone to strive and succeed." Remarks at a White House Briefing for Members of the Deficit Reduction Coalition (July 10, 1987).

1361   "[W]e in the United States believe that the place to look first for shape of the future is not in continental masses and sea lanes, although geography is, obviously, of great importance. Neither is it in national reserves of blood and iron or, on the other hand, of money and industrial capacity, although military and economic strength are also, of course, crucial. We begin with something that is far simpler and yet far more profound: the human heart." Address to the 42d Session of the United Nations General Assembly in New York, New York (September 25, 1987).

1362   "We have been revolutionaries, and for 7 years the so-called sophisticates have at every turn said our revolution had failed. But again and again they've been wrong, because they've forgotten our secret weapon — the human spirit. Yes, ours is a revolution for the most powerful yearnings of the spirit: yearning for opportunity, for a better life for your children, for freedom, for true and lasting peace. The yearning of the spirit — in all the history and humanity, no force is stronger or more blessed." Remarks at the 1988 Reagan Administration Executive Forum (January 19, 1988).

IMMIGRATION AND ETHNIC DIVERSITY

1363   "I think it is important that we have teachers equipped who can get at them [non–English speaking students] in their own language and understand why it is they don't get the answer to the problem and help them in that way. But it is absolutely wrong and against the American concept to have a bilingual education program that is openly, admittedly dedicated to preserving their native language and never getting them adequate in English, so that they can go out into the job market and participate." Remarks at the Mid-Winter Congressional City Conference of the National League of Cities (March 2, 1981).

1364   "Americans, perhaps because of our own cultural and racial variety, believe that beneath the world's diversity most people have similar goals. They look for dignity, freedom, peace, and a chance to prosper. These common dreams and aspirations can serve as our strength." Remarks at a White House Dinner Honoring the Chiefs of Diplomatic Missions (February 18, 1982).

1365   "Our people include every race, creed, and ethnic background, yet we're bound by shared values and a love of freedom. Somewhere in the history of every American family is a person like you, who became an American not by birth but by choice." Remarks at the Swearing-In Ceremony for New United States Citizens in White House Station, New Jersey (September 17, 1982).

1366   "Americans have always opened their hearts to those coming from distant lands to make a new life here, to live in freedom, and to improve their lot." Remarks on Signing a Bill Providing for the Immigration of Certain Amerasian Children (October 22, 1982).

1367   "We weren't the people who stayed on the shores of the Old World. Instead, we were the Italians, the Frenchmen, the Dutchmen, the men and women of every race, nationality, and religion who came here to push back the limits and in the process became Americans one and all." Remarks at the 25th Anniversary Celebration of the National Aeronautics and Space Administration (October 19, 1983).

1368   "America has always been a magnet for people seeking freedom and peace and the opportunity to better their lot and to go as far as their God-given talents will let them. Pioneers came to our shores with the courage to start all over again because they knew America offered a hope for the future." Remarks During a Meeting with Puerto Rican Leaders (March 15, 1984).

1369   "All of the immigrants who came to us brought their own music, literature, customs, and ideas. And the marvelous thing, a thing of which we are proud, is that they did not have to relinquish these things in order to fit in. In fact, what they brought to America became American. And this diversity has more than enriched us; it has literally shaped us." Remarks at Fundan University in Shanghai, China (April 30, 1984).

1370   First of all, America is really many Americas. We call ourselves a nation of immigrants, and that's what we are. We have drawn people from every corner of the Earth. We're composed of virtually every race and region, and not in small numbers, but large." Remarks at Fundan University in Shanghai, China (April 30, 1984).

1371   "Maybe today, someone will put his hand on the shoulder of one of those new citizens [those who had just taken the oath of citizenship] and say, 'Welcome,' and not just as a courtesy, but to say welcome to a great land, a place of unlimited possibilities. Welcome to the American family." Address to the Nation on the Observance of Independence Day (July 4, 1984).

1372   "[S]omewhere in the history of every American family is a person or persons who became American not by birth, but by choice." Remarks at a Reagan-Bush Rally in Elizabeth, New Jersey (July 26, 1984).

1373 "[W]hat distinguished these groups of immigrants [who came to America] is that they yielded more than their share of genius. In fact, you might say that Ellis Island was one big incubator for American greatness. All of these immigrants ... changed our country by adding to the sum total of what we are. They did not take from, they added to." Remarks at the Annual Dinner of the National Italian Foundation (September 15, 1984).

1374 "Only those who most yearned for freedom would make the terrible trek that it took to get here. America has drawn the stoutest hearts from every corner of the world, from every nation of the world. And that was lucky for America, because if it was going to endure and grow and protect its freedoms for 200 years, it was going to need stout hearts." Remarks at Naturalization Ceremonies for New United States Citizens in Detroit, Michigan (October 1, 1984).

1375 "So, you know, every now and then academics talk about assimilation and how various ethnic groups have, with time, dropped their ethnicity and become more 'American.' Well, I don't know about that. It seems to me that America is constantly reinventing what 'America' means. We adopt this country's phrases and that country's art, and I think it's really closer to the truth to say that America has assimilated as much as her immigrants have. It's made for a delightful diversity, and it's made us stronger and a more vital nation." Remarks at Naturalization Ceremonies for New United States Citizens in Detroit, Michigan (October 1, 1984).

1376 "Of all the things that a President does, nothing is as rewarding as events such as this [a naturalization ceremony]. This is a ceremony of renewal. With you, today the American dream is reborn." Remarks at Naturalization Ceremonies for New United States Citizens in Detroit, Michigan (October 1, 1984).

1377 "We Americans come from many lands; we represent just about every race, religion, and ethnic group that's found on this planet. We take pride in our family heritage, passing it on to our children.... Yet, what keeps us together, what cements our national unity, is our abiding love freedom. And I think that's what America is all about." Remarks to the Heritage Council in Warren, Michigan (October 10, 1984).

1378 "America is committed to the world because so much of the world is inside America. After all, only a few miles from this very room [the General Assembly Hall at the United Nations] is our Statue of Liberty, past which life began anew for millions, where the peoples from nearly every country in this hall joined to build these United States. The blood of each nation courses through the American vein and feeds the spirit that compels us to involve ourselves in the fate of this good Earth." Address to the 40th Session of the United Nations General Assembly in New York, New York (October 24, 1985).

1379 "Diversity is one of our great strengths. This is partly why we're confusing to outsiders." Radio Address to the Nation and the World on the Upcoming Soviet–United States Summit Meeting in Geneva (November 9, 1985).

1380 "[E]very time we swear in a new citizen, America is rededicating herself to the cause of human liberty." Radio Address to the Nation on Independence Day and the Centennial of the Statue of Liberty (July 5, 1986).

1381 "Distance has not discouraged illegal immigration to the United States from all around the globe. The problem of illegal immigration should not, therefore, be seen as a problem between the United States and its neighbors. Our objective is only to establish a reasonable, fair, orderly, and secure system of immigration into this country and not to discriminate in any way against particular nations or people." Remarks on Signing the Immigration Reform and Control Act of 1986 (November 6, 1986).

1382 "Future generations of Americans will be thankful for our efforts to humanely regain control of our borders and thereby preserve the value of one of the most sacred possessions of our people: American citizenship." Remarks on Signing the Immigration Reform and Control Act of 1986 (November 6, 1986).

1383 "[I] think that the Federal Government has a part that is played in this, and not a good part — that we have come to the point where we're talking about teaching both languages and teaching students in their native language, instead of what the move should be if they're going to be in America: They have to learn our language in order to get along. And I will do anything that I can to help to get rid of any Federal interference that is trying to force local school districts to continue teaching students in their native tongue. Their job is to teach them English." Remarks to the National Governors' Association — Department of Education Conference in Columbia, Missouri (March 26, 1987).

1384 "Look at us; we've crossed all those borders. We're a melting pot, and we've found out we're all human beings, and it works." Remarks to Participants in the People to People International Youth Exchange Program (June 24, 1987).

1385 "[T]his great nation of ours is made up of immigrants, immigrants who have brought their culture, their traditions, and their values. They were attracted to this nation by a common element: by the love of liberty and justice." Remarks on Signing the National Hispanic Heritage Week Proclamation (September 11, 1987).

1386 "I received a letter from a man one day. He pointed out something I had never thought of. He said, 'You can go to live in France; you cannot become a Frenchman. You can go to live in Germany or Spain, and you cannot become a German or a Spaniard.' And he went on, naming Japan, China, and other countries. But he said, 'Anyone from any corner of the world can come to America and become an American.' And this country is the only one you can say has that peculiar melding of people together, revealing as no other area ever has, that we are all the sons and daughters of God." Remarks to the Students and Faculty of Archbishop Carroll and All Saints High Schools (October 17, 1988).

INTERNATIONAL RELATIONS

1387 "God made Mexico and the United States neighbors, but it is our duty and the duty of generations yet to come to make sure that we remain friends." Remarks at the Welcoming Ceremony for President José López Portillo of Mexico (June 8, 1981).

1388 "Canadians and citizens of the United States are more than neighbors; we're friends in the truest and deepest meaning of the word." Remarks at a White House Luncheon for the National Hockey League All-Stars (February 8, 1982).

1389 "[T]he people of the Caribbean and Central America are in a fundamental sense fellow Americans. Freedom is our common destiny. And freedom cannot survive if our neighbors live in misery and oppression. In short, we must do it (provide economic support) because we're doing it for each other." Remarks to the Permanent Council of the Organization of American States (February 24, 1982).

1390 "Our countries [the United States and the countries of Central America] are neighbors, linked geographically, politically, economically, culturally, and strategically. We have our differences, as neighbors always do, but we can deal directly with and manage these differences because we're neighbors." Remarks at a Celebration Sponsored by the Caribbean Basin Initiative Coalition (July 21, 1982).

1391 We [the United States and Mexico] have every reason to be proud of the distinct cultural traditions of our two peoples. Yet our differences need never diminish our good will and our respect for one another because good will and mutual respect always should be the hallmark of relations between the United States and Mexico." Remarks Following Meetings with President Miguel de la Madrid Hurtado of Mexico in La Paz (August 14, 1983).

1392 "It's our sacred responsibility to see that Central America does not become a string of anti-

American, Marxist dictatorships." Remarks at a Fundraising Reception for Representative Robert J. Lagomarsino in Santa Barbara, California (August 26, 1983).

1393   "Japan and America are separated by thousands of miles of oceans, different languages, and different cultures, yet in our robust trade — everything from food to computers — we've found a way to help each other create abundance." Remarks at a Reception for American and Japanese Businessmen in Tokyo, Japan (November 10, 1983).

1394   "We [America and Japan] are like climbers who begin their ascents from opposite ends of the mountain. The harder we try, the higher we climb and the closer we come together — until that moment we reach the peak and we are as one." Address Before the Japanese Diet in Tokyo (November 11, 1983).

1395   "I have not come to China to hold forth on what divides us, but to build on what binds us. I have not come to dwell on a closed-door past, but to urge that Americans and Chinese look to the future, because together we can and will make tomorrow a better way." Remarks to Chinese Community Leaders in Bejing, China (April 27, 1984).

1396   "The United States and Mexico have a common border and a common American heritage as well. The people of our countries ... represent the values and culture of the new world...." Remarks at the Welcoming ceremony for President Miguel de la Madrid Hurtado of Mexico (May 15, 1984).

1397   "We value deeply our close friendship with Japan. As economic powers and as democratic nations, we're committed to the search for peace and prosperity for our own people and for all people. As leaders of two great nations, we have the mutual responsibility to work together in partnership to help people throughout the world secure the blessings of freedom and prosperity that we enjoy." Remarks Following Discussions with Prime Minister Yasuhiro Nakasone of Japan in Los Angeles, California. (January 2, 1985).

1398   "[F]ree and democratic government is the birthright of every citizen of this hemisphere. The Americas should be, and by right of heritage, ought to be populated by free and independent people." Remarks at the Western Hemisphere Legislative Leaders Forum (January 24, 1985).

1399   "I cannot overstate the value America places on our friendship with Australia. We share a commitment to democratic ideals. In fact, at the heart of our election process is the secret ballot, which, by no coincidence, was referred to as the Australian ballot when it was first introduced into our country." Remarks Following Discussions with Prime Minister Robert Hawke of Australia (February 7, 1985).

1400   "Australia is a reliable ally, an important trading partner, a trusted friend, and a fellow democracy. We've stood together through trials and tribulations. We've rejoiced together in triumph." Remarks Following Discussions with Prime Minister Robert Hawke of Australia (February 7, 1985).

1401   "[T]he United States and the United Kingdom are bound together by inseparable ties of ancient history and present friendship. Our language, our law — even though you do use our language with an accent, our law, our democratic system of government, and our fierce belief in the God-given right of all men to be free — all of these the United States shares with your proud island." Toasts of the President and Prime Minister Margaret Thatcher of the United Kingdom at a Dinner at the British Embassy (February 20, 1985).

1402   "Our two countries [the United States and Great Britain] are bound together by innumerable ties of ancient history and present friendship. Our language, our law, our democratic system of government, our fierce belief in the God-given right of men to be free — all of these we owe to you." Toasts at a White House Dinner for the Prince and Princess of Wales (March 9, 1985).

1403   "No country is more important to the United States [than Canada]. Sometimes we overlook that fact." Radio Address to the Nation on the Upcoming Trip to Canada (March 16, 1985).

1404   "Perhaps nowhere in the world is the contrast between our [the United States and Korea] shared democratic values and communism clearer than it is there on the DMZ. And nowhere is it clearer that strength is the surest path to peace." Remarks Following Discussions with President Chun Doo-hwan of the Republic of Korea (April 26, 1985).

1405   "Ours is an increasingly productive re-lationship based not on personality or momentary concerns, but on a recognition that our nations share significant common interests and an under-standing of the many benefits we've reaped from the good will between us. Now, this doesn't mean that there are no areas of disagreement; however, we will continue to put any differences in per-spective." Remarks at the Welcoming Ceremony for President Li Xiannian of China (July 23, 1985).

1406   "As free peoples, it is unthinkable that the Japanese and Americans will ever again go to war. Where there are differences, as there are in the relations of any two great nations, they can be settled in the spirit of good will." Radio Address to the Nation on the 40th Anniversary of the End of the Second World War in the Pacific (August 10, 1985).

1407   "As a genuinely nonaligned nation, Singapore is independent and beholden to no country; we respect this.... We also admire that, although nonaligned and independent, you have demonstrated a sense of responsibility that few can match — playing a constructive role in the world community of nations and in the Asian-Pacific region." Remarks at the Welcoming Cer-emony for Prime Minister Lee Kuan Yew of Sin-gapore (October 8, 1985).

1408   "Our citizens have grown to expect positive relations between Canada and the United States; however, I would suggest that we must never take our friendship for granted. It must be fostered and nurtured to keep it strong, vibrant, and relative to those areas which most interest our peoples." Remarks at the Welcoming Ceremony for Prime Minister Brian Mulroney of Canada (March 18, 1986).

1409   "Our countries [the United States and Australia] share many historical experiences: our love of democracy, our frontier heritage, and our common defense of freedom from the First and Second World Wars through Korea and Vietnam. All this had nurtured the bonds of friendship be-tween our two peoples." Remarks Following Dis-cussions with Prime Minister Robert Hawke of Australia (April 17, 1986).

1410   "Canada and the United States, as you see, share much more than a common border; we share a democratic tradition, and we share the

hopes, dreams, and aspirations of free people." Radio Address to the Nation on Canada–United States Relations (April 4, 1987).

1411   "No two countries [the United States and Canada] in the world ... have as great a range of trade and investment exchanges at all levels — from an individual's vacation trip to a mammoth contract for electric power — as the United States and Canada. No two countries trade more with each other. No two countries invest in each other's industry or engage in leisure activities in our neighbor's playgrounds to the extent that we do. And the citizens of both our countries — as busi-nessmen, farmers, workers, and consumers — have benefited accordingly." Remarks at the Welcom-ing Ceremony in Ottawa, Canada (April 5, 1987).

1412   "As two proud and independent peoples [the United States and Canada], there is much that distinguishes us one from the other, but there is also much that we share: a vast con-tinent, with its common hardships and uncom-mon duties; generations of mutual respect and support; and an abiding friendship that grows ever stronger. We are two nations, each built by im-migrant refugees from tyranny and want, pioneers of a new land of liberty." Address to a Joint Ses-sion of Parliament in Ottawa, Canada (April 6, 1987).

1413   "[T]here's an unseen bridge that spans the vast Pacific, a bridge built by the hard work, commercial genius, and productive powers of our two peoples [the United States and Japan]. We must strive to see that it is maintained in good order and is traveled with equal intensity in both directions, carrying the goods and services that improve lives and increase happiness." Remarks at the Welcoming Ceremony for Prime Minister Yasuhiro Nakasone of Japan (April 30, 1987).

1414   "As a neutral nation, Sweden is not an ally of the United States, but it is a partner in our pursuit of a free and peaceful world. We recognize and appreciate that Sweden provides amply for its own strong defense and works vigorously for the cause of peace. We respect that ... even though on some issues we may differ in views." Remarks at the Welcoming Ceremony for Prime Minister Ing-var Carlsson of Sweden (September 9, 1987).

1415   "Sweden and America share the same basic vales and the same hopes for a more peaceful and prosperous world. We often pursue our similar goals through different means, but our democratic traditions have bred in us both an appreciation for a diversity and an understanding that there is often more than one way to achieve a goal." Toasts at the State Dinner Honoring Prime Minister Ingvar Carlsson of Sweden (September 9, 1987).

1416   "In Canada there are those who fear that their national identity might be damaged by a closer association with such a large country as the United States. Well, experience says otherwise. European countries have for decades cooperated closely on trade, yet the national character of each member nation still remains vital and distinctive. Canada, too, has a national character that will not only survive but flourish in an environment of free trade and expanding opportunity." Radio Address to the Nation on the United States–Canada Free Trade Agreement (January 9, 1988).

1417   "Ours [the United States and Canada] is a relationship of people and their ability to hold personal relationships across a national border. They form them easily and quickly, in good times and during times of stress." Remarks at the Welcoming Ceremony for Prime Minister Brian Mulroney of Canada (April 27, 1988).

1418   "The essence and the strength of the relations between our two countries [the United States and Canada] are people. Our people naturally get along well together. We share our triumphs and victories as we share our adversities. And when at times we spar, we do so without rancor, and we work out our differences." Toasts at the State Dinner for Prime Minister Brian Mulroney of Canada (April 27, 1988).

INTERNATIONAL TRADE

Free Trade

1419   "When governments get too involved in trade, economic costs increase and political disputes multiple. Peace is threatened." Radio Address to the Nation on International Free Trade (November 20, 1982).

1420   "[A]merica must be an unrelenting advocate of free trade. As some nations are tempted to turn to protectionism, our strategy cannot be to follow them, but to lead the way toward freer trade." Address Before a Joint Session of the Congress on the State of the Union (January 25, 1983).

1421   "[T]he freer the flow of trade across borders, the greater the world economic progress and the greater the impetus for world peace." Remarks and a Question-and-Answer Session with Members of the Commonwealth Club of California in San Francisco (March 4, 1983).

1422   "We can improve the well-being of our people, and we can enhance the forces for democracy, freedom, peace, and human fulfillment around the world, if we stand up for principles of trade expansion through freer markets and greater competition among nations." Remarks and a Question-and-Answer Session with Members of the Commonwealth Club in San Francisco (March 4, 1983).

1423   "We believe in free trade, but we're no longer going to play patsy for those who would use this commitment as leverage against us. Free trade means access for those trading with us and it also means access for Americans to their markets, those foreign markets." Remarks to Department of Agriculture Employees on National Agriculture Day (March 21, 1983).

1424   "Free trade is in all our interests, but because of foreign subsidies and protections, our farmers are being pitted against the economic strengths of the national treasuries of other countries. All nations, particularly our friends in Europe and Japan, must be made to understand that trade is a two-way proposition." Remarks at the Weeries Family Farm in Chopin, Illinois (October 20, 1982).

1425   "The winds and waters of commerce carry opportunities that help nations grow and bring citizens of the world closer together. Put simply, increased trade spells more jobs, higher earnings, better products, less inflation, and cooperation over confrontation." Radio Address to the Nation on International Trade (August 6, 1983).

1426   "America's future growth and prosperity depend on how well we develop and compete in foreign markets." Remarks at the Presentation Ceremony for the President's "E" and "E Star" [Excellence in Exporting] Awards (May 23, 1984).

1427   "Yes, we believe in free trade, but only if it's fair trade." Remarks at an Agricultural Forum in Decatur, Illinois (August 20, 1984).

1428   "We know that if America wants more jobs, greater prosperity, and a dynamic, competitive economy, the answer is more world trade, not less." Remarks on Signing the Trade and Tariff Act of 1984 (October 30, 1984).

1429   "Like the global economy, our national economies benefit from freedom and suffer in its absence." Remarks to Community Leaders in Madrid, Spain (May 7, 1985).

1430   "We can either balance the trade deficit up by encouraging our trading partners to adopt the high-growth policies of tax cuts and open markets, or we can balance down by adopting the no-growth policies of tax hikes and protectionism. The choice is clear. Let's take the high road to prosperity by fighting for an open, free, and fair trading system with our economic partners and by encouraging them to adopt low tax, high employment growth policies." Radio Address to the Nation on Free and Fair Trade (September 7, 1985).

1431   "We do not seek an America that is closed to the world; we seek a world that is open to America. We do not dream of protecting America from others' success; we seek to include everyone in the success of the American dream."

Radio Address to the Nation on the Farm Industry (September 14, 1985).

1432   "Above all else, free trade is, by definition, fair trade. When domestic markets are closed to the exports of others, it is no longer free trade. When governments subsidize their manufacturers and farmers so that they can dump goods in other markets, it is no longer free trade. When governments permit counterfeiting or copying of American products, it is stealing our future, and it is no longer free trade. When governments assist their exporters in ways that violate international laws, then the playing field is no longer level, and there is no longer free trade. When governments subsidize industries for commercial advantage and underwrite costs, placing an unfair burden on competitors, that is not free trade." Remarks at a White House Meeting with Business and Trade Leaders (September 23, 1985).

1433   "And the way to correct the trade imbalance is not to decrease imports but to increase exports. Rather than erect trade barriers of our own, let's go to work dismantling those obstacles in other countries. Let's balance up and not down. And that way everyone is better off." Remarks at a Senate Campaign Fundraiser for Former Governor Christopher S. (Kit) Bond in St. Louis, Missouri (February 12, 1986).

1434   "There is no reason to doubt America's ability to compete, no reason to lack confidence in our working men and women and our corporate leaders. When everyone plays with the same rules, our people have what it takes: the ingenuity, the hard work, and the integrity to compete with anyone, anytime, anywhere." Radio Address to the Nation on the President's Trip to Indonesia and Japan (May 4, 1986).

1435   "The main question is not how to shelter the American economy but how to bring it into still wider contact with the rest of the world; not how to protect it from competition but how to release our boundless talent, creativity, and know-how so that America comes out of the competition a winner." Remarks at a White House Briefing for Trade Association Representatives on Free and Fair Trade (July 17, 1986).

1436   "[O]ur motto is: free and fair trade with free and fair traders." Radio Address to the Nation on Free and Fair Trade (August 2, 1986).

1437 "No nation can expect to continue freely exporting to others if its own domestic markets are closed to foreign competition. Prosperity must be built not at the expense of others, but on the principle of mutual benefit." Remarks at the Welcoming Ceremony for President Jose Sarney Costa of Brazil (September 10, 1986).

1438 "Our country is also victimized by the international theft of American creativity. Too many countries turn a blind eye when their citizens violate patent and copyright laws designed to protect intellectual property rights. If we permit the product of our best minds to be stolen, we will pay the price in ingenuity, vision, and creativity—the core of all human progress." Radio Address to the Nation on Free and Fair Trade (September 13, 1986).

1439 "Our fundamental belief in the power of the market remains unquestioned. We will not sit idly by when other countries close their markets to our products, subsidize their exports, or fail to trade fairly." Remarks to Business Leaders at a White House Briefing on Economic Competitiveness (February 17, 1987).

1440 "It's no good being the tallest one around just because everybody else is flat on his back. And we went to great lengths with the Marshall plan ... to help other nations [after World War II] get back on their economic feet. But, yes, this new prosperity on the part of other nations does involve certain challenges. By the way, I'd like to stress that I used the word 'challenges,' not 'threats.' Threats are something you need to beat back; challenges are something you can rise to." Radio Address to the Nation on Economic Competitiveness (February 21, 1987).

1441 "As I've often said: Our commitment to free trade is also a commitment to fair trade." Radio Address to the Nation on Free and Fair Trade (April 25, 1987).

1442 "The best way to meet foreign competition is also the right way: by sticking to our agreements with other countries and not breaking our promises, by making sure other countries also stick to their agreements with us, and by being the best." Remarks to Harley-Davidson Company Employees in York, Pennsylvania (May 6, 1987).

1443 "This profound movement in recent years toward more limited government and freer trade has not only kept the global economy moving along at a steady pace, it's made it possible for the democratic nations to stand together and keep our defenses strong, while we promote the growth of democratic institutions in the world spread of freedom and peace." Remarks and a Question-and-Answer Session with Economic Reporters (June 16, 1987).

1444 "[A]nd the United States cannot and will not allow itself to become party to a trade war." Remarks to Reporters on the Proposed International Trade Bill (June 19, 1987).

1445 "Trade and commerce are the lifeblood of job creation. The flow of goods and services between countries and peoples is a stimulus to growth and prosperity. This isn't a time for us to be afraid, to be erecting barriers, or to be trying to shut out the world. Instead, we should be working to open markets, to increase our productivity, and to meet the competition head-on. And don't let anyone tell you we can't do it." Radio Address to the Nation on Free and Fair Trade (September 5, 1987).

1446 "I believe that the birth of a truly global economy, such as we're seeing happen now, will mark the birth of a new age of peace." Remarks at the Swearing-In Ceremony for C. William Verity, Jr., as Secretary of Commerce (October 19, 1987).

1447 "[S]ome time ago—way back in those prehistoric times known as the seventies—I called for what I named a North American accord that would embrace our whole continent—the United States, Canada, and Mexico.... I said then that it's time we stopped thinking of our nearest neighbors as foreigners. Let us instead think of them as partners, independent and sovereign, but united in a common purpose. Unity, I need hardly say, does not imply homogeneity. In a true alliance of friendship, the differences—the unique characters and national identities of our northern and southern neighbors—would only broaden our understanding and strengthen the mandate of freedom." Remarks to Business Leaders at a White House Briefing on the Canada–United States Free Trade Agreement (November 4, 1987).

1448 "What the world and the United States need now is more trade and more open trade." Remarks to Business Leaders at a White House Briefing on International Trade (March 11, 1988).

1449 "I can't think of a recent economic issue that has generated more heat and less light, yet has more importance to our long-term national interest, than trade." Radio Address to the Nation on International Trade (March 12, 1988).

1450 "Part of the difficulty in accepting the good news about trade is in our words. We too often talk about trade while using the vocabulary of war. In war, for one side to win, the other must lose. But commerce is not warfare. Trade is an economic alliance that benefits both countries. There are no losers, only winners. And trade helps strengthen the free world." Radio Address to the Nation on the Canadian Elections and Free Trade (November 26, 1988).

Protectionism

1451 "It's imperative that all of us work together to reduce the growing tide of protectionism and export subsidies overseas. If other countries can't understand an evenhanded approach is in everybody's best interest, if they're not willing to play by the rules of the game, then let there be no mistake: We must and we will counter with strong measures of our own to permit American farmers to realize the benefits of their extraordinary productivity." Radio Address to the Nation on Agriculture and Grain Exports (October 15, 1982).

1452 "We're in the same boat with our trading partners. If one partner shoots a hole in the boat, does it make sense for the other one to shoot another hole in the boat? Some say, yes, and call it getting tough. Well, I call it stupid. We shouldn't be shooting holes; we should be working together to plug them up. We must strengthen the boat of free markets and fair trade so it can lead the world to economic recovery and greater political stability." Radio Address to the Nation on International Trade (November 20, 1982).

1453 "Free trade can only survive if all parties play by the same rules.... Defending workers in industries from unfair and predatory trade practices is not protectionism, it's legitimate action under U.S. and international law." Remarks and a Question-and-Answer Session with Members of the Commonwealth Club in San Francisco (March 4, 1983).

1454 "Protectionism only opens the door to retaliation. We would buy less from our partners, they would buy less from us. The world economic pie would shrink and political tensions would multiply." Remarks and a Question-and-Answer Session During a United States Chamber of Commerce Teleconference (May 10, 1983).

1455 "Protectionism is not a problem solver; it is a problem creator. Protectionism invites retaliation. It means you will buy less from your trading partner, they will buy less from you, the world economic pie will shrink, and the danger of political turmoil will increase." Remarks at the Annual Meeting of the Boards of Governors of the World Bank Group and the International Monetary Fund (September 27, 1983).

1456 "We oppose protectionism because, like so many other forms of government intervention, it doesn't work. Protectionism brings higher prices, it provokes retaliation, and it insulates inefficiencies in production." Remarks at the Presentation Ceremony for the President's "E" and "E Star" [Excellence in Exporting] Awards (May 23, 1984).

1457 "The lessons of history are clear. The costs of protectionism for one group would automatically be passed on to another. Inflation would be reignited, jobs would be destroyed, not saved, and foreign countries would retaliate against our exporters, like our farmers. And America doesn't need that kind of help." Radio Address to the Nation on Agricultural and Steel Industries (September 22, 1984).

1458 "[A] blunderbuss approach of quotas and trade barriers, encouraging stagnation by stifling competition, is not the way to a better future. It's a giant step back into the misery of a failed past." Remarks at the Timken Faircrest Steel Plant in Canton, Ohio (September 26, 1984).

1459 "Protectionism almost always ends up making the protected industry weaker and less able to compete against foreign imports." Radio Address to the Nation on Free and Fair Trade (August 31, 1985).

1460 "Our objective will always be to make world trading partnerships freer and fairer for all. So, while we will use our powers as a lever to open closed doors abroad, we will continue to resist protectionist measures that would only raise prices, lock out trade, and destroy the jobs and prosperity trade brings to all. There are no winners in a trade war, only losers." Radio Address to the Nation on Free and Fair Trade (September 7, 1985).

1461   "[T]here's another path that can only lead away from opportunity and progress: A mindless stampede toward protectionism will be a one-way trip to economic disaster. That's the lesson of the Smoot-Hawley tariff in 1930, which helped to trigger a worldwide trade war that spread, deepened, and prolonged the worst depression in history. And I know; I lived through that period. I've seen and felt the agony this nation endured because of that dreadful legislation. If we repeat that same mistake, we'll pay a price again." The President's News Conference [prepared statement] (September 17, 1985).

1462   "Now is not the time to be closing markets and retreating; now is the time to let the world know we mean business. The era of the all-providing, never-complaining America is over. Fair trade means fair trade for us, too. I don't care if we're talking about microchips, potatoes, chemicals, or any other product. It has to be free, fair, and open trade for all." Remarks at a Fundraising Event for Senator Steven D. Symms in Boise, Idaho (October 15, 1985).

1463   "The solution we seek is not decreasing what others send us, but increasing what we send them. Balancing the trade deficit up means a better life for all. Balancing it down through protectionism and weaker economic growth means stagnation and decline. I firmly believe that if the deck is not stacked against us, the American people can outproduce and outcompete anyone in the world." Remarks at a Fundraising Luncheon for Senator Slade Gorton in Seattle, Washington (December 2, 1985).

1464   "Protectionist moves basically profit special interests at the expense of the consumer and at the risk of retaliation — costing Americans their jobs." Remarks to the International Forum of the Chamber of Commerce of the United States (April 23, 1986).

1465   "[E]ver since the disaster of the 1930 Smoot-Hawley tariffs, we've known that protectionism doesn't work. No, the way to promote worldwide prosperity is not to erect barriers, but

to bring them down; not to decrease international trade, but to expand it." Remarks at a White House Ceremony for World Trade Week and the "E" and "E Star" Awards (May 19, 1986).

1466   "No one who has lived through or learned the lessons of this century doubts how dangerous it is to play a game of chicken with our trading partners. Because it won't be long until we're both driving over that cliff." Remarks to the Annual Meeting of the National Association of Manufacturers (May 29, 1986).

1467   "[I]nternational trade is one of those issues that politicians find an unending source of temptation. Like a 5-cent cigar or a chicken in every pot, demanding high tariffs or import restrictions is a familiar bit of flimflammery in American politics." Radio Address to the Nation on International Trade (June 29, 1986).

1468   "Yes, there is such a thing as unfair trade, but you don't fix it by inviting our trading partners to take a snipe at American agriculture." Remarks at the Illinois State Fair in Springfield (August 12, 1986).

1469   "Our basic trade policy remains the same: We remain opposed as ever to protectionism, because America's growth and future depend on trade. But we would insist on trade that is fair and free. We are always willing to be trade partners but never trade patsies." Address Before a Joint Session of Congress on the State of the Union (January 27, 1987).

1470   "Yes, we have a trade deficit that's too big, and part of the reason is unfair trading practices. But, no, the way to solve that is not to lash out at our trading partners." Remarks at the 75th Annual Meeting of the United States Chamber of Commerce (April 27, 1987).

1471   "Well, the way up and out of the trade deficit is not protectionism, not bringing down the competition, but instead the answer lies in improving our products and increasing our exports. The Government should work to create the conditions in which trade will flourish." Radio Address to the Nation on Free and Fair Trade and the Budget Deficit (May 16, 1987).

1472   "Our countries should move forward to end unsustainable trade imbalances, to reform agricultural policies, and restore stability to the international currency markets. The major economic powers of the world must also work to eliminate inequities in the international trade environment to keep markets open and to keep commerce flowing. Economic growth and free markets are everybody's business." Remarks on Departure for the Venice Economic Summit (June 3, 1987).

1473   "[A]ll nations must resist calls for protectionism. So-called protectionism is like the evil of drugs: It will end up destroying all those who use it. And that's why I call it destructionism, because all it does is slow growth, wipe out jobs, and close the door on progress." Address to Western Europe from the Venice Economic Summit (June 5, 1987).

1474   "Well, restricting trade in the long run is bad for everybody, especially for the working people of America. Protecting one domestic industry risks retaliation against another." Radio Address to the Nation on Free and Fair Trade (September 5, 1987).

1475   "Protectionism destroys jobs. It destroys growth. It undermines the entire global economy, and it undermines our own economy." Remarks at the Swearing-In Ceremony for C. William Verity, Jr., as Secretary of Commerce (October 19, 1987).

1476   "A creative, competitive America is the answer to a changing world, not trade wars that would close doors, create greater barriers, and destroy millions of jobs. We should always remember: Protectionism is destructionism. America's jobs, America's growth, America's future depend

on trade — trade that is free, open, and fair." Address Before a Joint Session of Congress on the State of the Union (January 25, 1988).

1477   "[S]ort of summing it all up, a kind of golden rule, don't pass any trade law that we wouldn't want another nation to pass in just the same form, regulating Americans who do business there. The golden rule — it's not a bad way to do business, in the home or in the marketplace, around the world." Remarks to Business Leaders at a White House Briefing on International Trade (March 1, 1988).

1478   "Legislation can reduce a trade deficit only if it reduces economic activity. If people are not working, they're not trading." Radio Address to the Nation on International Trade (March 12, 1988).

1479   "Government can create opportunities by knocking down unfair barriers, but businesses themselves must follow through with the proposals, creativity, and workmanship that made America the leader in this field [large scale public works projects]." Remarks at a White House Meeting with the Associated General Contractors of America (April 18, 1988).

1480   "Protectionism has no future; it's a dead and discredited idea. In a global economy, there can be no surer way of impoverishing ourselves than to try to make America go it alone, by cutting us off from trade and investment with the other countries of the world." Remarks to the American Coalition for Trade Expansion with Canada (June 16, 1988).

ISRAEL AND THE MIDDLE EAST

1481   "Israel and America may be thousands of miles apart, but we are philosophical neighbors

sharing a strong commitment to democracy and the rule of law." Remarks at the Welcoming Ceremony for Prime Minister Menachem Begin of Israel (September 9, 1981).

1482   "Our dream, our challenge, and, yes, our mission, is to make the golden age of peace, prosperity, and brotherhood a living reality in all countries of the Middle East." Remarks at the Welcoming Ceremony for Prime Minister Menachem Begin of Israel (September 9, 1981).

1483   "Our involvement in the search for Mideast peace is not a matter of preference; it's a moral imperative." Address to the Nation on United States Policy for Peace in the Middle East (September 1, 1982)

1484   "[T]he security of all the states in the area can only be guaranteed through freely negotiated peace treaties between Israel and its neighbors." Remarks to Reporters on Lebanon and the Middle East (September 8, 1982).

1485   "No people have fought longer, struggled harder, or sacrificed more to survive, to grow, and to live in freedom than the people of Israel." Remarks at the Jewish Community Center of Greater Washington During the Observance of Hanukkah (December 4, 1983).

1486   "Whether we be Americans or Israelis, we are all children of Abraham, children of the same God. The bonds between our two peoples are growing stronger, and they must not and will never be broken." Remarks at the Jewish Community Center of Greater Washington During the Observance of Hanukkah (December 4, 1983).

1487   "[A]merica will stand by her friends. And this is especially true concerning our commitment to the one Western-style democracy in the Middle East, the state of Israel. There have been moves afoot to kick Israel out of the United Nations. And let me just say one thing and make it very plain: If Israel is ever forced to leave the United Nations, we will leave together." Remarks at a New York Republican Party Fundraising Dinner (March 6, 1984).

1488   "[T]he strength and well-being of the United States and Israel are bound inextricably together." Remarks at the International Convention of B'nai B'rith (September 6, 1984).

1489   "Israel and the United States are bound together by the ties of family, friendship, shared ideals, and mutual interests. We're allies in the de-

fense of freedom in the Middle East." Remarks to Members of the Congregation of Temple Hillel and Jewish Community Leaders in Valley Stream, New York (October 26, 1984)

1490   "Israelis and Americans can be proud of the relationship between our two countries. The common values and interests that bring us together sustain us both, and the many levels of cooperation between us provide a rich substance to our ties. We look forward to building on the good will and trust so evident between our governments and peoples." Remarks Following Discussions with Prime Minister Shimon Peres of Israel (September 15, 1986).

1491   "Our deep commitment to Israel's security is one with our commitment to freedom of religion in our own country. Underlying both are the unchanging moral and spiritual values to which Jews and Judaism continue to make an incalculable contribution." Message on the Observance of the Jewish High Holy Days (October 3, 1986).

1492   "[T]he road to peace lies through bilateral negotiations between Israel and its neighbors, including representative Palestinians." Remarks Following Meetings with Prime Minister Yitzhak Shamir of Israel (February 18, 1987).

1493   "The United States and Israel share many common values and traditions. We have developed a warm friendship that encompasses close mutual and strategic cooperation. This relationship, in which each gives special consideration to the other's interests, strengthens us both. It's unshakable, and we're proud of it." Remarks Following Meetings with Prime Minister Yitzhak Shamir of Israel (February 18, 1987).

1494   "Our goal is to seek peace rather than provocation, but our interests and those of our friends must be preserved. We're in the gulf to protect our national interests and, together with our allies, the interests of the entire Western World. Peace is at stake; our national interest is at stake. And we will not repeat the mistakes of the past. Weakness, a lack of resolve and strength, will only encourage those who seek to use the flow of oil as a tool, a weapon, to cause the American people hardship at home, incapacitate us abroad, and promote conflict and violence throughout the Middle East and the world." Remarks on United States Policy in the Persian Gulf (May 29, 1987).

1495   "Our wider role in the Middle East — perhaps more than in any other region — is that of peacemaker. We are doing our best to help narrow the differences between Israel and her Arab neighbors so that real negotiations for peace can get started. The desire for peace and the will to make peace are growing in the region. Our job is to help." Radio Address to the Nation on Foreign Policy (October 17, 1987).

1496   "We share the conviction that Israel can be secure and realize its full promise and genius only when security and lasting peace are achieved. The United States remains undeterred in the quest for such a peace, a negotiated settlement of the Arab-Israeli conflict that would assure the security and well-being of the people of Israel and its Arab neighbors. That goal will be realized when people of good will from all sides find a way to bridge a crevasse of hatred and distrust." Remarks at the Welcoming Ceremony for President Chaim Herzog of Israel (November 10, 1987).

1497   "We know what Israel is. We know what Israel means. And as I will tell the Prime Minister tomorrow, when it comes to Israel, the United States is not a bargainer or a broker: The United States is a friend and an ally." Remarks to Supporters of Israel at a White House Briefing on United States Foreign Policy (March 15, 1988).

1498   "And let me underscore one point that I hope needs no underscoring: Our policy has as its basis — and this is a first principle in any negotiation — the assuring of Israel's freedom and security. We will not leave Israel to stand alone, nor will we acquiesce in any effort to gang up on Israel. Peace will not be imposed by us or by anyone else. It will and must come from the genuine give-and-take of negotiations." Remarks to Supporters of Israel at a White House Briefing on United States Foreign Policy (March 15, 1988).

1499   "We must defend ourselves against the evil of totalitarianism. We must follow his example and never waver in our pursuit of justice, never waver in our pursuit of resolve. We must remain strong, and we must be willing to use force when we're under threat. This is a lesson that binds us still closer to the State of Israel, for the fact is: a strong Israel depends upon a strong America. An America that loses faith in the idea of a strong defense is an America that will lose faith in a nation at arms like Israel." Remarks at the Simon Wiesenthal Center Awards Presentation Ceremony in Los Angeles, California (October 30, 1988).

JUDICIARY

Rule of Law

1500   "Our very freedom is secure because we're a nation governed by laws, not men. We have the means to change the laws if they become unjust or onerous. We cannot, as citizens, pick and choose the laws we will or will not obey." Remarks in Chicago, Illinois, at the Annual Convention and Centennial Observance of the United Brotherhood of Carpenters and Joiners (September 3, 1981).

1501   "Our heritage of individual liberty is dependent on the rule of law." Remarks at a White House Reception for District and Appellate Court Judges and Supreme Court Justices (September 24, 1981).

1502   "Any progress that our generation has brought to our people and to the world rests on the foundation of law and justice laid by earlier generations of Americans, beginning with those courageous, far-sighted individuals who two centuries ago had the faith to believe that men and women could live in freedom under law." Remarks on Signing Proclamation 4931, Proclaiming Law Day U.S.A., 1982 (April 16, 1982).

1503 "Law is the handmaiden of liberty, essential to preserving order in freedom." Remarks at the Annual Meeting of the American Bar Association in Atlanta, Georgia (August 1, 1983).

1504 "The rule of law represents the civil discourse of a free people. Crime is the uncivilized shout that threatens to drown out and ultimately silence the language of liberty." Remarks at the Annual Meeting of the American Bar Association in Atlanta, Georgia (August 1, 1983).

1505 "Our commitment to freedom has meant commitment to the rule of law, and commitment to the law has created opportunity...." Remarks at the Annual Meeting of the American Bar Association in Atlanta, Georgia (August 1, 1983).

1506 "[W]ithout law there can be no freedom, only chaos and disorder. And without freedom, law is but a cynical veneer for injustice and oppression." Remarks on Signing Law Day Proclamation (April 9, 1984).

1507 "[O]ver the years, tort law has helped us drive the malevolent and the negligent out of the marketplace. This, in turn, has permitted legitimate economic innovation to take its course and raise living standards throughout the Nation. More recently, however, tort law began to go terribly wrong. Twisted and abused, tort law has become a pretext for outrageous legal outcomes — outcomes that impede our economic life, not promote it." Remarks to Members of the American Tort Reform Association (May 30, 1986).

1508 "Outlandish court awards have placed tremendous burdens on U.S. companies as they try to compete in an international marketplace. If Congress is serious about enhancing the competitiveness of American firms, it should pass meaningful product liability law reform this year — reform that protects legitimate claims by consumers, but limits the level of awards to reasonable losses." Remarks at the Business Roundtable Annual Dinner (June 22, 1988).

Federal Judiciary

1509 "Those who sit on the Supreme Court interpret the laws of our land and truly leave their footprints on the sands of time. Long after the policies of Presidents and Senators and Congressmen of any given era may have passed away from public memory, they'll be remembered." Remarks Announcing the Intention to Nominate Sandra Day O'Connor to Be an Associate Justice of the Supreme Court of the United States (July 7, 1981).

1510 "Wisdom is the quality we look for most in our judges. In an age of mounting judicial workloads and increasing technicality, we demand of our judges a wisdom that knows no time, has no prejudice, and wants no other reward." Remarks at a White House Reception for District and Appellate Court Judges and Supreme Court Justices (September 24, 1981).

1511 "[T]he Supreme Court of the United States is the only group of ... men and women in history that has exercised significant authority over such a long period of time without having need for battalions of fighting men to enforce their decisions." Remarks at a White House Luncheon for the Supreme Court Justices (October 1, 1982).

1512 "I'll tell you what I believe, and that is that we ought to appoint judges who restore respect for the laws and make criminals think twice before they commit a crime." Remarks at a Reagan-Bush Rally in Cleveland, Ohio (November 2, 1984).

1513 "[I] intend to go right on appointing highly qualified individuals of the highest personal integrity to the bench, individuals who understand the danger of short-circuiting the electoral process and disenfranchising the people through judicial activism. I want judges of the highest intellectual standing who harbor the deepest regard for the Constitution and its traditions, one of which is judicial restraint." Remarks During a White House Briefing for United States Attorneys (October 21, 1985).

1514 "[W]e've sought to appoint judges who look at the law as something to be honored, respected, and interpreted according to legislative intent, not whim or ideology." Radio Address to the Nation on the Federal Judiciary (June 21, 1986).

1515 "[T]oo many judges were taking upon themselves the prerogatives of elected officials. Instead of interpreting the law according to the intent of the Constitution and the Congress, they were simply using the courts to strike down laws that displeased them politically or philosophically. I argued [during the campaign] the need for judges who would interpret law, not make it. The people, through their elected representatives, make our laws; and the people deserve to have these laws enforced as they were written." Radio Address to the Nation on the United States Supreme Court Nominations (August 9, 1986).

1516   "We don't need a bunch of sociology majors on the bench. What we need are strong judges who will aggressively use their authority to protect our families, communities, and our way of life; judges who understand that punishing wrongdoers is our way of protecting the innocent; and judges who do not hesitate to put criminals where they belong — behind bars." Remarks at a Campaign Rally for Senator James T. Broyhill in Raleigh, North Carolina (October 8, 1986).

1517   "The Supreme Court of the United States is the custodian of our Constitution. Justices of the Supreme Court must not only be jurists of the highest competence; they must be attentive to the specific rights guaranteed in our Constitution and proper role of the courts in our democratic system." Remarks Announcing the Nomination of Robert H. Bork to Be an Associate Justice of the Supreme Court of the United States (July 1, 1987).

1518   "The great safeguard of our liberty is the totality of the constitutional system, with no one part getting the upper hand. And that's why the judiciary must be independent. And that's why it also must exercise restraint." Remarks at the "We the People" Bicentennial Celebration in Philadelphia, Pennsylvania (September 17, 1987).

1519   "Too many theorists believe that the courts should save the country from the Constitution. Well, I believe it's time to save the Constitution from them. The principal errors in recent years have had nothing to do with the intent of the framers who finished their work 200 years ago last month. They've had to do with those who have looked upon the courts as their own special province to impose by judicial fiat what they could not accomplish at the polls." Address to the Nation on the Supreme Court Nomination of Robert H. Bork (October 14, 1987).

1520   "The American people do not want judges picked for special interests. They do not want to return to leniency in the courtroom and unsafe streets. They want judges and laws that reflect common sense attitudes about crime. The simple truth is: crime is far too common. Lenient laws and lenient judges have been greatly to blame for it." Remarks at a White House Briefing on Proposed Criminal Justice Reform Legislation (October 16, 1987).

1521   "[T]he proper role of the judiciary is to interpret the laws, not make them." Radio Address to the Nation on the Supreme Court Nomination of Douglas H. Ginsburg and the Federal Budget (October 31, 1987).

1522   "[T]o the extent that judges make the law — no matter how high or fine their intentions — to that extent, we cease to be a democracy governed by the people and become governed instead by the very few. This is not what the Founders like Madison intended. To keep faith with their noble experiment in democracy, to keep faith with the generations of Americans who for two centuries have labored and sacrificed to keep this nation free, American judges must submit themselves to the Constitution and the original intent of those who founded it." Remarks to Ethnic and Minority Administration Supporters on the Supreme Court Nomination of Douglas H. Ginsburg (November 6, 1987).

1523   "[T]he struggle between political parties and political points of view is important, even vital, to the health of the Nation. But the Federal judiciary is not that place. On the contrary, the Federal judiciary must remain impartial in order to command the respect of the Nation and to ensure that we remain governed by laws properly enacted, not by the views of whatever group happens to hold temporary power." Remarks to Ethnic and Minority Administration Supporters on the Supreme Court Nomination of Douglas H. Ginsburg (November 6, 1987).

1524   "[J]udges should interpret the law, not make it — that, in other words, judges should be umpires, not players." Radio Address to the Nation on the Supreme Court Nomination of Anthony M. Kennedy, Central America, and Deficit Reduction (November 14, 1987).

1525   "[A]ny man who teaches law school in a tricorner hat and a powdered wig [U.S. Supreme Court nominee Anthony Kennedy] is okay by me on original intent." Remarks at the Annual Conservative Political Action Conference Dinner (February 11, 1988).

1526   "[T]he role assigned to judges in our system was to interpret the Constitution and lesser laws, not to make them. It was to protect the integrity of the Constitution, not to add to it or subtract from it — certainly not to rewrite it. For as the framers knew, unless judges are bound by the text of the Constitution, we will, in fact, no longer have a government of laws, but of men and women who are judges. And if that happens, the words of the documents that we think govern us will be just masks for the personal and capricious rule of a small elite." Remarks at the Swearing-In Ceremony for Anthony M. Kennedy as an Associate Justice of the Supreme Court of the United States (February 18, 1988).

1527   "If judges don't do their job right, criminals feel like they can run rampant." Remarks at a Republican Campaign Rally in San Diego, California (October 27, 1988).

Judicial Nominations Process

1528   "[T]oo often character assassination has replaced debate in principle here in Washington. Destroy someone's reputation, and you don't have to talk about what he stands for." Remarks at the Annual Meeting of the National Alliance of Business (September 14, 1987).

1529   "Our Founding Fathers intended the courts to be above partisan politics. But in the last few weeks we've seen an attempt to turn the confirmation of a Justice into a partisan issue. No expense has been spared, and we all know the reason. A few special interests consider the courts their private preserve. Communities all over the Nation have seen how these special interests get through the courts what they can't get through the ballot box." Remarks on Signing the German-American Day Proclamation (October 2, 1987).

1530   "[T]he special interests are determined to pack the Supreme Court and to distort the reputation of anyone who disagrees. Some say they're compromising and demeaning the judicial selection process. I hope we haven't come to a time when good men and women are afraid to accept nominations to the bench...." Remarks on Signing

the German-American Day Proclamation (October 2, 1987).

1531   "At stake here [in the Senate confirmation hearings concerning Robert H. Bork's nomination to the U.S. Supreme Court] is the integrity and independence of the American system of justice." Remarks on Signing the German-American Day Proclamation (October 2, 1987).

1532   "[L]iberal special interest groups seek to politicize the court system; to exercise a chilling effect on judges; to intimidate them into making decisions, not on the basis of the law or the merits of the case, but on the basis of a litmus test or a response to political pressure." Radio Address to the Nation on Voluntarism and the Supreme Court Nomination of Robert H. Bork (October 3, 1987).

1533   "They [liberal special interest groups] are determined to thwart the desire of the American people for judges who understand the real role of the judiciary; judges who seek to interpret the law, not make it; judges who will enforce the law and bring criminals to justice, not turn them loose and make our streets unsafe." Radio Address to the Nation on Voluntarism and the Supreme Court Nomination of Robert H. Bork (October 3, 1987).

1534   "[W]hat's at issue here [in connection with the nomination of Robert H. Bork to the U.S. Supreme Court] is not one man and what happened to him. What's at issue is that we make sure that the process of appointing and confirming judges never again is turned into such a political joke. And if I have to appoint another one, I'll try to find one that they'll object to just as much as they did for this one." Remarks to the New Jersey Republican State Committee in Whippany (October 13, 1987).

1535   "It takes leadership from the Supreme Court to help shape the attitudes of the courts in our land and to make sure that principles of law are based on the Constitution. That is the standard to judge those who seek to serve on the courts: qualifications, not distortions; judicial temperament, not campaign disinformation." Address to the Nation on the Supreme Court Nomination of Robert H. Bork (October 14, 1987).

1536   "I do not believe that nominees to the Supreme Court should have to pass litmus tests administered by single-interest lobbies. Such tactics are better suited for campaigns and elections than for Supreme Court nominations." Remarks at the Republican Governors Club Annual Dinner(October 15, 1987).

1537 "The Federal judiciary is too important to be made a political football." Remarks at the 1988 Reagan Administration Executive Forum (January 19, 1988).

DR. MARTIN LUTHER KING, JR.

1538 "Dr. Martin Luther King, Jr., was born into a world where bigotry and racism still held sway. Before he died, he had touched the conscience of a nation and had contributed immeasurably to the human rights of black Americans. He was a man of character and a man of courage." Radio Address to the Nation on the Anniversary of the Birth of Martin Luther King, Jr. (January 15, 1983).

1539 "Martin Luther King, Jr., burned with the gospel of freedom, and that flame lit the way for millions. What he accomplished — not just for black Americans, but for all Americans — he lifted a heavy burden from this country. As surely as black Americans were scarred by injustice, American was scarred by injustice. Many Americans didn't fully realize how heavy America's burden was until it was lifted. Dr. King did that for us, all of us." Remarks on the Anniversary of the Birth of Martin Luther King, Jr. (January 15, 1983).

1540 "[L]et us resolve anew to do everything we can, in our time, to continue to fulfill Dr. King's dream — a dream that all men and women of good will, black and white alike, share with all their hearts." Statement on the 20th Anniversary of the March on Washington for Jobs and Freedom (August 27, 1983).

1541 "[E]ach day on Martin Luther King Day, let us not only recall Dr. King, but rededicate ourselves to the Commandments he believed in and sought to live every day: Thou shall love thy God with all thy heart, and thou shall love thy neighbor as thyself." Remarks on Signing the Bill

Making the Birthday of Martin Luther King, Jr., a National Holiday (November 2, 1983).

1542 "Martin Luther King knew that America's democracy was imperfect, but he also knew that America's conscience was a powerful force for reform. His unique combination of moral leadership and practical political wisdom enlisted America's conscience on the side of peaceful change." Statement on the Birthday of Martin Luther King, Jr. (January 15, 1985).

1543 "Dr. King forged a dream out of the values of his religion and the ideals of our nation's founders. He cherished the dream of a world where human dignity was respected, human rights were protected, and all stood equal before the law. Like Lincoln, he sought the full realization of the principles set forth in our Declaration of Independence." Message on the [First] Observance of Martin Luther King, Jr., Day (January 14, 1986).

1544 "Ultimately, the great lesson of Martin Luther King, Jr.'s life was this: He was a great man who wrested justice from the heart of a great country, and he succeeded because that great country had a heart to be seized. Martin Luther King, Jr., really helped make our nation freer." Remarks to the Students and Faculty at Martin Luther King, Jr., Elementary School (January 15, 1986).

1545 "[L]et us not forget that he [Dr. King] was once jeered and threatened, fined and jailed. But through it all he never sought revenge, only reconciliation. His unshakable faith enabled him to conquer the temptation to hate and the temptation to fear. His was a triumph of courage and love." Message to the Congress of Racial Equality on the Observance of Martin Luther King, Jr., Day (January 16, 1986).

1546   "His memory should serve not just as an inspiration to black Americans but to each and every one of us to stand firm for our principles and to strive to better ourselves and our country." Address to High School Students on Martin Luther King, Jr.'s Birthday (January 15, 1987).

1547   "In honoring one man's commitment, we're also rededicating ourselves to the fundamental principle behind that dream. That principle, which goes to the very essence of America, is simply this: that it is self-evident that all men are created equal and that they are endowed by their Creator with certain unalienable rights." Remarks on Signing the Martin Luther King, Jr., Day Proclamation (January 12, 1988).

1548   "Today we honor a man who dedicated his life to the pursuit of a dream — a dream not just for himself but for you, for all of us, for America. And in honoring his commitment, his dedication, his life, we rededicate ourselves to the fundamental principle behind that dream and to the challenge that history has given every American from the founding of our country to the present: the challenge of making that principle and that dream, the American dream, an enduring reality." Address to the Nation's Students on the Observance of Martin Luther King, Jr., Day (January 15, 1988).

1549   "Let us resolve that future generations will know a new birth of freedom and that this land that Reverend King loved so well and gave so much to will continue to shine with the brilliant hope of all mankind." Address to the Nation's Students on the Observance of Martin Luther King, Jr., Day (January 15, 1988).

LABOR

1550   "America depends on the work of labor, and the economy we build should reward and encourage that labor as our hope for the future." Remarks at the National Conference of the Building and Construction Trades Department, AFL-CIO (March 30, 1981).

1551   "Let me make one thing plain. I respect the right of workers in the private sector to strike.... But we cannot compare labor-management relations in the private sector with government. Government cannot close down the assembly line. It has to provide without interruption the protective services which are government's reason for being." Remarks and a Question-and-Answer with Reporters on the Air Traffic Controllers Strike (August 3, 1981).

1552   "[T]his administration will not fight inflation by attacking the sacred right of American workers to negotiate their wages. We propose to control government, not people." Remarks in Chicago, Illinois, at the Annual Convention and Centennial Observance of the United Brotherhood of Carpenters and Joiners (September 3, 1981).

1553   "[I]f there's one challenge that I have for organized labor today, it is that they ... not become the handmaiden of one political party." Remarks in Chicago, Illinois, at the Annual Convention and Centennial Observance of the United Brotherhood of Carpenters and Joiners (September 3, 1981).

1554   "Collective bargaining ... has played a major role in America's economic miracle. Unions represent some of the freest institutions in this land. There are few finer examples of participatory democracy to be found anywhere." Remarks in

Chicago, Illinois, at the Annual Convention and Centennial Observance of the United Brotherhood of Carpenters and Joiners (September 3, 1981).

1555 "America's trades men and women are the pistons that drive the engine of our economy. This country was built with the sweat and determination of hard-working men and women who ... love to work with their hands as well as their minds.... We're a nation of people who believe it's not enough to be good; you've got to be good at something." Remarks at the Annual National Leadership Conference of the Vocational Industrial Clubs of America in Louisville, Kentucky (June 29, 1983).

1556 "We know that what is good for the American worker is good for America." Radio Address to the Nation on the Observance of Labor Day (September 1, 1984).

1557 "If we can lead a revolution in technology and push back the frontiers of space, then we can provide our workers in industries old and new all that they need, because I believe with all my heart that if we give American workers the proper tools, they can outproduce, outcompete, and outsell anybody, anywhere in this world." Remarks at a Reagan-Bush Rally in Media, Pennsylvania (October 29, 1984).

1558 "[W]orkers have contributed as much to America's social greatness as they have to our economic strength. Their dedication to humanitarian goals, conscientious craftsmanship and technical excellence have improved virtually every aspect of our lives — from jobs and working conditions to education, national defense, housing, medical care and transportation." Message on the Observance of Labor Day, 1985 (September 1, 1985).

1559 "You know, some people say it's America's natural resources that make our country so great, but the greatest resource of all is our working men and women — their skill, hard work, guts, and determination." Radio Address to the Nation on Economic Growth (August 30, 1986).

1560 "Nobody works as hard as the American worker. And forgive my pride, but when given half a chance American business and labor can outcompete any country or people in the world." Remarks to Broan Manufacturing Company Employees in Hartford, Wisconsin (July 27, 1987).

1561 "Our working people are still the most productive on the planet. I've always believed that, given the tools and equipment they need and on a level playing field, American workers can outcompete and beat the pants off anybody, anywhere." Radio Address to the Nation on Free and Fair Trade (September 5, 1987).

NATIONAL SECURITY

Military Strength

1562 "Our forbearance should never be misunderstood. Our reluctance for conflict should not be misjudged as a failure of will. When action is required to preserve our national security, we will act. We will maintain sufficient strength to prevail if need be, knowing that if we do so

we have the best chance of never having to use that strength." Inaugural Address (January 20, 1981).

1563 "A truly successful army is one that because of its strength and ability and dedication will not be called upon to fight, for no one will dare to provoke it." Address at Commencement Exercises at the United States Military Academy (May 27, 1981).

1564   "There have been four wars in my lifetime. None of them came about because the United States was too strong." Address at Commencement Exercises at the United States Military Academy (May 27, 1981).

1565   "The search for peace must go on, but we have a better chance of finding it if we maintain our strength while we're searching." Address at Commencement Exercises at the United States Military Academy (May 27, 1981).

1566   "Government's first responsibility is national security...." Address to the Nation on the Program for Economic Recovery (September 24, 1981).

1567   "Military inferiority does not avoid a conflict, it only invites one and then ensures defeat." Remarks at the Bicentennial Observance of the Battle of Yorktown in Virginia (October 19, 1981).

1568   "Those who must fight when war comes know better than others that peace is not achieved through platitudes or excessive emotion. It requires hard work, resolution, and sacrifice." Toasts of President Reagan and President Hosni Mubarak of Egypt at the State Dinner (February 3, 1982).

1569   "When we build up our national defenses, it isn't with the idea that some day you're [the young people in the audience] going to go fight a war. The idea in building them up is that we will be so strong that no other generation of young Americans will have to bleed their lives into foreign battlefields or beachheads someplace out in the oceans." Remarks at a Rally for United States Senator David D. Durenberger in Bloomington (February 8, 1982).

1570   "We must not resign ourselves to life as a second-rate power, tempting aggression with our weakness. America has never gone to war because it was too strong." Remarks at a Rally for Senator Malcolm Wallop of Wyoming in Cheyenne (March 2, 1982).

1571   "[L]et us as a people take the lead in preserving peace and a safer world for mankind. But let us do so not just with a good heart, but with a clear head." Address Before a Joint Session of the Tennessee State Legislature in Nashville (March 15, 1982).

1572   "We can no longer choose between national security and national welfare — the two have become one and the same." Address Before a Joint Session of the Tennessee State Legislature in Nashville (March 15, 1982).

1573   "[N]o American President must ever sit across the negotiating table from someone dedicated to the destruction of our way of life unless our military strength is such that those on the other side of the table have a darn good reason to legitimately negotiate a reduction of weapons for their own feeling of security." Address Before a Joint Session of the Tennessee State Legislature in Nashville (March 15, 1982).

1574   "The top priority of the Federal Government is the safety of this country. If the choice must be made between balancing the budget — and I want to do that — or national security, I must come down on the side of national security." Address Before a Joint Session of the Oklahoma State Legislature in Oklahoma City (March 16, 1982).

1575   "Every penny we spend [on defense] is for one sacred purpose; to prevent that first shot from being fired, to prevent Americans from dying in battle." Remarks at the National Legislative Conference of the Building and Construction Trades Department, AFL-CIO (April 5, 1982).

1576   "I also believed back when we still had the draft that we would be better off if we used that same American volunteer spirit for our military." Remarks on Private Sector Initiatives at a White House Briefing for National Service Organization Leaders (April 27, 1982).

1577   "We Americans — we Americans are optimists, but we are also realists. We're a peaceful people, but we're not a weak or gullible people." Remarks to the People of Berlin (June 11, 1982).

1578   "The record of history is clear: Citizens of the United States resort to force reluctantly and only when they must." Remarks in New York, New York, Before the United Nations General Assembly Special Session Devoted to Disarmament (June 17, 1982).

1579   "The scourge of tyranny cannot be stopped with words alone." Remarks in New York, New York, Before the United Nations General Assembly Special Session Devoted to Disarmament (June 17, 1982).

1580   "We found [when President Reagan took office] that half our airplanes couldn't fly on any given day for lack of spare parts. We found that on any given day there were Navy vessels that couldn't leave port either because they didn't have enough crew or they didn't have enough parts. And we set out to do something about that." Remarks at a Fundraising Dinner in Los Angeles, California, for United States Senate Candidate Pete Wilson (August 23, 1982).

1581   "But let the world understand: Our purpose is not belligerency, but respect; not conflict, but deterrence; and not war, but peace." Remarks on Presenting the Presidential Citizens Medal to Raymond Weeks at a Veterans Day Ceremony (November 11, 1982).

1582   "Our status as a free society and world power is not based on brute strength. When we've taken up arms, it's been for the defense of freedom for ourselves and for other peaceful nations who needed our help. But now, faced with the development [by the Soviet Union] of weapons with immense destructive power, we've no choice but to maintain ready defense forces that are second to none. Yes, the cost is high, but the price of neglect would be infinitely higher." Remarks at the Re-Commissioning Ceremony for the U.S.S. *New Jersey* in Long Beach, California (December 28, 1982).

1583   "Americans will no longer tolerate just a facade of security. They expect our planes to fly, our ships to sail, and our helicopters to stay aloft." Remarks and a Question-and-Answer Session at a Luncheon Meeting of the St. Louis Regional Commerce and Growth Association in Missouri (February 1, 1983).

1584   "[H]istory teaches us that weakness only tempts aggression." Remarks via Satellite to *Newsweek* Magazine Employees and Press on the 50th Anniversary of the Magazine (February 24, 1983).

1585   "The defense policy of the United States is based on a simple premise: The United States does not start fights. We will never be an aggressor. We maintain our strength in order to deter and defend against aggression — to preserve freedom and peace." Address to the Nation on Defense and National Security (March 23, 1983).

1586   "[O]ur security is based on being prepared to meet all threats." Address to the Nation on Defense and National Security (March 23, 1983).

1587   "I believe it's immoral to ask the sons and daughters of America to protect this land with second-rate equipment and bargain-basement weapons. If they can put their lives on the line to protect our way of life, then, by golly, we can give them the weapons, the training, and the money they need to do the job right." Remarks at the Annual Members Banquet of the National Rifle Association in Phoenix, Arizona (May 6, 1983).

1588   "We can only keep our families safe and our country at peace when enemies of democracy know that America has the courage to stay strong." Remarks at a Republican Fundraising Dinner for Congressional Campaign Committees (May 12, 1983).

1589   "We're not belligerent people. We've always sought peace. We occupy no country, we build no walls to keep our people in, we have no armies of secret police to keep them quiet. But we must understand [that] our foes will do everything they can to divide us and to undermine our will. To keep our families safe, to keep our country at peace, the enemies of democracy must know that America has the courage to stay strong." Remarks at a California Republican Party Fundraising Dinner in Long Beach (June 30, 1983).

1590   "[W]eakness on the part of those who cherish freedom inevitably leads to trouble — that it only encourages the enemies of both peace and freedom. On the other hand, history teaches us that by being strong and resolute we can keep the peace — and even reduce the threat of peace." Remarks at the Annual Convention of the American Legion in Seattle, Washington (August 23, 1983).

1591   "Today's so-called peace movement — for all its modern hype and theatrics — makes the same old mistake. They would wage peace by weakening the free. And that just doesn't make sense." Remarks at the Annual Convention of the American Legion in Seattle, Washington (August 23, 1983).

1592   "'Peace' is a beautiful word, but it is also freely used and sometimes even abused. As I've said before, peace is an objective, not a policy. Those who fail to understand this do so at their peril. Neville Chamberlain thought of peace as a vague policy in the thirties, and the result brought us closer to World War II." Remarks at the Annual Convention of the American Legion in Seattle, Washington (August 23, 1983).

1593   "We can't build a safer world with honorable intentions and good will alone. Achieving the fundamental goals our nation seeks in world affairs — peace, human rights, economic progress, national independence, and international stability — means supporting our friends and defending our interests. Our commitment as peacemaker is focused on these goals." Remarks at the Annual Convention of the American Legion in Seattle, Washington (August 23, 1983).

1594   "[W]e didn't return to the draft, and today our volunteer military is back on its feet and prouder than ever." Remarks to Republican Women's Leadership Forum in San Diego, California (August 26, 1983).

1595   "Too often the demands of prosperity and security are viewed as competitors when, in fact, they're complementary, natural, and necessary allies. We cannot prosper unless we're secure, and we cannot be secure unless we're free." Remarks at the Annual Meeting of the Boards of Governors of the World Bank Group and the International Monetary Fund (September 27, 1983).

1596   "Weakness does not offer the chance for success; strength does. And that strength is based on military capability, strong alliances, a willingness to speak the truth and to state our hope that someday all peoples of the world will enjoy the right to self-government and personal freedom." Remarks at a Dinner Marking the 10th Anniversary of the Heritage Foundation (October 3, 1983).

1597   "The development of democratic political institutions is the surest means to build the national consensus that is the foundation of true security." Address Before the Korean National Assembly in Seoul (November 12, 1983).

1598   "History teaches that wars begin when governments believe the price of aggression is cheap. To keep the peace, we and our allies must be strong enough to convince any potential aggressor that war could bring no benefit, only disaster." Address to the Nation and Other Countries on United States–Soviet Relations (January 16, 1984).

1599   "Only the strong are free, and peace comes only through strength." Remarks at an Event Sponsored by the America Legion Auxiliary (March 1, 1984).

1600   "Peace through strength is not a slogan; it's a fact of life." Remarks at the National Legislative Conference of the Independent Insurance Agents of America (March 27, 1984).

1601   "Reality is often harsh. We will not make it less so, if we do not first see it for what it is." Remarks at the National Leadership Forum of the Center for International and Strategic Studies of Georgetown University (April 6, 1984).

1602   "[W]e know that strength alone is not enough, but without it there can be no effective diplomacy and negotiations, no secure democracy and peace. Conversely, weakness or hopeful passivity are only self-defeating. They invite the very aggression and instability that they would seek to avoid." Remarks at the National Leadership Forum of the Center for International and Strategic Studies at Georgetown University (April 6, 1984).

1603   "[T]oday's [defense] expenditures pay for tomorrow's security — the security of our children and our children's children." Remarks at the Midyear Meeting of the National Association of Realtors (May 10, 1984).

1604   "If the sons and daughters of this nation can risk their lives to protect our freedom in a dangerous world, then we have a moral obligation to give them, in the way of protection, the finest we can in weaponry, in machinery." Remarks at a Reagan-Bush Rally in Austin, Texas (July 25, 1984).

1605   "History shows that weakness invites tyrants to believe that the price of aggression will be cheap. And while military strength alone is not enough to ensure a more secure world, without military strength, there can be no effective diplomacy, no meaningful negotiations, no real security, no lasting peace." Remarks at the National Convention of the Veterans of Foreign Wars in Chicago, Illinois (August 24, 1984).

1606   "Simply stated: if we're strong, we will discourage those who would disrupt the peace. If we maintain our strength, we will maintain the peace, and there is no threat to the world in this."

Remarks and a Question-and-Answer Session at the "Choosing a Future" Conference in Chicago, Illinois (September 5, 1984).

1607 "If history teaches us anything, it is that a strong defense is a prerequisite to a lasting peace, the only credible deterrent against aggression." Statement on the Observance of National Peace Through Strength Week (September 22, 1984).

1608 "The world is a dangerous place. We try to be a good neighbor, but we must be strong enough and confident enough to be patient when provoked. But we must be equally clear that past a certain point, our adversaries push us at their peril. Uncle Sam is a friendly old man, but he has a spine of steel." Remarks and a Question-and-Answer Session at Bowling Green State University in Bowling Green, Ohio (September 26, 1984).

1609 "As long as I'm President, we're not going to quibble about supplying the weapons and the equipment that they [America's armed forces] need to do the job their doing. We'll continue our strenuous efforts to cut waste and fraud and to get the very best deal we can, but we aren't going to play politics with the lives of those who are defending our country." Remarks at a Reagan-Bush Rally in Corpus Christi, Texas (October 2, 1984).

1610 "We are free. We are the land of the free, because we are the home of the brave." Remarks to Members of the Congregation of Temple Hillel and Jewish Community Leaders in Valley Stream, New York (October 26, 1984).

1611 "[I]f we make sure that America remains strong and prepared for peace, then we can begin to reduce nuclear weapons and, one day, banish them from the Earth entirely." Remarks at a Reagan-Bush Rally in Parkersburg, West Virginia (October 29, 1984).

1612 "You know, we only have a military-industrial complex until a time of danger, and then it becomes the arsenal of democracy. Spending for defense is investing in things that are priceless — peace and freedom." Address Before a Joint Session of the Congress on the State of the Union (February 6, 1985).

1613 "And I've said before, I don't know of a single war — one of those four — that was fought because the United States was too strong. The truth of the matter is, the two World Wars were because people on the other side looked at us, looked at our military weakness, and decided we wouldn't fight." Remarks to Private Sector Leaders During a White House Briefing on the MX Missile (March 6, 1985).

1614 "National security is not just another category on the budget; it's the first duty of the Federal Government to the American people." Remarks at a Senate Republican Policy Committee Luncheon (March 19, 1985).

1615 "Americans don't want to take chances with our national security. It's just one of the strongest impulses in our body politic." Radio Address to the Nation on Armed Forces Day and Defense Spending (May 18, 1985).

1616 "[T]oday as throughout our history, it is strength not weakness, resolve not vacillation, that will keep the peace." Address at the United States Naval Academy Commencement Exercises in Annapolis, Maryland (May 22, 1985).

1617 "It is time to stop treating our Defense Establishment and intelligence agencies like enemies and concentrate our attention and anger on the true enemies of freedom and democracy in the world." Radio Address to the Nation on the Federal Budget (June 22, 1985).

1618 "[T]he maintenance of a strong national defense [is] the first duty of government to the people." Radio Address to the Nation on Economic Growth (January 11, 1986).

1619 "Defense is not just another budget expense. Keeping America strong, free, and at peace is solely the responsibility of the Federal Government; it is government's prime responsibility." Address Before a Joint Session of Congress on the State of the Union (February 4, 1986).

1620 "[S]trength is the most persuasive argument we have to convince our adversaries to give up their hostile intentions, to negotiate seriously, and to stop bullying other nations. In the real world, peace through strength must be our motto." Remarks at a White House Meeting with the Board of Directors of the United States Institute of Peace (February 26, 1986).

1621 "American power is the indispensable element of a peaceful world...." Address to the Nation on National Security (February 26, 1986).

1622 "America must never again slide back into helpless insecurity. America must never become ... a paper tiger." Radio Address to the Nation on the Defense Budget (March 1, 1986).

1623 "Militaristic states perceive unilateral concessions as a sign of weakness, not good faith. Serious negotiations flow not from proving sincerity but from resolve and leverage. In short, peace through strength is a fact of life...." Remarks at a Senate Campaign Fundraiser for Representative W. Henson Moore in New Orleans, Louisiana (March 27, 1986).

1624 "Europeans who remember history understand better than most that there is no security, no safety, in the appeasement of evil." Address to the Nation on the United States Air Strike Against Libya (April 14, 1986).

1625 "Yes, we Americans have our disagreements, sometimes noisy ones, almost always in public — that's the nature of an open society. But no foreign power should mistake disagreement for disunity or disputes for decadence. Those who are tempted to do so should reflect on our national character, on our record of littering history with the wreckage of regimes who've made the mistake of underestimating the will of the American people, their love for freedom, and their national valor." Remarks at the Heritage Foundation Anniversary Dinner (April 22, 1986).

1626 "Here in America we've been fortunate to be the keeper and custodian of a dream — a dream that began this nation, a dream that millions of people hope to share in someday. And every member of America's Armed Forces has a special part in keeping that dream alive. The dream, of course, is freedom, and truly those of you in uniform today are freedom's honor guard." Radio Address to the Nation on Armed Forces Day (May 17, 1986).

1627 "If we really care about peace, we must stay strong. If we really care about peace, we must, through our strength, demonstrate our unwillingness to accept an ending of the peace. We must be strong enough to create peace where it does not exist and strong enough to protect it where it does." Remarks at a Memorial Day Ceremony at Arlington National Cemetery in Virginia (May 26, 1986).

1628 "If we ask our military personnel to put their lives on the line for us, we're not going to give them anything less than the top quality equipment they need to do their job and come home safely." Remarks at a Republican Party Rally in Miami, Florida (July 23, 1986).

1629 "I say a weaker America is not a safer America. And I say when we negotiate with our adversaries, we should do it from a position of strength." Remarks at a Senate Campaign Rally for James Abdnor in Sioux Falls, South Dakota (September 29, 1986).

1630 "When the next agreement is finally reached with the Soviet Union — and I say when, not if— it will not be the result of weakness or timidity on the part of Western nations. Instead, it will flow from our strength, realism, and unity." Remarks at the Welcoming Ceremony for Chancellor Helmut Kohl of the Federal Republic of Germany (October 21, 1986).

1631 "[P]eace through strength is more than a policy; it's a promise, a promise we've made to the people and a promise we intend to keep. Hope alone can never lead to agreement with the Soviets. We must maintain our military preparedness...." Remarks at a White House Briefing for Senior Staff on the Congressional and Gubernatorial Election Results (November 5, 1986).

1632 "Nothing could be more important than this: When it comes to America's national security, politics must stop at the water's edge. America must remain united in spirit and strong in purpose." Radio Address to the Nation on Administration and Congressional Goals (November 15, 1986).

1633 "Too often many Members of Congress treat defense like it was someone else's responsibility. It's always the first thing to be sacrificed, to be canceled or cut, or delayed, even while wasteful boondoggles and pork-barrel spending sail right through untouched." Radio Address to the Nation on Defense Spending (May 9, 1987).

1634 "We're a tolerant people, but we do not bow to intimidation, and we've consistently throughout our history been willing to defend ourselves. Our tolerance should not be mistaken for a lack of resolve." Radio Address to the Nation on Administration Goals (August 15, 1987).

1635 "Admittedly, defense is expensive. But it's not so expensive when you understand that it represents an investment in our own freedom and in world peace, and it's not so expensive when you consider what would happen if our defenses were permitted to fail." Remarks at the Annual Convention of the National Association of Broadcasters in Las Vegas, Nevada (April 10, 1988).

1636 "We came into office convinced that the word 'peace' is just an empty slogan unless the word 'strength' follows hard upon it. Peace is a godly thing, but men are seldom godly. What we've learned is that peace is hard to achieve unless the forces of good have the strength to stand firmly for it." Radio Address to the Nation on Foreign Policy Achievements (August 27, 1988).

1637 "Our policy of peace through strength has been vindicated wherever it's been tried." Radio Address to the Nation on Foreign Policy Achievements (August 27, 1988).

1638 "When it comes to our own security and the cause of freedom, we cannot accept naive, liberal notions that fail to keep faith with the American people and their dedication to peace through strength." Remarks at the Swearing-In Ceremony for Nicholas F. Brady as Secretary of the Treasury (September 16, 1988).

1639 "One thing is certain. If we're to continue to advance world peace and human freedom, America must remain strong. We must turn a deaf ear to those born-again patriots who talk about strength while serving up the same old menu of weakness. If we have learned anything these last 8 years, it's that peace through strength works." Radio Address to the Nation on Foreign Policy (September 24, 1988).

Negotiating the Arms Race with the Soviets

1640 "So long as our adversaries continue to arm themselves at a pace far beyond the needs of defense, so the free world must do whatever is necessary to safeguard its own security." Remarks at the Welcoming Ceremony for Prime Minister Margaret Thatcher of the United Kingdom (February 26, 1981).

1641 "They [the Soviets] are squealing like they're sitting on a sharp nail simply because we are now showing the will that we're not going to let them get to the point of dominance, where they can someday issue to the free world an ultimatum of 'surrender or die,' and they don't like that." Remarks on Signing the Economic Recovery Tax Act of 1981 and the Omnibus Reconciliation Act of 1981, and a Question-and-Answer Session with Reporters (August 13, 1981).

1642 "We take no joy in using our resources to produce weapons of war." Remarks to the People of Foreign Nations on New Year's Day (January 1, 1982).

1643 "As President, I can't close my eyes, cross my fingers, and simply hope that the Soviets behave themselves." Address Before a Joint Session of the Indiana State Legislature in Indianapolis (February 9, 1982).

1644 "[W]e're trying to redress our defensive structure so we can sit down at the bargaining table with the Soviet union for once in which they'll have a legitimate reason for wanting to engage in arms reductions along with us. So far we've had nothing to offer them. They are so far ahead. But if they find out that we mean it, then maybe we can reduce those threatening weapons, particularly those nuclear weapons that are aimed back and forth at each other. And that's my dream." Remarks at a White House Reception for Members of the National Newspaper Association (March 11, 1982).

1645 "To preserve peace, to ensure it for the future, we must not just freeze the production of nuclear weapons, we must reduce the exorbitant level that already exists." Address Before a Joint Session of the Oklahoma State Legislature in Oklahoma City (March 16, 1982).

1646 "[L]et's not fool ourselves. The Soviet Union will not come to any conference table bearing gifts. Soviet negotiators will not make unilateral concessions. To achieve parity, we must make it plain that we have the will to achieve parity by our own effort." Radio Address to the Nation on Nuclear Weapons (April 17, 1982).

1647 "Disarmament and international security are inextricably related." Toasts of the President and Secretary-General Javier Perez de Cuellar at a Luncheon at the United Nations in New York City (June 17, 1982).

1648   "[I] don't think the Soviet Union would have been at the bargaining table in Geneva if they had not seen our determination to go ahead building up our ability to defend ourselves." Remarks at a Kansas Republican Party Fundraising Luncheon in Topeka (September 9, 1982).

1649   "[W]hen I arrived in office there was virtually no hope that we could expect the Soviets to bargain seriously for real reductions. After all, they had all the marbles. We hadn't designed a new missile in 15 years. We hadn't built a new submarine in the same period, although they'd built more than 60. Our bombers were older than the pilots who flew them. Today that's no longer the case." Remarks and a Question-and-Answer Session with Reporters on Strategic Arms Reduction and Military Resistance (January 14, 1983).

1650   "Deep down, the Soviets must know it's in their interest as well as ours to prevent a wasteful arms race." Address Before a Joint Session of Congress on the State of the Union (January 25, 1983).

1651   "We cannot negotiate strategic arm reductions ... with only trust and good will." Remarks and a Question-and-Answer Session at a Luncheon Meeting of the St. Louis Regional Commerce and Growth Association in Missouri (February 1, 1983).

1652   "If we continue our past pattern of only rebuilding our defenses in fits and starts, we will never convince the Soviets that it's in their interests to behave with restraint and negotiate genuine arms reductions. We will also burden the American taxpayer time and time again with the high cost of crash armament. Sooner or later, the bills fall due." Radio Address to the Nation on Defense Spending (February 19, 1983).

1653   "Too many of our leaders saw the Soviets as a mirror image of themselves. If we would simply disarm, the Soviets would do likewise. They spent all their time viewing the world they wished it was, not the way it really is. And that's no way to protect the peace." Remarks at the Annual Washington Conference of the American Legion (February 22, 1983).

1654   "[L]et us be aware that while they [Soviet leaders] preach the supremacy of the state, declare its omnipotence over individual man, and predict its eventual domination over the peoples of the earth, they are the focus of evil in the modern world.... I urge you to beware the temptation ... to ignore the facts of history and the aggressive impulses of an evil empire, to simply call the arms race a giant misunderstanding and thereby remove yourself from the struggle between right and wrong, good and evil." Remarks at the Annual Convention of the National Association of Evangelicals in Orlando, Florida (March 8, 1983).

1655   "We know that the ideology of the Soviet leaders does not permit them to leave any Western weakness unprobed, any vacuum of power unfilled. It would seem that to them negotiation is only another form of struggle." Remarks and a Question-and-Answer Session at the Los Angeles World Affairs Council Luncheon in California (March 31, 1983).

1656   "[A]s Commander in Chief, I have an obligation to protect this country, and I will not let political expedience influence those crucial [nuclear weapons] negotiations. We will restore equality of strength with the Soviet Union either one way or the other, and the choice is theirs." Remarks at the Fundraising Dinner of the Republican National Hispanic Assembly (September 14, 1983).

1657   "Well, you know, there was a cartoon back when we first started the rebuilding of the military that said it all for me. It was a picture of a couple of Russian generals talking to each other, and one of them said, 'I liked it better when we were the only ones in the arms race.'" Remarks at a Reagan-Bush Rally in Louisville, Kentucky (October 7, 1984).

1658   "[I]'m proud to say that that during the last four years, not one inch of territory has been lost to Communist aggression." Remarks at a Reagan-Bush Rally in Rochester, New York (November 1, 1984).

1659   "In order for arms control to have meaning and credibly contribute to national security and to global or regional stability, it is essential that all parties to agreements fully comply with them." Message to the Congress Transmitting a Report on Soviet Noncompliance with Arms Control Agreements (February 1, 1985).

1660   "[O]ur security and our hopes for success at the arms reduction talks hinge on the determination that we show here to continue our program to rebuild and refortify our defenses." Remarks to Business and Trade Representatives During a White House Briefing on the Fiscal Year 1986 Budget (February 4, 1985).

1661   "The Soviets aren't going to compromise out of the goodness of their hearts, but only if they calculate that an agreement is in their immediate self-interest. We'd be doing the American people a disservice if we imagined otherwise." Remarks to Members of Congress During a White House Briefing on the MX Missile and the Soviet–United States Nuclear and Space Arms Negotiations (March 25, 1985).

1662   "The only way to resolve differences is to understand them. We must have candid and complete discussions [with the Soviets] of where dangers exist and where peace is being disrupted." Address to the 40th Session of the United Nations General Assembly in New York, New York (October 24, 1985).

1663   "History has shown that progress is more surely made through confidential negotiations...." Remarks Announcing the Presentation of a New United States Proposal at the Nuclear and Space Arms Negotiations with the Soviet Union (October 31, 1985).

1664   "The Soviets must know that if America reduces her defenses, it will be because of a reduced threat, not a reduced resolve." Address Before a Joint Session of Congress on the State of the Union (February 4, 1986).

1665   "We want to reduce arms. We want agreements that truly diminish the nuclear danger. We don't just want signing ceremonies and color photographs of leaders toasting each other with champagne. We want more. We want real agreements, agreements that really work, with no cheating." Address to the Nation on National Security (February 26, 1986).

1666   "Clearly, by making offensive nuclear missiles less reliable [through the SDI initiative], we make agreements to reduce their number more attainable. Particularly is that true where one side now is an economic basket case because of the massive arms buildup that it's been conducting over the last few decades — the Soviet Union." Remarks at a White House Briefing for Supporters of the Strategic Defense Initiative (August 6, 1986).

1667   "Some Congressmen seem to believe that peace and American weakness mean the same thing. Didn't it ever occur to anyone what the Soviets must be thinking? They're thinking, if we wait long enough, they'll do our work for us — meaning we will do their work for them." Remarks at a White House Briefing for Private Sector Supporters of United States Defense Policies (September 23, 1986).

1668   "Nations don't mistrust each other because they're armed; they're armed because they mistrust each other." Radio Address to the Nation on the Meeting with Soviet General Secretary Gorbachev in Reykjavik, Iceland (October 4, 1986).

1669   "[W]e will not sacrifice our values, principles, or vital interests for the sake of merely signing agreements. And that's just another way of making it clear to the Soviets we harbor no illusions about them or their geopolitical intentions." Radio Address to the Nation on the Meeting with Soviet General Secretary Gorbachev in Reykjavik, Iceland (October 4, 1986).

1670   "In order to be successful in negotiations, an American President must be perceived by the Soviets as realistic and firm and, above all, a President speaking for a united people, a united country. In the past this has been one of the Nation's noblest traditions. When it came to matters of national security, politics usually stopped at the water's edge. Americans stood together and the fabric of bipartisan cooperation was untearable, the bond of national unity unbreakable." Radio Address to the Nation on the Meeting with Soviet General Secretary Gorbachev in Reykjavik, Iceland (October 4, 1986).

1671   "If we hadn't begun to rebuild our defenses, there would have been no negotiations [with the Soviet Union]. It's only through strength that we can protect the peace and rid the world of nuclear weapons." Remarks on Departure for a Campaign Trip to Wisconsin, Missouri, Oklahoma, and Florida (October 23, 1986).

1672   "I simply can't go along with those who would hand the Soviets, free of charge, what they can't win at the bargaining table. This is no way to run America's foreign policy, and I would be compelled to veto any legislation that endangers our arms reduction efforts or undermines our national defense." Remarks to Congressional Leaders on Defense Spending (May 12, 1987).

1673   "The Soviet Union ... has a poor record of compliance with past arms control agreements. So, any new treaty will contain ironclad provisions for effective verification, including on-site inspection of facilities before and during reductions and short-notice inspections afterward." Address to the People of Western Europe on Soviet–United States Relations (November 4, 1987).

1674   "I have even learned a couple of Russian words that I have used in my previous meetings with the General Secretary. It is a proverb. It says, Dovorey no provorey. That means 'Trust but verify.' And we will." Remarks on the Strategic Defense Initiative to Martin Marietta Denver Astronautics Employees in Waterton, Colorado (November 24, 1987).

1675   "Building up our defensive strength was designed to convince the Soviet leadership that they couldn't win an arms race. The second half of the formula is reaching agreements to reduce weapons on both sides to an equal and verifiable level." Remarks Announcing Senate Minority Leader Dole's Endorsement of the Intermediate-Range Nuclear Forces Treaty (December 17, 1987).

1676   "Our approach is not to seek agreement for agreement's sake but to settle only for agreements that truly enhance our national security and that of our allies. We will never put our security at risk — or that of our allies — just to reach an agreement with the Soviets. No agreement is better than a bad agreement." Address Before a Joint Session of Congress on the State of the Union (January 25, 1988).

1677   "We cannot expect diplomacy to work if we ourselves lack the will to negotiate from a position of strength. We cannot go to the bargaining table empty-handed." Remarks to Members of the Reserve Officers Association (January 27, 1988).

1678   "[I] understand the justifiable apprehension about dealing with the Soviet Union. Will Rogers used to say we never lost a war, and we never won a conference. Well, let me just note: The cornerstones of any bargaining with the Soviets are strength and realism. I believe, however, there are potential areas, even with a government

that is so fundamentally contrary to our own ideals, where it will be mutually beneficial for us to come to an agreement of some kind." Remarks to Members of the Reserve Officers Association (January 27, 1988).

1679   "There is a role for arms control negotiations here, but as a supplement to a policy of strength, not as a substitute. We have learned from experience: The only effective way to negotiate with the Soviets is from a position of strength." Remarks at the Annual Leadership Conference of the American Legion (February 29, 1988).

1680   "Arms reduction can only succeed if it is backed up by a strong defense." Remarks on Departure for the North Atlantic Treaty Organization Summit Meeting in Brussels, Belgium (March 1, 1988).

1681   "In noting the differences that still stand between us [the United States and the Soviet Union], therefore, my desire has not been to sound a note of discouragement but one of realism, not to conduct a tutorial but to give the kind of emphatic testimony to the truth that, over the long run, removes illusion and moves the process of negotiation forward." President's News Conference Following the Soviet–United States Summit Meeting in Moscow [prepared statement] (June 1, 1988).

1682   "[O]ur relationship with the Soviets is like a table. It's built on four legs: arms reduction, resolving of regional conflicts, improvement of human rights within the Soviet Union, and expansion of bilateral exchanges." Remarks and a Question-and-Answer Session at a Luncheon with Radio and Television Journalists (June 8, 1988).

1683   "Weapons are a sign of tensions, not a cause of them. I know all of you have heard me say this time and again, but let me repeat it here: Nations do not distrust each other because they're armed; they are armed because they distrust each other." Remarks and a Question-and-Answer Session at a Luncheon with Radio and Television Journalists (June 8, 1988).

1684   "[O]nce the Soviets learned they could not intimidate us or cajole us into giving them the advantage, they came to the bargaining table. They did business because we proved we meant business." Radio Address to the Nation on Foreign Policy Achievements (August 27, 1988).

Nuclear War and Its Deterrence

1685 "Those who've governed America throughout the nuclear age and we who govern it today have had to recognize that a nuclear war cannot be won and must never be fought." Radio Address to the Nation on Nuclear Weapons (April 17, 1982).

1686 "My duty as President is to ensure that the ultimate nightmare never occurs, that the prairies and the cities and the people who inhabit them remain free and untouched by nuclear conflict." Address at Commencement Exercises at Eureka College, Eureka, Illinois (May 9, 1982).

1687 "Those who advocate that we renounce the use of a crucial element of our deterrent strategy [nuclear weapons] must show how this would decrease the likelihood of war. It is only by comparison with nuclear war that the suffering caused by conventional war seems a lesser evil. Our goal must be to deter war of any kind." Address Before the Bundestag in Bonn, Federal Republic of Germany (June 9, 1982).

1688 "What do we mean when we speak of 'nuclear deterrence'? Certainly, we don't want such weapons for their own sake. We don't desire excessive forces or what some people have called 'overkill.' Basically, it's a matter of others knowing that starting a conflict would be more costly to them than anything they might hope to gain. And, yes, it is sadly ironic that in these modern times, it still takes weapons to prevent war. I wish it did not." Address to the Nation on Strategic Arms Reduction and Nuclear Deterrence (November 22, 1982).

1689 "Now, when a potential enemy knows that by starting a war he'll lose more than he hopes to gain, he just won't start a war in the first place. That's what deterrence is all about." Radio Address to the Nation on Production of MX Missile (December 11, 1982).

1690 "There is no higher moral goal than to rid the world of a nuclear nightmare." Remarks via Satellite to *Newsweek* Magazine Employees and Press on the 50th Anniversary of the Magazine (February 24, 1983).

1691 "'Deterrence' means simply this: making sure any adversary who thinks about attacking the United States, or our allies, or our vital interests, concludes that the risks to him outweigh any potential gains. Once he understands that, he won't attack. We maintain the peace through our strength; weakness only invites aggression." Address to the Nation on Defense and National Security (March 23, 1983).

1692 "[N]ations should turn their best energies to moving away from a nuclear nightmare. We must not resign ourselves to a future in which security on both sides depends on threatening the lives of millions of innocent men, and women, and children." Remarks and a Question-and-Answer Session at the Los Angeles World Affairs Council Luncheon in California (March 31, 1983).

1693 "I can't believe that this world can go on beyond our generation and on down to succeeding generations with this kind of [nuclear] weapon on both sides poised at each other without someday some fool or some maniac or some accident triggering the kind of war that is the end of the line for all of us." Remarks at a White House Briefing for Chief Executive Officers of Trade Associations and Corporations on Deployment of the MX Missile (May 16, 1983).

1694 "Above all, our goal is to maintain a stable nuclear balance in order to reduce the risk of war." Remarks Announcing Changes in the United States Position at the Strategic Arms Reduction Talks (June 8, 1983).

1695 "[W]e must never depart from the ultimate goal of banning them [nuclear weapons] from the face of the Earth." Radio Address to the Nation on Arms Control and Reduction (July 16, 1983).

1696 "[W]e must ensure that world security is not undermined by the further spread of nuclear weapons. Nuclear nonproliferation must not be the forgotten element of the world's arms control agenda." Address Before the 38th Session of the United States General Assembly (September 26, 1983).

1697 "Any American President, anyone charged with the safety of the American people, any person who sits in the Oval Office and contemplates the horrible dimensions of a nuclear war must, in conscience, do all in his power to seriously pursue and achieve effective arms reduction agreements. The search for genuine, verifiable arms reduction is not a campaign pledge or a sideline item in my national security agenda. Reducing the risk of war and the level of nuclear arms is an imperative, precisely because it enhances our security." Remarks at a Dinner Marking the 10th Anniversary of the Heritage Foundation (October 3, 1983).

1698   "There is simply no sensible alternative to the parallel goal of deterrence and arms reduction." Radio Address to the Nation on Arms Control and Reduction (October 22, 1983).

1699   "We have no higher priority than the reduction of nuclear weapons. Arms reductions are the only sound course to a safer world." Statement on Soviet Union Withdrawal from the Intermediate-Range Nuclear Force Negotiations (November 23, 1983).

1700   "The only value in our two nations [the United States and the Soviet Union] possessing nuclear weapons is to make sure they will never be used. But then would it not be better to do away with them entirely?" Address Before a Joint Session of the Congress on the State of the Union (January 25, 1984).

1701   "Since the dawn of the nuclear age, we've sought to reduce the risk of war by maintaining a strong deterrent and by seeking genuine arms control." Remarks and a Question-and-Answer Session with Reporters on Foreign and Domestic Issues (May 14, 1984).

1702   "We recognize that there is no sane alternative to negotiations on arms control and other issues between our two nations [the United States and the Soviet Union] which have the capacity to destroy civilization as we know it." Address to the 39th Session of the United Nations General Assembly in New York, New York (September 24, 1984).

1703   "It's frustrating, but here is the truth of the nuclear age: There are no cheap solutions, no easy answers. The only path to progress on this is the open door, the honest proposal, and such a path takes patience. But patience isn't inappropriate. Each day the world turns completely. Each day the world is reborn. Possibilities that yesterday didn't exist emerge and startle us." Remarks and

a Question-and-Answer Session at Bowling Green State University in Bowling Green, Ohio (September 26, 1984).

1704   "And every once in awhile, I see people put posters up in front of me — Nuclear Freeze. Okay, a nuclear freeze — when we have reduced the nuclear weapons on both sides down to an equal, verifiable level, then we will have a nuclear freeze." Remarks at Reagan-Bush Rally Center in Milwaukee, Wisconsin (November 3, 1984).

1705   "Now, for decades, we and the Soviets have lived under the threat of mutual assured destruction — if either resorted to the use of nuclear weapons, the other could retaliate and destroy the one who started it. Is there any logic or morality in believing that if one side threatens to kill tens of millions of our people our only recourse is to threaten killing tens of millions of theirs?" Inaugural Address (January 21, 1985).

1706   "It is my firm conviction that preventing the spread of nuclear explosives to additional countries is essential to world peace and stability. It forms an indispensable complement to the efforts we have undertaken to bring about deep reductions in strategic and intermediate-range nuclear weapons. It is no exaggeration to say that the future of mankind may well depend on the achievement of these goals, and I intend to pursue them with unflagging determination and a deep sense of personal commitment." Message to the Congress Transmitting the Annual Report on Nuclear Nonproliferation (February 12, 1985).

1707   "I happen to believe — logic forces me to believe — that this new defense system, the Strategic Defense Initiative, is the most hopeful possibility of our time. Its primary virtue is clear. If anyone ever attacked us, Strategic Defense would be there to protect us. It could conceivably save millions of lives." Remarks at the Annual Dinner of the Conservative Political Action Conference (March 1, 1985).

1708   "Nuclear war would be the greatest tragedy, I think, ever experienced by mankind, in the history of mankind. And we've avoided that tragedy because we've maintained a credible deterrent force. We can't afford to play political games with the delicate balance of deterrence. No room should be left for doubt about a nuclear exchange; no one would win." Remarks to Private

Sector Leaders During a White House Briefing on the MX Missile (March 6, 1985).

1709   "Since the dawn of the nuclear era, all God's children have lived with the fear of nuclear war and the danger of nuclear devastation. Our moral imperative is to work with all our power for that day when the children of the world can grow up without the fear of nuclear war." Remarks to the United States Negotiating Team for the Nuclear and Space Arms Negotiations with the Soviet Union (March 8, 1985).

1710   "The Strategic Defense Initiative has been labeled 'Star Wars,' but it isn't about war; it's about peace. It isn't about retaliation; it's about prevention. It isn't about fear; it's about hope. And in that struggle, if you'll pardon my stealing a film line: The force is with us." Remarks at the National Space Club Luncheon (March 29, 1985).

1711   "We cannot and should not seek to build our peace and freedom perpetually upon the basis of expanding nuclear arsenals." Address to a Special Session of the European Parliament in Strasbourg, France (May 8, 1985).

1712   "Today our deterrent, our war deterrent, is based on: They have missiles, we have missiles; and if they fire their missiles and kill millions of our people, we will fire ours and kill millions of theirs. That's no way to go." Remarks at a Fundraising Dinner for Senator Robert W. Kasten, Jr., in Milwaukee, Wisconsin (October 15, 1985).

1713   "Our goal is to make the world safer through development of nonnuclear security shields that would protect people by preventing weapons from reaching their targets and, hopefully, render ballistic missiles obsolete." Radio Address to the Nation and the World on the Upcoming Soviet–United States Summit Meeting in Geneva (November 9, 1985).

1714   "Since the dawn of the nuclear age, every American President has sought to limit and end the dangerous competition in nuclear arms. I have no higher priority than to finally realize that dream." Address to the Nation on the Upcoming Soviet–United States Summit Meeting in Geneva (November 14, 1985).

1715   "Well, MAD spells what it is — it's really mad, but it was mutual assured destruction,

and the idea being that there would be peace between us as long as each one of us knew that the other fellow could retaliate if we shot first — and blow us up, too." Remarks at a White House Briefing for Republican Student Interns on Soviet–United States Relations (July 29, 1986).

1716   "Mutual assured destruction — those three words — that is the system that was adopted by our two governments a few years ago.... And as Washington is prone to do, that shortened down to its initials; mutual assured destruction comes out a MAD policy. And that's just what it is: stark, staring, mad policy. It's little more than a threatened slaughter of millions of innocent people." Remarks to Representatives of the Young Astronauts Council on Their Departure for the Soviet Union (October 16, 1986).

1717   "[N]o responsible President should rely solely on a piece of paper for our country's safety. We know the record on Soviet treaty violations. We can either have American technology as insurance for keeping us safe, or we can rely on Soviet promises alone. Our technology and their promises each have their own track record. And I'll take our technology any day." Radio Address to the Nation on Soviet–United States Relations (November 1, 1986).

1718   "Peace based on strategic defenses that can absorb and blunt an attack, coupled with radical reductions in offensive missiles — that is the safest course of all." Remarks and a Question-and-Answer Session at a Los Angeles World Affairs Council Luncheon in California (April 10, 1987).

1719   "We [the Reagan Administration] sought more than a shaky world peace atop the volcano of potential nuclear destruction; we sought something beyond accepted spheres of influence and tense standoffs between the totalitarian and the democratic worlds. In short, we sought ways to dispel rather than to live with the two great darkening clouds of the postwar era: the danger of nuclear holocaust and the expansion of totalitarian rule." Remarks on Soviet–United States Relations at the Town Hall of California Meeting in Los Angeles (August 26, 1987).

1720   "Arms reduction — if done with care to ensure the continuing credibility of our deterrent, both nuclear and conventional — is in the interest of all Western countries." Address to the People of Western Europe on Soviet–United States Relations (November 4, 1987).

1721 "Building a defense against nuclear weapons is a moral as well as strategic imperative, and we will never give it up. Our bottom line on SDI is simple: We will research it; we will test it. And when it is ready, we will deploy it." Radio Address to the Nation Following the Soviet–United States Summit Meeting (December 12, 1987).

1722 "It can be said that the old discredited policy of MAD is like two adversaries holding loaded guns to each other's head. It may work for awhile, but you sure better hope you don't make a slip. People who put their trust in MAD must trust it to work 100 percent — forever, no slip-ups, no madmen, no unmanageable crises, no mistakes — forever." Remarks to the Institute for Foreign Policy Analysis at a Conference on the Strategic Defense Initiative (March 14, 1988).

NORTH ATLANTIC TREATY ORGANZATION

1723 "For us, our NATO partnership is an anchor, a fixed point in a turbulent world. And it's our sincere hope that the Soviet leadership will finally realize it is pointless to continue its efforts to divide the alliance. We will not be split. We will not be intimidated. The West will defend democracy and individual liberty. And the West will protect the peace." Remarks on the 35th Anniversary of the North Atlantic Council (May 31, 1984).

1724 "Every alliance involves burdens and obligations, but these are far less than the risks and sacrifices that will result if the peace-loving nations were divided and neglectful of their common security." Address to the 39th Session of the United Nations General Assembly in New York, New York (September 24, 1984).

1725 "It is just such strength as NATO has demonstrated that is a precondition to such progress [toward peace]. Weakness, vulnerability, and wishful thinking can undo what has been accomplished by standing firm." Address to the People of Western Europe on Soviet–United States Relations (November 4, 1987).

1726 "Any philosophy or leader suggesting that there is a predetermined course of history and that conflict between our peoples [the United States and the Soviet Union] and systems is inevitable is wrong. We are not condemned by forces beyond our control. We, all peoples in every land, can shape the world in which we live and determine the future." Address to the People of Western Europe on Soviet–United States Relations (November 4, 1987).

1727 "NATO has too often seemed an alliance between a number of partners and one very senior partner. Well, now the alliance must become more and more an alliance among equals; indeed, an alliance between two continents." Remarks to the Board of Trustees of the Center for Strategic and International Studies (December 14, 1987).

1728 "The Atlantic alliance is the core of America's foreign policy and of America's own security. Preservation of a peaceful, free, and democratic Europe is essential to the preservation of a peaceful, free, and democratic United States. If our fellow democracies are not secure, we cannot be secure. If you are threatened, we're threatened. If you're not at peace, we cannot be at peace. An attack on you is an attack on us. This is not simply a matter of treaty language, important as treaty language is. It is an enduring reality — as enduring as the reality that a threat to the security of the State of Maine or New York or California is a threat to the security of all 50 American States. Simply put: An attack on Munich is the same as an attack on Chicago." Address to the Citizens of Western Europe (February 23, 1988).

1729   "NATO's strategy for peace has always been simple: Prevent aggression before it starts. Be strong enough, be determined enough so that no adversary would think even for a moment that war might pay." Address to the Citizens of Western Europe (February 23, 1988).

1730   "[O]ur goal is not a nuclear-free or a tank-free or an army-free Europe but a war-free Europe. A war-free Europe is what we have today; a war-free Europe is what we want to preserve." Address to the Citizens of Western Europe (February 23, 1988).

1731   "[A]s Abraham Lincoln said ... 'no man is good enough to govern another without that other's consent.' All of us [NATO members] honor this truth. All of us are united in defending

it. We have raised high the roof beam of this great structure of an alliance to shelter that truth from all the winds that blow and all the bears and wolves that prowl." Address to the Citizens of Western Europe (February 23, 1988).

1732   "Yes, the Atlantic community is the house of democracy. The Atlantic alliance is the guardian of Europe's greatest legacy to the ages — human freedom and democratic rule." Address to the Citizens of Western Europe (February 23, 1988).

1733   "Our first priority is to maintain a strong and healthy partnership between North America and Europe, for this is the foundation on which the cause of freedom so crucially depends. We will never sacrifice the interests of this partnership in any agreement with the Soviet Union." Remarks on Departure for the North Atlantic Treaty Organization Summit Meeting in Brussels, Belgium (March 1, 1988).

1734   "The North Atlantic alliance is the most successful in history. While other alliances have been formed to win wars, our fundamental purpose is to prevent war while preserving and extending the frontiers of freedom." Remarks to Reporters Following the North Atlantic Treaty Organization Summit Meeting in Brussels, Belgium (March 3, 1988).

OLYMPICS

1735   "Wrapped up in all the difficult nuts-and-bolts work that goes with an event like these great games [the Olympics] is the importance, the overriding importance of the contestants themselves, the young men and women learning the importance of honest striving, fair play, love of country, and, yes, love of their fellow man." Remarks at a United States Olympic Committee Dinner Honoring August A. Busch III in St. Louis (July 22, 1982).

1736   "[C]ountries throughout the world have been brought together by one great event, the

winter Olympics. The competition is fierce and we cheer for the men and women on our respective teams. But we can and should celebrate the triumphs of all athletes who compete in the true spirit of sportsmanship and give the very best of themselves. And when each race or event is done and our teams come together in friendship, we will remember that we are meant to be one family of nations." Radio Address to the Nation on United States–Soviet Relations (February 11, 1984).

1737   "[The 1984 U.S. Winter Olympic Team] reminded us that the qualities of personal commitment — courage, character, and heart — are the mark of greatness in sport." Remarks at a White House Reception for Members of the United States Winter Olympic Team (February 29, 1984).

1738 "We consider sport to be one of the finest opportunities for people of all nations to come and to know and to understand each other. And in sport, nothing can match the competition of the Olympics." Remarks at a White House Ceremony on the 1984 Olympic Torch Relay (May 14, 1984).

1739 "[T]he success of the Olympics ... in no way depend[s] on political machinations of powerbrokers in countries that are less than free. The games are moving forward, and they'll be successful [despite the Soviet boycott]." Remarks During a Visit to the United States Olympic Training Center in Colorado Springs, Colorado (May 29, 1984).

1740 "One of the things I noted and liked so much as I watched the games on TV was that ... you could sort out or figure out who represented what country, except for the American athletes. With the American athletes, we almost always had to see the U.S.A. on [their] uniforms, because our team came in all shapes and sizes, all colors and nationalities, and all races and ethnics groups. And I was thinking ... you can talk on and read forever about the melting pot; but the last 2 weeks, there it was winning gold medals for us...." Remarks at the United States Olympic Medal Winners in Los Angeles, California (August 13, 1984).

1741 "The mark of greatness in sports is the quality of personal commitment, drive, and determination that all Olympians share. The athletes who competed in Sarajevo may have posted faster times or combined more spins into their routines, but sports has less to do with things like times and double toe loops than with courage of the human heart." Remarks at a White House Ceremony for Participants in the Special Olympics from the Washington Metropolitan Area (March 23, 1985).

1742 "The heart of the Olympics is the sport and the competition.... It's striving with the support and love of family and community to be the best you possibly can be, because you love your sport and — win, lose, or draw — you love the competition. And for that, all of you get gold medals. There's one thing you can remember above all. Just being here in those uniforms and being where you were puts you a world apart from just literally millions of other people, and every one of you has a right to be proud." Remarks to Members of the United States Winter Olympic Team (March 8, 1988).

1743 "[Y]ou can see the American spirit in the lives of every one of our team members at these games. This team comes from all over our nation, from the rough and tumble streets of our brawny cities to the quiet lanes of our vast countryside, from the suburban hills of southern California to riverfront towns in the Midwest. They represent every aspect of our country's life and a shining hope, too, a crystalline beacon of opportunity that we know is the heart of America." Radio Address to the Nation on the Summer Olympic Games (September 17, 1988).

PATRIOTISM

General

1744 "[T]here are a lot of reasons ... why this good spirit [patriotism] has returned to our land.

But it got a lot of encouragement from Nashville. It's the people of this city who never forgot their country, who never thought patriotism was out of style." Remarks at a Birthday Celebration for Roy Acuff in Nashville, Tennessee (September 13, 1984).

1745 "Call it confidence, self-assurance, what you will. It's a renewed understanding that, for all our faults, ours is a nation of goodness and greatness; that despite our mistakes in the world, we've stood for human freedom with greater consistency and courage than any other nation in history; that if only we have faith, if only we look not to government but to ourselves, we can build upon this economic expansion to create a new and lasting era of prosperity. Now, come to think of it, what I've seen has a name. It's called patriotism." Remarks at a Fundraising Luncheon for Carroll A. Campbell and Thomas F. Hartnett in Columbia, South Carolina (July 24, 1986).

1746 "Now, you know, some people — and without wanting to flatter me — have referred to me as a super patriot. Well, I guess maybe I'm old-fashioned, but I don't think you can love America too much." Remarks at a Senate Campaign Rally for Representative W. Henson Moore in Metairie, Louisiana (September 18, 1986).

1747 "Let no one charge, however, that ours is blind nationalism. We do not hide our short-comings. Yes, we have our imperfections, but there are no people on this planet who have more reason to hold their heads high than do the citizens of the United States of America." Remarks Announcing America's Economic Bill of Rights (July 3, 1987).

1748 "I've often said that there is something unique about the American form of patriotism.... It is not an exclusive attachment; it is not jealous or chauvinistic: It's the affirmation of man's deepest desires for the rights and liberties given him by his Creator. American patriotism is, quite simply, the call to freedom, everywhere, for all peoples. And that's why the American flag is more than a national flag. It has been, throughout our history, the hope and encouragement of freedom-loving peoples everywhere." Remarks at the Annual Leadership Conference of the American Legion (February 29, 1988).

1749 "[I]f patriotism is not the only thing, it is one of the best things." Remarks Upon Returning from the Soviet–United States Summit Meeting in Moscow (June 3, 1988).

National Symbols

1750 "I don't know or have[n't] heard all the national anthems of the world, but I do know this: The only anthem of those I do know that ends with a question is ours, and may it ever be thus. Does that banner still wave 'o'er the land of the free and the home of the brave.'" Remarks at the Republican Congressional "Salute to President Ronald Reagan Dinner" (May 4, 1982).

1751 "Well, I've been accused of having that problem, myself [of being too nationalistic], back over the years. The best answer I know is the one attributed to George M. Cohan. He was asked why there was so much flag-waving in his plays, and he gave a pretty good answer. He said, 'Can you think of a better flag to wave?'" Remarks at a Reception Marking the First Edition of *USA Today.* (September 15, 1982).

1752 "[O]ur own national anthem is the only one I know that ends with a question, 'Does that banner sill wave o'er the land of the free and the home of the brave?' We must always be able to answer that question affirmatively." Remarks on Signing the Human Rights and Day of Prayer for Poland Proclamations (December 10, 1982).

1753 "The Red, White, and Blue is a testament to the unity and patriotism of our people and to the deep love and commitment we have for our country, our freedom, and our way of life." Message to the Nation on the Observance of Independence Day (July 3, 1983).

1754 "[I]t's up to us to see that it [the American flag] continues to fly over a land that is free and brave." Remarks at Convocation Ceremonies at the University of South Carolina in Columbia (September 20, 1983).

1755 "It's the one symbol of all that we are and all that we hope to be." Remarks on Presenting a Flag to the United States Olympic Committee (June 14, 1984).

1756 "The Statue of Liberty — made in Europe, erected in America — helps remind us not only of past ties but present realities. It is to those realities we must look in order to dispel whatever doubts may exist about the course of history and the place of free men and women within it. We live in a complex, dangerous, divided world; yet a world which can provide all of the good things we require — spiritual and material — if we but have the confidence and courage to face history's challenge." Address to a Special Session of the European Parliament in Strasbourg, France (May 8, 1985).

1757 "I don't know about you, but I always get a chill up and down my spine when I say that Pledge of Allegiance...." Remarks at a Flag Day Ceremony in Baltimore, Maryland (June 14, 1985).

1758 "[T]he Statue of Liberty or simply Miss Liberty ... [is] cherished across America, and the torch that she bears is recognized throughout the world as a symbol of human freedom." Remarks on Signing the Bill Designating the Centennial Year of Liberty in the United States (October 28, 1985).

1759 "And let us never forget that in honoring our flag, we honor the American men and women who have courageously fought and died for it over the last 200 years, patriots who set an ideal above any consideration of self. Our flag flies free today because of their sacrifice." Radio Address to the Nation on Flag Day and Father's Day (June 14, 1986).

1760 "[M]iss Liberty, like the many millions she's welcomed to these shores, is of foreign birth, the gift of workers, farmers, and shopkeepers and children who donated hundreds of thousands of francs to send her here. They were the ordinary people of France. This statue came from their pockets and from their hearts." Remarks at the Opening Ceremonies of the Statue of Liberty Centennial Celebration in New York, New York (July 3, 1986).

1761 "Some people look to the source of the American miracle in our abundant natural resources, others in the accident of history. But if you want to know the secret, you don't have to look any farther than that grand lady standing in New York Harbor. Freedom is the key. Freedom is what allowed individuals to make America great." Radio Address to the Nation on Independence Day and the Centennial of the Statue of Liberty (July 5, 1986).

1762 "The 31 words of the Pledge of Allegiance to our flag takes only a moment to recite, yet their meaning reaches across the many decades of our history as a free people." Radio Address to the Nation on International Trade (June 13, 1987).

1763 "Our hope, our prayer, remains the same as that heard on the lips of so many millions who looked up once, as we did yesterday, to see the outstretched lamp of Liberty and who felt for the first time its warmth and glow: a prayer that someday freedom will light the world and become the blessing and birthright of every people, everywhere." President's News Conference [prepared statement] (December 8, 1988).

1764 "Yes, the torch of Lady Liberty symbolizes our freedom and represents our heritage, the compact with our parents, our grandparents, and our ancestors. It is that lady who gives us our great and special place in the world. For it's the great life force of each generation of new Americans that guarantees that America's triumph shall continue unsurpassed into the next century and beyond. Other countries may seek to compete with us; but in one vital area, as a beacon of freedom and opportunity that draws the people of the world, no country on Earth comes close." Remarks at the Presentation Ceremony for the Presidential Medal of Freedom (January 19, 1989).

PEACE

1765 "As for the enemies of freedom, those who are our potential adversaries, they will be reminded that peace is the highest aspiration of the American people. We will negotiate for it, sacrifice for it; we will not surrender for it, now or ever." Inaugural Address (January 20, 1981).

1766 "Working for peace is both a moral duty and a practical necessity. We should have no illusions. This task is immensely difficult, and we can no more solve the world's problems than we can isolate ourselves from them. But the search for peace is the surest way to preserve all that we cherish and avoid the nightmares that we fear." Remarks at the Annual Meeting of the United States Chamber of Commerce (April 26, 1982).

1767 "I happen to believe that the foreign policy of this country must have one goal and one only, and that is world peace." Remarks on Private Sector Initiatives at a White House Briefing for National Service Organization Leaders (April 27, 1982).

1768 "Peace is not the absence of conflict, but the ability to cope with conflict by peaceful means." Address at Commencement Exercises at Eureka College, Eureka, Illinois (May 9, 1982).

1769 "[L]ike prosperity, peace comes from commitment and hard work." Remarks in Los Angeles at a California Republican Party Fundraising Dinner (May 25, 1982).

1770 "To those who march for peace, my heart is with you. I would be at the head of your parade if I believed marching alone could bring about a more secure world." Address Before the Bundestag in Bonn, Federal Republic of Germany (June 9, 1982).

1771 "We desire peace. But peace is a goal, not a policy. Lasting peace is what we hope for at the end of our journey; it doesn't describe the steps we must take nor the paths we should follow to reach that goal." Address to the Nation on Strategic Arms Reductions and Nuclear Deterrence (November 22, 1982).

1772 "Our goal is peace with justice. We search for a means to resolve differences without resort to war, without resort to violence, and with assurance of compliance with the agreements made." Remarks at the Swearing-In Ceremony for Kenneth L. Adelman as Director of the United States Arms Control and Disarmament Agency (April 22, 1983).

1773 "[I] speak not only as the President of the United States but also as a husband, a father,

a grandfather, and as a person who loves God and whose heart yearns deeply for a better future — my dream is for our peoples to come together in a spirit of faith and friendship, to help build and leave behind a far safer world." Radio Address to the Nation and the Peoples of Other Countries on Peace (September 24, 1983).

1774 "People don't make wars; governments do." Radio Address to the Nation and the Peoples of Other Countries on Peace (September 24, 1983).

1775 "We commit our resources and risk the lives of those in our Armed Forces to rescue others from bloodshed and turmoil and to prevent humankind from drowning in a sea of tyranny." Remarks to Military Personnel at Cherry Point, North Carolina, on United States Casualties in Lebanon and Grenada (November 4, 1983).

1776 "Peace through strength is not a slogan; it's a fact of life." Remarks at the National Legislative Conference of the Independent Insurance Agents of America (March 27, 1984).

1777 "[T]he American people seek to act as a force for peace in the world and to further the cause of human freedom and dignity." Remarks at the Welcoming Ceremony for Pope John Paul II in Fairbanks, Alaska (May 2, 1984).

1778 "We in America have learned bitter lessons from two World Wars: It is better to be here ready to protect the peace, than to take blind shelter across the sea, rushing to respond only after freedom is lost. We've learned that isolationism never was and never will be an acceptable response to tyrannical governments with an expansionist intent." Remarks at a Ceremony Commemorating the 40th Anniversary of the Normandy Invasion, D-Day (June 6, 1984).

1779 "While we remain strong, we must always be ready for reconciliation, ready to resolve differences with our adversaries and resolve them peacefully at the negotiating table." Remarks at a Meeting with Conservative Members of the British Parliament (June 6, 1984).

1780 "America has always been a peaceable country. We've never loved war. We're the least warlike powerful nation in the history of the world. We can be trusted with the military power that is our responsibility to hold. We maintain it only for the good, never for territorial gain or imperialistic desires. We work for peace by staying strong, so that we may be a nation at peace with ourselves and at peace with the world." Remarks and a Question-and-Answer Session at the "Choose a Future" Conference in Chicago, Illinois (September 5, 1984).

1781   "Our friends know well something that we know and something that our adversaries know: America can be trusted with military might. We don't like war; we never have. We're not an expansionist country or an imperial country. We seek only to protect, never to act as the aggressor." Remarks at the Annual Dinner of the National Italian American Foundation (September 15, 1984).

1782   "[W]e seek no territorial expansion and are making no effort to impose our will on anyone. But we will never again allow the United States of America to let down its guard." Remarks at a Reagan-Bush Rally in Cedar Rapids, Iowa (September 20, 1984).

1783   "We hold on. We remain prepared for peace. We know that we have an absolute moral obligation to try and try again. We know that in the quest for peace the work of man is the work of God. And He will bless us, and bless one of our efforts and make our prayer of peace come true." Remarks and a Question-and-Answer Session at Bowling Green State University in Bowling Green, Ohio (September 26, 1984).

1784   "[O]ur opponents ... keep mistaking weakness for peace." Remarks at a "Victory '84" Fundraising Dinner in Houston, Texas (October 2, 1984).

1785   "Nothing could make our hearts more glad than to see the day when there will be no more walls, no more guns to keep loved ones apart. Nothing could bring greater happiness than to reach an agreement that will rid the Earth of nuclear weapons forever, and we will never stop praying, never stop working, never stop striving one moment to bring that day closer." Remarks to Citizens in Hambach, Federal Republic of Germany (May 6, 1985).

1786   "Yes, we Americans have our disagreements, sometimes noisy ones, almost always in public — that's the nature of our open society — but no foreign power should mistake disagreement for disunity. Those who are tempted to do so should reflect on our national character and our history — a history littered with the wreckage of regimes who made the mistake of underestimating the vigor and will of the American people." Remarks at the Annual Convention of the American Bar Association (July 8, 1985).

1787   "The differences between communism and democracy are profound. There will inevitably be competition between us, but it's the central responsibility of the leaders of the United States and the U.S.S.R. to ensure that this competition is peaceful." Radio Address to the Nation on Foreign Policy (September 21, 1985).

1788   "Peace based on mutual fear cannot be true peace, because staking our future on a precarious balance of terror is not good enough. The world needs a balance of safety." Address to the 40th Session of the United Nations General Assembly in New York, New York (October 24, 1985).

1789   "It's in the nature of Americans to hate war and its destructiveness. We would rather wage our struggle to rebuild and renew, not to tear down. We would rather fight against hunger, disease, and catastrophe. We would rather engage our adversaries in the battle of ideals and ideas for the future. These principles emerge from the innate openness and good character of our people and from our long struggle and sacrifice for our liberties and the liberties of others. Americans always yearn for peace. They have a passion for life. They carry in their hearts a deep capacity for reconciliation." Address to the 40th Session of the United Nations General Assembly in New York, New York (October 24, 1985).

1790   "Now, I know that much has been written in your [Soviet] press about America's hostile intentions toward you. Well, I reject these distortions. Americans are a peace-loving people; we do not threaten your nation and never will. The American people are tolerant, slow to anger, but staunch in defense of their liberties and, like you, their country." Radio Address to the Nation and the World on the Upcoming Soviet–United States Summit Meeting in Geneva (November 9, 1985).

1791   "Peace fails when we forget what we stand for. It fails when we forget that our Republic is based on firm principles, principles that have real meaning, that with them, we are the last, best hope of man on Earth; without them, we're little more than the crust of a continent. Peace also fails when we forget to bring to the bargaining table God's first intellectual gift to man: common sense. Common sense gives us a realistic knowledge of human beings and how they think, how they live in the world, what motivates them. Common sense tells us that man has magic in him, but also clay. Common sense can tell the difference between right and wrong. Common sense forgives error, but it always recognizes it to be error first." Remarks at the Veterans Day Wreath-Laying Ceremony at Arlington National Cemetery (November 11, 1985).

1792 "We endanger the peace and confuse all issues when we obscure the truth; when we refuse to name an act for what it is; when we refuse to see the obvious and seek safety in Almighty. Peace is only maintained and won by those who have clear eyes and brave minds. Peace is imperiled when we forget to try for agreements and settlements and treaties; when we forget to hold out our hands and strive; when we forget that God gave us talents to use in securing the ends He desires. Peace fails when we forget that agreements, once made, cannot be broken without a price." Remarks at the Veterans Day Wreath-Laying Ceremony at Arlington National Cemetery (November 11, 1985).

1793 "When we speak of peace, we should not mean just the absence of war. True peace rests on the pillars of individual freedom, human rights, national self-determination, and respect for the rule of law." Address to the Nation on the Upcoming Soviet–United States Summit Meeting in Geneva (November 14, 1985).

1794 "Surely no people on Earth hate war or love peace more than we Americans. But we cannot stroll into the future with childlike faith." Address Before a Joint Session of Congress on the State of the Union (February 4, 1986).

1795 "We live in a dangerous world. If peace is to be maintained and if our country is to be secure, we must have the courage to face facts and act." Remarks at a Senate Campaign Fundraiser

for Representative W. Henson Moore in New Orleans, Louisiana (March 27, 1986).

1796 "Being free and prosperous in a world at peace — that's our ultimate goal. That is, as you might say, the business at hand here in Washington." Remarks at a White House Briefing for Republican Student Interns on Soviet–United States Relations (July 29, 1986).

1797 "[W]e persevere, and in the end, freedom will triumph. Our victory will not be realized in the crossing of borders by well-equipped armies, certainly not in the launching of missiles or the occupation of other countries. Our victory will come, perhaps little by little, as walls are torn down, missiles dismantled, and as people are freed. Free peoples everywhere share this vision." Toasts at the State Dinner for Chancellor Helmut Kohl of the Federal Republic of Germany (October 21, 1986).

1798 "I believe that if America remains firm and strong, if we don't give up in squabbles among ourselves things that should be the subject of negotiations with the Soviets, we can usher in a new age of peace and freedom." Remarks at the Annual Meeting of the American Council of Life Insurance (November 16, 1987).

1799 "[T]here is a saying in your country that a poor peace is better than a good quarrel." Remarks at the Welcoming Ceremony for General Secretary Mikhail Gorbachev of the Soviet Union (December 8, 1987).

1800 "In working for a safer world and a brighter future for all people, we know arms agreements alone will not make the world safer; we must also reduce the reasons for having arms." Radio Address to the Nation on the Soviet–United States Summit Meeting in Moscow (May 28, 1988).

1801 "Nations do not mistrust each other because they're armed; they're armed because they mistrust each other." Address to the 43d Session of the United Nations General Assembly in New York, New York (September 26, 1988).

POLITICAL LEADERSHIP

General

1802   "From time to time we've been tempted to believe that society has become too complex to be managed by self-rule, that government by an elite group is superior to government for, by, and of the people. Well, if no one among us is capable of governing himself, then who among us has the capacity to govern someone else? All of us together, in and out of government, must bear the burden. The solutions we seek must be equitable, with no one group singled out to pay a higher price." Inaugural Address (January 20, 1981).

1803   "Evil is powerless if the good are unafraid." Remarks at the Conservative Political Action Conference Dinner (March 20, 1981).

1804   "So often in history great causes have been won or lost at the last moment, because one side or the other lacked that reserve of character and stamina, of faith and fortitude, to see the way through to success." Address to Nation on the Fiscal Year 1983 Federal Budget (April 29, 1982).

1805   "If history teaches anything it teaches self-delusion in the face of unpleasant facts is folly." Address to Members of the British Parliament (June 8, 1982).

1806   "Fostering the faith and character of our people is one of the great trusts of responsible leadership." Remarks at a Candle-Lighting Ceremony for Prayer in Schools (September 25, 1982).

1807   "I'm not interested in playing the political blame game. It's not who to blame that's the problem; it's what to blame, and the American people realize that." Remarks at the Weeries Family Farm in Chapin, Illinois (October 20, 1982).

1808   "Well, as I said before, we didn't go to Washington with more snake-oil remedies for quick fixes, and we don't suffer from paralysis by analysis." Remarks at the Annual Convention of the United States League of Savings Associations in New Orleans, Louisiana (November 16, 1982).

1809   "Hard work, a knowledge of the facts, the willingness to listen and be understanding, a strong sense of duty and direction, and a determination to do your best on behalf of the people you serve — these are hallmarks of good leadership at every level, whether the political arena is high school student council or the capital of the mightiest nation on Earth." Remarks and a Question-and-Answer Session with Participants in the National Conference of the National Association of Student Councils in Shawnee Mission, Kansas (June 29, 1983).

1810   "I firmly believe that we can and must go forward together, hand in hand not looking for easy villains to explain our problems...." Remarks at the Annual Meeting of the Boards of Governors of the World Bank Group and the International Monetary Fund (September 27, 1983).

1811   "Sometimes the one who straightens out a situation uses up so many brownie points he or she is no longer the best one to carry out the duties of day-to-day management." Radio Address to the Nation on the Resignation of Secretary of the Interior James G. Watt (November 26, 1983).

1812   "You know, I keep a sign on my desk that says, 'It CAN be done,' and the 'can' is spelled out in capital letters." Remarks on Receiving the Final Report of the President's Private Sector Survey on Cost Control in the Federal Government (January 16, 1984).

1813   "For this administration, it isn't going to matter that this is a political year. We'll do what is best for the people and let the politics take care of themselves. And won't some of the people in this town be surprised when they find out that doing what's good for the people also turns out to be good politics." Remarks to the Reagan Administrative Executive Forum (January 20, 1984).

1814   "[P]eople don't want to hear so much about where we've been, but about where we're going; not so much about what's been done, but what needs to be done." Remarks at an Event Sponsored by the American Legion Auxiliary (March 1, 1984).

1815   "There's no compassion in snake oil cures." Remarks at the Ford Claycomo Assembly Plant in Kansas City, Missouri (April 11, 1984).

1816   "Few things worthwhile ever happen without commitment and effort by good people." Toast at Dinner Hosted by President Li Xiannian of China in Beijing (April 26, 1984).

1817   "[G]overnment owes the people an explanation and needs their support for its actions at home and abroad." Remarks at Memorial Day Ceremonies Honoring an Unknown Serviceman of the Vietnam Conflict (May 28, 1984).

1818   "[I]f this administration deserves credit, it's only for having the kind of trust in the people that made us willing to take our case to them and seek their support." Remarks at the Annual Convention of the Texas State Bar Association in San Antonio (July 6, 1984).

1819   "Four years ago we raised a banner of bold colors — not pale pastels." Remarks Accepting the Presidential Nomination at the Republican National Convention (August 23, 1984).

1820   "[W]hen you lose faith in the people, you can go wrong in a hurry." Remarks at Dedication Ceremonies for Santa Maria Towers in Buffalo, New York (September 12, 1984).

1821   "No army is as powerful as an idea whose time has come." Remarks at a Reagan-Bush Rally in Grand Rapids, Michigan (September 20, 1984).

1822   "[Q]uick fixes don't solve problems. The more difficult path is to resist the temptation of politically expedient solutions or the pressure of powerful interest groups, and to instead make the hard choices necessary to advance the long-term good of all people." Remarks at the Annual Meeting of the Boards of Governors of the International Monetary Fund and the World Bank Group (September 25, 1984).

1823   "[E]ven though economic matters are important — well, the old saying is true: Man does not live by bread alone. Man lives by belief, by faith in things that are larger than himself. We really almost diminish all the things we are when

limit the debate to money and how it's distributed in our country. We lose a sense of the mystery in men's souls and the mystery of life." Remarks at a Reagan-Bush Rally in Brownsville, Texas (October 2, 1984).

1824   "Our country needs leadership that can see beyond the demands of the special interest groups and prepare America for a better tomorrow." Remarks at a Dedication Ceremony for a Statue of Christopher Columbus in Baltimore, Maryland (October 8, 1984).

1825   "It's always a struggle for those of us in political life to take the long view and to brave decisions without regard to personal political cost. There are times when we fail in the struggle and times when we succeed." Remarks at a Senate Republican Unity Dinner (November 28, 1984).

1826   "The challenge of statesmanship is to have the vision to dream of a better, safer world and the courage, persistence, and patience to turn that dream into reality." Remarks to the United States Negotiating Team for the Nuclear and Space Arms Negotiations with the Soviet Union (March 8, 1985).

1827   "Do not be afraid to admit and consider your doubts, but don't be paralyzed by them. Be brave. Make your judgment and then move forward with confidence, knowing that although there's never 100-percent certainty, you have honestly chosen what you believe to be ... the right course. Do this, and the American people will always back you up." Address at the United States Naval Academy Commencement Exercises in Annapolis, Maryland (May 22, 1985).

1828   "Many men are great, but few capture the imagination and the spirit of the times. The ones who do are unforgettable." Remarks at a Fundraising Reception for the John F. Kennedy Library Foundation (June 24, 1985).

1829   "You know, last fall I fought the last election of my political life, and for the rest of my time in this high office, there can be no doubt that all decisions will be guided by a single question: What's best for America? I've tried to do that all along, but no one really believes it of a politician. But now they can't doubt it because I am not going any place." Remarks at a Senior Citizens Forum on Tax Reform in Tampa, Florida (September 12, 1985).

1830   "[I]n government you can't let the perfect be the enemy of the good. You can't let your desire for a superior product lead you to kill a bill that's really pretty good." Remarks and a Question-and-Answer Session with Broadcasters and Editors on the Food Security Act of 1985 and the Farm Credit Amendments Act of 1985 (December 23, 1985).

1831   "Private values must be at the heart of public policies." Address Before a Joint Session of Congress on the State of the Union (February 4, 1986).

1832   "And I don't mind asking you a favor: Win one for the Gipper [by re-electing Jim Thompson Governor of Illinois]." Remarks at a Fundraiser for Gov. James R. Thompson, Jr., in Rosemont, Illinois (August 12, 1986).

1833   "[A] true leader is one who does not lose sight of goals and ideals. He keeps the spirit of his people high and the course set in the right direction." Toasts at the State Dinner for President Jose Sarney Costa of Brazil (September 10, 1986).

1834   "Now, what should happen when you make a mistake [the Iran Arms and Contra Aid Controversy] is this: You take your knocks, you learn your lessons, and then you move on. That's the healthiest way to deal with a problem. This in no way diminishes the importance of the other continuing investigations, but the business of our country and our people must proceed." Address to the Nation on the Iran Arms and Contra Aid Controversy (March 4, 1987).

1835   "Whenever there is change, even for the better, there are segments of society that resist — small groups that have a special interest in keeping things the way they are — even at the expense of keeping everybody else from moving forward." Radio Address to the Nation on the United States–Canada Free Trade Agreement (January 9, 1988).

1836   "Just as those who created this Republic pledged to each other their lives, their fortunes, and their sacred honor, so, too, America's leaders today must pledge to each other that we will keep foremost in our hearts and minds not what is best for ourselves or for our party but what is best for America." Address Before a Joint Session of Congress on the State of the Union (January 25, 1988).

1837   "[O]ne of the things I've been intrigued by while I've held this job is an attitude in government that says every approach to public policy issues must be complicated and indirect." Remarks to Media Executives at a White House Briefing on Drug Abuse (March 7, 1988).

1838   "Well, leadership means making hard choices, even in an election year." Radio Address to the Nation on the Federal Role in Scientific Research (April 2, 1988).

1839   "As I see it, political leadership in a democracy requires seeing past the abstractions and embracing the vast diversity of humanity and doing it with humility, listening as best you can not just to those with high positions but to the cacophonous voices of ordinary people and trusting those millions of people, keeping out of their way, not trying to act the all-wise and all-powerful, not letting government act that way. And the word we have for this is freedom." Remarks at a Luncheon Hosted by Artists and Cultural Leaders in Moscow (May 31, 1988).

1840   "The American people want to hear straight talk about where our leaders plan to take the country, not personal attacks." Radio Address to the Nation on the Democratic National Convention and the Administration's Achievements (July 23, 1988).

1841   "The American people expect straight talk about real issues. That's what they deserve, and that's what they ought to get." Radio Address to the Nation on the Democratic National Convention and the Administration's Achievements (July 23, 1988).

1842   "If a candidate is in politics just for the power of excitement ... he's bound to be disappointed. The power never lasts forever. And as for excitement, well, there's a lot less of excitement in government than there is in just plain work. But if someone enters politics in the name of ideals and principles, then it's all worthwhile." Remarks to Members of the American Legion's Boys Nation (July 25, 1988).

Bipartisanship

1843   "[E]conomic recovery must not be a concern of one party or one President, but of all parties and indeed all Americans. It shouldn't simply be my plan, it should be our plan." Remarks During a White House Briefing on the Program for Economic Recovery (February 24, 1981).

1844 "[I]f we just remember that if every once in a while we get together and break bread and realize how much we have in common, we'll discover that everything will be all right as long as we talk to each other instead of about each other." Remarks at a White House Reception and Barbeque for the California and Texas Congressional Delegations (September 23, 1981).

1845 "[M]ost problems can be solved when people are talking to each other instead of about each other." Remarks at the 1981 White House Conference on Aging (December 1, 1981).

1846 "You know, for too many years our adversaries were successful in convincing us that they had the right to criticize or accuse us of any kind of outrage, but that any attempt on our part to point out the evils of totalitarianism was somehow an act of belligerence. I've never been able to understand those people who could say, 'How dare you call someone a Communist, you Fascist.'" Remarks and a Question-and Answer Session in Los Angeles with Editors and Broadcasters from the Western Region of the United States (July 1, 1982).

1847 "Compromise must not mean incremental retreat on principle." Remarks at the Annual Convention of the United States League of Savings Associations in New Orleans, Louisiana (November 16, 1982).

1848 "When it comes to keeping our country safe, there must be no Republicans, no Democrats, just Americans." Remarks at the Annual Convention of the United States Hispanic Chamber of Commerce in Tampa, Florida (August 14, 1983).

1849 "I'm a firm believer in the need for bipartisan cooperation, especially in foreign policy where politics should stop at the water's edge." Remarks at a Fundraising Dinner for Senator Strom Thurmond in Columbia, South Carolina (September 20, 1983).

1850 "We must restore bipartisan consensus in support of U.S. foreign policy. We must restore America's honorable tradition of partisan politics stopping at the water's edge, Republicans and Democrats standing united in patriotism and speaking with one voice as responsible trustees for peace, democracy, individual liberty, and the rule of law." Remarks at the National Leadership Forum of the Center for International and Strategic Studies at Georgetown University (April 6, 1984).

1851 "No single sector of our nation — government, business, labor, or nonprofit organizations — can solve our problems alone. But by working together, pooling our resources, and building our strengths, we can accomplish great things." Remarks at the Annual Legislative Conference of the National Association of Counties (March 4, 1985).

1852 "The security of the family and the security of our country should not be the focus of partisan debate." Remarks at a Fundraising Dinner for Senator Mack Mattingly in Atlanta, Georgia (June 5, 1985).

1853 "I may be a Republican President, and be mighty proud of it, but I need the help of Republicans and Democrats in the Congress if we're going to solve the serious problems confronting our nation." Radio Address to the Nation on the State of the Union (January 25, 1986).

1854 "Some people might think having a Democrat Senator and a Republican Senator is part of our system of checks and balances. It is no such thing." Remarks at a Senate Campaign Fundraiser for Representative Ed Zschau in Los Angeles, California (September 7, 1986).

1855 "I think the best policy is America's time-tested tradition of leaving politics at the water's edge. It's great to know when I look over my shoulder [while in Iceland at summit meeting with General Secretary Gorbachev] that the folks back home are with me. I won't be seeing Republicans or Democrats, I'll be seeing Americans." Remarks at a Campaign Rally for Senator James T. Broyhill in Raleigh, North Carolina (October 8, 1986).

1856 "[W]e're only in trouble when we're talking about each other, instead of talking to each other." Remarks at a White House Luncheon for Members of the Volunteer International Council of the United States Information Agency (October 9, 1987).

1857   "The world is looking to Washington for leadership. So, I say to the leaders in Congress: Let's roll up our sleeves, pull together. The things we want aren't all that different — a better life for all Americans." Radio Address to the Nation on the Supreme Court Nomination of Douglas H. Ginsburg and the Federal Budget (October 31, 1987).

1858   "We may be Republicans or Democrats, but when it comes to a strongly defended nation, we must all be simply Americans." Radio Address to the Nation on the Veto of the National Defense Authorization Act, Fiscal Year 1989 (August 6, 1988).

Learning from the Past

1859   "May I suggest, don't discard the time-tested values upon which civilization was built simply because they are old." Address at the Commencement Exercises at the University of Notre Dame (May 17, 1981).

1860   "It's right that each generation looks at the preceding one and is critical of its shortcomings.... But as the years pass, we learn not to cast aside proven values simply because they are old. At least we should learn that if civilization is to continue." Remarks at the 1981 White House Conference on Aging (December 1, 1981).

1861   "Each generation sees farther than the one before, because it's standing on the shoulders of those who have gone before." Remarks at the 1981 White House Conference on Aging (December 1, 1981).

1862   "Let our children and our children's children one day say of us, the world that they live in is better because we were here before them." Remarks at the 1981 White House Conference on Aging (December 1, 1981).

1863   "In many ways the good old days never were." Address at Commencement Exercises at the United States Air Force Academy in Colorado Springs, Colorado (May 30, 1984).

1864   "In America we learn from our setbacks as well as our successes. And although the lessons of failure are hard, they are often the most impor-

tant on the road to progress." Remarks on Receiving the Final Report of the Presidential Commission on the Space Shuttle *Challenger* Accident (June 9, 1986).

1865   "You know every generation is critical of the generation that preceded it and feels it must discard many of the mores and customs of those who had gone before. Our generation felt that way, and so will yours. But in casting aside the old, don't throw out those values that have been tested by time just because they're old. They're old because their value has been proven by many generations over the years and, yes, the centuries." Remarks at the High School Commencement Exercises in Glassboro, New Jersey (June 19, 1986).

1866   "Every generation has to face challenges as it comes of age. But you need only to be true to the values that made our nation great." Remarks to the Junior Livestock Competition Participants at the Illinois State Fair in Springfield (August 12, 1986).

1867   "Yes, I feel certain that, despite all the challenges that beset us, this nation of freedom will flourish. But if we're to succeed in the future, we must first learn our own past." Remarks to the Volunteers and Staff of "We the People" in Philadelphia, Pennsylvania (April 1, 1987).

1868   "[I]f we're to succeed in the future, we must learn our own past and learn to look at these and other documents and hear the echoes and sense the greatness and draw strength. For to study American history is, in a sense, to study free will. It is to see that all our greatness has been built up by specific acts of choice and determination, and it is to see how very fragile our nation is, how very quickly so much that we cherish could be lost." Remarks at the Swearing-In Ceremony of Don W. Wilson as Archivist of the United States (December 4, 1987).

1869   "[C]hange would not mean rejection of the past. Like a tree growing strong through the seasons, rooted in the Earth and drawing life from the Sun, so, too, positive change must be · rooted in traditional values — in the land, in culture, in family and community — and it must take its life from the eternal things, from the source of all life, which is faith. Such change will lead to new understandings, new opportunities, to a broader future in which the tradition is not supplanted but finds its full flowering." Remarks and a Question-and-Answer Session with the Students

and Faculty at Moscow State University (May 31, 1988).

POLITICS

General

1870   "[T]he blacks of America should not be patronized as just one more voting bloc to be wooed and won." Remarks in Denver, Colorado, at the Annual Convention of the National Association for the Advancement of Colored People (June 29, 1981).

1871   "Baseball of course is our national pastime, that is if you discount political campaigning." Remarks at a White House Ceremony Observing National Amateur Baseball Month (May 11, 1983).

1872   "Of course, the real sign of spring is our national pastime—nine guys galloping out on the field: the Democratic Presidential candidates. No runs, no hits, just errors." Remarks at a Republican Fundraising Dinner for Congressional Campaign Committees (May 12, 1983).

1873   "They [Members of Congress] don't have to see the light; they have to feel the heat." Remarks at the Annual Conference of the National League of Cities (March 5, 1984).

1874   "Arguing is something of a tradition here. We like to disagree. But it's usually pretty good-natured arguing, and it doesn't tear us apart." Remarks at Naturalization Ceremonies for New United States Citizens in Detroit, Michigan (October 1, 1984).

1875   "Two great American sports are taking place this fall: politics and football." Remarks at a Reagan-Bush Rally in Parkersburg, West Virginia (October 29, 1984).

1876   "You know, I've become convinced over the years that the [distinction] between right

and left ... is false. There is no real right or left. There's only an up or down—up to the ultimate in individual freedom consistent with an orderly society or down through statism and the welfare state to the darkness of totalitarian tyranny and human misery." Remarks at a Fundraising Luncheon for Senator Don Nickles in Oklahoma City, Oklahoma (June 5, 1985).

1877   "[I]n America a lot of people are sort of born into a political party. Their families belong to the same party for generation after generation. And it seems like heresy or a renunciation of who you are and where you're from to switch. Well, this kind of fidelity to traditions and old ties is good; Americans are a faithful people. But the thing is ... when the party you were born into no longer represents the hopes and aspirations of the people you came from, well, then that party left you—you didn't leave it. And that has happened." Remarks at a White House Reception for New Republicans (June 10, 1985).

1878   "Now, the biggest obstacle between America and the future she deserves is ... special interests." Remarks to the Students and Faculty at North Carolina State University in Raleigh (September 5, 1985).

1879   "Maybe I've said it to you before; I'll say it again: You don't have to make them see the light. Just make them feel the heat!" Remarks to Business Leaders During a White House Briefing on Budget Reform (March 13, 1987).

1880   "The fact is gerrymandering has become a national scandal. The Democratic-controlled State legislatures have so rigged the electoral process that the will of the people cannot be heard. They vote Republican but elect Democrats." Remarks at the Republican Governors Club Annual Dinner (October 15, 1987).

1881 "A look at the district lines shows how corrupt the whole process has become. The congressional map is a horror show of grotesque, contorted shapes. Districts jump back and forth over mountain ranges, cross large bodies of water, send out little tentacles to absorb special communities and ensure safe seats. One Democratic Congressman who helped engineer the gerrymandering of California once described the district lines there as his contribution to modern art. But it isn't just the district lines the Democrats have bent out of shape: it's the American values of fair play and decency. And it's time we stopped them." Remarks at the Republican Governors Club Annual Dinner (October 15, 1987).

1882 "I've heard people that have interpreted our system of checks and balances to mean that, well, that's fine: You have people on one side out there in the legislature, then people on the other side in the Executive Office. That isn't what the checks and balances were supposed to be." Remarks at the Republican Governors Club Annual Dinner (October 15, 1987).

1883 "The fact is gerrymandering has become a national scandal. The Democratic-controlled State legislatures have so rigged the electoral process that the will of the people cannot be heard. They vote Republican but elect Democrats.... The congressional map is a horror show of grotesque, contorted shapes. Districts jump back and forth over mountain ranges, cross large bodies of water, send out little tentacles to absorb special communities and ensure safe seats." Remarks to State and Local Republican Officials on Federalism and Aid to the Nicaraguan Democratic Resistance (March 22, 1988).

1884 "You know, it reminds me of reading about a poll about another candidate in January 1980. It was taken at the National Press Club luncheon here in Washington on the eve of the primary season. Jimmy Carter got a large number of votes, and so did Teddy Kennedy. But there was one candidate on the Republican side who got so few votes from the wise men of Washington that it wasn't even reported in the lineup. I'm not going to tell you who that was — his initials happen to be RR." Remarks at a Campaign Fundraising Dinner for Senator David K. Karnes of Nebraska (July 11, 1988).

1885 "After the 1990 census, it will be time for the reapportionment.... We must go to the voters now. We must tell them that never again must they permit the kind of obscene redistricting plans that we saw in 1981 in places like California, where the map was shattered like a pane of glass and each district was a different shape. We've got to let them know how it was done, why it was done, and why it must never be done again." Remarks at the Republican Governors Club Dinner (October 4, 1988).

Democrats

1886 "After being in Washington for a year and a half there's one thing I know for sure; there are two sides to every question. And come election year, the Democrats turn up on both sides." Remarks in New York City at a Reception for Delegates to the State Republican Convention (June 17, 1982).

1887 "The opposition has been saying some terrible things about [our Republican] political ideas, and yet you'll find that they're friendly and cordial, personally. It's like being confronted by a dog who's showing its teeth and snarling, and its tail is wagging at the same time. You don't know which end to believe." Remarks at a Dinner Honoring the Republican Majority in the Senate (December 9, 1982).

1888 "[T]hese people [the Democrats] who talk so much about fairness for all Americans [are] the same ones who can't see you unless you belong to a special interest group." Remarks at an Iowa Caucus Rally in Waterloo (February 20, 1984).

1889 "We [Republicans] take no one for granted. We do not think we 'own' any group. We consider nobody 'ours.' We do not appeal to envy, and we don't seek to divide and conquer." Remarks at a Reagan-Bush Rally in Cupertino, California (September 3, 1984).

1890 "We're really talking about two different worlds. They see America wringing her hands; we see America raising her hands. They see America divided by envy, each of us challenging our neighbor's success; we see America inspired by opportunity, each of us challenging the best in ourselves. We believe in knowing when opportunity knocks; they seem determined only to knock opportunity." Radio Address to the Nation on the Presidential Campaign (September 15, 1984).

1891 "You know, the people of Milwaukee are as well known for your love of good beer as the liberal Democrats are for their taxing and spending. The difference is you know when to stop." Remarks at the Annual Family Oktoberfest in Milwaukee, Wisconsin (September 26, 1984).

1892 "For longer than anyone can remember, the Democratic Party has held the allegiance of a large number of Americans who were not well-served by the policies of that party. Yet voting habits are hard to change. I know; I was a Democrat myself for most of my adult life." Remarks at a Meeting with Reagan-Bush Campaign Leadership Groups (October 30, 1984).

1893 "The Democratic Party's politics of envy has been consigned to the trash heap of economic history." Remarks at the Annual Republican Senate/House Fundraising Dinner (May 21, 1986).

1894 "As predicted, liberalism was about as good for America as Mrs. O'Leary's cow was for Chicago." Remarks at a Senate Campaign Fundraiser for Representative Ed Zschau in Los Angeles, California (September 7, 1986).

1895 "[I] believe that the liberals who've taken control of that once great party [the Democrat Party] don't represent the vast majority of hard-working, patriotic Democrats. I know I couldn't face a throng this large without knowing that many of you are Democrats and many of you also were Democrats and changed, including me — I was one, too." Remarks at a Senate Campaign Rally for Representative W. Henson Moore in Metairie, Louisiana (September 18, 1986).

1896 "[W]e couldn't have been elected in 1980, we couldn't have brought America back, without the help of those Democrats. Because like us, they believe in the values of family and faith and love of country. Our Democratic allies deserve a vote of thanks, a real round of applause for all they're doing for America." Remarks at a Senate Campaign Fundraising Luncheon for Representative W. Henson Moore in New Orleans, Louisiana (September 18, 1986).

1897 "The truth of the matter is, there are millions of patriotic Democrats across this country who are totally out of step with the leadership of their party, which is still going down that old-fashioned road of taking your money and giving you orders." Remarks at a Republican Party Rally in Detroit, Michigan (September 24, 1986).

1898 "The truth is, the liberal Democratic leaders never met a tax they didn't like. And when it comes to spending your hard-earned money, those liberals act like they've got your credit card in their pocket; and believe me, they never leave home without it." Remarks at a Campaign Rally for Senator Robert W. Kasten, Jr., in Waukesha, Wisconsin (October 23, 1986).

1899 "For so long, the liberal message to our national culture was tune in, turn on, let it all hang out." Remarks at the Annual Conservative Political Action Conference Dinner (February 11, 1988).

1900 "There are only two things that the liberals don't understand: the things that change and the things that don't. The economy, technology, industry — these things change. But America's basic moral, spiritual, and family values — they don't change." Remarks at the Annual Republican Congressional Fundraising Dinner (May 11, 1988).

1901 "Our leaders [in the Carter Administration] answered not that there was something wrong with our government but that our people were at fault because of some malaise. Well, facts are stubborn things." Remarks at the Republican National Convention in New Orleans, Louisiana (August 15, 1988).

1902 "Our liberal friends seem to love to fiddle around making big government even bigger. But they never seem to achieve their goals. And so, they fiddle around some more, but they still don't get anywhere. And then, before you know it, they've fiddled around so much that they've sent the ship of state into drydock." Remarks at a Fundraiser for Representative Robert J. Lagomarsino in Santa Barbara, California (August 27, 1988).

1903 "America has traveled such a remarkable distance in the last 8 years that the memory has faded of the economic and foreign policy crises that we faced when Vice President Bush and I took office. The truth is that when you take a walk down our opposition's memory lane it starts to look like 'Nightmare on Elm Street.'" Remarks at a Republican Party Rally in Cape Girardeau, Missouri (September 14, 1988).

1904 "[T]he liberals have tried to hide their philosophy behind our words. When they say 'opportunity,' they mean subsidies. When they say 'closing the deficit,' they mean raising taxes. When they say 'strong defense,' they mean cut defense spending — no wonder their favorite machine is the snowblower." Remarks at a Republican Party Rally in Waco, Texas (September 22, 1988).

1905 "What it all comes down to is a clash [between conservatives and liberals] of principles, of values, and of visions. The liberals look at this country and see problems, woes, gloom and doom. And you know, that's the kind of thinking that can turn into a self-fulfilling prophecy." Remarks at a Republican Party Fundraising Dinner in Detroit, Michigan (October 7, 1988).

1906 "[T]he liberal leadership in Washington has replaced the idea of checks and balances with a philosophy of adversarial government. Now, when they lose in the national election, they fight a political guerrilla war for the next 4 years to block the policies that the American people have chosen at the ballot box. That's what the liberal Democrats have been doing in Congress for the last 8 years." Remarks at a Republican Campaign Rally in Raleigh, North Carolina (October 21, 1988).

1907 "When they [the liberals] say 'family,' they mean 'Big Brother in Washington.' When we say 'family,' we mean 'honor thy father and mother.'" Remarks at a Republican Campaign Rally in Bowling Green, Kentucky (October 21, 1988).

Republicans

1908 "I also believe that we conservatives, if we mean to continue governing, must realize that it will not always be so easy ... to place the blame on the past for our national difficulties. The point is we must lead a nation, and that means more than just criticizing the past. As T.S. Eliot once said, 'only by acceptance of the past will you alter its meaning.'" Remarks at the Conservative Political Action Conference Dinner (March 20, 1981).

1909 "We want to rebuild America, not from the government down, but from the people up, all of us together as partners, community by community...." Remarks at a Meeting with Chief Executive Officers of National Organizations to Discuss Private Sector Initiatives (March 24, 1982).

1910 "[W]hen the chips are down and decisions are made as to who the candidates will be, then the 11th commandment prevails and everybody goes to work, and that is: Thou shalt not speak ill of another Republican." Remarks in New York City at a Reception for Delegates to the State Republican Convention (June 17, 1982).

1911 "There's no room in the Republican Party for bigots...." Remarks at a National Black Republican Council Dinner (September 15, 1982).

1912 "[I]t was not our task as conservatives to just point out the mistakes made over all the decades of liberal government, not just to form an able opposition, but to govern, to lead a nation." Remarks at the Conservative Political Action Conference Dinner (February 18, 1983).

1913 "Let us remain united and true to the Republican vision of progress, a vision that begins with the people and their families, churches, synagogues, schools, and neighborhoods. We don't ask them to trust us. We say trust yourselves, trust the values that made us a good and loving people." Remarks and Question-and-Answer Session During a Teleconference with Members of the Republican Northeast Regional Leadership Conference (September 23, 1983).

1914 "There is going to be a woman President of the United States one of these days soon, and she's going to be a Republican. Why? Because we have the great talent." Remarks at a White House Luncheon for Elected Republican Women Officials and Candidates (July 13, 1984).

1915 "We Republicans want to keep going forward, and we want to bring America's heritage with us. We say without embarrassment that we seek to honor traditions, that we believe our fellow citizens are good and decent people. And their lives and aspirations deserve to be respected — not patronized. For us, words like faith, family, work, and neighborhood are not slogans to be dragged out of the closet every 4 years. They are values to respect and to live by every day." Remarks at a Reagan-Bush Welcoming Rally at the Republican National Convention in Dallas, Texas (August 22, 1984).

1916 "[I]n the party of Lincoln, there is no room for intolerance and not even a small corner for anti-Semitism or bigotry of any kind. Many people are welcome in our house, but not the bigots." Remarks Accepting the Presidential Nomination at the Republican National Convention in Dallas, Texas (August 23, 1984).

1917 "We're not a party of special interests that divides America into camps. We're a party of people who share the same love of country and God, who have the same respect for family and hard work. We're people who appreciate our freedom and are not ashamed to admit that we still feel a stirring inside every time we see the flag waving in the wind." Remarks to the Republican National Hispanic Assembly in Dallas, Texas (August 23, 1984).

1918 "To all those Democrats who have been loyal to the party of F.D.R., Harry Truman, and J.F.K, but who believe its current leaders have changed that party, that they no longer stand firmly for America's responsibilities in the world, that they no longer protect the working people of this country, we say to them, 'Join us. Come walk with us down the new path of hope and opportunity.'" Remarks at a Reagan-Bush Rally in Endicott, New York (September 12, 1984).

1919 "[W]e made the right move when we made our great turn in 1980. We were right to take command of the ship, to stop its aimless drift, and to get moving again. And we were right when we stopped sending out S.O.S. and started saying U.S.A.!" Remarks at a Reagan-Bush Rally in Springfield, Illinois (November 2, 1984).

1920 "The truth is, conservative thought is no longer over here on the right; it's the mainstream now." Remarks at the Annual Dinner of the Conservative Political Action Conference (March 1, 1985).

1921 "[I]n 1964 came a voice in the wilderness — Barry Goldwater; the great Barry Goldwater, the first major party candidate of our time who was a true-blue, undiluted conservative. He

spoke from principle, and he offered a vision. Freedom — he spoke of freedom: freedom from the Government's increasing demands on the family purse, freedom from the Government's increasing usurpation of individual rights and responsibilities, freedom from the leaders who told us the process of world peace is continued acquiescence to totalitarianism. He was ahead of his time. When he ran for President, he won 6 states and lost 44. But his candidacy worked as a precursor of things to come." Remarks at the Annual Dinner of the Conservative Political Action Conference (March 1, 1985).

1922 "You've joined the party that can speak of and glory in the best of American tradition and American culture because it believes in those traditions and that culture. You've joined a party that looks at our vast and imperfect nation and sees that it's precious and to be protected, a party that still feels the old tug of the immigrants' love for America — the pure, unalloyed love of those who have experienced less free places and who adored America for giving them freedom and opportunity." Remarks at a White House Reception for New Republicans (June 10, 1985).

1923 "The party of Lincoln [the Republican Party] will not be whole until those who were with us once before rejoin us again, until they taste the emancipation of full economic justice and economic power." Remarks at a White House Meeting with Reagan-Bush Campaign Leadership Groups (October 7, 1985).

1924 "[T]oday we Republicans are demonstrating to the Nation that the GOP is the true party of opportunity, the party to all Americans — women and men, black and white — who believe that individual enterprise, not big government, is the true source of prosperity and freedom." Remarks at a Gubernatorial Campaign Rally for Kay Orr in Omaha, Nebraska (September 24, 1986).

1925 "Modern conservatism is an active, not a reactive philosophy. It's not just in opposition to those vices that debase character and community, but affirms values that are at the heart of civilization." Remarks at the Conservative Political Action Conference Luncheon (February 20, 1987).

1926 "No longer can it be said that conservatives are just anti-Communist. We are, and proudly so, but we are also the keepers of the flame of liberty. And as such, we believe that America should be a source of support, both moral and material, for all those on God's Earth who struggle for freedom." Remarks at the Conservative Political Action Conference Luncheon (February 20, 1987).

1927 "Proud of our accomplishments, we Republicans have made the mistake in believing the public will naturally reward us at the polls. Well, unfortunately, as we learned last fall [when Republicans lost control of the Senate], the fastest drying liquid known to man are tears of gratitude. The American people will cast their ballots based not on what we did yesterday, but on what we will do tomorrow." Remarks at the Annual Republican Congressional Fundraising Dinner (April 29, 1987).

1928 "But back in 1966, we gave birth to something in California that turned out to be so successful in the whole history of our party politics — the 11th commandment: 'Thou shalt not speak ill of another Republican.' And we observed it." Remarks at a White House Briefing for Administration Supporters (June 29, 1987).

1929 "The American people now look to the Republican Party as the party of new ideas." Remarks at the Republican Governors Club Annual Dinner (October 15, 1987).

1930 "The real friends of the conservative movement are an entity that gets heard from in a big way every 4 years ... those who, if the case is aggressively put before them, will vote for limited government, family values, and a tough, strong foreign policy every single time. I'm talking about those believers in common sense and sound values, your friends and mine, the American people." Remarks at the Annual Conservative Political Action Conference Dinner (February 11, 1988).

1931 "[T]hose who underestimate the conservative movement are the same people who always underestimate the American people." Remarks at the Annual Conservative Political Action Conference Dinner (Feb. 11, 1988).

1932 "[T]he differences between the liberals and conservatives have become clear to the American people. We want to keep taxes low; they want to raise them. We send in budgets with spending cuts, and they want to ignore them. We want the balanced budget amendment and the line-item veto, and they oppose them. We want tough judges and tough anticrime legislation; they hold them both up in the Congress.... We want a prayer amendment; they won't let it come to a vote in the House. We stress firmness with the Soviets; they try to pass legislation that would tie our hands in arms negotiations and endanger our defenses." Remarks at the Annual Conservative Political Action Conference Dinner (February 11, 1988).

1933 "It's natural in politics — when there's a perceived need in the country, when people are calling out for solutions, they look to government first. Often government has a role, a crucial and a necessary one. Still, maybe it's my conservative bent, but I can't help but feel uneasy sometimes. Some describe a conservative as he who would rather sit and think, and others describe him as someone who would rather just sit." Remarks to Members of the National Governors' Association (February 22, 1988).

1934 "If I may, I'd like to take a moment to say just a word about my future plans. In doing so, I'll break a silence I've maintained for some time with regard to the Presidential candidates. I intend to campaign as hard as I can. My candidate is a former Member of Congress, Ambassador to China, Ambassador to the United Nations, Director of the CIA, and National Chairman of the Republican Party. I'm going to work as hard as I can to make Vice President George Bush the next President of the United States. Thank you, and God bless you." Remarks at the Annual Republican Congressional Fundraising Dinner (May 11, 1988).

1935 "[I]t was a faith in the people they [liberals] had lost, a faith in the basic goodness, decency, and wisdom of the American people and what our founders called the American experiment. We conservatives brought that faith back to Washington. And today America's in the longest economic peacetime expansion on record." Remarks at a White House Briefing for Conservative Political Leaders (July 5, 1988).

1936 "You know, I'll be addressing the Republican convention on Monday, the opening night, and taking an active role in the coming campaign. But even so, my name won't appear on any ballot this fall. What's at stake for me in this election is my love for America and my dreams for her future. And that's what my support for Vice President Bush comes down to. You see, George Bush understands that the question for America today is not 'What's different?' but 'What's next?'" Radio Address to the Nation on the Administration's Goals and Achievements (August 13, 1988).

1937   "Our party speaks for human freedom, for the sweep of liberties that are at the core of our existence. We do not shirk from our duties to preserve freedom so it can unfold across the world for yearning millions. We believe that lasting peace comes only through strength and not through the good will of our adversaries. We have a healthy skepticism of government, checking its excesses at the same time we're willing to harness its energy when it helps improve the lives of our citizens. We have pretty strong notions that higher tax receipts are no inherent right of the Federal Government. We don't think that inflation and high interest rates show compassion for the poor, the young, and the elderly. We respect the values that bind us together as families and as a nation. For our children, we don't think it's wrong to have them committed to pledging each day to the 'one nation, under God, indivisible, with liberty and justice for all.' And we have so many requirements in their classrooms; why can't we at least have one thing that is, voluntary, and that is allow our kids

to repair quietly to their faith to say a prayer to start the day, as Congress does. For the unborn, quite simply, shouldn't they be able to live to become children in those classrooms?" Remarks at the Republican National Convention in New Orleans, Louisiana (August 15, 1988).

1938   "[A] liberal senator from the other party stormed into my office, pounded my desk, and he said, 'I consider giving that money back to the people an unnecessary expenditure of public funds.' Well, there again is the difference, as I say, between our two philosophies. To them, everything belongs to the Government; to us, everything belongs to the people." Remarks at a Republican Party Rally in Waco, Texas (September 22, 1988).

1939   "[A]s you're thinking over how you'll vote this year, I wish you'd consider something else as well: Since we must ride two horses, Congress and the President, across every stream, shouldn't they both be going the same way? ... If we don't want a tax-and-spend liberal in the White House, shouldn't we give the President we do want a Congress that will work with him?" Radio Address to the Nation on the Federal Budget and the Congressional Elections (October 15, 1988).

PRESIDENCY

1940   "Of all the responsibilities of the Presidency, shaping American foreign policy is the most awesome. It's in this arena that we come to grips with the decisions which most directly affect the delicate balance of peace and which secure both the immediate and long-term well-being of the United States." Remarks at the Swearing-In Ceremony for George P. Shultz as Secretary of State (July 16, 1982).

1941   "A President's first duty is protecting the peace by guarding us from foreign attack and

ensuring the safety of our country and the future of our children." Remarks in Columbus to Members of Ohio Veterans Organizations (October 4, 1982).

1942   "Let us always remember that we have no higher responsibility than safeguarding the security and freedom of our country." Radio Address to the Nation on Economic Recovery and National Defense. (December 18, 1982).

1943   "It is my duty as President, and the duty of all of us as citizens, to make sure that

America is strong enough to remain free and at peace." Remarks and a Question-and-Answer Session at a Luncheon Meeting of the St. Louis Regional Commerce and Growth Association in Missouri (February 1, 1983).

1944   "[T]he most basic duty that any President and any people share [is] the duty to protect and strengthen the peace." Address to the Nation on Defense and National Security (March 23, 1983).

1945   "It is my duty as President, and all our duties as citizens, to keep this nation's defenses second to none, so that America can remain strong...." Remarks at the Biennial Convention of the National Federation of Republican Women in Louisville, Kentucky (October 7, 1983).

1946   "[A]s Commander in Chief, I have an obligation to protect this country, and I will never allow political expedience to influence these crucial negotiations [with the Soviets]." Remarks at the Annual Conservative Political Action Conference Dinner (March 2, 1984).

1947   "One cannot sit in the Oval Office without realizing the awesome responsibility of protecting peace and freedom and preserving human life. The responsibility cannot be met with halfway wishes. It can only be met by a determined effort to pursue and protect peace with all the strength that we can bring to bear." Remarks at the National Convention of the Veterans of Foreign Affairs in Chicago, Illinois (August 24, 1984).

1948   "To place one's hand on the Bible and solemnly swear to defend the Constitution of the United States is to be reminded of how strong the will of our free people, guided by faith, can be." Radio Address to the Nation on Economic Growth (January 26, 1985).

1949   "The first responsibility of an American President is to see that this country is securely defended in a world in which trouble is, unfortunately, not the exception but the rule. All the great leaders of our time, from Winston Churchill to John Kennedy, have understood that to maintain the peace we must maintain our strength. If we don't, our adversaries will be inspired to wild action by our weakness." Remarks to the Students and Faculty at St. John's University in New York, New York (March 28, 1985).

1950   "Keeping our country secure is government's first job, and as long as I'm President, I intend to see that job gets done." Remarks at the Annual Meeting of the Chamber of Commerce of the United States (April 29, 1985).

1951   "My first responsibility as President is the safety and security of the American people." Radio Address to the Nation on Armed Forces Day and Defense Spending (May 18, 1985).

1952   "[T]he President and the Vice President are the only ones in Washington elected by all the people. In a way then, the President should be the people's lobbyist, your lobbyist. And any President who wants to succeed should remember his first obligation is to the people. They elected him, and only they can give him the support he needs to get things done." Radio Address to the Nation on Tax Reform (June 1, 1985).

1953   "No one in a free country likes to spend money on weapons. I'd much rather see that money left in the hands of those who work for it, but as long as I'm President, I will not see our free country relegated to a position of weakness or inferiority to any other country." Remarks at a Fundraising Event for Senator Steven D. Symms in Boise, Idaho (October 15, 1985).

1954   "[M]y highest duty as President: to preserve peace and defend these United States." Address to the Nation on National Security (February 26, 1986).

1955   "My foremost responsibility is our national security, just as it is the prime duty of Congress to appropriate the necessary resources to keep our defenses strong. This is our duty, not only to America but to the cause of human freedom." Radio Address to the Nation on the Defense Budget (March 1, 1986).

1956   "As President of the United States, the security of our country is, by law, my paramount responsibility." Remarks at a Dinner for the Republican Congressional Leadership (March 10, 1986).

1957   "[I]'ve had one rule from the very first day in office: We will never send our young service people anyplace in the world where there is danger without them understanding that if somebody shoots at them, they can shoot back." Remarks at a Senate Campaign Fundraiser for Representative W. Henson Moore in New Orleans, Louisiana (March 27, 1986).

1958   "You know, part of a President's job is to prepare our nation for the future, for the years and even the decades ahead." Remarks to Members of the American Legion Auxiliary's Girls Nation (July 18, 1986).

1959   "But I'm going to tell you what I think. I think that any President who will try to get the Constitution changed should not be doing it for himself. He should be doing it for those who will follow him. Well, I have to tell you I think it should be changed, because I think it's only democratic for the people to be able to vote for someone as many times as they want." Remarks at a Republican Party Rally in Miami, Florida (July 23, 1986).

1960   "America's at peace today, and for any President that's cause for real satisfaction. Still, a President's job is more than that — it's to make the peace we enjoy today even more secure." Radio Address to the Nation on Soviet–United States Relations (November 1, 1986).

1961   "No, no [in response to chants of 'four more years']. The Constitution says no." Remarks at a Senate Campaign Rally for James Santini in Las Vegas, Nevada (November 3, 1986).

1962   "One of the joys of my current job has been getting to know America's young people. I've met you here at the White House, and everywhere I've traveled throughout this land — on campuses, in churches, on military bases — young people were there. Your idealism and confidence, your gusto for life, have been an energy source this not-so-young President has been able to tap." Address to High School Students on Martin Luther King, Jr.'s Birthday (January 15, 1987).

1963   "The Congress is a large, amorphous institution; it can't be held as accountable as an individual [the President] can." Remarks and a Question-and-Answer Session with Southeast Regional Editors and Broadcasters (May 15, 1987).

1964   "Sometimes people ask me whether I ever weary of the controversy that seems to surround so much of public life and especially this job. Well, the truth is that more than anything else, the Presidency becomes a source of satisfaction if you can look back and see a far distance

traveled." Remarks at a White House Briefing on Proposed Criminal Justice Reform Legislation (October 16, 1987).

1965   "The United States, as the most powerful of the free nations, is looked to for leadership by those who live in freedom and as a mighty source of hope to those who languish under tyranny. This is a weighty responsibility that no American, especially a President, can take lightly." Remarks at a White House Briefing for Human Rights Supporters (December 3, 1987).

1966   "The modern Presidency is, like everything else in our system, the product of both the founders' design and later practice." Remarks and a Question-and-Answer Session with the Members of the Center for the Study of the Presidency (March 25, 1988).

1967   "You may have heard me say before that one of the things I like most about my job as President is visiting and talking with our young men and women in uniform. I've met them all over the world...." Radio Address to the Nation on Armed Forces Day (May 21, 1988).

1968   "You know, every morning they hand me a schedule that tells me where I'm supposed to be." Remarks Congratulating the Eastern High School Choir (August 1, 1988).

1969   "You know, maybe it'll sound a little like bragging, but I have to tell you, I really have a great job." Remarks at the Presentation Ceremony for the Presidential Medal of Freedom (October 17, 1988).

1970   "Well, thank you [in response to the chant 'Four More Years'], but you know — yes, that's very kind of you, but you know there's a 22d amendment that makes that impossible. But I'll give you a little secret. When I'm out of here, so they can't accuse me of doing it for myself, I'm going to see if I can't talk the people of America into canceling that amendment because it is not an infringement on the man in office, it's an infringement on the democratic rights of the people of America." Remarks at a Republican Campaign Rally in Berea, Ohio (November 2, 1988).

1971   "No one knows better than a man who has sought the highest office in this land what an awesome responsibility it is to be the vessel of change, the selection of a people in control of their present and their future. It's truly humbling." Radio Address to the Nation on the Upcoming Elections (November 5, 1988).

1972 "The Presidency of the United States is a trust — a public trust from the great people of this land, who every 8 years vest that trust in someone who must be humble enough to do their will and firm enough to make sure their will is not thwarted by the twin demons of expediency and fear." Remarks at the Groundbreaking Ceremony for the Ronald Reagan Presidential Library and Center for Public Affairs in Simi Valley, California (November 21, 1988).

1973 "Today we live in a world in which America no longer enjoys preponderant power, but must lead by example and persuasion; a world of pressing new challenges to our economic prosperity; a world of new opportunities for peace and of new dangers. In such a world, more than ever, America needs strong and consistent leadership,

and the strength and resilience of the Presidency are vital." Remarks and a Question-and-Answer Session at the University of Virginia in Charlottesville (December 16, 1988).

1974 "One of the things about the Presidency is that you're always somewhat apart. You spend a lot of time going by too fast in a car someone else is driving, and seeing the people through tinted glass — the parents holding up a child, and the wave you saw too late and couldn't return. And so many times I wanted to stop and reach out from behind the glass, and connect." Farewell Address to the Nation (January 11, 1989).

1975 "It's been my responsibility, my duty, and very much my honor to serve as Commander in Chief of this nation's Armed Forces these past 8 years. That is the most sacred, most important task of the Presidency." Remarks at the Armed Forces Farewell Salute in Camp Springs, Maryland (January 12, 1989).

REAGAN ON REAGAN

Hard Work and Self-Reliance

1976 "Too often, people forget a basic fact of life: All those good things we enjoy come from the ache in [our] backs and the willingness to shoulder great personals risks." Radio Address to the Nation on Agriculture and Grain Exports (October 15, 1982).

1977 "The first job I ever had was working on a construction crew.... I was 14 years old. And I want you to know I haven't forgotten something. I was swinging a pickax on that job; and I wasn't swinging it to help somebody in Washington live better, I was working so our family could live a little better." Remarks at a Reagan-Bush Rally in Decatur, Illinois (August 20, 1984).

1978 "Four years ago we came here knowing what was wrong, but in truth, as conservatives who'd been out of power for a great many years, some of us had limited practical experience in how exactly to right all the wrongs that had preceded us. But we had a philosophy, and we had a vision. Our philosophy could be boiled down to one word: freedom. Freedom was at the heart of our plans for our economy, for individuals, for our country, and for all the nation states of the world. And so we pulled up our sleeves and went to work." Remarks at the 1985 Reagan Administration Executive Forum (January 25, 1985).

1979 "Our goal must be an open society in which hope is nourished and effort rewarded, where the promise of tomorrow is found in opportunity today." Radio Address to the Nation on Economic Growth (January 26, 1985).

1980 "Great challenges demand heroic struggles." Radio Address to the Nation on the Federal Budget (February 1, 1986).

1981 "Let us have the courage to live up to our ideals, the energy to reach our potential, and the commitment to do the job that has to be done." Remarks at the 1986 Reagan Administration Executive Forum (February 6, 1986).

1982 "Remember the lessons you've learned this season, the lessons about hard work and never quitting, about digging down into yourselves when you seem to be behind. Because what you've learned in basketball will be a strength to you all your lives. Especially here, in this great land of opportunity. Because it's true, if you keep your head up and work hard in America, anything can happen." Remarks on Greeting the 1988 National Collegiate Athletic Association Men's and Women's Basketball Champions (April 11, 1988).

1983 "Everyone who's been blessed with talent has the responsibility to put it to good use. And in America, I've always believed that each of us has a special responsibility because we have the freedom to use our talents to the fullest." Remarks to Members of the American Legion's Boys Nation (July 25, 1988).

His Age

1984 "I've already lived some two decades longer than my life expectancy when I was born. That's a source of annoyance to a number of people." Remarks at Convocation at the University of South Carolina in Columbia (September 20, 1983).

1985 "One of my favorite quotations about age comes from Thomas Jefferson. He said that we should never judge a President by his age, only by his work. And ever since he told me that — I've stopped worrying. And just to show you how youthful I am, I intend to campaign in all 13 States." Remarks at a White House Briefing for the National Alliance of Senior Citizens (February 29, 1984).

1986 "[I] hope that when you're my age, you'll be able to say as I have been able to say: We lived in freedom, we lived lives that were a state-ment, not an apology." Remarks to the Students and Faculty at St. John's University in New York, New York (March 28, 1985)

1987 "One fascinating aspect of space travel is, as Einstein pointed out: The faster you travel, the less you age. And now you know my real motive for supporting space exploration." Remarks at the National Space Club Luncheon (March 29, 1985).

1988 "I've already surpassed my own life expectancy at my birth by 20 years. Now, there are a lot of people that find that a source of annoyance, but I appreciate it very much." Remarks to Participants in the President's Inaugural Bands Parade at Walt Disney's EPCOT Center Near Orlando, Florida (May 27, 1985).

1989 "And if you'll forgive me, during lunch I overheard one or two references to my age. And it's true, as of last week, I'd been around for three-quarters of a century. And many of you have quoted the fact that I said that's only 24 Celsius. But I have another description of it, also: that if I'm ever in need of any transplants, I got parts they don't make anymore." Remarks and a Question-and-Answer Session with Regional Editors and Broadcasters (February 10, 1986).

1990 "[I]t's hard to believe it has been 5 years since we first met here in Washington. But you probably didn't know that I count my years now in blocks of five so it doesn't seem quite so long to me." Remarks at a White House Meeting with the Associated General Contractors of America (April 14, 1986).

1991 "Having celebrated my 39th birthday 36 times now — I've been around to witness a sizable chunk of this century." Remarks to the Annual Meeting of the National Association of Manufacturers (May 29, 1986).

1992 "[Y]our principal, Mr. Holland, showed me your American history book, and I was startled to see that it took almost 400 pages to tell the story of our nation. When I was your age, it only took two stone tablets." Remarks at the High School Commencement Exercises in Glassboro, New Jersey (June 19, 1986).

1993 "[I]'m particularly glad to be here during your sesquicentennial. Then, I'm always happy to be anyplace that's twice as old as I am." Remarks at a Campaign Fundraiser for William Clements in Dallas, Texas (July 23, 1986).

1994   "You'll discover when you get to be my age that quite a few things remind you of a story." Remarks at the Republican Governors Association Dinner (October 7, 1986).

1995   "You get along toward this time in life and you do have a lot of stories you delight in telling if there's half a chance." Remarks at a Republican Party Rally in Costa Mesa, California (November 3, 1986).

1996   "The last time we met ... I reminded you of my first small business venture — renting out a canoe for 35 cents an hour on the Rock River back in Dixon, Illinois, where I was lifeguarding. Contrary to what some of my young staffers may have thought when I said that, I want to clear the record now. I was not outfitting the Lewis and Clark expedition." Remarks on Receiving the Report of the National White House Conference on Small Business (December 23, 1986).

1997   "My birthday cake's beginning to look more and more like a bonfire every year." Remarks at the Conservative Political Action Conference Luncheon (February 20, 1987).

1998   "You know, by the time you reach my age, you've made plenty of mistakes. And if you've lived your life properly — so, you learn. You put things in perspective. You pull your energies together. You change. You go forward." Address to the Nation on the Iran Arms and Contra Aid Controversy (March 4, 1987).

1999   "But I am aware of my age. When I go in for a physical now they no longer ask me how old I am, they just carbon date me." Remarks at the White House Correspondents Association Annual Dinner (April 22, 1987).

2000   "It's a pleasure to be here today. It's particularly a pleasure on this, the chamber's 75th anniversary. Isn't there anything around here that's older than I am?" Remarks at the 75th Annual Meeting of the United States Chamber of Commerce (April 27, 1987).

2001   "It's a great honor to be here with you on this the 100th anniversary of your convention. The truth is, it's always a great pleasure to be addressing something older than I am." Remarks to the 100th Annual Convention of the American Newspaper Publishers Association in New York, New York (May 3, 1987).

2002   "You know, I hope you won't mind if I pause for a minute, but that reminds me of something. At my age, everything reminds you of something." Remarks at the Uniformed Services University of Health Sciences Commencement Ceremony (May 16, 1987).

2003   "No, I didn't take any classes with Socrates." Remarks at the Commencement Ceremony for Area High School Seniors in Chattanooga, Tennessee (May 19, 1987).

2004   "For 92 years, the National Association of Manufacturers has spoken for the concerns of industry. Ninety-two years — you know, it's great to find something older than I am." Remarks at the Annual Meeting of the National Association of Manufacturers (May 28, 1987).

2005   "[M]y birthday cake is beginning to look more like a celestial phenomenon every year...." Remarks at the Presentation Ceremony for the National Medals of Science and Technology (June 25, 1987).

2006   "It's great to be in New Orleans. You know, I always feel at home here in Louisiana because, you know, I'm the fella that talked Tom Jefferson into buying it." Remarks at the Welcoming Rally at the Republican National Convention in New Orleans, Louisiana (August 14, 1987).

2007   "History's no easy subject. Even in my day it wasn't, and we had so much less of it to learn then." Remarks to the Winners of the Bicentennial of the Constitution Essay Competition (September 10, 1987).

2008   "I appreciate this opportunity to join in celebrating *USA Today*'s fifth birthday. When you get my age, it always feels good to be celebrating someone else's birthday." Remarks at the Fifth Anniversary Celebration of *USA Today* in Arlington, Virginia (September 15, 1987).

2009   "Thank you very much, Governor Kean, and ... no, I wasn't at the Little Big Horn, but I was in the horse cavalry." Remarks at a Luncheon Hosted by the New Jersey Chamber of Commerce in Somerset (October 13, 1987).

2010   "It was back in the thirties that I joined the Army Reserves as a member of the 14th Regiment of the — get ready now — horse cavalry. It's not true that I was at the Battle of the Little Big Horn." Remarks at the United States Military Academy in West Point, New York (October 28, 1987).

2011 "Well, welcome to the Old Executive Office Building. It's even older than I am." Remarks to Business Leaders at a White House Briefing on the Canada–United States Free Trade Agreement (November 4, 1987).

2012 "There are more of you here [at the President's birthday gathering at the White House South Portico] than there lived in the town where I was born. There isn't any way to express it. And you know something: It ain't bad having another birthday, even at this stage. Here I am, 39 years old. I've been that old 39 times now. And I wouldn't mind going another 39." Remarks During the White House Staff's Celebration of the President's 77th Birthday (February 5, 1988).

2013 "[B]roadcasting and I go back a long way. I mean a very long way. Come to think of it, the first group like this that I ever addressed was called the National Association of Town-criers." Remarks at the Annual Convention of the National Association of Broadcasters in Las Vegas, Nevada (April 10, 1988).

2014 "I was looking over my notes from our last meeting, back in 1986, and I noticed that I told you about one of my first jobs as a young man, working for a contractor who was remodeling old homes. I was just 14 years old — by the way, it's not true that the homes that we were remodeling were log cabins." Remarks at a White House Meeting with the Associated General Contractors of America (April 18, 1988).

2015 "We [President Reagan and the visiting Presidential Scholars] do have something in common though this morning: All of you are seniors, and I'm a sort of senior myself. Believe me, when you get to be my kind of senior status there's no greater fun than a chance to meet your kind of senior." Remarks at the Presentation Ceremony for the Presidential Scholars Awards (June 16, 1988).

2016 "Well, while we're all sorry to see Senator Stennis leave Washington, I want you to know that I have a special reason. You see, Senator, you're one of the few fellows left in this town who calls me kid." Remarks at a Dinner

Honoring Senator John C. Stennis of Mississippi (June 23, 1988).

2017 "When you get to my age, you discover that quite a few things remind you of stories. My only fear is that I've told this so often that maybe I've told it to you already. Don't let me know if I have." Remarks at the Presentation Ceremony for the National Medals of Science and Technology (July 15, 1988).

2018 "The truth is that I had a special reason for wanting to be here for this occasion. You see, I was very moved at my own 55th birthday when President Abraham Lincoln showed up and said a few kind words." Remarks at a Campaign Fundraising Luncheon for Senator Pete Wilson in Irvine, California (August 23, 1988).

2019 "But another Gray, the British poet Thomas Gray, who died in 1771— I know what you're thinking, but, no, I never met him — wrote...." Remarks at the Dedication of the C.J. and Marie Gray Center for the Communications Arts at Hastings College in Nebraska (September 6, 1988).

2020 "Isn't it amazing how time flies when you're having fun? I still remember when Betsy Ross told me that the years would travel fast — of course I was too young then to really know what she meant." Remarks to Executive Women in Government (September 8, 1988).

2021 "I have a great affection for Georgetown. After all, it's one of the few things in this country that are older than I am." Remarks at Georgetown University's Bicentennial Convocation (October 1, 1988).

2022 "This bill is a landmark in the quest for alternative forms of energy. And believe me, when you're my age you just love hearing about alternative sources of energy." Remarks on Signing the Alternative Motor Fuels Act of 1988 (October 14, 1988).

2023 "You know, I have to tell you, I was president of the student body in my high school, and I always had a dream that one day the President of the United States might come visit our school. Of course, every time we invited him, President Washington said he was busy." Remarks to the Students and Faculty of Archbishop Carroll and All Saints High Schools (October 17, 1988).

2024 "It's great to be here in Baltimore. You know, as we were coming here, I turned to one of my fellows that was with me and said, 'I really love this city.' I remember the first time I came here. I said to my host, Francis Scott Key — I said, 'Francis, I just love Baltimore.' Francis, you know, was the guy who served me my very first crab cake." Remarks at a Fundraising Luncheon for Senatorial Candidate Alan Keyes in Baltimore, Maryland (October 26, 1988).

2025 "The United States is the world's oldest democratic government. And at my age, when I tell you something is the oldest in the world, you can take my word for it; I'm probably talking from personal experience." Remarks and a Question-and-Answer Session with Area Junior High School Students (November 14, 1988).

2026 "There hasn't been a transition like this since Inauguration Day in 1837, when Andrew Jackson turned the keys to the store over to Martin Van Buren. And, no, I don't remember that day. When you get to be my age, you don't remember anything that recent." Remarks to Administration Officials on Domestic Policy (December 13, 1988).

2027 "You know, just after he left the Presidency, George Washington said — and these are his words — 'Rural employments will now take place of toil, responsibility, and the solicitudes of public life.' And I told George then it sounded good to me." Remarks at the Nancy Reagan Drug Abuse Center Benefit Dinner in Los Angeles, California (January 4, 1989).

His Critics

2028 "I have to tell you, though, I'm more than a little self-conscious facing you [an audience of African-American women] here and saying these things [the importance of unity]. There's been such a case made that I am prejudiced, if not an outright bigot, that I find myself wondering if maybe you're thinking that I don't mean what I'm saying, and this is just another dose of political hot air. Well, believe me, it is not. Nothing has frustrated me more than the totally false image that has been created of me. I've lived a long time, but I can't remember a time in my life when I didn't believe that prejudice and bigotry were the worst of sins." Remarks at a White House Reception for the Council of Negro Women (July 28, 1983).

2029 "Critics have claimed that in opposing our administration on the issues, they're at some kind of an unfair disadvantage, that this Presidency is somehow based more on personality than on policy. Well, the truth is, no President can remain popular unless he retains the fundamental support of the American people on the issues. So, I invite my critics — I welcome my critics — to go after me on the issues just as hard as they please. We'll let the people decide who's right and who's wrong." Remarks at the Annual Convention of the National Association of Counties in Indianapolis, Indiana (July 13, 1987).

2030 "Sometimes they [Reagan's critics] dismiss the strong economy as a sign of my luck and then keep right on with their old talk of new programs and more spending. Well, maybe they ought to take a moment to look at the facts. I know that may come as a surprising suggestion to many of our critics. I'm not saying they're hostile to the facts, just apathetic about them." Remarks at the Annual Meeting of the National Alliance of Business (September 14, 1987).

2031 "Well, these days when those same critics talk about the last 6½ years, they remind me of a joke among dissidents in the Soviet Union. This one begins with a question: What is a Soviet historian? And the answer: someone who can accurately predict the past." Remarks at a Luncheon Hosted by the New Jersey Chamber of Commerce in Somerset (October 13, 1987).

2032 "It's been a time of increasing hope, of rising standards of living, of economic expansion. And don't let anyone tell you it's all over. We were told it couldn't be done even before we started. The doomsayers then claimed it could never last, yet it has been one of the longest, as I said, peace-time expansions in history." Remarks at the 1988 Reagan Administration Executive Forum (January 19, 1988).

2033 "The doomsayers, who can't make the front page or network news unless they've got something bad to say, have been wrong for the last 7 years." Remarks at the 1988 Reagan Administration Executive Forum (January 19, 1988).

2034   "So, believe me, I welcome this approach [criticizing Reagan's record] by the opposition. And I promise you every time they use it I'll just tell the story of a friend of mine who was asked to a costume ball a short time ago. He slapped some egg on his face and went as a liberal economist." Remarks at the Annual Conservative Political Action Conference Dinner (February 11, 1988).

2035   "We throw at them [Reagan's critics] a three-punch combination of surging manufacturing exports, the longest peacetime expansion on history, and the reality that more Americans are at work today than ever before. And after all this, you'd think they'd stay on the mat and wait for the bell, slip back into the locker room in shame. But, no, they just keep coming up with new charges and new demands for a return to old and discredited policies. You know, this Washington sparring match — in one form or another, it's been going on since the day I took office." Remarks to Business Leaders at a White House Briefing on International Trade (March 11, 1988).

2036   "You've probably heard that some of our political opponents are very concerned about the state of our economy. And I have to tell you I don't blame them. If I were in their shoes, I'd be worried too. You see, April marks the 65th straight month of the longest peacetime expansion in U.S. history." Radio Address to the Nation on Economic Growth and the Intermediate-Range Nuclear Forces Treaty (April 9, 1988).

2037   "I've heard a lot about this being the era of greed, usually from those who really mean that taxes are too low and government is too small." Remarks at the Annual Dinner of the Knights of Malta in New York, New York (January 13, 1989).

His Faith

2038   "I'm accused of being simplistic at times with some of the problems that confront us. But I've often wondered: Within the covers of that single Book are all the answers to all problems that face us today, if we'd only look there." Remarks at the Annual Convention of National Religious Broadcasters (January 31, 1983).

2039   "Inside its pages [the Bible] lie all the answers to all the problems that man has ever known." Remarks at the Annual National Prayer Breakfast (February 3, 1983).

2040   "Nelle Reagan, my mother, God rest her soul, had an unshakable faith in God's goodness. And while I may not have realized it in my youth, I know now that she planted that faith very deeply in me." Remarks and a Question-and-Answer Session with Women Leaders of Christian Religious Organizations (October 13, 1983).

2041   "[H]ardly a day goes by that I'm not told — sometimes in letters and sometimes by people that I met and perfect strangers — and they tell me that they're praying for me. Well, thanks to Nelle Reagan, I believe in intercessory prayer. And I know that those prayers are giving me strength that I otherwise would not possess." Remarks and a Question-and-Answer Session with Women Leaders of Christian Religious Organizations (October 13, 1983).

2042   "I know there are those who recognize Christmas Day as the birthday of a great and good man, a wise teacher who gave us principles to live by. And then there are those of us who believe that he was the son of God, that he was divine. If we live our lives for truth, for love, and for God, we never need be afraid. God will be with us, and He will be part of something much larger, much more powerful and enduring than any force here on Earth." Remarks on Lighting the National Community Christmas Tree (December 15, 1983).

2043   "My experience in this office I hold has only deepened a belief I've held for many years: Within the covers of that single Book are all the answers to all the problems that face us today if we'd only read and believe." Remarks at the Annual Conference of Religious Broadcasters (January 30, 1984).

2044   "For many of us, Christmas is a deeply holy day, the birthday of the promised Messiah, the Son of God who came to redeem our sins and teach us that most needed of all lessons, 'Peace on Earth, good will among men.' For others of us, Christmas marks the birth of a good, great man, a prophet whose teachings provide a pattern of living pertinent to all times and to all people. Either way, his message remains the guiding star of our endeavors." Remarks on Lighting the National Christmas Tree (December 13, 1984).

2045   "The clerk and the king and the Communist were made in His image. We all have souls, and we all have the same problems. I'm convinced, more than ever, that man finds liberation only when he binds himself to God and commits himself to his fellow man." Remarks at the Annual National Prayer Breakfast (January 31, 1985).

2046   "Prayer, of course, is deeply personal. Many of us have been taught to pray by people we love. In my case, it was my mother. I learned quite literally at her knee. My mother gave me a great deal, but nothing she gave me was more important than that special gift, the knowledge of the happiness and solace to be gained by talking to the Lord." Remarks on Signing the 1987 National Day of Prayer Proclamation (December 22, 1986).

2047   "The way we pray depends both on our religious convictions and our own individual dispositions, but the light of prayer has a common core — our hopes and our aspirations, our sorrows ... our deep remorse and renewed resolve, our thanks and joyful praise, and most especially our love, all turned towards loving God — for recognition of the supreme reality of God and his love." Remarks on Signing the 1987 National Day of Prayer Proclamation (December 22, 1986).

2048   "[I]t's important to remember that prayer doesn't always mean asking God to give us something. Prayer can also be a vehicle for worship — for recognition of the supreme reality, the reality of God and His love." Remarks on Signing the 1987 National Day of Prayer Proclamation (December 22, 1986).

2049   "I have long been unable to understand the atheist in this world of so much beauty. And I've had an unholy desire to invite some atheists to a dinner and then serve the most fabulous gourmet dinner that has ever been concocted and, after dinner, ask them if they believe there was a cook." Remarks at the Annual National Prayer Breakfast (February 4, 1988).

2050   "His truth is the ultimate power source, and it's always there. It's available to ministers of the Gospel, Presidents, and the local grocery clerk. His comforting hand — well, I could never carry the responsibilities of this high office without it." Remarks at the Annual National Prayer Breakfast (February 4, 1988).

2051   "The history of the 20th century has too often been brutal and tragic, but it has taught us one lesson that should fill our hearts with hope and joy, for we have found that the more religion is oppressed, the greater the attempt to extinguish that life principle, that divine spark — the more it glows. History is etched with stories of those who suffered religious persecution, yes, but it also tells of transcendence, devotion, and sanctity, even conversion." Remarks at a White House Briefing on Religious Freedom in the Soviet Union (May 3, 1988).

2052   "During the Civil War, perhaps our nation's darkest hour, Abraham Lincoln said, 'I have been driven many times to my knees by the conviction that I have nowhere else to go.' Well, believe me, no one can serve in this office without understanding and believing exactly what he said." Remarks to the Student Congress on Evangelism (July 28, 1988).

2053   "The Bible says: 'If my people who are called by my name humble themselves and pray and seek my face and turn from their wicked ways, then I will hear from Heaven and forgive their sins and heal their land.' Many, many years ago, my mother had underlined that particular passage in the Bible. And I had her Bible that I could place my hand on when I took the oath of office in 1980. And I had it opened to that passage that she had underlined. Today more and more Americans are seeking His face. And, yes, He has begun to heal our land." Remarks to the Student Congress on Evangelism (July 28, 1988).

2054   "[I] know in our land of freedom everyone — if they want to choose atheism instead of a belief in God, that's their right to do so. But I have always felt that I would like someday to entertain an atheist at dinner and serve the most gourmet, perfect dinner that has ever been served and then, at the end of the meal, ask that atheist if he believes there's a cook. We must cherish our nation, work to make her better still, and never stop saying this simple prayer: God bless America." Remarks to the Student Congress on Evangelism (July 28, 1988).

2055   "You know, hardly a day goes by that I'm not told — sometimes in letters, sometimes by people I meet — that they're praying for me. It's a warm but humbling feeling. I know that many of you pray probably for me and for all our government leaders. Well, I appreciate your prayers more deeply than I can say. I grew up in a home where I was taught to believe in intercessory prayer." Remarks to the Student Congress on Evangelism (July 28, 1988).

2056 "It is a truth that I hope now you'll permit me to mention ... a truth embodied in our Declaration of Independence: that the case for inalienable rights, that the idea of human dignity, that the notion of conscience above compulsion can be made only in the context of higher law, only in the context of what one of the founders of this organization, Secretary-General Dag Hammarskjold, has called devotion to something which is greater and higher than we are ourselves. This is the endless cycle, the final truth to which humankind seems always to return: that religion and morality, that faith in something higher, are prerequisites for freedom and that justice and peace within ourselves is the first step toward justice and peace in the world and for the ages." Address to the 43d Session of the United Nations General Assembly in New York, New York (September 26, 1988).

2057 "[H]er [Nelle Reagan] most important gift was the knowledge of happiness and solace to be gained in prayer. It's the greatest help I've had in my Presidency...." Address to the 43d Session of the United Nations General Assembly in New York, New York (September 26, 1988).

2058 "When we grow weary of the world and its troubles, when our faith in humanity falters, it is then that we must seek comfort and refreshment of spirit in a deeper source of wisdom, one greater than ourselves." Address to the 43d Session of the United Nations General Assembly in New York, New York (September 26, 1988).

2059 "[T]he deliberations of great leaders and great bodies are but overture, that the truly majestic music — the music of freedom, of justice, and peace — is the music made in forgetting self and seeking in silence the will of Him who made us." Address to the 43d Session of the United Nations General Assembly in New York, New York (September 26, 1988).

2060 "I believe that if we have faith in Him who created us and if we're true to the values of family, work, and community that He has taught us and that have always been America's guiding stars on the seas of history, then America's future

and your future hold promises bigger than the sky and more vast than the galaxies." Remarks to Area High School Students and Faculty in Upper Darby, Pennsylvania (October 12, 1988).

2061 "[I] believe that Lincoln spoke the truth I've learned in these 8 years as never before when he said, 'I could not perform the functions of this office for 15 minutes if I did not know that I could call upon one who is stronger and wiser than all others.'" Remarks to the Students and Faculty of Archbishop Carroll and All Saints High Schools (October 17, 1988).

2062 "Christmas casts its glow upon us, as it does every year. And it reminds us that we need not feel lonely because we are loved, loved with the greatest love there has ever been or ever will be." Remarks on Lighting the National Christmas Tree (December 15, 1988).

2063 "And so, goodbye, God bless you, and God bless the United States of America." Farewell Address to the Nation (January 11, 1989).

Jellybeans

2064 "You'd be surprised ... we're beginning to run the government with them. They get us through a lot of late afternoon meetings, and you'd be surprised at the very important affairs that are being discussed and the jar of jellybeans is going around the table." Remarks at a Meeting with Disabled Climbers Following Their Ascent of Mount Rainier (July 8, 1981).

2065 "And sometimes when a Cabinet meeting starts to drag, I wonder what would happen if the jellybean jar there [at] ... the Cabinet table was filled with jalapeno jellybeans." Remarks at the Annual Convention of the American G.I. Forum in El Paso, Texas (August 13, 1983).

2066 "I have to tell you, someone gave me one the other day [an unusual gift] — it was new to me. It was a little duck. And if you squeezed it, it laid jellybeans." Remarks During a White House Briefing for Members of the American Retail Federation (May 22, 1986).

2067 "It seems that when I told somebody to expect the Hurricanes on Friday some of the

White House staffers battened down the storm doors and ordered up emergency reserves of jellybeans. And I had to explain that I wasn't talking about tropical storms, that I'd invited the best college football team in America to come by." Remarks to the University of Miami Hurricanes, the National Collegiate Athletic Association Football Champions (January 29, 1988).

His Legacy

2068   "[I] hope our political victory will be remembered as a generous one and our time in power will be recalled for the tolerance we showed for those with whom we disagree." Remarks at the Conservative Political Action Conference Dinner (March 20, 1981).

2069   "Well, at my age I didn't come to Washington to play politics as usual. I didn't come here to reward pressure groups by spending other people's money. And most of all, I didn't come here to further mortgage the future of the American people just to buy a little short-term political popularity. I came to Washington to try to solve problems, not to sweep them under the rug and leave them for those who follow." Address to the Nation on the Economy (October 13, 1982).

2070   "We were sent here to move America forward again by putting people in charge of their own country, to promote growth by placing limits on the size and power of government, to give individuals the opportunities to reach their dreams, to strengthen institutions of family, school, church, and community, to make the United States a stronger leader for peace, freedom, and progress abroad, and, through it all, to renew our faith in the God who has blessed our land." Remarks to the Reagan Administration Executive Forum (January 20, 1983).

2071   "You know, I was once asked how I hoped, personally, to be remembered for my time as custodian of this office ... [and] I said I would hope that I would be remembered as having given the government of this country back to the people." Remarks and a Question-and-Answer Session at the Economic Club of Detroit in Detroit, Michigan (October 1, 1984).

2072   "I'd like my Presidency to be remembered as the one that gave the Government back to the people." Remarks at a Reagan-Bush Rally in Charlotte, North Carolina (October 8, 1984).

2073   "The great change that we began 4 years ago has been called the Reagan Revolution." Remarks at a Senate Republican Unity Dinner (November 28, 1984).

2074   "Let history say of us: 'These were the golden years — when the American Revolution was reborn, when freedom gained new life, and America reached for her best.'" Inaugural Address (January 21, 1985).

2075   "[O]ur New Beginning is a continuation of that beginning created two centuries ago when, for the first time in history, government, the people said, was not our master, it is our servant; its only power that which we the people allow it to have." Inaugural Address (January 21, 1985).

2076   "Well, as long as I'm President, we're not going back to the days when America was fast becoming an impotent democracy, too weak to meet defense commitments or to resist Communist takeovers and, yes, too weak to stop a Federal spending machine from impoverishing families and destroying our economy with runaway taxes and inflation." Radio Address to the Nation on the Fiscal Year 1986 Budget (March 2, 1985).

2077   "My fellow Americans, I hope history says of us that we were worthy of our past, worthy of our heritage. We can seize the moment; we can do our best for America to keep our future strong, secure, and free. Our children will thank us, and that's all the thanks we'll ever need." Address to the Nation on the Federal Budget and Deficit Reduction (April 24, 1985).

2078   "[T]here is nothing I'd like better than to be remembered as a President who did everything he could to bust up the syndicates and give the mobsters a permanent stay in the jailhouse, courtesy of the United States Government." Remarks During a White House Briefing for United States Attorneys (October 21, 1985).

2079   "[R]eal reductions in nuclear weapons and a real chance at lasting peace. That would be the finest legacy we could leave behind for our children and for their children." Address to the Nation on National Security (February 26, 1986).

2080 "You know, as we looked at the second half of this second term, I sometimes think of the quip that Mark Twain is supposed to have made about listening to an opera in German. He said, 'You have to wait until the end to hear the verb.' So it is with this administration. There's a great deal left to be accomplished before the final curtain. And when we do reach that curtain, my friends, I'm confident our verb will be 'done,' 'well done.'" Remarks During a White House Briefing for Members of the American Retail Federation (May 22, 1986).

2081 "[W]e promised the American people a government that stopped doing what it shouldn't be doing and did well whatever was left." Remarks at the Presentation Ceremony for the Presidential Distinguished Executive Rank Awards (December 8, 1986).

2082 "Increasingly, the real action in the country is going to be coming from the States. The *Christian Science Monitor* put it this way: 'Decentralization of power could be one of the most long-lasting effects of the Reagan Presidency.' I'd be very proud if that were so." Remarks at a White House Briefing for the American Legislative Exchange Council (December 12, 1986).

2083 "Well, you know, I had to smile when they called it the Reagan revolution, because, yes, those values may have been revolutionary, but they were from a revolution much older than me — the revolution that started with the Declaration of Independence and the Constitution, the revolution continued by every American who ever plowed the land or worked in a factory, an office, or a store, or built a business or stayed home and built a family." Radio Address to the Nation on the Fiscal Year 1988 Budget (January 3, 1987).

2084 "The pundits, you know, the pundits told us that we couldn't expect to get anything accomplished, even before we got to Washington. Now, they're trying to bring the curtain down before the show is over. Well, I learned a lesson in my former profession. So, let me give you a tip: We're saving the best stuff for the last act." Remarks at the Conservative Political Action Conference Luncheon (February 20, 1987).

2085 "There will be no post–Reagan era, because there's been no Reagan era in the way those people mean it. This has been the era of the

American people. Leaders may come and go. When it comes to the American people, their truth keeps marching on." Remarks at a White House Briefing for Administration Supporters (June 29, 1987).

2086 "I went to Washington to do a job: lower taxes, restore our defenses, cut the size and intrusiveness of government, tune up the carburetor and step on the gas of the greatest engine against poverty and for opportunity in the history of man — the free enterprise system of the United States of America. We've achieved a great deal of that." Remarks to Community Leaders in New Britain, Connecticut (July 8, 1987).

2087 "Now, you may have heard of some people, maybe even some that are present, talk about a certain lame duck and the end of an era. Well, all that lame duck is for the birds. The era we've begun won't end any time soon, because it's not my era, it's yours, the era of the American people. You did this. And in America, when you, the people, put your foot down, you're the boss." Remarks to Citizens in New Britain, Connecticut (July 8, 1987).

2088 "My fellow Americans, I have a year and a half before I have to clean out this desk. I'm not about to let the dust and cobwebs settle on the furniture in this office or on me. I have things I intend to do, and with your help, we can do them." Address to the Nation on the Iran Arms and Contra Aid Controversy and Administration Goals (August 12, 1987).

2089 "Well, could I give you just a little lesson in civics and politics? The President can't spend a nickel; only Congress can appropriate money to be spent. And there are some things I think you should know. The President is required to submit a budget every year. I have never had one of my budgets approved by Congress since I've been there. And if they had passed the budget I first proposed for 1982, the cumulative deficits from there through 1986 would have been $207 billion less than they were." Remarks to Civic and Community Leaders in North Platte, Nebraska (August 13, 1987).

2090 "In looking back over these 6½ years, then, I cannot help but reflect on the most dramatic change to my own eyes: the exciting new prospects for the democratic cause. A feeling of energy and hope prevails. Statism has lost the intellectuals, and everywhere one turns, nations and people are seeking the fulfillment of their age-old aspirations for self-government and self-determination." Remarks on Soviet–United States Relations at the Town Hall of California Meeting in Los Angeles (August 26, 1987).

2091 "Our economic expansion will go on the record books as America's all-time, peacetime champion — 59 months of peace and economic growth. This land of opportunity has never recorded a run like that before." Remarks at a Luncheon Hosted by the New Jersey Chamber of Commerce in Somerset (October 13, 1987).

2092 "If anyone expects just a proud recitation of the accomplishments of my administration, I say let's leave that to history; we're not finished yet. So, my message to you tonight is put on your work shoes; we're still on the job." Address Before a Joint Session of Congress on the State of the Union (January 25, 1988).

2093 "No legacy would make me more proud than leaving in place a bipartisan consensus for the cause of world freedom, a consensus that prevents a paralysis of American power from ever occurring again." Address Before a Joint Session of Congress on the State of the Union (January 25, 1988).

2094 "Getting the Federal Government's fiscal house in order is part of the unfinished business of our revolution. And despite the odds, I'm convinced that, one way or another, it'll be done. You see, on this issue, as on so many others, we've changed the terms of national debate." Remarks at a White House Briefing for the American Legislative Exchange Council (April 22, 1988).

2095 "One of the great lessons of the last 7 years is that when people in free economies are allowed to trade with one another around the world the result is greater prosperity for us all." Radio Address to the Nation on Economic Growth and Free and Fair Trade (June 11, 1988).

2096 "Several years ago, I said to you that we could spark a great prairie fire that would sweep across this nation and the world. Well, by golly, we have! Others would like to extinguish the flame of hope, but if we stand together, it won't happen. America will know a new morning of growth, and the world will know a new birth of freedom." Remarks at a White House Briefing for Conservative Political Leaders (July 5, 1988).

2097 "The American model of low tax rates, deregulation, and privatization are the policies being emulated around the world. Today's news [employment is at an all-time high] is more solid evidence that the policies of this administration work, that our philosophy works." Remarks on Economic Growth and a Question-and-Answer Session with Reporters (July 8, 1988).

2098 "Yes, America is in a new era of opportunity. Some have called it the Reagan era...." Remarks at a Fundraising Reception for Senator William V. Roth, Jr., of Delaware (August 1, 1988).

2099 "I hope that history will record that this former Governor went on to practice what he'd preached and to fight the use of Federal dollars, first as bait and then as a club, and to return power and responsibility to the States, where they belong." Remarks at the Annual Meeting of the National Governors' Association in Cincinnati, Ohio (August 8, 1988).

2100 "When our children turn the pages of our lives, I hope they'll see that we had a vision to pass forward a nation as nearly perfect as we could, where there's decency, tolerance, generosity, honesty, courage, common sense, fairness, and piety." Remarks at the Republican National Convention in New Orleans, Louisiana (August 15, 1988).

2101 "[S]ome people have been kind enough to say that I'm a great communicator." Remarks at a Presidential Campaign Rally for George Bush in Los Angeles, California (August 24, 1988).

2102 "America has traveled such a remarkable distance in the last 8 years that the memory has faded of the economic and foreign policy crises that we faced when Vice President Bush and I took office. The last time so many things went wrong all at once was right after Mrs. O'Leary's cow decided to do the cancan." Remarks at a Republican Party Fundraiser in Chicago, Illinois (September 30, 1988).

2103 "This is not the end of an era but a time to refresh and strengthen our new beginning. In fact, to those who sometimes flatter me with talk of a Reagan revolution, today my hope is this:

You ain't seen nothin' yet." Remarks and an Informal Exchange with Reporters at a White House Ceremony for President-Elect George Bush and Vice President–Elect Dan Quayle (November 9, 1988).

2104 "The journey has not just been my own. It seems I've been guided by a force much larger than myself, a force made up of ideas and beliefs about what this country is and what it could be. The story that'll be told inside the walls that are yet to be built here is the story not only of a Presidency but of a movement — a determined movement dedicated to the greatness of America and faith in its bedrock traditions; in the essential goodness of its people; in the essential soundness of its institutions; and, yes, faith in our very essence as a nation." Remarks at the Groundbreaking Ceremony for the Ronald Reagan Presidential Library and Center for Public Affairs in Simi Valley, California (November 21, 1988).

2105 "[I]f I were to offer a toast of my own, it would be this: From economics to foreign policy to defense, what we believe and have fought for so long has now been tried — and, yes, it works." Remarks at a Dinner Honoring Representative Jack F. Kemp of New York (December 1, 1988).

2106 "[I] would echo Churchill and say we have not come this far through lack of strength or any weakness in our resolve, nor has there been anything inevitable about what we've achieved. The unity, confidence, power, and firmness of the democracies has brought us forward, and maintaining a strong alliance will keep us moving forward." Radio Address to the Nation on Soviet–United States Relations (December 10, 1988).

2107 "The way I see it, there were two great triumphs, two things that I'm proudest of. One is the economic recovery, in which the people of America created — and filled —19 million new jobs. The other is the recovery of our morale. America is respected again in the world and looked to for leadership." Farewell Address to the Nation (January 11, 1989).

2108 "And in all of that time I won a nickname, 'The Great Communicator.' But I never thought it was my style or the words I used that made a difference: it was the content. I wasn't a great communicator, but I communicated great things, and they didn't spring full bloom from my brow, they came from the heart of a great nation — from our experience, our wisdom, and our belief in the principles that have guided us for two centuries. They called it the Reagan revolution. Well, I'll accept that, but for me it always seemed more like the great rediscovery, a rediscovery of our values and our common sense." Farewell Address to the Nation (January 11, 1989).

2109 "Once you begin a great movement, there's no telling where it will end. We meant to change a nation, and instead, we changed a world." Farewell Address to the Nation (January 11, 1989).

Life's Plan

2110 "I've always believed that we were, each of us, put here for a reason, that there is a plan, somehow a divine plan for all of us. I know that whatever days are left to me belong to Him." Remarks at Annual National Prayer Breakfast (February 4, 1982).

2111 "[W]e're lucky not to live in pale and timid times. We've been blessed with the opportunity to stand for something — for liberty and freedom and fairness. And these are things worth fighting for, worth devoting our lives to." Remarks at the Annual Dinner of the Conservative Political Action Conference (March 1, 1985).

2112 "The miracle of life is given by One greater than ourselves, but once given, each life is ours to nurture and preserve, to foster, not only for today's world but for a better one to come." Address to the 40th Session of the United Nations General Assembly in New York, New York (October 24, 1985).

2113 "You know, in Hollywood, if you don't sing or dance, you become an after-dinner speaker. And look where I wound up." Remarks at the American Film Institute's Preservation Ball Honoring Fred Astaire (May 21, 1988).

2114 "I've found there are two kinds of people in this world: those absorbed in themselves and those who give love — love to their families, to their friends, to their communities, to their country, and to God. Yes, we show love in many ways: by saying we love, of course, and by putting our arms around someone, but even more, by how we live, by our courtesy, by our integrity, by studying and preparing for the future, and by service to humanity. Add it all up, and you'd say: by our values." Remarks to the Students and Faculty of Archbishop Carroll and All Saints High Schools (October 17, 1988).

On Becoming a Republican

2115 "I was a Democrat once; in fact, for a good share of my life. But in those days, the leaders of the Democratic Party weren't in that 'blame America first' crowd. Its leaders were men like Harry Truman, Senator Scoop Jackson, John F. Kennedy — men who understood the challenges of the times. They didn't reserve all their indignation for America. They knew the difference between freedom and tyranny, and they stood for one and damned the other." Remarks at a Reagan-Bush Rally in Milwaukee, Wisconsin (November 3, 1984).

2116 "There was a Democratic fundraiser. And when the people were coming out of the affair at the end of it, there was a kid outside with some puppies. And he was holding up these puppies one by one, and he was saying, 'Pups for sale. Democratic pups for sale.' And 2 weeks later the Republicans held a fundraiser in the same place, and the same kid was there with the puppies. And he was now holding up Republican puppies for sale. And a newspaper reporter who had seen him 2 weeks before said, 'Hey, kid, wait a minute. Last time here, 2 weeks ago, you were trying to sell those puppies as Democrat puppies. Now you say they're Republican puppies. How come?' The kid said, 'Now they got their eyes open.'" Remarks at a Campaign Rally for Senator Mack Mattingly in Columbus, Georgia (October 28, 1986).

2117 "And as you may know, I used to be a Democrat myself until I learned that the liberal leadership of that party had become completely out of step with the hard-working and patriotic men and women who make up the Democratic Party. [I] know how tough it can be to break with tradition...." Remarks at a Campaign Rally for Senator James Abdnor in Rapid City, South Dakota (October 29, 1986).

2118 "[Y]ou know, in this thing of changing parties, though, I know how tough it can be to break with tradition. But remember, there's a great example set for us: the great statesman, Winston Churchill. As a Member of Parliament, Winston Churchill changed parties, and he was criticized for it. But he gave an answer that says it all. He said very simply, 'Some men change principle for party, others change party for principle.'" Remarks at a Campaign Rally for Senator Slade Gorton in Spokane, Washington (October 31, 1986).

2119 "I know many of you are Democrats or maybe Independents. Well, I was a Democrat, but like millions of others I became dismayed with the liberal leadership that was completely out of step with the hard-working and patriotic men and women who make up the Democratic Party." Address to the Nation on the Congressional and Gubernatorial Elections (November 2, 1986).

2120 "[I]'ve seen them across the country, patriotic Democrats who realize they could no longer follow the policies of the liberal leadership of their party; that it had become completely out of step with the hard-working and patriotic men and women who make up the mainstream of the Democratic Party. Now, I know how tough it can be to break with tradition...." Remarks at a Republican Party Rally in Costa Mesa, California (November 3, 1986).

2121 "I remember back in the days when, well, when I'd first become a Republican, because I was in the other party. Then, as the Bible says, I put aside childish things." Remarks at the Annual Senate Republican Dinner (November 21, 1986).

2122 "But like so many of us ... I started out in the other party. But 40 years ago, I cast my last vote as a Democrat. It was a party in which Franklin Delano Roosevelt promised the return of power to the States. It was a party where Harry Truman committed a strong and resolute America to preserving freedom. F.D.R. had run on a platform of eliminating useless boards and commissions and returning autonomy and authority to local governments and to the States. That party changed, and it will never be the same. They left me; I didn't leave them. So, it was our Republican Party that gave me a political home." Remarks at the Republican National Convention in New Orleans, Louisiana (August 15, 1988).

2123   "Now, you know ... I'm a former Democrat. But I think you know what I mean when I raise questions about the distinction between the rank-and-file Democrats — many of whom I hope are here — and the liberal leadership of that party in Washington, a liberal leadership that has turned a once-proud party of hope and affirmation into one dominated by strident liberalism and negativism." Remarks at a Republican Party Rally in Waco, Texas (September 22, 1988).

2124   "I know there are rank-and-file Democrats that if— once the facts are pointed out, they'll do what I did, because I was one of them once, and then I saw the light. As a matter of fact, I could quote the Scriptures: 'When I was a child, I spake as a child, I thought as a child. When I was an adult, I put aside childish things.'" Remarks at a Republican Party Fundraising Reception (October 11, 1988).

2125   "You see, the secret is that when the left took over the Democratic Party leadership, we took over the Republican Party. We made the Republican Party into the party of working people; the family; the neighborhood; the defense of freedom; and, yes, 'one nation under God.' So, you see, the party that so many of us grew up with still exists, except today it's called the Republican Party. And I'm asking all of you to come home and join me." Remarks at a Republican Campaign Rally in Raleigh, North Carolina (October 21, 1988).

Optimism

2126   "We have every right to dream heroic dreams. Those who say that we're in a time when there are no heroes, they just don't know where to look." Inaugural Address (January 20, 1981).

2127   "In times of trouble, fear is a disease of the spirit that can slow recovery and be exploited by those who are more interested in taking advantage of our problems than in helping solve them. And there are such people. Some are seeking political profit, and others are just naturally given to doom crying." Radio Address to the Nation on the Economy (October 16, 1982).

2128   "There are no such things as limits to growth, because there are no limits on the human capacity for intelligence, imagination, and wonder." Remarks at Convocation Ceremonies at the University of South Carolina in Columbia (September 20, 1983).

2129   "Send away the handwringers and the doubting Thomases." Address Before a Joint Session of the Congress on the State of the Union (June 25, 1984).

2130   "Am I optimistic? Well, you bet I am. I believe our best days are yet to come. With faith, freedom, courage, there's no limit to what the American people can do and will accomplish." Remarks to Participants in the Agricultural Communicators Congress (June 25, 1984).

2131   "Now, I've been accused of being an optimist, and it's true. All my life I've seen that when people like Mary Lou [Retton] have a dream, when they have the courage and opportunity to work hard, when they believe in the power of faith and hope, they not only perform great feats, they help pull all of us forward as well." Radio Address to the Nation on Administration Policies (August 18, 1984).

2132   "All my life, I've believed in miracles. I believe that if you truly have faith, your dream will come true." Remarks and a Question-and-Answer Session at the "Choosing a Future" Conference in Chicago, Illinois (September 5, 1984).

2133   "You know, it can be said that investing in the future is the most faithful act a man or woman can make. And when you invest your hard work and your money and your effort and your time, you show an extraordinary faith in our system, our culture, and our country. This is the faith of the heartland, and it's what our future is built on." Remarks at a Community Picnic in Fairfax, Iowa (September 20, 1984).

2134   "Now, I've often been accused of being an optimist, and I hope so. All my life I've seen that when people have freedom and a vision, when they have the courage and opportunity to work hard, and when people believe in the power of faith and hope, they can accomplish great things." Remarks and a Question-and-Answer Session at St. Agatha High School in Detroit, Michigan (October 10, 1984).

2135 "And one last thing ... and I know this will drive them [the Democrats] up the wall: You ain't seen nothin' yet." Remarks at a Reagan-Bush Rally in Media, Pennsylvania (October 29, 1984).

2136 "You know, I've been accused, I know, of being a believer in Norman Rockwell's America; and that's one charge that, as a small-town boy and a reader of the old *Saturday Evening Post*, I've always willingly pled guilty to that charge." Remarks and a Question-and-Answer Session During a White House Briefing for Members of the Magazine Publishers Association (March 14, 1985).

2137 "I'm not optimistic about the future of America because I have a sunny disposition. I'm not optimistic because I don't know the realities. I'm optimistic because I do know them. I'm optimistic because I have witnessed the American experience for more than seven decades, and I know that the American people can do anything." Remarks to Citizens in Bloomfield, New Jersey (June 13, 1985).

2138 "If I have one piece of advice for you: Dare to dream big dreams. Follow your star." Remarks to the Students and Faculty at North Carolina State University in Raleigh (September 5, 1985).

2139 "Each day brings new opportunities for great dreams and great feats. Let's begin now — united, confident, and determined to get the job done." Radio Address to the Nation on the State of the Union (January 25, 1986).

2140 "You'd be surprised how much gets done when you find out you could do all those things they said can't be done." Remarks at the 1986 Reagan Administration Executive Forum (February 6, 1986).

2141 "I've had many wonderful experiences during my time in office, but the greatest thrill has been meeting and getting to know this generation out there of young Americans. I've met them on the campuses and high schools and in churches, in factories, and, just last week, at a Marine base in South Carolina. They're the best darn bunch of kids we've ever had." Remarks at a White House Briefing for Supporters of Tax Reform (June 10, 1986).

2142 "Remember this: When we come to the edge of our known world, we're standing on the shores of the infinite. Dip your hand in that limitless sea; you're touching the mystery of God's universe. Set sail across its waters, and you embark on the boldest, most noble adventure of all. Out beyond our present horizons lie whole new continents of possibility, new worlds of hope waiting to be discovered. We've traveled far, but we've only begun our journey." Remarks to Participants in the Young Astronauts Program (June 11, 1986).

2143 "Believe me, if there's one impression I carry with me after the privilege of holding for 5½ years the office held by Adams and Jefferson and Lincoln, it is this: that the things that unite us — America's past of which we're so proud, our hopes and aspirations for the future of the world and this much-loved country — these things far outweigh what little divides us." Address to the Nation on Independence Day (July 4, 1986).

2144 "Imagine it — in a single lifetime — from Charles Lindbergh in that solo flight across the Atlantic to moon landings. And they wonder why I'm an optimist." Remarks to National and State Officers of the Future Farmers of America (July 22, 1986).

2145 "America didn't become great being pessimistic and cynical. America is built on a can-do spirit that sees every obstacle as a challenge, every problem as an opportunity." Radio Address to the Nation on Tax Reform (August 23, 1986).

2146 "Call it confidence, self-assurance, what you will. It's a renewed understanding that, for all our faults, ours is a nation of goodness and greatness; that despite our mistakes in the world we've stood for human freedom with greater consistency and courage than any other nation in history; that if only we have faith, if only we look not to government, but to ourselves to create a new and lasting era of prosperity." Remarks at a Campaign Rally for Senator Jeremiah A. Denton in Montgomery, Alabama (September 18, 1986).

2147 "[S]ome have accused me of telling people what they want to hear, of urging them not to engage the day but to escape it. Yet, to hope is to believe in humanity and in its future. Hope remains the highest reality, the age-old power. Hope is at the root of all the great ideas and causes that have bettered the lot of humankind across the centuries. History teaches us to hope, for it teaches us about man and about the irrepressible human spirit." Address to the 41st Session of the United Nations General Assembly in New York, New York (September 22, 1986).

2148 "[I] always thought being an American meant never being mean or small or giving in to prejudice or bigotry; that it did mean trying to help the other fella and working for a world where every person knows freedom is both a blessing and a birthright; that being an American also means that on certain special days, for a few precious moments, all of us — black or white, Jew or gentile, rich or poor — we are all equal, with an equal chance to decide our destiny, to determine our future, to cast our ballot. Tell them, too, of my fondest hope, my greatest dream for them: that they would always find here in America a land of hope, a light unto the nations, a shining city upon a hill. So that they would be able to say in their time as we've said in ours: I'm proud to be an American, where at least I know I'm free. And I won't forget the men who died, who gave that right to me. And I'll gladly stand up next to you and defend her still today. Cause there ain't no doubt I love this land; God bless the U.S.A.!" Remarks at a Republican Party Rally in Costa Mesa, California (November 3, 1986).

2149 "[A]merica has a great future ahead. We have a future of more opportunity, more growth. We have a future of a stronger America and a freer world. And that's what we're building toward, and this is what we can achieve." Remarks at a White House Briefing for Women Entrepreneurs (December 3, 1986).

2150 "We hear the cynics, but pay them no mind. We pass by the pessimists and the doomsayers knowing that they'll always be with us, but confident that they no longer can hold our country back unless we let them. We see before us a future worthy of our past and a tomorrow greater than all our yesterdays. If there's any message that I wish to convey today it is: be of good cheer." Remarks at the Conservative Political Action Conference Luncheon (February 20, 1987).

2151 "I believe in an America that can meet the challenge of the 21st century, and this means better educating our young people, better training our workers, protecting our intellectual property, reforming our antitrust laws and trade laws when necessary, and pursuing multilateral trade negotiations — and, yes, taking tough actions to open foreign markets that are closed to American exports." Remarks at a Meeting with Members of the Advisory Committee for Trade Negotiations (April 8, 1987).

2152 "Well, one of the worst mistakes anybody can make is to bet against Americans." Radio Address to the Nation on Free and Fair Trade and the Budget Deficit (May 16, 1987).

2153 "Well, on my desk in the Oval Office, there sits a plaque that says, 'It can be done.' It's a belief that I deeply hold true." Remarks at the Presentation Ceremony for the "C" Flag Awards (July 23, 1987).

2154 "Political life has always reminded me a little of my former career. And the whole philosophy was when you come to town open big. And now, well, it's time for an even bigger finish and a good curtain call." Remarks on Administration Goals to Senior Presidential Appointees (September 8, 1987).

2155 "But history doesn't just happen; it's made. And even in the most difficult moments of these past months, we went right on making history, right on striving to turn our vision of America into reality." Remarks on Administration Goals to Senior Presidential Appointees (September 8, 1987).

2156 · "In this world there are many conflicting visions of man's economic life.... One sees the resources and potential of this world as finite, and most likely insufficient for the needs of a growing humanity. It posits a world of limits and describes not only a present of insufficiency but a future of increasing scarcity, and insists on cruel but, in its view, necessary choices. That's the life raft view of humanity. We're adrift here, at the mercy of natural forces, our food is running low and not much hope of rescue. In the meantime, we don't have room for the luxuries of the past. In fact, to keep from sinking, we may have to throw them overboard. And it's our freedom that is always the first luxury to be jettisoned. Thankfully, that deeply pessimistic view ... has never really taken hold in North America." Remarks to Business Leaders at a White House Briefing on the Canada–United States Free Trade Agreement (November 4, 1987).

2157 "Well, whether we're skeptical Yankees, or recent immigrants to the Sunbelt, we know too much about America to believe in limits, to believe that the future isn't ours for the making. There's too much hope, too much possibility on this continent of ours for us to believe in the zero-sum philosophies of the Old World. Whether it's communism or socialism or what used to be called social Darwinism, we know that one person's achievement doesn't subtract from another, but adds each to the other in an expanding cycle of prosperity." Remarks to Business Leaders at a White House Briefing on the Canada–United States Free Trade Agreement (November 4, 1987).

2158 "Are America's best days ahead? You bet they are, and together we're making certain of that." Remarks to the United States Chamber of Commerce on the Economy and Deficit Reduction (November 19, 1987).

2159 "There is no such thing as inevitability in history." New Year's Messages of President Reagan and Soviet General Secretary Gorbachev (January 1, 1988).

2160 "The only thing that can keep America back is an unwillingness to do what needs to be done, to do what is within our ability to do." Remarks at the 1988 Reagan Administration Executive Forum (January 19, 1988).

2161 "One more year, not for the Gipper but for Americans and for all mankind. As they say in showbiz: Let's bring them to their feet with our closing act." Remarks at the 1988 Reagan Administration Executive Forum (January 19, 1988).

2162 "Not everything has been made perfect in 7 years, nor will it be made perfect in seven times 70 years, but before us, this year and beyond, are great prospects for the cause of peace and world freedom." Address Before a Joint Session of Congress on the State of the Union (January 25, 1988).

2163 "I believe that America is standing before the brightest future the world has ever known...." Remarks at the United States Coast Guard Academy Commencement Ceremony in New London, Connecticut (May 18, 1988).

2164 "[S]kepticism and doubt bring a barren harvest." Remarks at the Exchange of Documents Ratifying the Intermediate-Range Nuclear Forces Treaty (June 1, 1988).

2165 "[I]t makes somebody feel good who's kind of coming to the end of the job to see a lineup of the kind of people [participants at Boys Nation] that will be taking over as these years go by. And I can assure you, I have a great faith from what I've seen in how our country is going to do in the years to come." Remarks to Members of the American Legion's Boys Nation (July 25, 1988).

2166 "But when I pack up my bags in Washington, don't expect me to be happy to hear all this talk about the twilight of my life. Twilight? Twilight? Not in America. Here, it's a sunrise every day — fresh new opportunities, dreams to build. Twilight? That's not possible, because I confess there are times when I feel like I'm still little Dutch Reagan racing my brother down the hill to the swimming hole under the railroad bridge over the Rock River. You see, there's no sweeter day than each new one, because here in our country it means something wonderful can happen to you. And something wonderful happened to me." Remarks at the Republican National Convention in New Orleans, Louisiana (August 15, 1988).

2167 "I believe America's future and your future hold promises bigger than the sky and more vast than the galaxies — if we have faith and if we're true to the values of family, work, and community that have always been America's guiding stars on the path of history." Remarks to High School Students and Citizens in Sterling Heights, Michigan (October 7, 1988).

2168 "[W]e who live in democracy are all our own masters, and we know that the future is ours to build and that the only limits upon us are those we place on ourselves." Radio Address to the Nation on the Upcoming Elections (November 5, 1988).

2169 "[B]ecause we're a great nation, our challenges seem complex. It will always be this way. But as long as we remember our first principles and believe in ourselves, the future will always be ours." Farewell Address to the Nation (January 11, 1989).

Race Relations

2170 "Well, I usually try to ignore personal attacks, but one charge I will have to admit strikes at my heart every time I hear it. That's the suggestion that we Republicans are taking a less active approach to protecting the civil rights of all Americans. No matter how you slice it, that's just plain baloney." Remarks at a National Black Republican Council Dinner (September 15, 1982).

2171   "[I]f those who share my philosophy have had any failure, it's been a failure to communicate what's in our hearts to the black community. This has led to misunderstanding and, sometimes, mistrust." Remarks at a Meeting with Officials of Black Colleges and Universities (September 22, 1982).

SCHOOL PRAYER

2172   "The first amendment was not written to protect the people from religious values; it was written to protect those values from government tyranny." Remarks at the Annual Convention of National Religious Broadcasters (February 9, 1982).

2173   "To those who cite the first amendment as reason for excluding God from more and more of our institutions and everyday life, may I just say: The first amendment of the Constitution was not written to protect the people of this country from religious values; it was written to protect religious values from government tyranny." Address Before a Joint Session of the Alabama State Legislature in Montgomery (March 15, 1982).

2174   "No one must ever be forced or coerced or pressured to take part in any religious exercise [prayer in school], but neither should the government forbid religious practice." Remarks at White House Ceremony in Observance of National Day of Prayer (May 6, 1982).

2175   "We believe that school children deserve the same protection, the same constitutional consensus that permits prayer in the Houses of Congress, chaplains in our armed services, and the motto on our coinage, 'In God We Trust.'" Remarks at the Centennial Meeting of the Supreme Council of the Knights of Columbus in Hartford, Connecticut (August 3, 1982).

2176   "No one will ever convince me that a moment of voluntary prayer can harm a child or

threaten a school or a state." Remarks at Kansas State University at the Alfred M. Landon Lecture Series on Public Issues (September 9, 1982).

2177   "The Constitution was never meant to prevent people from praying: its declared purpose was to protect their freedom to pray." Radio Address to the Nation on Prayer (September 18, 1982).

2178   "Now, no one is suggesting that others should be forced into any religious activity, but to prevent those who believe in God from expressing their faith is an outrage. And the relentless drive to eliminate God from our schools can and should be stopped." Remarks at a Candle-Lighting Ceremony for Prayer in Schools (September 25, 1982).

2179   "The public expression through prayer of our faith in God is a fundamental part of our American heritage and a privilege which should not be excluded from our schools." Radio Address to the Nation on Domestic Social Issues (January 22, 1983).

2180   "[I]t's not good enough to have equal access to our law; we must also have equal access [in our schools] to the higher law — the law of God." Remarks at the Annual Meeting of the American Bar Association in Atlanta, Georgia (August 1, 1983).

2181   "[I] just have to believe that the loving God who has blessed this land and thus made us a good and caring people should never have been expelled from America's classrooms. It's time to welcome Him back, because whenever we've opened ourselves and trusted Him, we gained not only moral courage but intellectual strength." Remarks at Convocation Ceremonies at the University of South Carolina in Columbia (September 20, 1983).

2182   "Government is not supposed to wage war against God and religion, not in the United States." Remarks and a Question-and-Answer Session with Women Leaders of Christian Religious Organizations (October 13, 1983).

2183   "[W]e're told that to protect the first amendment, we must expel God, the source of all knowledge, from our children's classrooms. Well, pardon me, but the first amendment was not written to protect the American people from religion; the first amendment was written to protect the American people from government tyranny." Remarks at a Spirit of America Rally in Atlanta, Georgia (January 26, 1984).

2184   "Sometimes I can't help but feel the first amendment is being turned on its head. Because ask yourselves: Can it really be true that the first amendment can permit Nazis and Ku Klux Klansmen to march on public property, advocate the extermination of people of the Jewish faith and the subjugation of blacks, while the same amendment forbids children from saying a prayer in school?" Radio Address to the Nation on Prayer in School (February 25, 1984).

2185   "Now, let me make it plain that we seek voluntary vocal prayer, not a moment of silent prayer. We already have the right to remain silent: we can take the fifth amendment." Remarks at the Annual Conservative Political Action Conference Dinner (March 2, 1984).

2186   "Today prayer remains a vital part of American public life. The Congress begins each day with prayer, and the Supreme Court begins each sitting with an invocation. Now, I just have to believe that if Members of Congress and the Justices can acknowledge the Almighty, our children can, too." Remarks at the Annual Convention of the National Association of Evangelicals in Columbus, Ohio (March 6, 1984).

2187   "[T]hose who are fighting to make sure that voluntary prayer is not returned to the class-

rooms ... are attacking religion ... claim they are doing it in the name of tolerance, freedom, and open mindedness. Question: Isn't the real truth that they are intolerant of religion? They refuse to tolerate its importance in our lives." Remarks at an Ecumenical Prayer Breakfast in Dallas, Texas (August 23, 1984).

2188   "We establish no religion in this country, nor will we ever. We command no worship. We mandate no belief. But we poison our society when we remove its theological underpinning. We court corruption when we leave it bereft of belief. All are free to believe or not believe; all are free to practice a faith or not. But those who believe must be free to speak of and act on their beliefs, to apply moral teaching to public questions." Remarks at an Ecumenical Prayer Breakfast in Dallas, Texas, (August 23, 1984).

2189   "Now, I can't think of anyone who favors the Government establishing a religion. I know I don't.... The unique thing about America is that every single American is free to choose and practice his or her own religion, or to choose no religion at all, and that right must not and shall not be questioned or violated by the state." Remarks at the Annual Convention of the American Legion in Salt Lake City, Utah (September 4, 1984).

2190   "The unique thing about America is a wall in our Constitution separating church and state. It guarantees that there will never be a state religion in this land, but at the same time it makes sure that every single American is free to choose and practice his or her religious beliefs or to choose no religion at all. Their rights shall not be questioned or violated by the state." Remarks at the International Convention of B'nai B'rith (September 6, 1984).

2191   "[T]he real walls of separation we need in this country are prison walls that will keep criminals off the streets and away from our children." Remarks at a Fundraising Luncheon for Virginia Gubernatorial Candidate Wyatt Durrette in Arlington, Virginia (October 9, 1985).

2192   "[L]et's stop suppressing the spiritual core of our national being. Our nation could not have been conceived without divine help. Why is it that we can build a nation with our prayers, but we can't use a schoolroom for voluntary prayer?" Address Before a Joint Session of Congress on the State of the Union (January 27, 1987).

2193   "When I read the writings of our Founding Fathers ... I always note how openly they gave praise to God and sought His guidance. And I just can't believe that it was ever their intention to expel Him from our schools.... When we explain to our students for the first time the marvel of the semiconductors or share with them any of God's wonders or the fact that they live in the freest, most prosperous nation in the history of the world, don't you think they may want to utter words of prayer, and shouldn't we let them"? Remarks at a White House Ceremony Honoring the Winners of the Secondary School Recognition Program and the Exemplary Private School Recognition Project (October 5, 1987).

2194   "So many of our greatest statesmen have reminded us that spiritual values alone are essential to our nation's health and vigor. The Congress opens its proceedings each day, as does the Supreme Court, with an acknowledgment of the Supreme Being. Yet we are denied the right to set aside in our schools a moment each day for those who wish to pray. I believe Congress should pass our school prayer amendment." Address Be-

fore a Joint Session of Congress on the State of the Union (January 25, 1988).

2195   "The first amendment protects the rights of Americans to freely exercise their religious beliefs in an atmosphere of toleration and accommodation. As I have noted in the past, certain court decisions have, in my view, wrongly interpreted the first amendment so as to restrict, rather than protect, individual rights of conscience. What greater legacy could we leave our children than a new birth of religious freedom in this one nation under God? Now, I hear the smart money in this town say we haven't got a prayer, but somehow I believe the man upstairs is listening and that He'll show us how to return to America's schoolchildren the right that every member of Congress has: to begin each day with a simple, voluntary prayer." Remarks at the Annual Convention of the National Religious Broadcasters Association (February 1, 1988).

2196   "To this day, it astonishes me that some would so misread the Constitution as to claim that it forbids us from displaying in public symbols of God's promise to mankind or prevents us from mentioning His name in the Pledge of Allegiance in our schools." Remarks to the Student Congress on Evangelism (July 28, 1988).

SCIENCE AND TECHNOLOGY

2197   "Technology, plus freedom, equals opportunity and progress." Address at Commencement Exercises at the United States Air Force Academy in Colorado Springs, Colorado (May 30, 1984).

2198   "[F]reedom is not a luxury, but a necessity; not a privilege, but the source of our life's bread. In science, just as in our economy, our object must be to maximize freedom, to open up new avenues of inquiry and new areas of experi-

mentation." Remarks at a White House Luncheon for the New Pioneers (February 12, 1985).

2199   "[T]here are no limits to discovery and human progress when men and women are free to follow their dreams." Remarks at the Presentation Ceremony for the National Medal of Science (February 27, 1985).

2200   "We're moving from an age of things to an age of thoughts, of mind over matter. It is the mind of man, free to invent, free to experiment, free to dream, that will shape the economy and the world of the future." Address to Western Europe from the Venice Economic Summit (June 5, 1987).

2201   "Our country's greatest asset is not our vast expanse of land and not our abundant resources or our temperate climate. Instead, what will serve America most in the years ahead, our most precious possession, is the genius of our people. It will be the inventions, the ideas, the innovations developed by our fellow Americans...." Remarks at the Presentation Ceremony for the National Medals of Science and Technology (June 25, 1987).

2202   "We're increasingly moving from an age of things to an age of thoughts, an age of mind over matter. In this new age, it's the mind of man, free to invent, free to experiment, that is our most precious resource. Gold, steel, oil — these were the treasures of the past that made people rich and nations strong. Today the premium is on the human heart and mind. They can't be locked in a vault, nationalized, or expropriated. They can only be let free, and then, really, the sky is the only limit." Remarks at the Federal Conference on Commercial Applications of Superconductivity (July 28, 1987).

2203   "You know, I can't help thinking that the goals Americans set for themselves in the days of my own youth seem so modest: indoor plumbing, electricity, a family car, a telephone. I remember living in a home without indoor plumbing. Today jet airplanes carry passengers — even those of modest means — from coast to coast and overseas, while our engineers are busy developing crafts that one day will take off from a runway and carry us into space." Remarks on Signing the National Historically Black Colleges Week Proclamation (September 24, 1987).

2204   "Science is shrinking distances, overcoming obstacles, and opening borders. Today individuals in distant lands are working, trading, and even playing together on a global scale. We are, as would never have been thought possible a century ago, truly becoming a community — perhaps even a family — of free people, united by humane values and democratic ideals, and sharing in a prosperity that is closely linked to the trade and commerce between us." Address to the People of Western Europe on Soviet–United States Relations (November 4, 1987).

2205   "We're in an age when the common man can do and experience what in past times was enjoyed only by royalty, aristocracy, and the elite.... It's been technology and freedom, together, that have pushed America forward and made her the land of abundance and progress that we love so dearly." Remarks on the Strategic Defense Initiative to Martin Marietta Denver Astronautics Employees in Waterton, Colorado (November 24, 1987).

2206   "Technology in these last decades has reshaped our lives. It's opened vast opportunity for the common man and has brought all of mankind into one community." Remarks at the Unveiling of the Knute Rockne Commemorative Stamp at the University of Notre Dame in Indiana (March 9, 1988).

2207   "I think one of the reasons I've always had so little patience with those who talk about the limits to growth is that in my lifetime I've seen those limits shattered again and again by questing minds. When I was very young, horsepower was still the kind you fed with hay." Remarks to Science Honors Students on the Supercollider Program (March 30, 1988).

2208   "We cannot know where scientific research will lead. The consequences and spin-offs are unknown and unknowable until they happen. In research, as Albert Einstein once said, imagination is more important than knowledge. We can travel wherever the eye of our imagination can see. But one thing is certain: If we don't explore, others will, and we'll fall behind." Radio Address to the Nation on the Federal Role in Scientific Research (April 2, 1988).

2209   "You see, America's greatest resource is not the land, vast and beautiful though it is. It's not our climate, nor even our abundant natural resources. America's greatest resource is the genius of her people." Remarks at the Presentation Ceremony for the National Medals of Science and Technology (July 15, 1988).

2210   "Technology does not leave people behind; it carries everyone along." Remarks at the Johnson Space Center in Houston, Texas (September 22, 1988).

SENIOR CITIZENS

2211   "[O]lder Americans possess a reservoir of experience and a depth of knowledge that is a great national treasure." Remarks on Signing Proclamation 4918, Proclaiming Older Americans Month, 1982 (April 2, 1982).

2212   "When it comes to retirement, the criterion should be fitness for work, not year of birth." Remarks on Signing Proclamation 4918, Proclaiming Older Americans Month, 1982 (April 2, 1982).

2213   "Senior citizens provide invaluable skill, talent, and wisdom that can come only with years." Remarks at a White House Briefing for the National Alliance of Senior Citizens (February 29, 1984).

2214   "One of the great challenges of our time is to improve the quality for all Americans, and especially our older Americans. The folks who've paid their dues, who kept the world going during the tough years of the thirties and the Depression, and the forties and the war, and the fifties and sixties and seventies and beyond — all of you have earned the right to sit back and take it easy and let the world take care of itself. But you don't. You're in there swinging. You're contributing to things that no one else could. You're our most valuable asset, and I'm proud to be one of you." Remarks to Chapter Presidents of the Catholic Golden Age Association (August 31, 1984).

2215   "Our senior citizens want and deserve to be full participants in American life. They want and deserve independence, quality health care, and economic security." Remarks on Signing the Older Americans Act Amendments of 1984 (October 9, 1984).

SOCIAL SECURITY

2216   "[Y]ou can understand my frustration over the last couple of years ... to be portrayed as somehow an enemy of my own generation. Most of the attack has been centered around one issue, social security. There's been political demagoguery and outright falsehood, and as a result, many who rely on social security for their livelihood have been needlessly and cruelly frightened. And those who did that frightening either didn't know what they were talking about or they were deliberately lying." Remarks at the 1981 White House Conference on Aging (December 1, 1981).

2217   "With bipartisan cooperation and political courage, social security can and will be saved. For too long, too many people dependent on social security have been cruelly frightened by individuals seeking political gain through demagoguery and outright falsehood, and this must stop. The future of social security is much too important to be used as a political football." Remarks Announcing the Establishment of the National Commission on Social Security Reform (December 16, 1981).

2218   "The entitlement programs that make up our safety net for the truly needy have worthy goals and many deserving recipients. We will protect them. But there's only one way to see to it that these programs really help those whom they were designed to help. And that is to bring their spiraling costs under control." Address Before a Joint Session of the Congress Reporting on the State of the Union (January 26, 1982).

2219   "[I]f I was guilty of all the things with regard to social security that I've read about myself or heard said about myself, I wouldn't like me either." Remarks and a Question-and-Answer Session with Senior Citizens in Los Angeles, California (July 6, 1982).

2220   "Maintenance of that system [Social Security] is a duty we must never shirk." Remarks at a Fundraising Dinner for Senator Charles Percy (January 19, 1983).

2221   "I have pledged repeatedly that we have only one goal — to save a system badly in need of repair. The best thing that could happen to social security is to get it out of the news, out of politics, and back into the confidence of the American people." Radio Address to the Nation on the Fiscal Year 1984 Budget (February 12, 1983).

2222   "[I] have repeatedly pledged that no American who depends on social security would ever be denied his or her check ... [b]ut the system [does] have problems and ... only through hard work, not demagoguery, [will] we be able to solve them." Remarks and a Question-and-Answer Session with Reporters on Domestic and Foreign Policy Issues (March 25, 1983).

2223   "The social security system must be preserved. And rescuing the system has meant reexamining its original intent, purposes, and practical limits." Remarks on Signing the Social Security Amendments of 1983 (April 20, 1983).

2224   "This [enacting programs that care for the elderly] is not just a matter of economic common sense, it's a matter of basic human dignity." Remarks to Members of the Sheriff's Posse in Sun City, Arizona (May 6, 1983).

2225   "There is no one in this administration — and if there was, they wouldn't be here long — that has any intention of taking Social Security away from those people who have it and who deserve it." Remarks During a Whistlestop Tour of Ohio [Sidney] (October 12, 1984).

2226   "There is no secret plan to do anything about depriving people who are dependent on Social Security, and there never will be as far as I have anything to say about it. Those who are dependent on this program are going to be able to depend on it." Remarks at the Wesley Park Senior Center in Milwaukee, Wisconsin (November 3, 1984).

2227   "We've made so much economic progress in our country, but it will mean very little if your children look back at your days as a time of materialism and selfishness and looking out for number one. The people you're sitting with right now, they're your brothers and sisters. Someday you'll have a home or an apartment, and your neighbors will be your brothers and sisters then. And it's up to us, as members of the American family, to take care of each other and love each other." Remarks at Northside High School in Atlanta, Georgia (June 6, 1985).

2228   "[L]et us remove a financial specter facing our older Americans: the fear of an illness so expensive that it can result in having to make an intolerable choice between bankruptcy and death." Address Before a Joint Session of Congress on the State of the Union (January 27, 1987).

SOVIET UNION

2229   "I think the greatest description of the difference between the two countries [the United States and the Soviet Union] is simply that one [the Soviet Union] has to put up fences and walls to keep its people in, and there's nothing like that that has to keep anyone in America. And thanks be to God." Remarks at the Opening Ceremony for the Knoxville International Energy Exposition (World's Fair) in Tennessee (May 1, 1982).

2230 "[T]hey [the Soviets] must be made to understand we will never compromise our principles and standards. We will never give away our freedom. We will never abandon our beliefs in God. And we will never stop searching for a genuine peace." Remarks at the Annual Convention of the National Association of Evangelicals (March 8, 1983).

2231 "I've developed a new hobby. It is one of finding and then verifying from some of the dissidents who are here in our country, who've escaped, the jokes that the Russian people are telling among themselves which shows their cynicism about their own government. And one of the recent ones is that they were saying that if the Soviet Union let another political party come into existence, they would still be a one-party state, because everybody'd join the other party." Remarks to Polish Americans in Chicago, Illinois (June 23, 1983).

2232 "What can we think of a regime that so broadly trumpets its vision of peace and global disarmament and yet so callously and quickly commits a terrorist act [shooting down a Korean civilian airliner] to sacrifice the lives of innocent human beings." Remarks to Reporters on the Soviet Attack on a Korean Civilian Airliner (September 2, 1983).

2233 "[W]hile the Soviets accuse others of wanting to return to the cold war, it's they who have never left it behind." Radio Address to the Nation on the Soviet Attack on a Korean Civilian Airliner and on the Observance of Labor Day (September 3, 1983).

2234 "[T]hey [the Soviets] have openly and publicly declared the only morality they recognize is what will further world communism; that they reserve unto themselves the right to commit any crime, to lie, to cheat, in order to attain that. [W]e should keep this in mind when we deal with them." Radio Address to the Nation on International Broadcasting (September 10, 1983).

2235 "[W]e recognize the fundamental differences in our [and the Soviet's]values and in

our perspective on many international issues. We must be realistic and not expect that these differences can be wished away. But realism should also remind us that our two peoples share common bonds and interests. We are both relatively young nations with rich ethnic traditions and a pioneer philosophy. We have both experienced the trauma of war. We have fought side by side in the victory over Nazi Germany. And while our governments have very different views, our sons and daughters have never fought each other. We must make sure they never do." Radio Address to the Nation on United States–Soviet Relations (February 11, 1984).

2236 "The differences between America and the Soviet Union are deep and abiding. The United States is a democratic nation. Here the people rule. We build no walls to keep them in, nor organize any system of police to keep them mute. We occupy no country. The only land abroad we occupy is beneath the graves where our heroes rest. What is called the West is a voluntary association of free nations, all of whom fiercely value their independence and their sovereignty. And as deeply as we cherish our beliefs, we do not seek to compel others to share them." Address to the 40th Session of the United Nations General Assembly in New York, New York (October 24, 1985).

2237 "The United States and the Soviet Union are as different as any two nations can be. These differences are based on opposing philosophies and values and no differences could be more profound or meaningful." Remarks to the Students and Faculty at Fallston High School in Fallston, Maryland (December 4, 1985).

2238 "The Soviet Union is not a democracy. The hopes and aspirations of the Soviet people have little or no direct effect on government policy." Remarks to the Students and Faculty at Fallston High School in Fallston, Maryland (December 4, 1985).

2239 "[W]ith its secrecy and stubborn refusal to inform the international community of the common danger from this disaster [Chernobyl], is stark and clear. The Soviets' handling of this incident manifests a disregard for the legitimate concerns of people everywhere. A nuclear accident that results in contaminating a number of countries with radioactive material is not simply an internal matter. The Soviets owe the world an explanation." Radio Address to the Nation on the President's Trip to Indonesia and Japan (May 4, 1986).

2240   "I've long believed that if we're to be successful in pursuing peace, we must face the tough issues directly and honestly and with hope. We cannot pretend the differences aren't there, seek to dash off a few quick agreements, and then give speeches about the spirit of Reykjavik." Remarks on Departure for Reykjavik, Iceland (October 9, 1986).

2241   "[T]here are many fundamental differences between our two ... countries ... and our political and economic systems. Yet being different does not preclude better relations." Remarks to Representatives of the Young Astronauts Council on Their Departure for the Soviet Union (October 16, 1986).

2242   "[T]here are enormous differences between our two systems, but there is also something the American and the Soviet people share — something as universal and eternal as what a mother feels when she hears the cry of her newborn child — and it is those common hopes." New Year's Radio Address to the People of the Soviet Union (December 31, 1986).

2243   "You know, we Americans have always preferred dialog to conflict, and so, we always remain open to more constructive relations with the Soviet Union. But more responsible Soviet conduct around the world is a key element of the U.S.–Soviet agenda." Address Before a Joint Session of Congress on the State of the Union (January 27, 1987).

2244   "[I]n the past I've often talked about what would happen if ordinary Americans and people from the Soviet Union could get together — get together as human beings, as men and women who breathe the same air, share the same concerns about making life better for themselves and their children." Remarks at a Ceremony Honoring the Coast Guard for the Rescue of the Crew of the Soviet Merchant Ship *Komsomolets Kirgizii* (March 17, 1987).

2245   "From the very first days of this administration, I have insisted that our relations with the Soviets be based on realism rather than illusion. Indeed, the basis for our foreign policy has been, from the very beginning, an insistence upon enunciating the truth about U.S.–Soviet relations and upon making it clearly understood what we think the Soviets stand for and what we stand for." Remarks and a Question-and-Answer Session at a Los Angeles World Affairs Council Luncheon in California (April 10, 1987).

2246   "If I had to characterize U.S.–Soviet relations in one word it would be this: proceeding. No great cause for excitement; no great cause for alarm." Remarks and a Question-and-Answer Session at a Los Angeles World Affairs Council Luncheon in California (April 10, 1987).

2247   "We've heard a lot lately about the Soviet desire to participate in the world economy, to no longer be the odd man out. Well, the ground rules remain the same as they were 40 years ago. No playing the spoiler. No manipulation of world organizations for political gain. Open your economy. Open your political system. Open your borders. Let your people go. Let them travel where they wish, live where they want to. Let them bathe in the light of freedom. And one thing further: Leave your weapons at home. Quit Afghanistan; you have no business there. Dismantle your weapons pointed at Europe. Then we will gladly welcome you as a constructive partner in our 21st-century enterprise." Address to Western Europe from the Venice Economic Summit (June 5, 1987).

2248   "In Europe, only one nation and those it controls refuse to join the community of freedom. Yet in this age of redoubled economic growth, of information and innovation, the Soviet Union faces a choice: It must make fundamental changes, or it will become obsolete. Today thus represents a moment of hope. We in the West stand ready to cooperate with the East to promote true openness, to break down barriers that separate people, to create a safer, freer world." Remarks on East-West Relations at the Brandenburg Gate in West Berlin (June 12, 1987).

2249   "If the world is to know true peace, the Soviets must give up these imperial adventures [in Afghanistan, Cambodia, Angola, and Nicaragua]." Radio Address to the Nation on Soviet–United States Relations (August 29, 1987).

2250   "We [the United States and the Soviet Union] continue to have our differences and probably always will. But that puts a special responsibility on us to find ways — realistic ways — to bring greater stability to our competition and to show the world a constructive example of the value of communication and of the possibility of peaceful solutions to political problems." Address to the 42d Session of the United Nations General Assembly in New York, New York (September 21, 1987).

2251   "We are concerned with human rights in the Soviet Union itself. This has always been at the top of my agenda. It's impossible to have a constructive relationship with a government that tramples upon the rights of its people." Radio Address to the Nation on Foreign Policy (October 17, 1987).

2252   "I've always felt that, even between systems as different as ours, if we remain true to our principles and firm in the advocacy of our own interests, some common ground can be found." Radio Address to the Nation on Foreign Policy (October 17, 1987).

2253   "Denial of the right to emigrate is only a small part of the problem of the repressive Soviet system. A recognition of freedom of speech, religion, and press; a release of all prisoners of conscience; an ending of the practice of sending perfectly sane political dissidents to psychiatric hospitals; tolerance of real opposition; and freedom of political choice — these things, which we all take for granted, would signal that a true turning point has been reached...." Address to the People of Western Europe on Soviet–United States Relations (November 4, 1987).

2254   "Make no mistake, the Soviets are and will continue to be our adversaries, the adversaries, indeed, of all who believe in human liberty. Yet as we work to advance the cause of liberty, we must deal with the Soviets soberly and from strength and in the name of peace." Radio Address to the Nation on Soviet–United States Relations (November 28, 1987).

2255   "Yes, deep, fundamental differences separate us from the Soviets, differences that

center upon our own belief in God and human freedom, differences that we cannot compromise. Yet even as we Americans strive to spread freedom through the world, we must also recognize our obligation to ensure the peace, in particular, to search for areas where America and the Soviet Union can act together to reduce the risk of war." Radio Address to the Nation on Deficit Reduction and Soviet–United States Relations (December 5, 1987).

2256   "[L]et us have the courage to recognize that there are weighty differences between our governments and systems, differences that will not go away by wishful thinking or expressions of good will no matter how sincerely delivered. This uncomfortable reality need not be reason for pessimism, however; it should provide us with a challenge, an opportunity to move from confrontation toward cooperation." Remarks at the Welcoming Ceremony for General Secretary Mikhail Gorbachev of the Soviet Union (December 8, 1987).

2257   "The quest for human rights and personal freedom is very much a part of the agenda of American-Soviet relations." Remarks Upon Departure for a Meeting with Soviet President Gorbachev in New York, New York (December 7, 1988).

2258   "[I]f we're to understand each other better [the United States and the Soviet Union], we must be able to talk freely with each other, and listen freely as well." New Year's Messages of President Reagan and President Mikhail Gorbachev of the Soviet Union (January 1, 1989).

2259   "What it all boils down to is this: I want the new closeness [with the Soviet Union] to continue. And it will, as long as we make it clear that we will continue to act in a certain way as long as they continue to act in a helpful manner. If and when they don't, at first pull your punches. If they persist, pull the plug. It's still trust but verify. It's still play, but cut the cards. It's still watch closely. And don't be afraid to see what you see." Farewell Address to the Nation (January 11, 1989).

SPACE PROGRAM

2260   "Through our history, we've never shrunk before a challenge. The conquest of new frontiers for the betterment of our homes and families is a crucial part of our national character.... The space program in general and the shuttle program in particular have gone a long way to help our country recapture its spirit of vitality and confidence. The pioneer spirit still flourishes in America. In the future as in the past, our freedom, independence, and national well-being will be tied to new achievements, new discoveries, and pushing back new frontiers." Remarks at Edwards Air Force Base, California, on Completion of the Fourth Mission of the Space Shuttle *Columbia* (July 4, 1982).

2261   "Perhaps NASA's greatest gifts have been the moments of greatness that [it has] allowed all of us to share." Remarks at the 25th Anniversary Celebration of the National Aeronautics and Space Administration (October 19, 1983).

2262   "Nowhere is more important than our next frontier, space. Nowhere do we so effectively demonstrate our technological leadership and ability to make life better on Earth." Address to a Joint Address of a Joint Session of the Congress on the State of the Nation (January 25, 1984).

2263   "Just as the Yankee Clipper ships of the last century symbolized American vitality, our space shuttles today capture the optimistic spirit of our times." Radio Address to the Nation on the Space Program (January 28, 1984).

2264   "[T]he first landing on the Moon was not just a crowning achievement but a great beginning. The dream of regular space travel, the use of space to enrich life on Earth is becoming a reality, a working part of our everyday lives." Remarks on Signing an Executive Order on Commercial Expendable Launch Vehicle Activities (February 24, 1984).

2265   "I believe we will be leaders in space because the American people would rather reach for the stars than reach for excuses why they shouldn't." Remarks and a Question-and-Answer

Session at the "Choose a Future" Conference in Chicago, Illinois (September 5, 1984).

2266   "The grandeur of the space shuttle taking off and then landing after a successful mission has been a source of inspiration to America. We can't put a price tag on this." Remarks at the National Space Club Luncheon (March 29, 1985).

2267   "The challenge of pushing back frontiers is part of our national character. And as we face the vast expanses of space, let us recapture those stirrings in our soul that make us Americans. Space, like freedom, is a limitless, never-ending frontier on which our citizens can prove that they are indeed Americans." Remarks at the National Space Club Luncheon (March 29, 1985).

2268   "I know it is hard to understand, but sometimes painful things like this happen. It's all part of the process of exploration and discovery. It's all part of taking a chance and expanding man's horizons. The future doesn't belong to the fainthearted; it belongs to the brave. The *Challenger* crew was pulling us into the future, and we'll continue to follow them." Address to the Nation on the Explosion of the Space Shuttle *Challenger* (January 28, 1986).

2269   "The crew of the space shuttle *Challenger* honored us by the manner in which they lived their lives. We will never forget them, nor the last time we saw them, this morning, as they prepared for their journey and waved goodbye and 'slipped the surly bonds of earth' to 'touch the face of God.'" Address to the Nation on the Explosion of the Space Shuttle *Challenger* (January 28, 1986).

2270   "The future is not free; the story of all human progress is one of a struggle against all odds." Remarks at the Memorial Service for the Crew of the Space Shuttle *Challenger* in Houston, Texas (January 31, 1986).

2271   "America has a claim to stake on the future. We've suffered a tragedy and a setback, but we'll forge ahead, wiser this time, and undaunted — as undaunted as the spirit of the *Chal-*

lenger and her seven heroes." Remarks on Receiving the Final Report of the Presidential Commission on the Space Shuttle *Challenger* Accident (June 9, 1986).

2272   "For our journey into space we have a copilot now: the memory, the spirit of the *Challenger* Seven." Remarks to Participants in the Young Astronauts Program (June 11, 1986).

2273   "The space station is vital to our leadership in space and contributes to our preeminence in manned space flight. Some say we can't afford the space station. I ask you: Can America ever afford to stop dreaming great dreams?" Remarks at the Electronic Industries Association's Annual Government-Industry Dinner (April 19, 1988).

2274   "Yes, there have been setbacks and tragedy and heroism along the way. And the journey ahead is not for the faint-hearted; it's for the brave. But there are wonders that lie before us, wonders that the human heart has yearned to know since the dawn of time. Ours is the first generation in human history that has had the tools to bring mankind into the heavens, into space; and America intends to stay there as long as the human soul can dream and wonder, as long as our ancient destiny draws us toward the stars." Remarks Congratulating the Crew of the Space Shuttle *Discovery* (October 14, 1988).

2275   "Today vistas beyond imagination are being opened for humanity in space. A new future of freedom, both peaceful and bountiful, is being created. And America is telling the world: Follow us. We'll lead you there. This is the mission for which our nation itself was created, and we ask for God's guidance. America's as large as the universe, as infinite as space, as limitless as the vision and courage of her people." Remarks Congratulating the Crew of the Space Shuttle *Discovery* (October 14, 1988).

TERRORISM

2276   "Let terrorists be aware that when rules of international behavior are violated, our policy will be one of swift and effective retribution. We hear it said that we live in an era of limit to our powers. Well, let it also be understood, there are limits to our patience." Remarks at the Welcoming Ceremony for the Freed American Hostages (January 27, 1981).

2277   "Let no terrorist question our will or no tyrant doubt our resolve. Americans have courage and determination, and we must not and will not be intimidated by anyone, anywhere." Remarks to Military Personnel at Cherry Point, North Carolina, on United States Casualties in Lebanon and Grenada (November 4, 1983).

2278   "[T]he worst outcome of all is one in which terrorists succeed in transforming an open democracy into a closed fortress." Remarks to Military Personnel at Cherry Point, North Carolina, on United States Casualties in Lebanon and Grenada (November 4, 1983).

2279   "The problem of terrorism will not disappear if we run from it." Remarks and a Question-and-Answer Session with Reporters on the Pentagon Report on the Security of United States Marines in Lebanon (December 27, 1983).

2280   "For terrorists to be curbed, civilized countries must begin a new effort to work together, to share intelligence, to improve our training and security and our forces, to deny havens or legal protection for terrorist groups and, most important of all, to hold increasingly accountable those countries which sponsor terrorism and terroristic activity around the world." Remarks and a Question-and-Answer Session with Reporters on the Pentagon Report on the Security of United States Marines in Lebanon (December 27, 1983).

2281 "[A]ll the economic aid in the world won't be worth a dime if Communist guerrillas are determined and have the freedom to terrorize and to burn, to bomb, and destroy everything...." Radio Address to the Nation on Central America (March 24, 1984).

2282 "[T]errorists are not guerrillas or commandos or freedom fighters or anything else. They're terrorists, and should be identified as such." Remarks at the International Convention of B'nai B'rith (September 6, 1984).

2283 "[T]he cowardly act of terrorism ... against our Embassy annex in East Beirut [this morning] has saddened us all [and is] another painful reminder of the persistent threat of terrorism in the world." Remarks to Employees of Westinghouse Furniture Systems in Grand Rapids, Michigan (September 20, 1984).

2284 "When terrorism strikes, civilization itself is under attack; no nation is immune. There's no safety in silence or neutrality. If we permit terrorism to succeed anywhere, it will spread like a cancer, eating away at civilized societies and sowing fear and chaos everywhere. This barbarism is abhorrent, and all of those who support it, encourage it, and profit from it are abhorrent. They are barbarians." Remarks to Citizens in Chicago Heights, Illinois (June 28, 1985).

2285 "The United States gives terrorists no rewards and no guarantees. We make no concessions; we make no deals.... Terrorists, be on notice, we will fight back against you...." Remarks Announcing the Release of the Hostages from the Trans World Airlines Hijacking Incident (June 30, 1985).

2286 "Hijacking is a crime; kidnapping is a crime; murder is a crime; and holding our people prisoner is a crime. When cruelty is inflicted on innocent people, it discredits whatever cause in whose name it is done. And those who commit such deeds are enemies of the peace." Remarks to the Freed Hostages from the Trans World Airlines Hijacking Incident (July 2, 1985).

2287 "There is a temptation to see the terrorist act as simply the erratic work of a small group of fanatics. We make this mistake at great peril, for the attacks on America, her citizens, her allies, and other democratic nations in recent years ... form a pattern of terrorism that has strategic implications and political goals. And only by moving our focus from the tactical to the strategic perspective, only by identifying the pattern of terror and those behind it, can we hope to put into force a strategy to deal with it." Remarks at the Annual Convention of the American Bar Association (July 8, 1985).

2288 "So, the American people are not — I repeat — not going to tolerate intimidation, terror, and outright acts of war against this nation and its people. And we're especially not going to tolerate these attacks from outlaw states run by the strangest collection of misfits, loony tunes, and squalid criminals since the advent of the Third Reich." Remarks at the Annual Convention of the American Bar Association (July 8, 1985).

2289 "You can run but you can't hide." Remarks and a Question-and-Answer Session with Reporters (October 11, 1985).

2290 "[T]he United States of America isn't about to be pushed around by the nickel-and-dime cowards who commit acts of terror." Remarks at a White House Meeting with 1984 Reagan-Bush Campaign Supporters (November 6, 1985).

2291 "Terrorists and those who harbor them must be denied sympathy, safe haven, and support." President's News Conference [prepared statement] (January 7, 1986).

2292 "I warned that there should be no place on Earth where terrorists can rest and train and practice their deadly skills. I meant it. I said that we would act with others, if possible, and alone if necessary to ensure that terrorists have no sanctuary anywhere. Tonight, we have." Address to the Nation on the United States Air Strike Against Libya (April 14, 1986).

2293 "Terrorism is the preferred weapon of weak and evil men." Remarks at a White House Meeting with Members of the American Business Conference (April 15, 1986).

2294 "These vicious, cowardly acts [of terrorism] will, if we let them, erect a wall of fear around nations and neighborhoods. It will dampen the joy of travel, the flow of trade, the exchange of ideas. In short, terrorism undeterred will deflect the winds of freedom." Remarks to the International Forum of the Chamber of Commerce of the United States (April 23, 1986).

2295   "Well, America will never watch passively as our innocent citizens are murdered by those who would do our country harm. We're slow to wrath and hesitant to use the military power available to us. By nature we prefer to solve problems peacefully. But as we proved last week [with the air strike against Libya], no one can kill Americans and brag about it — no one." Remarks to the International Forum of the Chamber of Commerce of the United States (April 23, 1986).

2296   "The decent people of the world ... are not just standing together in this war against terrorism. We're committed to winning the war and wiping this scourge from the face of the Earth." Remarks Upon Returning from Trip to Indonesia and Japan (May 7, 1986).

2297   "For too long, the world [has been] paralyzed by the argument that terrorism could not be stopped until the grievances of terrorists were addressed. The complicated and heartrending issues that perplex mankind are no excuse for violent, inhumane attacks, nor do they excuse not taking aggressive action against those who delib-

erately slaughter innocent people. Radio Address to the Nation on Terrorism (May 31, 1986).

2298   "Terrorists are always the enemies of democracy." Radio Address to the Nation on Terrorism (May 31, 1986).

2299   "Something else, I just have to believe it will be one long stretch before any nickel-and-dime dictator or terrorist chooses to tangle with the United States of America." Remarks at a Fundraising Luncheon for Carroll A. Campbell and Thomas F. Hartnett in Columbia, South Carolina (July 24, 1986).

2300   "[T]he grave threat of terrorism also jeopardizes the hopes for peace. No cause, no grievance, can justify it. Terrorism is heinous and intolerable. It is the crime of cowards — cowards who prey on the innocent, the defenseless, and the helpless." Address to the 41st Session of the United Nations General Assembly in New York, New York (September 22, 1986).

2301   "You know, America used to wear a 'Kick Me' sign around its neck. We threw that sign away. Now it reads, 'Don't Tread on Me.' Today every nickel-and-dime dictator around the world knows that if he tangles with the United States of America, he'll have to pay a price." Remarks at a Senate Campaign Rally for James Santini in Las Vegas, Nevada (November 3, 1986).

UNEMPLOYMENT

2302   "Maybe those of us who went through the Great Depression have some kind of complex, but to me as long as there is one single person able and willing to work but unable to find work, that is too high an unemployment rate." Radio Address to the Nation on Federal Budget Legislation and Unemployment Figures (May 8, 1982).

2303   "[S]omething must be done and can be done about unemployment if Congress will get

off the dime and adopt the deficit-reducing budget it now has before it. Interest rates will come down when it does, and so will unemployment. This is no time for politics as usual. There are too many people hurting." Radio Address to the Nation on Federal Budget Legislation and Unemployment Figures (May 8, 1982).

2304   "[W]e believe that economic recovery, not government social programs, is the best and most permanent solution to the problem of unemployment. The best social program we can have is a job." Remarks at a Fundraising Dinner for Governor William P. Clements, Jr., in Houston, Texas (June 15, 1982).

2305 "We're not training for jobs that don't exist. I have spoken of this before and was criticized for doing it, as if it showed no compassion for the unemployed. There's no one in the world who has more compassion for the unemployed than I do. I was looking for a job in 1932; I'd seen my father lose his on Christmas Eve." Remarks at a Meeting with Participants in the American Business Conference (September 28, 1982).

2306 "[S]tructural [un]employment is not the result of temporary slips in the economy.... It's caused by deep and lasting changes in science, technology, competitiveness, and skills. And you just can't cure that with a quick-fix solution." Remarks at the National Conference on the Dislocated Worker in Pittsburgh, Pennsylvania (April 6, 1983).

2307 "I believe that we as a nation owe an obligation as well as a helping hand to those who pay the price of economic readjustment." Remarks at the National Conference on the Dislocated Worker in Pittsburgh, Pennsylvania (April 6, 1983).

2308 "[T]he enterprise zone concept ... harnesses the energy of the private sector, pumping new life into depressed areas. Rather than creating jobs in Washington, enterprise zones will provide results where they're needed, right in our local communities." Remarks at Cinco de Mayo Ceremonies in San Antonio, Texas (May 5, 1983).

2309 "[T]hose [the House Democrats] who refuse to take action on a bill that's to create jobs and opportunity are the last people who should be giving speeches about their compassion for the unemployed." Remarks During a Meeting with Puerto Rican Leaders (March 15, 1984).

2310 "America needs jobs and opportunities, not make-work and handouts." Text of the President's Remarks During a Meeting with Cuban-American Leaders (March 19, 1984).

2311 "We, of course, need to remain concerned about each and every citizen who is seeking work and should not be satisfied until everyone who wants a job — a good job — has one. One person enduring the pressures and frustrations of unemployment is too many." Radio Address to the Nation on the Federal Budget (February 20, 1988).

UNITED NATIONS

2312 "Whatever challenges the world was bound to face, the founders intended this body to stand for certain values, even if they could not be enforced, and to condemn violence, even if it could not be stopped. This body was to speak with the voice of moral authority. That was to be its greatest power." Address Before the 38th Session of the United Nations General Assembly in New York, New York (September 26, 1983).

2313 "From the 1970s on, the United Nations has too often allowed itself to become a forum for the defamation of Israel." Remarks at the International Convention of B'nai B'rith (September 6, 1984).

2314 "For our part, we in the United States still hold firm to the belief that within the structure of this institution [United Nations General Assembly] we can improve the chances for peace on this planet. And whether we succeed in doing so is not dependent on luck or any inevitable pattern of history. We have it within our power to make history; let's not be afraid to do so." Remarks at a Reception for Heads of Delegations to the 39th Session of the United Nations General Assembly in New York, New York (September 23, 1984).

2315 "The responsibilities of this assembly [the United Nations]— the peaceful resolution of disputes between peoples and nations — can be discharged successfully only if we recognize the great common ground upon which we all stand: our fellowship as members of the human race, our oneness as inhabitants of this planet, our place as representatives of billions of our countrymen whose fondest hope remains the end to war and to the repression of the human spirit." Address to the 39th Session of the United Nations General Assembly in New York, New York (September 24, 1984).

2316 "The United Nations' founders understood that true peace must be based on more than just reducing the means of waging war. It must address the sources of tension that provoke men to take up arms. True peace is based on self-determination, respect for individual rights, open and honest communications...." Radio Address to the Nation on the 40th Anniversary of the United Nations General Assembly (October 19, 1985).

2317 "The nations and the peoples of the world value the United Nations for many things, but most, perhaps, for what it symbolizes. The U.N. began as a symbol of hope and reconciliation 40 years ago after the worst war in history; it's no less a symbol today. The United Nations is still a symbol of man's great hope that some day he'll be able to resolve all disputes through peaceful discussion and never again through the force of arms. The United Nations is a symbol of man's long struggle to rise beyond his own flawed nature and live by the high ideals that the best of mankind have defined and declared down through the ages." Toast at a Luncheon for the Heads of Delegations to the 40th Session of the United Nations General Assembly in New York, New York (October 23, 1985).

2318 "The vision of the U.N. Charter — to spare succeeding generations this scourge of war — remains real. It still stirs our soul and warms our hearts, but it also demands of us a realism that is rock hard, clear-eyed, steady, and sure — a realism that understands the nations of the United Nations are not united." Address to the 40th Session of the United Nations General Assembly in New York, New York (October 24, 1985).

VETERANS

General

2319 "The men and women in our armed forces are the final protection against those who wish us ill. The soldier, the sailor, the airman, and the marine in the United States and around the world are the ultimate guardians of our freedom to say what we think, go where we will, choose who we want for our leaders, and pray as we wish." Radio Address to the Nation on Armed Forces Day (May 15, 1982).

2320 "Nothing is more important to the soul of America than remembering and honoring those who gave of themselves so that we might enjoy the fruits of peace and liberty." Remarks on Presenting the Presidential Citizens Medal to Raymond Weeks at a Veterans Day Ceremony (November 11, 1982).

2321 "You know, there are some pleasures in being President. But one of the things that makes me proudest is our men and women in uniform.... I see them doing their part for our country, and I want to grab their hands and tell them how much the Nation appreciates their services — to tell how honored we are to have them defending us. You can't look at their faces and do anything but burst with pride in these young people." Remarks at a Tribute to Bob Hope at the Kennedy Center (May 20, 1983).

2322   "The world looks to America for leadership. And America looks to the men in its Armed Forces...." Remarks to Military Personnel at Cherry Point, North Carolina, on United States Casualties in Lebanon and Grenada (November 4, 1983).

2323   "Veterans know better than anyone else the price of freedom, for they've suffered the scars of war. We can offer them no better tribute than to protect what they have won for us. That is our duty. They have never let America down. We will not let them down." Radio Address to the Nation on America's Veterans (November 5, 1983).

2324   "I'm going to say something right now that — I know I run a risk because there are so many people that want to portray me as trigger happy. I want to tell you something — I never see these young men and women in our Armed Forces uniform without having a swell of pride that puts a lump in my throat. And how anyone could think that any man would want to send them out to lose their lives — it's just impossible." Remarks at the Annual Convention of the Texas State Bar Association in San Antonio (July 6, 1984).

2325   "The men and women veterans who've proudly served their country in the military have earned more than simply the respect of their countrymen, they have earned the benefits to which they're entitled, including veterans preference in government employment." Remarks at the Annual Convention of the American Legion in Salt Lake City, Utah (September 4, 1984).

2326   "[A]merica's debt to those who would fight for her defense doesn't end the day the uniform comes off. For the security of our nation, it must not end. Every time a man or woman enlists in the Army, Navy, Air Force, Marines, or Coast Guard, he or she is ready to lay down his or her life for our nation. We must be ready to show that America appreciates what that means." Remarks at the National Defense University on Signing the Department of Veterans Affairs Act (October 25, 1988).

Vietnam Veterans

2327   "They [Vietnam veterans] came home without a victory not because they'd been defeated, but because they'd been denied permission to win." Remarks on Presenting the Medal of Honor to Master Sergeant Roy P. Benavidez (February 24, 1981).

2328   "For too long, America closed its heart to those who served us in valor. It's time that Vietnam veterans take their rightful place in our history along with other American heroes who have put their lives on the line for their country. Certainly, mistakes were made. But the reality of Vietnam today ... all this suggests the cause for which our Vietnam veterans fought was an honorable one." Remarks on Presenting the Presidential Citizens Medal to Raymond Weeks at a Veterans Day Ceremony. (November 11, 1982).

2329   "[T]hose veterans of Vietnam ... were never welcomed home with speeches and bands, but [they] ... were undefeated in battle and were heroes as surely as any who ever fought in a noble cause...." Remarks at the Conservative Political Action Conference Dinner (February 18, 1983).

2330   "The sacrifices they made and still may be making and the uncertainty their families still endure deeply trouble us all. We must not rest until we know their fate." Radio Address to the Nation on America's Veterans (November 5, 1983).

2331   "[W]e must remember that we cannot today, as much as some might want to, close this chapter in our history, for the war in Southeast Asia still haunts a small but brave group of Americans — the families of those still missing in the Vietnam conflict." Remarks at Memorial Day Ceremonies Honoring an Unknown Serviceman of the Vietnam Conflict (May 28, 1984).

2332   "Only those who have been POWs can realize the trauma of being captured and the indignities and hardships that [they] had to endure. And [their] families suffered with them." Remarks by Telephone to the Annual Convention of American Ex-Prisoners of War in Seattle, Washington (July 18, 1984).

2333   "Our prisoners of war have been and are the bravest of the brave. They kept a trusting heart, they retained their spirit and their will, and they kept the faith. They trusted us, and that trust did us great honor." Remarks at a White House Ceremony Marking the Observance of National P.O.W./M.I.A. Recognition Day (July 20, 1984).

2334 "Those who fought in Vietnam are part of us, part of our history. They reflected the best of us. No number of wreaths, no amount of music and memorializing will ever do them justice but it is good for us that we honor them and their sacrifice." Remarks at Dedication Ceremonies for the Vietnam Veterans Memorial Statue (November 11, 1984).

2335 "There were great moral and philosophical disagreements about the rightness of the war, and we cannot forget them because there is no wisdom to be gained in forgetting. But we can forgive each other and ourselves for those things that we recognize may have been wrong, and I think it's time we did." Remarks at Dedication Ceremonies for the Vietnam Veterans Memorial Statue (November 11, 1984).

2336 "When you [Vietnam veterans] returned home, you brought solace to the loved ones of those who fell, but little solace was given to you. Some of your countrymen were unable to distinguish between our native distaste for war and the stainless patriotism of those who suffered its scars. But there has been rethinking there, too. And now we can say to you and say as a nation: Thank you for your courage. Thank you for being patient with your countrymen. Thank you. Thank you for continuing to stand with us together." Remarks at Dedication Ceremonies for the Vietnam Veterans Memorial Statue (November 11, 1984).

2337 "[T]here can be no partisan or parochial views or any special interests, but only the interest of the entire American people to see to it that all of us do our duty toward those who served this Nation so well in time of war and their families who look to us to help secure the answers they so rightfully seek and deserve." Message to the Congress Transmitting a Report on POWs and MIAs in Southeast Asia (April 30, 1985).

2338 "They were quite a group, the boys of Vietnam — boys who fought a terrible and vicious war without enough support from home, boys who were dodging bullets while we debated the

efficacy of the battle. It was often our poor who fought in that war; it was the unpampered boys of the working class who picked up the rifles and went on the march. They learned not to rely on us; they learned to rely on each other. And they were special in another way: They chose to be faithful. They chose to reject the fashionable skepticism of their time. They chose to believe and answer the call of duty. They had the wild, wild courage of youth. They seized certainty from the heart of an ambivalent age; they stood for something." Remarks at a Memorial Day Ceremony at Arlington National Cemetery in Virginia (May 26, 1986).

2339 "They [those Americans who fought and died in Vietnam] were our loved ones and our fellow Americans; and they were, I'm certain time will tell, part of a noble cause and history's heroes." Radio Address to the Nation on POWs and MIAs in Southeast Asia (July 19, 1986).

2340 "These men died in battle for their country, and it's only right and fitting that they finally rest now in the Nation they loved so dearly and for which they so willingly sacrificed." Radio Address to the Nation on POWs and MIAs in Southeast Asia (July 19, 1986).

2341 "Those men were fighting a noble cause. They were fighting for America and for freedom. We will never forget them. And that's one reason why I'm renewing today the personal commitment I made to the families of our POWs and MIAs: We will not give up. We will not relent until we bring our American heroes home." Remarks at the Annual Leadership Conference of the American Legion (February 29, 1988).

2342 "I don't understand those who would so easily forget. I'm speaking about those who would turn their backs on the men missing in action in Southeast Asia. We have a moral bond as sacred as any a free people can make with one of their own to close no books, write no last chapters, reach no final conclusions until we have the fullest possible accounting of every soldier, airman, aviator, marine, and civilian lost in Laos, Cambodia, or Vietnam." Remarks at the Annual Conference of the Veterans of Foreign Wars (March 7, 1988).

2343 "[I]n Vietnam, you fought a noble battle for freedom. On the battlefield you knew only victory, only to have your victory lost by a failure of political will." Remarks at the Presentation Ceremony for the Prisoners of War Medal (June 24, 1988).

2344   "As former prisoners of war, you know what it is to lose your freedom and to recover it. You know that freedom has its enemies, you've stared them in the eye, and you've suffered at their hands. You've seen that those who hate America hate us not for our flaws but for our strengths. You know what it means to be Americans, and in fact to be punished for it by those who despise what our country stands for." Remarks at the Presentation Ceremony for the Prisoners of War Medal (June 24, 1988).

2345   "[T]here have always been those rushing to say that it was time to forget. Well, to those in a hurry to forget, your love for your fathers, brothers, husbands, and sons stands in the way. Those who want to close the door on the true history of the Vietnam war, to escape accountability and leave important questions unanswered — they would close the book on those Americans still missing. Well, this is more than a betrayal of the men. It's more than a breach of faith with their families and their loved ones. It's a denial of the truth. And to them I say: America cannot move forward by leaving her missing sons behind." Remarks at the Annual Meeting of the National League of POW/MIA Families (July 29, 1988).

2346   "Both sides spoke with honesty and fervor. And what more can we ask in our democracy? And yet after more than a decade of desperate boat people, after the killing fields of Cambodia, after all that has happened in that unhappy part of the world, who can doubt that the cause for which our men fought was just? It was, after all, however imperfectly pursued, the cause of freedom; and they showed uncommon courage in its service. Perhaps at this late date we can all agree that we've learned one lesson: that young Americans must never again be sent to fight and die unless we are prepared to let them win." Remarks at the Veterans Day Ceremony at the Vietnam Veterans Memorial (November 11, 1988).

2347   "Now before I go, as have so many others, Nancy and I wanted to leave a note at the wall. And if I may read it to you before doing so, we will put this note here before we leave: Our young friends — yes, young friends, for in our hearts you will always be young, full of the love that is youth, love of life, love of joy, love of country — you fought for your country and for its safety and for the freedom of others with strength and courage. We love you for it. We honor you. And we have faith that, as He does all His sacred children, the Lord will bless you and keep you, the Lord will make His face to shine upon you and give you peace, now and forever more." Remarks at the Veterans Day Ceremony at the Vietnam Veterans Memorial (November 11, 1988).

VOLUNTARISM

2348   "[I]'m a great believer in the spirit of voluntary service, cooperation of the private and community initiatives.... So we know that letting government handle it, as it has done, has done to our economy just about what Mrs. O'Leary's cow did to the city of Chicago...." Remarks at a Reception for Members of the Advertising Council (May 20, 1981).

2349   "Let us start by asking ourselves ... 'What did I do today to help a fellow American in need'? If the answer is nothing, then the next question is, 'What am I going to do about that today?' "Remarks at the New York City Partnership Luncheon in New York (January 14, 1982).

2350   "One of America's greatest strengths is our tradition of neighbor caring for neighbor in times of trouble." Remarks at the Annual Meeting of the United States Chamber of Commerce (April 26, 1982).

2351   "[V]olunteering is an old American tradition. We've always been a country of neighbors dependent on one another. A strong, competitive community spirit is the heart and soul of our democracy and the key to our quality of life." Remarks and a Question-and-Answer Session at a White House Reception for Participants in the Youth Volunteer Conference (November 12, 1982).

2352   "[T]he spirit of voluntarism moves like a deep and mighty river throughout our country." Remarks at the Presentation Ceremony for the Peace Corps Awards (April 18, 1983).

2353   "One of America's finest traditions is voluntarism — the belief that instead of expecting government to do it, we should ourselves get involved and do what we can to help our neighbors and community." Remarks at Cinco de Mayo Ceremonies in San Antonio, Texas (May 5, 1983).

2354   "[W]hen people are free the choice of helping others becomes meaningful. The choice of doing something to better one's community becomes a source of pride because it reflects the character of the donor and not the product of legal coercion." Remarks at the Annual Convention of the Concrete and Aggregates Industries Associations in Chicago, Illinois (January 31, 1984).

2355   "Americans are the most charitable people in the world. We reach out to the needy. We're a nation of volunteers. We seek community service. It's easy to have faith in America." Remarks During a Homecoming and Birthday Celebration in Dixon, Illinois (February 6, 1984).

2356   "People coming together in a spirit of community and neighborhood is what makes the smallest rural hamlet or the largest urban center worth living in." Remarks at the Annual Legislative Conference of the National Association of Counties (March 4, 1985).

2357   "Why is the freest nation on Earth also the one in which it is so common to see people from every walk of life — rich and poor, young and old — rolling up their sleeves and pitching in to help others? Maybe it's just that we want to say thank you to the Lord who blessed our country with freedom. And the best way to do that is to care for our fellow human beings." Remarks at the President's Volunteer Action Awards Luncheon (April 22, 1985).

2358   "Today we also understand that government cannot assume the responsibility for all good works without destroying the spirit of benevolence and sense of community so important to the well-being of any free society. Government, even with the best of intentions, sometimes does more harm than good." Remarks at the Annual Convention of the Lions Club International in Dallas, Texas (June 21, 1985).

2359   "[O]ne of the wellsprings of our greatness as a nation [is] our willingness to serve each other." Radio Address to the Nation on Voluntarism (May 24, 1986).

2360   "The spirit of voluntarism is deeply ingrained in us as a nation. Indeed, when asked by pollsters, most Americans state their belief that no matter how big government gets and no matter how many services it provides, it can never take the place of volunteers. In other words, the American people understand that there are no substitutes for gifts of service given from the heart." Remarks at a White House Presentation Ceremony for the President's Volunteer Action Awards (June 2, 1986).

2361   "[W]ith personal charity, there are two winners: the person who gives as well as the person who receives. And very often, it's the giver who receives the most precious gift. Personal, private charity humanizes a society. It makes us more aware of each other, of our hopes and needs and of our sorrows and our joys, and it makes us all more compassionate. I think we found that the cold, clinical, impersonal giving of government handouts can just never replace private voluntarism; sometimes it's even counterproductive." Remarks at the Presentation Ceremony for the "C" Flag Awards (June 18, 1986).

2362   "The good-hearted actions of individuals, of you and me, promote the public good, the welfare of the Nation as a whole, in ways that government never could. They ensure that the public-spiritedness of our people is harnessed to its full extent. If we let government take its place entirely, we would surely be wasting our most potent resource." Remarks at a White House Briefing for the United States Delegation to the International Conference on Private Sector Initiatives (November 6, 1986).

2363   "Americans live by the age-old truth that with personal charity there are two winners: the person who gives as well as the person who receives. And very often, it's the giver who receives the most precious gift." Remarks at a White House Briefing for the United States Delegation to the International Conference on Private Sector Initiatives (November 6, 1986).

2364   "Personal, private charity humanizes a society. It makes us more aware of each other, of our hopes and needs, and of our sorrows and our joys; and it makes us all more compassionate." Remarks at a White House Briefing for the United States Delegation to the International Conference on Private Sector Initiatives (November 6, 1986).

2365   "[I]f freedom, democracy, and the rights of man are to be preserved through the ages, free men and women must accept the responsibilities that go with their freedoms." Remarks at the Italian-American Conference on Private Sector Initiatives in Venice, Italy (June 11, 1987).

2366   "When individuals and organizations are willing to get involved, there's no limit to the good that can be done. It's a tradition as old as our country, that in America neighbors help neighbors." Remarks at the Presentation Ceremony for the "C" Flag Awards (July 23, 1987).

2367   "[V]oluntarism is something the administration has worked hard to encourage during the past few years. It's been part of our policy of cutting back government while giving free

markets and free people a chance to work their magic. And the results have been economic magic." Radio Address to the Nation on Voluntarism and the Supreme Court Nomination of Robert H. Bork (October 3, 1987).

2368   "There is always much to improve. But I can assure you that the spirit of good will and benevolence, an aspect of our national character recognized since the early days of our Republic, remains a vibrant part of the American way of life." Radio Address to the Nation on Voluntarism (December 26, 1987).

2369   "Helping others is just our way, part of our national character." Radio Address to the Nation on Voluntarism (December 26, 1987).

2370   "Volunteering to help your neighbor is an old American tradition — and among our most distinctive traditions. From the time of our founding to the present, it's one of the things that foreign visitors most often note when they come to visit this country." Remarks to Representatives of Volunteer Youth Groups (April 18, 1988).

2371   "America has been blessed in so many ways, but isn't it great that our greatest blessing, really, is that we have each other? There are few things more inspiring than the pure generosity of a neighbor's helping hand, that distinctively American spirit which says: We can; we care." Remarks at the Presentation Ceremony for the "C" Flag Awards (September 29, 1988).

2372   "Among life's deepest truths is that all that is done for you is but an opportunity and invitation to do something for others." Remarks to Area High School Students and Faculty in Upper Darby, Pennsylvania (October 12, 1988).

WASHINGTON, D.C.

2373   "You know, the difference between local government and Washington is very simple.

Recently, there was a little town. Their traffic signs were only 5 feet high, and they decided to raise them, for better visibility for the motorists, to raise them to 7 feet above the ground. And the Federal Government came in and said they had a program that would do that for them. They lowered the pavement 2 feet." Remarks at a Target '82 Republican Fundraising Reception in Los Angeles, California (August 17, 1981).

2374   "[W]ashington is a place of fads and one-week stories. It's also a company town, and the company's name is government, big government." Remarks at a Conservative Political Action Conference Dinner (February 26, 1982).

2375   "When I was a very small boy in a small town in Illinois, we lived above the store where my father worked. I have something of the same arrangement here." Remarks on Presenting the Small Business Person of the Year Award (May 11, 1983).

2376   "The problem is that Washington is full of special interest groups passing around self-serving studies that are then reported as fact. They serve up headlines, but too many of them don't serve up the truth." Remarks at the Annual Meeting of the American Medical Association House of Delegates in Chicago, Illinois (June 23, 1983).

2377   "You know, it's an odd thing, but the farther we get from Washington, the better I feel." Remarks at the Annual Convention of the American G.I. Forum in El Paso, Texas (August 13, 1983).

2378   "Today the people no longer look to Washington as an Emerald City with magic solutions to every problem. I've been here going on 5 years now, and I can tell you it's more like the Twilight Zone than the Land of Oz." Toast at a White House Dinner Honoring the Nation's Governors (February 24, 1985).

2379   "[T]he Potomac disease ... causes too many elected officials to give up a better tomorrow for America in order to placate special interests today." Remarks at a Fundraising Luncheon for Senator Slade Gorton in Seattle, Washington (December 2, 1985).

2380   "Good afternoon and welcome to the White House complex. That's what we call these buildings—the White House complex. It's also what you get when you've been around here working here too long." Remarks to Jewish Leaders During a White House Briefing on United States

Assistance for the Nicaraguan Democratic Resistance (March 5, 1986).

2381   "It's important for a President to get away from Washington every so often—away from the special interests and big government mentality, out among the people that don't believe that government is the only industry in the world." Remarks at the Illinois State Fair in Springfield (August 12, 1986).

2382   "It's going to take a lot to get us on that plane headed back to Washington. I've always said that had the Pilgrims landed on the west coast rather than where they did, the capital of this nation would be in California." Remarks at a Senate Campaign Fundraiser for Representative Ed Zschau in Los Angeles, California (September 7, 1986).

2383   "You know, as I often say when we're taking off in Air Force One, it's great to get out of Washington and back to where the real people are." Remarks at a Republican Party Rally in Costa Mesa, California (November 3, 1986).

2384   "[W]hite House complex ... sounds like a neurosis." Remarks at the Presentation Ceremony for the Presidential Distinguished Executive Rank Awards (December 8, 1986).

2385   "Most people think of it as an honor to be invited here, and that includes myself. I remember how humble I felt on that day in 1980 when the American people first asked me to come here." Remarks at a White House Ceremony Honoring the Citizens of Chase, Maryland, Who Assisted in the Amtrak Accident Rescue (February 3, 1987).

2386   "You know, living in the White House is kind of an experience. You can't ever be free of the knowledge of who and how many have preceded you there." Remarks to Students from Hine Junior High School on Abraham Lincoln (February 12, 1987).

2387   "But no one can live in this house for long without feeling the vibrant spirit of our French and American forebears, of Thomas Jefferson and Benjamin Franklin, of Lafayette and Rochambeau." Toasts at the State Dinner for Prime Minister Jacques Chirac of France (March 31, 1987).

2388   "I have to tell you, back there in those puzzle palaces on the Potomac, you can sometimes lose touch with the basic values that we're working so hard to try and defend." Remarks on Arrival in West Lafayette, Indiana (April 9, 1987).

2389 "And it's good to get out of Washington, where we spend a lot of time worrying about a lot of things that are only important there. Here you have perspective and realize what the important issues are: who's got a prom date and who hasn't." Remarks at the Commencement Ceremony for Area High School Seniors in Chattanooga, Tennessee (May 19, 1987).

2390 "Before we begin, I hope you'll forgive me for saying that it's good to be back in California. Actually, I didn't realize how completely I made the transition from Washington until I got on a helicopter yesterday and told the pilot, Giddy up!" Remarks on Soviet–United States Relations at the Town Hall of California Meeting in Los Angeles (August 26, 1987).

2391 "You know, it's good to get out of Washington, where we spend a lot of time worrying about things that are only important there. Here you have perspective and realize what the important issues are — who's got a Christmas dance date and who hasn't." Remarks and a Question-and-Answer Session with Area High School Seniors in Jacksonville, Florida (December 1, 1987).

2392 "I want to welcome all of you to the Capital, which in so many ways is a company town. But none of us should ever forget the real business of the company takes place in the far reaches of our country and even the world." Remarks at the Presentation Ceremony for the Presidential Rank Awards for the Senior Executive Service (January 5, 1988).

2393 "You know, when I was a kid, my family used to live over the store. Sometimes I feel like I haven't come all that way — only now, got elevators." Remarks on Signing the Housing and Community Development Act of 1987 (February 5, 1988).

2394 "Thank you all very much, and welcome to the White House complex. White House complex — that's what they call these buildings. That's because nothing in Washington is ever simple." Remarks to Business Leaders at a White House Briefing on International Trade (March 11, 1988).

2395 "It's good to have you all here in Washington. As you may have noticed, Washington, D.C., isn't like other cities. Harry Truman, a man famous for saying exactly what he meant in a very few words well chosen, once said of Washington, it's the kind of city that if you want a friend you should find a dog." Remarks to State and Local Republican Officials on Federalism and Aid to the Nicaraguan Democratic Resistance (March 22, 1988).

2396 "[W]ashington isn't always the easiest city in which to achieve a sense of shared purpose or common vision." Remarks at a White House Briefing for Members of the American Business Conference (March 23, 1988).

2397 "Thank you very much, and welcome to the White House. I know you don't think you're in the White House, but somehow — you know Washington. They call it the White House complex. Washington is complex." Remarks and a Question-and-Answer Session with the Members of the Center for the Study of the Presidency (March 25, 1988).

2398 "Well, thank you all very much, and welcome to the White House complex. White House complex — that's what our opponents have after 8 years out of power." Remarks at a White House Briefing for Conservative Political Leaders (July 5, 1988).

2399 "Welcome to the White House complex. White House complex — that's because nothing in Washington is ever simple — well, almost nothing." Remarks at the Presentation Ceremony for the Distinguished Rank Awards (August 2, 1988).

2400 "Every time I leave Washington to travel around the country, as I get out of the plane I half expect to see a sign waiting for me saying, 'Welcome to America.' You know, if I didn't get out of Washington often, it would be easy to lose touch with what's really going on." Remarks to the Employees of United States Precision Lens, Inc., in Cincinnati, Ohio (August 8, 1988).

2401 "Well, I've just come from another place, Washington, D.C., where some liberals seem to think that work is a dirty word." Remarks at a Republican Party Fundraising Dinner in Houston, Texas (September 22, 1988).

WELFARE

General

2402   "How can we love our country and not love our countrymen; and loving them, reach out a hand when they fall, heal them when they're sick, and provide opportunity to make them self-sufficient so they will be equal in fact and not just in theory." Inaugural Address (January 20, 1981).

2403   "'Entitlement programs' means the redistribution of your earnings." Remarks in Chicago, Illinois, at the Annual Convention and Centennial Observance of the United Brotherhood of Carpenters and Joiners (September 3, 1981).

2404   "The true test of civilization, it's been said, is not the census or the size of its crops, but the kind of people the country turns out." Remarks on Presenting the Young American Medals for Bravery and Service (September 11, 1981).

2405   "For too long the American people have been told that they are relieved of responsibility for helping their fellow man because government's taken over the job. Now, we don't believe in totally eliminating government's role in humanitarian efforts, but we are trying to recapture the spirit of generosity that suffocates under heavy taxation and bureaucratic red tape." Remarks at the Annual Ambassadors Ball to Benefit the Multiple Sclerosis Society (September 22, 1981).

2406   "[T]he extravagance that brought us inflation, unemployment, high interest rates, and intolerable debt [were] well-intentioned ... [but they] didn't eliminate poverty or raise welfare recipients from dependence to self-sufficiency, independence, and dignity." Address to the Nation on the Program for Economic Recovery (September 24, 1981).

2407   "Many people today are economically trapped in welfare. They'd like nothing better than to be out in the work-a-day world with the rest of us. Independence and self-sufficiency is what they want. They aren't lazy or unwilling to work.

They just don't know how to free themselves from that welfare security blanket." Remarks at the Annual Meeting of the National Alliance of Business (October 5, 1981).

2408   "Before the idea got around that government was the principle vehicle of social change, it was understood that the real source of progress as a people was the private sector. The private sector still offers creative, less expensive, and more efficient alternatives to solving our social problems." Remarks at the Annual Meeting of the National Business Alliance (October 5, 1981).

2409   "More can be done; more should be done. But doing more doesn't mean to simply spend more. The size of the Federal budget is not an appropriate barometer of social conscience or charitable concern." Remarks at the Annual Meeting of the National Alliance of Business (October 5, 1981).

2410   "[N]o one should have a vested interest in poverty or dependency, that these tragedies must never be looked at as a source of votes for politicians or paychecks for bureaucrats. They are blights on our society that we must work to eliminate, not institutionalize." Remarks at a Conservative Political Action Conference Dinner (February 26, 1982).

2411   "Well, I believe a safety net is essential for people who cannot help themselves. And I believe most of us in this country have a real compassion for such people. We're the most generous people on earth. But how about a little compassion left over for those Americans who sit around the table at night after dinner, trying to figure out how to pay their own bills, keep their kids in school, and keep up with higher inflation and higher taxes year after year?" Address Before a Joint Session of the Alabama State Legislature in Montgomery (March 15, 1982).

2412   "We must aid those who need us, but we must not hinder those who need only a chance." Remarks to the National Catholic Education Association in Chicago, Illinois (April 15, 1982).

2413 "[T]he best social program is a productive job for anyone who's willing to work." Remarks at a Luncheon with Local Elected Officials and Businessmen in Baltimore, Maryland (July 13, 1982)

2414 "The war on poverty created a great new upper-middle class of bureaucrats that found that they had a fine career as long as they could keep enough needy people there to justify their existence." Remarks at a Kansas Republican Party Fundraising Luncheon in Topeka (September 9, 1982).

2415 "What we've seen in too many cases in the inner city is the broken will of people who desire to be as proud and independent as any other American. And perhaps unintentionally, many government programs have been designed not to create social mobility and help the needy along the way, but instead to foster a state of dependency. Whatever their intentions, no matter their compassion, our opponents created a new kind of bondage for millions of Americans citizens." Remarks at a National Black Republican Council Dinner (September 15, 1982).

2416 "Over the past few decades, no greater harm has been done than by government programs designed so poorly that they maneuvered people in need into a terrible dependency. Instead of strengthening recipients and helping them along the way, many well-intentioned programs did nothing but destroy pride and create a feeling of helplessness among those who needed encouragement and hope." Remarks at a Meeting with Officials of Black Colleges and Universities (September 22, 1982).

2417 "[I] get a little irritated with that consistent refrain about compassion. I got an unsigned valentine in February, and I'm sure it was from Fritz Mondale. The heart on it was bleeding." Remarks at a Fundraising Dinner for Senator John Tower in Houston, Texas (April 29, 1983).

2418 "America is a wealthy nation, but our wealth is not unlimited. So we have to face up to the reality too many have ignored. Unless we prune nonessential programs, unless we end benefits for those who should not be subsidized by their fellow taxpayers, we won't have enough resources to meet the requirements of those who must have our help. And helping those who truly need assistance is what fairness in government spending should be all about." Radio Address to the Nation on Economic and Fair Housing Issues (July 9, 1983).

2419 "[T]here is only one compassionate, sensible, and effective policy for Federal assistance: We must focus domestic spending on the poor and bypass the bureaucracies by giving assistance directly to those who need it." Remarks at the Young Leadership Conference of the United Jewish Appeal (March 13, 1984).

2420 "Those who can do it on their own shouldn't be taking the money we need to help those who couldn't receive a higher education without it." Remarks at a Reagan-Bush Rally in Brownsville, Texas (October 2, 1984).

2421 "This government will meet its responsibility to help those in need. But policies that increase dependency, break up families, and destroy self-respect are not progressive; they're reactionary." Address Before a Joint Session of the Congress on the State of the Union (February 6, 1985).

2422 Let us resolve that we will stop spreading dependency and start spreading opportunity; that we will stop spreading bondage and start spreading freedom." Address Before a Joint Session of the Congress on the State of the Union (February 6, 1985).

2423 "Economic growth is our most powerful tool for reducing poverty and fostering vigor and self-esteem among the millions in America's work force." Remarks at the Presentation Ceremony for the National Technology Awards (February 19, 1985).

2424 "[I]t's the duty of the government to care for those in genuine need.... Shrinking the safety net is out." Remarks at the Annual Meeting of the Chamber of Commerce of the United States (April 29, 1985).

2425 "[T]he answer to poverty is not more government programs and redistribution. The answer to poverty is economic growth through greater freedom." Remarks and a Question-and-Answer Session with Regional Editors and Broadcasters (September 16, 1985).

2426 "[T]he success of welfare should be judged by how many of its recipients become independent of welfare." Address Before a Joint Session of Congress on the State of the Union (February 4, 1986).

2427   "We're in danger of creating a permanent culture of poverty as inescapable as any chain or bond; a second and separate America, an America of lost dreams and stunted lives. The irony is that misguided welfare programs instituted in the name of compassion have actually helped turn a shrinking problem into a national tragedy." Radio Address to the Nation on Welfare Reform (February 15, 1986).

2428   "[T]he right answer to helping the less fortunate is not handouts and welfare, but jobs and opportunity." Remarks at a Senate Campaign Fundraiser for Representative W. Henson Moore in New Orleans, Louisiana (March 27, 1986).

2429   "Now, we will never abandon those who, through no fault of their own, must have our help. But let us work to see how many can be freed from the dependency of welfare and made self-supporting, which the great majority of welfare recipients want more than anything else." Address Before a Joint Session of Congress on the State of the Union (January 27, 1987).

2430   "No one doubts that welfare programs were designed with the best of intentions, but neither can anyone doubt that they've failed — failed to boost people out of dependency." Radio Address to the Nation on Welfare Reform (February 7, 1987).

2431   "How compassionate is a welfare system that discourages families that are economically self-reliant, that takes 6,000 pages of Federal regulations to explain, and is so complex it confuses and demoralizes the poor? How compassionate is a system that robs the poor of the tools to break the cycle of dependency? Well, the emerging consensus on welfare is finally agreeing with us that the Federal welfare system has become a poverty trap, a trap that is wreaking havoc on the very support system the poor need most to lift themselves up and out of destitution — the family." Remarks at a White House Briefing for Supporters of Welfare Reform (February 9, 1987).

2432   "[I]n the past year we've been going around the country asking the experts about how the welfare system works and doesn't work. Now, asking experts is not a new thing in the area of

welfare reform. Time and again over the years, government has inquired of professors and welfare professionals why people are poor and why they stay poor. And, forgive me for saying this, but the result has been a welfare system that's very good at keeping people poor." Remarks and a Panel Discussion with Community Leaders on Welfare Reform (February 11, 1987).

2433   "A Federal welfare system, constructed in the name of helping those in poverty, wreaked havoc on the poor family — tearing it apart, eating away at the underpinnings of their community, creating fatherless children, and unprecedented despair. The liberal welfare state has been a tragedy beyond description for so many of our fellow citizens, a crime against less fortunate Americans. The welfare system cries out for reform, and reformed it will be." Remarks at the Conservative Political Action Conference Luncheon (February 20, 1987).

2434   "[T]he fundamental truth about the difference between dependency and self-sufficiency [is]: It hinges on the family. The fundamental principle that must guide all our efforts at reform is that anything we do, any change we make, must strengthen, support, and give encouragement to the family." Remarks to Members of the National Governors' Association (February 23, 1987).

2435   "We can't go into the competitive world of the next century with so many of our fellow citizens caught in a poverty trap — a trap that robs those in it of hope and dignity and robs all of us of the benefits of their minds and their work." Remarks at a White House Meeting with Members of the Council for a Black Economic Agenda (February 24, 1987).

2436   "[I] said that some years ago the Federal Government declared a War on Poverty and poverty won. Instead of providing a ladder out of poverty, welfare became a net of dependency that held millions back. Instead of hope, we've too often bred despair and futility." Remarks to State and Local Republican Officials on Federalism and Aid to the Nicaraguan Democratic Resistance (March 22, 1987).

2437   "The Federal Government does not know how to get people off of welfare and into productive lives. We had a war on poverty —

poverty won. But when we went around the Nation looking, we found States and communities that do know how. So, we don't plan to serve up another program from Washington. We want to give States and communities the room to experiment, room to find out more about what works." Remarks at a White House Briefing for Members of the American Legislative Exchange Council (May 1, 1987).

2438 "Well, government, of course, has its place, but we've seen in the last two decades that the impersonal giving of government can often do more harm than good, creating a welfare trap from which the poor and underprivileged can rarely escape." Remarks at a White House Presentation Ceremony for the President's Volunteer Action Awards (June 30, 1987).

2439 "The fact is, it's probably more important to give well and wisely than to simply give." Remarks at a White House Presentation Ceremony for the President's Volunteer Action Awards (June 30, 1987).

2440 "It's now common knowledge that our welfare system has itself become a poverty trap — a creator and reinforcer of dependency...." Radio Address to the Nation on Welfare Reform (August 1, 1987).

2441 "[F]rom that failure [the War on Poverty], we learned many lessons about poverty and getting out of it. We learned that work should be more rewarding than welfare, because work is the only genuine path to self-respect and independence. We learned that welfare should sustain and not disrupt families, because intact, self-reliant families are the best antipoverty insurance ever devised. And we learned that the Federal Government doesn't really know how to apply these and other lessons to the day-to-day problems of the welfare family that's trying to lift itself up." Remarks at the Annual Meeting of the National Alliance of Business (September 14, 1987).

2442 "My friends, some years ago, the Federal Government declared war on poverty, and poverty won." Address Before a Joint Session of Congress on the State of the Union (January 25, 1988).

2443 "Federal welfare programs have created a massive social problem. With the best of intentions, government created a poverty trap that wreaks havoc on the very support system the poor need most to lift themselves out of poverty: the family. Dependency has become the one enduring heirloom, passed from one generation to the next, of too many fragmented families." Address Before a Joint Session of Congress on the State of the Union (January 25, 1988).

2444 "Twenty years ago the Government declared a war on poverty. Poverty won. Too many poor people were sucked into a system that declared that the only sin is not to have enough money. Soon, too many became dependent on government payments and lost the moral strength that has always given the poor the determination to climb America's ladder of opportunity. In my view, the great lesson of that experience is that no war on poverty stands a chance unless it rises above the secular state and is guided by the power of love that moves through God's word." Remarks at the Annual Dinner of the Knights of Malta in New York, New York (January 13, 1989).

Welfare Reform

2445 "Clearly, decades of spending have done little more than subsidize the status quo and make wards of the government out of citizens who would rather have a job than a handout. It's time for us to find out if two of the most dynamic and constructive forces known to man — free enterprise and profit motive — can be brought to play where government bureaucracy and social programs have failed." Remarks on Signing a Message to the Congress Transmitting Proposed Enterprise Zones Legislation (March 23, 1982).

2446 "You can't create a desert and then hand someone in the middle of that desert a cup of water and call it compassion. You can't pour billions of dollars into dead end, make-work jobs and call that opportunity. You cannot build up years and years of degrading dependence by our citizens on the government and then call that hope. And believe me, you can't drive people to despair with crises that wipe them out or taxes which sap their energies and then boast that you've given them fairness." Remarks at a Meeting with Participants in the American Business Conference (September 28, 1982).

2447 "[T]he enterprise zone concept ... harnesses the energy of the private sector, pumping new life into depressed areas. Rather than creating jobs in Washington, enterprise zones will provide results where they're needed, right in our local communities." Remarks at Cinco de Mayo Ceremonies in San Antonio, Texas (May 5, 1983).

2448 "For too long, well-meaning Government programs had lured too many Americans into the deep, dark caverns of dependency. We want to help free them to climb out and walk in the sunlight of pride and independence." Remarks at a White House Briefing for Supporters and Presidents of Historically Black Colleges (September 19, 1986).

2449 "From dealing as a Governor closer at hand with welfare, and those people, I think truly that the bulk of the people on welfare aren't just lazy bums or cheaters — they want nothing more than to be independent, free of the social workers, and out on their own once again. So, we can help them do that." Remarks at a White House Briefing for Supporters of Welfare Reform (February 9, 1987).

2450 "More must be done to reduce poverty and dependency and, believe me, nothing is more important than welfare reform. It's now common knowledge that our welfare system has itself become a poverty trap — a creator and reinforcer of dependency...." Radio Address to the Nation on Welfare Reform (August 1, 1987).

2451 "Now the question I ask about any welfare reform proposal is: Will it help people become self-sufficient and lead a full life, or will it keep them down in a state of dependency?" Radio Address to the Nation on Welfare Reform (August 1, 1987).

2452 "[T]he principal issue in any welfare reform proposal is whether or not it'll help people become self-sufficient and lead a full life or keep them in a state of dependency." Remarks at a White House Meeting with the House of Representatives Republican Task Force on Welfare Reform (August 6, 1987).

2453 "[I]n welfare reform it's time to get the Federal Government to learn some humility and admit what it doesn't know and put its trust in the American people. At the very least, we should insist that the Government will not do more harm than good when it acts. It's time for us to look

carefully at the full range of government activities and ask which ones make it harder for the poor to escape poverty; which cut off rungs in the ladder of American opportunity; which make it more difficult to realize the American dream." Remarks at the Annual Meeting of the National Alliance of Business (September 14, 1987).

2454 "There are a thousand sparks of genius in 50 States and a thousand communities around the Nation. It is time to nurture them and see which ones can catch fire and become guiding lights.... Let's start making our welfare system the first rung on America's ladder of opportunity, a boost up from dependency, not a graveyard but a birthplace of hope." Address Before a Joint Session of Congress on the State of the Union (January 25, 1988).

2455 "Our aim is simple: to replace today's poverty trap with a welfare system that fosters genuine economic opportunity." Remarks to the National Conference of State Legislators (January 29, 1988).

2456 "But in this area [welfare reform], more than any other, government should tread carefully, humbly, because we're dealing with the most fundamental element of human society: the family." Remarks to Members of the National Governors' Association (February 22, 1988).

2457 "In the name of compassion, too many Americans on welfare have been robbed of the one priceless item with which they could build a future: hope. It's time to return hope to those on welfare...." Radio Address to the Nation on the Economy and Welfare Reform (September 3, 1988).

2458 "Any bill not built around work is not true welfare reform. If Congress presents me with a bill that replaces work with welfare expansion and that places the dignity of self-sufficiency through work out of the reach of Americans on welfare, I will use my veto pen." Radio Address to the Nation on the Economy and Welfare Reform (September 3, 1988).

2459 "For too long the Federal Government, with the best of intentions, has usurped responsibilities that appropriately lie with parents. In so doing, it has reinforced dependency and separated welfare recipients from the mainstream of American society." Remarks on Signing the Family Support Act of 1988 (October 13, 1988).

Index

References are to entry numbers